Welcome to

Spiralizer World

Unlock EVERY Secret of Cooking Through 500 AMAZING Spiralizer Recipes

(Unlock Cooking, Book 4)

Annie Kate

Contents

Introduction

***

"Your body is precious. It is your vehicle for awakening.

Treat it with care."

___Buddha___

This quote is found everywhere, which isn't surprising, since it reminds us of the importance of keeping the body in good health - something many of us neglect to do. No one can deny the importance of health in our lives. Its health, as Mahatma Gandhi said, that is the real wealth not pieces of gold and silver. A good health is not something you can buy, but a thing you can improve considerably with a few changes in your lifestyle. On speaking of *"healthy"*, we're always given a same advice that we should consume more fresh vegetables and fruits every single day. We follow this advice but quickly want to give up because:

We're sick of salads.

We can't stomach another crudité.

We feel hungry all day long because of consuming only juices.

We try to stir-fry vegetable but worry about cholesterol from additional oil and raw fat.

Luckily, thanks to spiralizer recipes, all of these problems are solved. Spiralizer, also called spiral vegetable slicer, seems to be latest must-have kitchen tool. You can use it to turn a whole vegetable, such as carrot, sweet potato into long noodle-like spirals that can replace for your favorite pasta. Spiralizer is *affordable, easy to use and able to make healthy eating in the funniest way.* It's the reason why spiralizer suddenly seems to be everywhere. When I first heard about spiralizer, I got kind of annoyed. I wondered why people had to buy a machine that would take up kitchen space just to make noodles out of vegetables. But then, after watching my friend inspiralizing, I caved in. I felt something warm and fuzzy inside my heart when watching a sweet potato turn into tiny little spirals and then proceeding to enjoy these tiny little spirals covered in cashew cream sauce. Until now, I still couldn't forget its flavor. It's a perfect combination of natural sweet from fresh potatoes and creamy tasty flavor of cashew cream sauce.

Not only is spiralizer a fun, inexpensive way to make delicious and nutritious meals but it's a scope for creativity. Only with a spiralizer does cooking become a land of real art where your creativity is strongly woken up. You can gather nearly everything from your weekly farmers' market trip to make a summery colorful salad. You also can combine crunchy Brussels sprouts and creamy avocado to make the dish which is surprisingly low in sodium. What's more, you can coat your carrots in a tasty tahini and tamari dressing. And then top it with grilled chicken, shrimp, or steak to make it a meal and many more delicacies. Your creativity in cooking together with a spiralizer will bring your family a heaven on plate and a rainbow on dining table. If you don't have much time to think of a new recipe, my cookbook is right here supporting you.

Until now, I have made spiralizer for hundreds of times. After failures, I got experiences. After successful times, I got tips and tricks. I gathered these experiences together with 500 amazing spiralizer recipes to write this book. "Welcome to the world of spiralizer" is the gift of health I send to you guys. In this cookbook, in addition to showing you amazing benefits of spiralizer, I will, as usual, give you some additional tips for making a great spiralizer. Final part of this book is 500 amazing spiralizer recipes throughout which you can see spiralizer recipes in all respects:

- *Chapter 1: Top 9 Benefits of Spiralizer Recipes*
- *Chapter 2: Breakfast*
- *Chapter 3: Dessert*
- *Chapter 4: Snack and Side Dish*
- *Chapter 5: Salad*
- *Chapter 6: Inspiralizer rice*
- *Chapter 7: Noodles*
- *Chapter 8: Pasta*
- *Chapter 9: Soup*

If you've just bought a spiralizer, then these recipes are a great starting point. If you've already inspiralized, I think you'll add these recipes to your "quick and easy" list. From now on, in freezing days, thanks to spiralizer, you can cook spicy soup from potato, cauliflower and a little mushroom for your family. Or In the nice weather, everyone can gather and enjoy some nutritious pasta for lunch and together prepare cupcakes for eventful party.

Errick Mcadams said:

"If you keep good food in your fridge, you will eat good food".

The same as him, whenever I get the chance, I spend a lot of time on filling up my kitchen by healthy foods and vegetables. It's a really good habit. Don't hesitate anymore, energize your life by getting in to this habit. Let spiralizer and my recipes help you. You'll surely receive a lot of wonderful things!

Sincerely

Annie Kate

Chapter 1: Top 9 Benefits of Spiralizer Recipes

***

In recent years, *healthy* is a very common but a confusing term. We almost miss the point of this concept and coat it in a strict diets dressing. Of course, for some of us, following a strict diet can help lose weight and manage illness. However, we all know that no diet is suitable in long term. It's essential for us to figure out what really works best for our own bodies. You guys may find out a lot of different answers for yourself, but I can make sure that you'll have a same one; it's advocating eating more vegetables. When you add more vegetables to your diet, the health benefits are immense. Spiralizer is the thing that helps your meal and you become a healthy, inspired version of the original. When you add vegetable noodle and vegetable rice into your diets, you'll notice the considerably positive changes: glowing skin, body fitness, better digestion, more and more energy and overall dietary satisfaction. These benefits of spiralizer are figured out below:

1. **Source of important nutrients**: The main ingredient of spiralizer is vegetable, which is a source of important nutrients. Most vegetables are naturally low in fat and calories. None have cholesterol. In addition, vegetables are important sources of man y nutrients, including potassium, dietary fiber, folic acid, vitamin A, and vitamin C. Potassium contained in vegetable may help to maintain healthy blood pressure. Dietary fiber from vegetables helps reduce blood cholesterol levels and may lower risk of heart disease.

2. **Disease prevention**: Eating a diet rich in vegetables and fruits as part of an overall healthy diet may reduce risk for heart disease, including heart attack and stroke. Diet rich in some vegetables and fruits as part of an overall healthy diet may protect against certain types of cancers, lower blood pressure, and also reduce the risk of developing kidney stones and help to decrease bone loss.

3. **Stress management:** Crunchy raw vegetables can help ease stress in a purely mechanical way. Munching celery or carrot sticks helps release a clenched jaw, and that can ward off tension. Vitamin E to bolster the immune system, plus B vitamins, which may make you more resilient during bouts of stress or depression. One of the best ways to reduce high blood pressure is to get enough potassium, and half an avocado has more potassium than a medium-sized banana. Using pistachios, walnuts, or almonds to make sauce for your spiralizer everyday may help lower your cholesterol, ease inflammation in your heart's arteries, make diabetes less likely, and protect you against the effects of stress.

4. **Beauty secrets**: The secret to being beautiful does not come with a high price. In fact, you only need to be more conscious about the foods you eat and make sure that what you put on your plate can benefit not only your health, but your skin as well. Most vegetables which are proven to make you look beautiful effectively such as beet, red cabbage, carrot can be

inspiralized. Therefore, spiralizer may help your meal and you become a pretty, inspired version of the original. When you add vegetable noodle and vegetable rice into your diets, you'll notice the considerably positive changes: glowing skin, body fitness, stronger hair and many more.

5. **Weight loss and health goals:** Spiralizing should be a lifestyle, not a diet, but you can certainly use spiralizer to *significantly reduce your calorie and carb* intake. It is extremely important to consume carbohydrates as they play a significant role in our bodily functions and health – but consuming the right kind of carbohydrates is imperative. It is not necessary to consumer carbs in the form of breads or pasta – in fact, I highly recommend spiralized sweet potatoes as one of the highest carbohydrate vegetables. Make it easier to eat more and weigh less by spiralizing.

6. **Dietary satisfaction:** We're ofter given an advice that "watch what we eat" or to "be aware" of how many calories are in our food so as not to overeat and put on weight. Spiralizing helps alleviate this concern. I will have a bowl of noodles and still have an appetite for more – which is actually a good thing! It means you can (and should) keep eating to get the calories and the carbs you need.

7. **Kids love spiralizer:** Colorful like a rainbow, delicious, funny. Ets. They're the reasons why kids love and eat spiralizer without complaint. In addition, spiralizing presents an opportunity for kids to get their feet wet in the kitchen without knives or the mess and bacteria of meat. It is safe, exciting, and fun for them. It's also good chance of teaching them about nutrition and developing their appetite for cooking from a young age.

8. **Cut some bills and save on electricity**: Hand-held spiralizer requires no electricity and is eco-friendly! This is particularly advantageous both in summer and winter. It's spiralizer that helps cut down a few bucks on electricity. Power outage? Make raw pasta! Trying to reduce your green footprint? Inspiralize!

9. **Waken up the creative beast in you:** By nature, spiralizing challenges us to come up with creative meals with our vegetable and fruit noodles. Each vegetable has its own flavors, textures and nutrients. Therefore, we can invent our own meals or reinvent our favorite classics, by picking a vegetable to spiralize. There are hundreds of types of meals you can make with all the different vegetables and fruits. Once you start spiralizing, you'll notice that you never get bored and you look forward to making something different each time! You may even find strat a blog about spiralizing.

Chapter 2: Breakfast

***

Almond Butter & Jelly Oatmeal Bowl with Spiralized Apples and Toasted Almonds

Prep time: 5 mins | Cook time: 5 mins | Total time: 10 mins | Serves: 2

Ingredients

- 1 tablespoon slivered almonds
- 1 cup gluten-free rolled oats
- 2 tablespoons almond butter
- 1 tablespoon grape jelly (no sugar added)
- ½ cup unsweetened almond milk
- 1 apple, Blade D

Directions

1. Place a small skillet over medium-high heat and add in the almonds. Let toast for 5 minutes or until fragrant and golden brown. Transfer to a bowl and set aside.
2. Bring two cups of water to a boil in a medium saucepot. Add in the oatmeal, bring to a boil again and then reduce heat to low and let simmer, letting cook until all water is absorbed.
3. Once oatmeal is done, drizzle evenly over with the almond butter and jelly. Pour ¼ cup of almond milk per bowl and then top with apples and garnish with toasted almonds. Serve immediately.

Asiago Kohlrabi Noodle Frittata With Corn, Bacon And Basil

Prep Time: 15 m | Cook Time: 35 m | Total Time: 50 m | Servings: 4

Ingredients

- 1 head of corn
- 5 pieces of bacon
- 10 eggs, beaten
- 5 pieces of basil, ribboned

- 1/4 cup shredded asiago cheese
- salt and pepper, to taste
- 1/2 tablespoon extra virgin olive oil
- 1 large garlic clove, minced
- pinch of red pepper flakes
- 1 kohlrabi, peeled, Blade C

Directions

1. Preheat the oven to 375 degrees.
2. Place the corn in a saucepan, cover with water and bring to a boil. Once boiling, cook for 2 more minutes or until easily pierced with a fork and drain into a colander. Rinse with cold water so it's easier to handle and then shave the kernels off with a knife into a bowl. Set bowl of kernels aside.
3. While the corn is cooking, place a large skillet over medium-high heat, coat with cooking spray and cook the bacon until crispy, in batches, if needed. Set aside on a paper towel lined plate and crumble.
4. Once bacon and corn are cooked, add to a bowl with the eggs, basil and asiago cheese. Season with salt and pepper and set aside.
5. Set a 10 or 12" skillet (preferably cast iron) over medium heat and add in the olive oil. Once oil heats, add in the garlic and red pepper flakes. Cook for 30 seconds or until fragrant and then add in the kohlrabi noodles and season with salt and pepper. Toss frequently for 3-5 minutes and cook until mostly wilted. Once wilted, pour in the egg mixture evenly over the kohlrabi.
6. Let cook for 2-3 minutes or until the bottom sets into the skillet.
7. Bake for 20-25 minutes or until when you pierce with a skewer (or fork), the skewer comes out clean and the edges of the frittata are lightly golden brown. Serve for 4 or 8

Bacon & Brussels Sprouts Potato Noodle Casserole

Prep Time: 15 m | Cook Time: 15 m | Total Time: 30 m | Servings: 4-6

Ingredients

- 6-8 brussels sprouts
- 4-5 strips of bacon
- 2 garlic cloves, minced
- 1/4 tsp red pepper flakes

- 1/2 cup diced red onion
- 2 large (320+g) Idaho potatoes, peeled, Blade C (or sweet potatoes!)
- 1.25 cup shredded cheddar cheese (optional)

Directions

1. Preheat the oven to high broil.
2. Chop the bottoms off of the brussel sprouts and then slice thinly, lengthwise. Set aside.
3. Place a large skillet over medium heat and place in the bacon slices. Cook the bacon until crispy and transfer to a paper towel lined plate. Drain the skillet of all bacon grease except 1 tbsp.
4. To the same skillet, add in the garlic, cook for 30 seconds and then add in the red pepper flakes and onions. Cook the onions for about 2 minutes and then add in the brussel sprouts. Cook the brussel sprouts for about 3 minutes, tossing frequently and then add in the potato noodles and crumble in the bacon.
5. Let the potato noodles cook for about 2 minutes, tossing frequently. Then, cover the skillet with a lid and let sit cooking for 3 minutes. Uncover, stir and cook another 3 minutes or until noodles are fully cooked and slightly browned.
6. Pour the contents of the skillet into a casserole dish in an even layer and serve! When serving, cut into sections first to cut up the noodles. Optional: Sprinkle cheddar cheese on top and broil for 2-3 minutes or until cheese melts into the casserole. Then, cut into sections and serve!

Bacon Potato Noodle Home "Fries"

Prep Time: 10 m | Cook Time: 10 m | Total Time: 20 m | Servings: 3-4

Ingredients

- 3 slices of bacon
- 1/2 tablespoon extra virgin olive oil
- 1 large waxy potatoes, peeled, Blade C, noodles trimmed
- 1 teaspoons smoked paprika
- ½ teaspoon garlic powder
- ¼ teaspoon onion powder
- coarse sea salt and pepper, to taste
- 1 tablespoon of minced parsley, to garnish

Directions

1. Heat a large skillet over medium heat. Flick water into the skillet and if it sizzles, it's ready. Coat skillet with cooking spray and add in the bacon slices and cook 3-4 minutes per side or until crispy. Set bacon aside on a paper towel lined plate and return skillet over medium heat, keeping all bacon fat.
2. While the bacon cooks, add the potato noodles to a large mixing bowl and pour over olive oil and toss until noodles are coated. Then, add in the paprika, garlic powder, onion powder and season generously with salt and pepper.
3. Add the potato noodles to the skillet with bacon fat, toss, and cover, cooking for 7-10 minutes or until potato noodles are cooked through. Uncover occasionally to toss and recover to continue cooking.
4. When done, uncover, crumble in bacon, toss and divide onto plates and garnish with parsley.

Baked Spanish Egg and Sweet Potato Noodle Bowls

The day after Thanksgiving, you tend to want something light, hence the single-serving nature of this recipe. This recipe also has a spicy Spanish-influenced flavor to it with paprika, jalapeño, cilantro and onions. The flavor from the spices and the tomatoes is sensational and the sweet potato noodles are fun to eat for breakfast.

Prep Time: *15 m* | **Cook Time:** *25 m* | **Total Time:** *40 m* | **Servings:** *5 (1) 6oz ramekin*

Ingredients

- 1 tablespoon extra virgin olive oil
- 1/2 small yellow onion, diced
- 1 jalapeno, seeded and finely chopped
- 2 large garlic cloves, finely minced
- 1 15oz can diced tomatoes
- 1/4 teaspoon smoked paprika
- ¼ teaspoon cumin
- salt and pepper, to taste
- 1 large sweet potato, peeled, Blade C, noodles trimmed
- 4 eggs
- 1.5 tablespoons chopped cilantro
- equipment needed: (5) 6oz ramekins

Directions

1. Preheat the oven to 375 degrees. Take out five 6oz ramekins and set aside.
2. Place a large skillet over medium heat and add in the oil. Once oil heats, add in the chili, onions and garlic and cook for 3 minutes or until onions are translucent. Add in the tomatoes, paprika, cumin, salt, pepper and sweet potato noodles and cook for 5-7 minutes or until the tomatoes thicken. The sweet potato noodles might break apart, but that's okay.
3. Portion the mixture into the ramekins and crack an egg in each one. Season the tops with pepper and bake for 10-15 minutes or until egg whites are completely set, careful not to overcook the yolks.
4. Sprinkle with cilantro and serve.

Bbq Chickpea Sweet Potato Noodle Breakfast Tacos With Eggs, Avocado Sauce And Scallions

*Prep time: 15 mins | **Cook time**: 15 mins | **Total time**: 30 mins | **Serves:** 4 tacos*

Ingredients

- For the avocado cream sauce:
- ½ the insides of 1 large very ripe avocado
- 1.5 tablespoons cilantro
- 1 small lime, juiced
- 1 teaspoon minced jalapeno
- salt and pepper, to taste
- For the tacos:
- 2 teaspoons extra virgin olive oil (or coconut oil)
- 1 medium (7.5oz) sweet potato, peeled, Blade D, noodles trimmed
- salt and pepper, to taste
- ¼ teaspoon ground paprika
- cooking spray
- 3 eggs, beaten (or don't beat them and do them up fried-style – just use 4 eggs instead!)
- ½ cup chickpeas, drained and rinsed
- ¼ cup Matty's BBQ Sauce by Tessemae's
- 4 corn tortillas (or lettuce wraps)
- 3 tablespoons sliced scallions, to garnish

Directions

1. Place all of the ingredients for the avocado sauce into a food processor and pulse until creamy. Taste and adjust, if necessary.
2. Heat the oil in a large skillet over medium-high heat. Once oil is shimmering, add in the sweet potato noodles and season with salt, pepper, and paprika. Cook until soft, 5-7 minutes, tossing occasionally.
3. Meanwhile, place a medium skillet over medium-high heat and coat with cooking spray. Once pan is hot (flick water and if it sizzles, it's ready), add in the eggs and scramble them. Season with pepper when done and transfer to a plate and set aside.
4. Immediately wipe down the medium skillet used to cook the eggs and add in the chickpeas and barbecue sauce. Stir for about 3 minutes or until chickpeas are warmed through. If the pan is too hot and the barbecue sauce starts to stick, just stir off heat.
5. If you're heating up your tortillas, do so (I like to simply warm mine in a skillet for about 30 seconds per side.)
6. Assemble your tacos: place two tortillas down on a large plate and spread out half of the avocado sauce among the two tortillas. Then, add half of the sweet potato noodles among the two tortillas. Do the same with the eggs and chickpeas and then garnish with scallions. Repeat until all tacos are done.
7. Serve two tacos per person.

Beet Noodle, Feta and Avocado Omelet

Prep Time: 10 min | Cook Time: 15 min | Total Time: 25 min | Servings: 1

Ingredients

- 1/2 tablespoon extra virgin olive oil
- 1 small beet, peeled, Blade C, noodles trimmed (only use about 1/4 cup of noodles - save the rest for future use)
- 3 eggs, beaten
- salt and pepper, to taste
- 3 tablespoons crumbled feta cheese
- 1/4 of the insides of an avocado, cubed
- freshly minced parsley, to garnish

Directions

1. Place a large skillet over medium heat and add in the olive oil. Once oil heats, add in the beet noodles. Toss to coat in the oil and cover and cook 5-7 minutes or until beet noodles soften completely, uncovering occasionally to toss.
2. For a scramble: Add the eggs and avocado into the pan with the beet noodles and scramble together. Once eggs are almost completely scrambled, add in the feta and finish scrambling. Serve.
3. For an omelet: Set the beet noodles aside and place a medium saucepan over medium heat (or your preferred omelet pan) and coat with cooking spray. Add in the eggs and let set, pulling in the edges of the eggs with a spatula to let the egg disperse and cook almost fully. Once most of the eggs are set, season with salt and pepper and add in the beet noodles, feta and avocado. Fold the omelet in half and press down to compress with the back of a spatula. Let cook another 2 minutes or until eggs are cooked through. Garnish with parsley and serve.

Butternut Squash Breakfast Risotto with Fried Egg and Bacon

Prep time: 20 mins | Cook time: 25 mins | Total time: 45 mins | Serves: 4

Ingredients

- 4 strips of bacon
- 4 whole large eggs
- about 2 tablespoons freshly minced parsley to garnish
- For the risotto:
- 1 large butternut squash, peeled, Blade C
- 1 tablespoon olive oil
- 2 cloves of garlic, minced
- salt and pepper, to taste
- ½ cup chicken broth + more if needed
- ¼ cup shredded mild cheddar cheese
- ¼ cup shredded Havarti cheese

Directions

1. Pulse the butternut squash noodles in a food processor until rice-like, then set aside.
2. Place a large skillet over medium-high heat. Once heated, add in the bacon and cook until crispy. Transfer to paper towel lined sheet and set aside.

3. Heat the 1 tablespoon olive oil in a large pot over medium heat. Once oil is shimmering, add the garlic and cook for 30 seconds or until fragrant. Add the butternut squash rice, season with salt and pepper and stir. Cook for 2 minutes to heat through, then add the broth. Lower heat to low to bring to a simmer. Cook for 10-15 minutes or until broth fully reduces. Remove the pot from heat and fold in the cheeses. Stir until cheese has fully melted and then crumble the bacon and add in and stir to combine.
4. Once risotto is almost done, using the same skillet used to cook the bacon, wipe it down and place over medium-high heat and once heated, add in the eggs. Cook the eggs until whites are set.
5. Spoon risotto into bowls and top with fried egg and garnish with parsley. Serve hot.

Butternut Squash Rice with Bacon, Caramelized Onions, and Grated Egg

*Prep time: 15 mins | **Cook time**: 25 mins | **Total time**: 40 mins | **Serves**: 4*

Ingredients

- 1 large butternut squash, peeled, Blade D
- 4 slices of bacon
- ½ red onion, peeled, Blade A, noodles trimmed
- salt and pepper
- ¼ teaspoon garlic powder
- ½ teaspoon paprika
- ¼ cup chicken broth, low-sodium
- 2 hard boiled eggs, peeled

Directions

1. Place the butternut squash noodles into a food processor and pulse until rice-like. Set aside.
2. Place a large skillet over medium-high heat and add in the bacon. Cook the bacon for 7 minutes or until crispy, flipping halfway through. When done, transfer to a paper towel lined plate.
3. Immediately add in the onions to the pan, season with salt and pepper, and cook for 10 minutes or until caramelized and starting to brown. Set aside on a plate.
4. Immediately add in the butternut squash rice and season with garlic powder, paprika, salt and pepper. Stir and pour in the chicken broth. Let

cook for 7 minutes or until rice softens and then stir in the cooked onions and crumble in the bacon. Cook for 1 more minute or until heated through.
5. Divide the rice mixture into bowls. Grate ½ egg over each bowl and serve.

Chocolate Chip Sweet Potato Noodle Waffles

Prep time: 10 mins | *Cook time:* 20 mins | *Total time:* 30 mins | *Serves:* 2 waffles

Ingredients

- 1 large sweet potato, peeled, Blade D, noodles trimmed
- salt, to taste
- ½ teaspoon cinnamon
- 1 large egg, beaten
- 2 tablespoons chopped dark chocolate (I used two rectangle pieces from ALOHA's Superfood Dark Chocolate)
- cooking spray
- optional, to top: maple syrup, blueberries, pecans, etc.

Directions

1. Preheat a Belgian waffle iron.
2. Place a large skillet over medium heat and add in the olive oil. Once oil heats, add in the sweet potatoes and season with salt and cinnamon. Toss and cook for about 10 minutes or until noodles are cooked through. You can cover to cook more quickly.
3. Transfer the noodles to a large mixing bowl and add in the egg and chocolate. Toss to combine.
4. Spray the preheated waffle iron with cooking spray and pack in the noodles carefully. You may have to play around with the noodles to get them to fit in all of the grooves.
5. Cook the waffle according to your iron's settings.
6. When done, carefully remove the waffles and transfer to plates. Top with any toppings you'd like, but don't forget the maple syrup.

Chorizo, Parsley and Potato Noodle Waffles

Prep time: 15 mins | *Cook time:* 20 mins | *Total time:* 35 mins | *Serves:* 2 waffles

Ingredients

- 2.25 oz chorizo, decased and crumbled
- 1 large red potato, peeled, Blade D, noodles roughly trimmed
- ¼ teaspoon garlic powder
- salt and pepper, to taste
- 1 large egg
- ¼ teaspoon smoked paprika
- 1 teaspoon minced parsley
- maple syrup, to drizzle

Directions

1. Preheat a Belgian waffle iron.
2. Meanwhile, place a large skillet over medium heat and once heated, add in the chorizo and cook for 5-7 minutes or until lightly browned. Set the chorizo aside in a plate and then add in the potato noodles and season with garlic powder, salt and pepper. Cover and cook for 5 minutes or until noodles are wilted and cooked through, tossing occasionally.
3. Once cooked, add the noodles to a large mixing bowl with the chorizo and let cool for two minutes. Then, add in the egg, smoked paprika and parsley and toss to combine fully. Spray the waffle iron with cooking spray and then pack in the potato mixture. Cook to the waffle iron's settings (about 7 minutes) and then remove carefully.
4. Serve each waffle topped with maple syrup

Mini Spiralized Butternut Squash and Feta Frittata

Prep time: 10 mins | Cook time: 20 mins | Total time: 30 mins | Serves: 4 slices (2 people)

Ingredients

- ½ tablespoon extra virgin olive oil
- 1 packed cup curly kale, chopped
- 1 small garlic clove, minced
- ¼ teaspoon red pepper flakes
- salt and pepper, to taste

- 1.5 cup butternut squash Blade D noodles (about ¼ of a small peeled butternut squash)
- ¼ teaspoon paprika
- 4 large eggs, beaten
- 2 tablespoons well-crumbled feta cheese (or goat cheese, or omit if dairy-free)

Directions

1. Preheat the oven to 425 degrees.
2. Place a large skillet over medium-high heat and add in the olive oil. Once oil heats, add in the kale, garlic and red pepper flakes and season with salt and pepper. Cook for 5 minutes or until kale is mostly wilted and place in an 8" oven-safe skillet. Then, in the skillet used to cook the kale, add in the butternut squash noodles and season with salt, pepper and paprika. Toss and cook for 5 minutes or until noodles are mostly wilted. Place the cooked noodles into the 8" skillet and make sure the kale and noodles are evenly distributed in the skillet.
3. While the butternut squash cooks, stir in the feta to the beaten eggs. Pour the eggs evenly over the frittata and season with pepper. Let cook for 1 minute or until eggs set on the bottom.
4. Bake the 8" skillet frittata for 10-13 minutes or until eggs are cooked through and edges are lightly brown and when pierced with a toothpick, the toothpick comes out clean. Remove from the oven and divide into four slices.

Mini Spiralized Scallion Hash Brown Cake

Prep time: 10 mins | Cook time: 25 mins | Total time: 35 mins | Serves: 2

Ingredients

- 2 slices bacon, chopped
- 2 scallions, chopped
- ½ pound red potato (or a little smaller)
- salt and pepper, to taste
- 1 egg, beaten
- 2 teaspoons extra virgin olive oil

Directions

1. Cook the bacon in a medium nonstick skillet over medium heat, stirring occasionally, until bacon begins to brown, about 5 minutes.
2. Reserve about 1 tablespoon of scallions and then add in the rest to the skillet and cook, stirring occasionally, until bacon is crisp and scallions are soft, about 5 minutes.
3. While the bacon cooks, spiralize the potatoes with Blade D and set aside in a large mixing bowl. Once bacon/scallion mixture is done, add to the large mixing bowl and toss together and season generously with salt and pepper. Let cool for 2 minutes and then add in the egg and toss again.
4. Heat a small 8" skillet over medium-low heat. Once heated, add in the potato noodle mixture and pat down with a spatula. Cook for 5-7 minutes. Then, put a plate on top and flip the skillet over and empty the noodle cake onto the plate. Then, add the olive oil to the skillet and slide the potato cake (browned side up) onto the skillet and let cook for another 5 minutes or until potatoes are cooked through. While it cooks, press down with the spatula to compress the potatoes.
5. Transfer the potato cake to a serving dish and garnish with reserved scallions.

Open-Faced Summer Bruschetta Omelet With Spiralized Zucchini

Prep time: 5 mins | *Cook time:* 10 mins | *Total time:* 15 mins | *Serves:* 1

Ingredients

For the omelet:

- ½ medium zucchini, Blade D, noodles trimmed
- 3 large eggs, beaten
- salt and pepper, to taste
- For the bruschetta:
- 1 garlic clove, minced
- ½ cup cherry tomatoes, halved
- 5 basil leaves, chopped
- ½ tablespoon red wine vinegar
- ½ tablespoon extra virgin olive oil
- salt and pepper, to taste

Directions

1. Place a small skillet over medium-high heat and coat with cooking spray. Once the pan heats, add in the zucchini noodles, and cook for 3 minutes or until wilted and al dente. Once cooked, make sure the noodles are evenly distributed on the bottom of the pan. Pour over the eggs, season with salt and pepper, and cook until the bottom sets, about 3 minutes. Cover and let cook another 5 minutes or until eggs are cooked all the way through.
2. Meanwhile, combine all of the ingredients for the bruschetta in a medium mixing bowl and toss to combine. Set aside.
3. When omelet is done cooking, transfer to a plate and top with prepared bruschetta. Serve immediately

Pear Noodle Yogurt Parfaits with Chobani

Prep Time: 5 minutes | Cook Time: 5 minutes | Servings: 3

Ingredients

- 3/4 cup diced fruit (bananas, blueberries or strawberries)
- Chobani Simply 100 Greek yogurt - vanilla, blueberry, strawberry
- 1 cup favorite granola
- 2 medium pears (bosc or anjou)

Directions

1. Divide your diced fruit at the bottom of three mason jars.
2. Top fruit with one container of Chobani Simply 100 Greek yogurt per mason jar.
3. Top greek yogurt with 1/3 cup of granola per mason jar.
4. Top granola with pear noodles in each mason jar.
5. Serve with a spoon.

Pizza Egg Muffins with Potato Noodles

Prep Time: 20 mins | Cook Time: 20 mins | Total Time: 40 mins | Servings: 12 large muffins

Ingredients

- 1 tablespoon extra virgin olive oil
- 2 large Yukon gold potatoes, peeled, Blade C
- salt and pepper, to taste
- 1/2 teaspoon garlic powder
- 1 dozen large eggs
- 1 cup canned diced tomatoes, drained
- ½ teaspoon dried oregano
- ½ teaspoon dried basil
- ¼ teaspoon onion powder
- ½ cup diced turkey pepperoni slices
- 1 cup shredded mozzarella cheese
- 12 slices of turkey pepperoni
- 2 tablespoons grated parmesan cheese, to garnish

Directions

1. Preheat the oven to 375 degrees.
2. Place a large skillet over medium heat and add in the olive oil. Once oil heats, add in the potato noodles. Season with salt, pepper and garlic powder and toss to combine. Cover and cook for 5-7 minutes or until potatoes are cooked to al dente, uncovering occasionally to toss.
3. Coat the muffin cavities with cooking spray and then pack each with potato noodles, about halfway-through, snipping the noodles with kitchen scissors as you go.
4. In a medium mixing bowl, beat the eggs. Add in the tomatoes, oregano, basil, onion powder and diced pepperoni and season with salt and pepper. Stir to mix and then pour into the muffin cavities, atop the potato noodles, filling the cavities about three-quarters of the way.
5. Top each cavity with a sprinkling of mozzarella cheese and top with a slice of pepperoni. Bake in the oven for 20-25 minutes or until eggs have set completely. Pop out of the muffin cavities and serve, garnished immediately with parmesan cheese.

Potato Noodle Bowl with Manchego, Egg & Serrano Ham

*Prep time: 10 mins | **Cook time:** 15 mins | **Total time:** 25 mins | **Serves:** 2*

Ingredients

- 1 tablespoon extra virgin olive oil
- salt and pepper, to taste
- ¼ teaspoon garlic powder
- 1 pinch chili powder (about ⅛ teaspoon), to taste
- ¾ pound red potatoes, Blade D, peeled, noodles trimmed
- 2 eggs
- 2 pieces Serrano ham
- ¼ cup finely grated manchego cheese (this can be prepared while potato noodles cook to save time)
- 1 tablespoon chopped chives

Directions

1. Place a medium skillet over medium-high and add in the olive oil. Once the oil heats, add in the potato noodles, season with salt, pepper, garlic and chili powder and toss. Let cook, covered, for 7-10 minutes or until cooked through. Once cooked, divide onto two plates and cover to keep warm.
2. While potato noodles cook, beat the eggs and set aside.
3. Once potatoes are done, immediately add in the eggs and scramble them. Divide the eggs onto the plates with potato noodles. Then, place 1 piece of Serrano ham per plate. Dust each plate with manchego and garnish with chives. Serve.

Potato Noodle Scramble Bowl with Lemon-Basil Pesto

Prep time: 15 mins | Cook time: 20 mins | Total time: 35 mins | Serves: 2

Ingredients

- 1 tablespoon extra virgin olive oil
- 1 large red potato, peeled, Blade D, noodles trimmed
- salt and pepper, to taste
- ¼ teaspoon chili powder
- ¼ teaspoon garlic powder
- 2½-inch thick beefsteak tomato slices
- 4 eggs, beaten
- ½ avocado, peeled, pitted insides sliced
- 2 tablespoons diced green onions
- For the pesto:

- 1 cup basil
- ½ teaspoon pine nuts
- 1 small garlic clove, minced
- 1 tablespoon extra virgin olive oil
- 1.5 tablespoon freshly squeezed lemon juice
- salt and pepper, to taste

Directions

1. Place a large skillet over medium heat and add in the olive oil. Once oil heats, add in the potato noodles and season with salt, pepper, chili powder and garlic powder. Toss to combine and cover, cooking 7-10 minutes or until potato noodles are lightly browned and cooked through. Divide the noodles into separate bowls and cover to keep warm.
2. While potatoes cook, place all of the ingredients for the pesto into a food processor and pulse until creamy. Taste and adjust, if necessary.
3. Immediately add in the tomato slices and cook for 30 seconds on each side. Place the tomato slices over the potato noodles (in the bowls).
4. Then, let the skillet cool down for 1-2 minutes (or just rinse quickly with cold water) and then coat with cooking spray. Add in the eggs and scramble and then season with salt and pepper. Top the tomato slices with the eggs and then garnish with avocado and drizzle of pesto

Savory Oatmeal with Spiralized Apples with DeLallo SaladSavors®

*Cook time: 5 mins| **Total time:** 5 mins | **Serves:** 3*

Ingredients

- 3 packs of instant oats
- 1 box of DeLallo's Salad Savors: fresh flavor*
- 1 apple of choice
- ¾ cup plain, unsweetened almond milk
  *If you want to make this recipe but don't have access to the Salad Savors, instead use:
- 3 tablespoons chopped walnuts
- 4 tablespoons dried cranberries
- 1 ounce goat cheese, crumbled

Directions

1. Empty the contents of the oats packets into three bowls. Pour over ⅔ cup of boiling water over each bowl and stir each until oats fluff up and absorb the moisture fully.
2. Spiralize the apple with Blade D and divide the apple noodles onto each bowl of oatmeal and top with equal amounts of the contents of the Salad Savors. Add the almond milk and serve.

Savory Parsnip Noodle Chive Waffles

Prep Time: 10 minutes | Cook Time: 15 minutes | Servings: 2 waffles

Ingredients

- ½ tablespoon extra virgin olive oil
- 2 large parsnips, peeled, Blade C, noodles roughly trimmed
- 1/4 teaspoon garlic powder
- salt and pepper, to taste
- 1 large egg, beaten
- 3 tablespoons chopped chives
- optional, to top: ¼ cup greek yogurt, 2 teaspoons lemon juice

Directions

1. Preheat a Belgian waffle iron.
2. Meanwhile, place a large skillet over medium heat and add in the olive oil. Once oil heats, add in the parsnip noodles and season with garlic powder, salt and pepper. Cover and cook for 5 minutes or until noodles are wilted and cooked through.
3. Once cooked, add to a bowl with the egg and chives and toss to combine. Spray the waffle iron with cooking spray and then pack in the parsnip mixture. Cook to the waffle iron's settings and then remove carefully.
4. Optional: while waffles are cooking, mix together Greek Yogurt and lemon juice and season with pepper.
5. When waffles are done, top with optional Greek yogurt or serve as is, ideally with salty bacon or maple syrup.

Savoy Cabbage "Breakfast Burrito" with Sweet Potato Noodles

Prep Time: 10 m | Cook Time: 15 m | Total Time: 25 m | Servings: 2

Ingredients

- 2 cabbage savoy leafs
- 1 avocado, insides cubed
- salt and pepper, to taste
- 4 pieces of bacon
- 1 sweet potato, peeled, Blade C
- 4 eggs, beaten

Directions

1. Rinse your cabbage leaves and pat dry. Set aside, on a plate.
2. Place your avocado into a bowl, mash and season with salt and pepper. Spread this over the center of each cabbage leaf.
3. Place a large skillet over medium heat and add in the bacon. Let cook until to your crispy preference and set aside on a paper-towel lined plate. Remove half of the oil left behind from the bacon and add in your sweet potato noodles. Cook the noodles, tossing occasionally, for 5-8 minutes or until they wilt. Once done, place onto the cabbage leaves, over the avocado.
4. Next, place the eggs into the same skillet and scramble. Once scrambled, place over the sweet potato noodles.
5. Top the eggs with two pieces of bacon per wrap. Then, roll like a burrito and enjoy.

Spicy Chorizo "Migas" with Sweet Potato Noodles

Prep Time: 15 minutes | Cook Time: 20 minutes | Servings: 3

Ingredients

- 1/2 tablespoon extra virgin olive oil
- 1 large sweet potato, peeled, Blade C, noodles trimmed
- ¼ teaspoon garlic powder
- salt and pepper, to taste
- ½ pound chorizo links, decased (about 2)
- 1 small onion, diced
- 1 large red bell pepper, diced
- 2 teaspoons minced jalapeno (if you don't like spicy, omit)

- ¼ teaspoon paprika
- 1 teaspoon oregano
- 6 eggs, beaten
- 1 tablespoon chopped cilantro

Directions

1. Place a large skillet over medium heat and add in the olive oil. Once oil heats, add in the sweet potato noodles and season with garlic powder, salt and pepper. Cover and cook, uncovering occasionally to toss, for 5-7 minutes or until potato noodles are cooked to al dente. Set the noodles aside in three plates and cover (with tinfoil or a plate) and then add the chorizo to the skillet, crumbling with a wooden spoon.
2. Cook the chorizo until browned, about 7 minutes. Set aside, using a slotted spoon. Immediately add in the onions, bell pepper and jalapeno. Season with paprika, oregano and salt and pepper and cook for about 3 minutes or until vegetables soften. Then, add in the cooked chorizo and the eggs. Cook until the eggs are scrambled.
3. Divide the chorizo-egg mixture on top of the sweet potato noodles. Garnish with cilantro and serve immediately.

Spiralized Paleo Eggs Benedict with Roasted Sweet Potato Noodles, Avocado and Chipotle Hollandaise

Prep Time: 15 m | Cook Time: 15 m | Total Time: 30 m | Servings: 3

Ingredients

- 1 large sweet potato, Blade C, noodles trimmed
- olive oil cooking spray
- ¼ teaspoon garlic powder
- salt and pepper, to taste
- 1 avocado, insides cubed
- 3 large eggs
- 1 tablespoon chopped cilantro
- For the sauce:
- 2 eggs yolks
- 1 tablespoon lemon juice
- ½ teaspoon sea salt
- 1 chipotle pepper + 1 teaspoon of adobo sauce (from canned chipotles in adobo sauce)

- 3 tablespoons melted coconut oil

Directions

1. Preheat the oven to 425 degrees. Place the sweet potato noodles on a baking sheet, lightly coat with cooking spray and season with garlic powder, salt and pepper. Sprinkle over with the avocado cubes and then roast for 10-13 minutes or until the sweet potato noodles are cooked to your preference.
2. Meanwhile, place the egg yolks, lemon juice, se salt, chipotle pepper and sauce in a blender and blend for about 10 seconds. Then, set the blender on medium and slowly pour in the coconut oil to thicken. Once thickened, set aside.
3. After the hollandaise sauce is made, fill a medium saucepan halfway with water and bring to a steady simmer. Crack the eggs individually into a ramekin or small bowl. Then, create a gentle whirlpool in the simmering water to help the egg white wrap around the yolk. Slowly tip the egg into the water. Let cook for three minutes. Remove with a slotted spoon and gently rest on a paper towel lined plate.
4. Once the sweet potato noodles and avocado are done, place like a "nest" on three plates. Top each with poached (or fried, if you don't feel like poaching!) egg and drizzle with hollandaise sauce. Serve immediately, garnished with cilantro.

Spiralized Parsnip Nests with Eggs, Bacon and Arugula

Prep time: *5 mins* | **Cook time:** *40 mins* | **Total time:** *45 mins* | **Serves:** *8*

Ingredients

- 2 strips of bacon
- 2 large parsnips, peeled, Blade D, noodles trimmed
- salt and pepper, to taste
- ½ teaspoon garlic powder
- 2 eggs, beaten
- 8 whole eggs
- 1 cup baby arugula
- hot sauce, to drizzle

Directions

1. Preheat the oven to 425 degrees. Grease a large muffin tin with cooking spray.
2. Place a large skillet over medium-high heat and once heated, add in the bacon. Cook the bacon, about 10 minutes, until cooked through and crispy. Set aside on a paper towel lined plate and when ready to cool, crumble into small "bits."
3. Remove all of the bacon fat except for one tablespoon and add in the parsnip noodles. Season with salt, pepper and garlic powder and toss. Let cook for 5-7 minutes or until cooked through and then transfer to a medium mixing bowl. Let cool for 2 minutes.
4. Add in the eggs to the bowl and toss thoroughly to combine. Pack the parsnip noodles into the muffin holes, trying your best to create a cavity in the center. Cook for 15 minutes.
5. Remove the parsnip nests from the oven and crack an egg in each. Place back in the oven and bake another 9-12 minutes or until the eggs set. Open the oven and check at 9 minutes - give the muffin pan a shake and if the egg whites are still not set, cook for another 2 minutes and then check again. When done, remove from the oven and immediately top with arugula, bacon and hot sauce.

Spiralized Potato Breakfast Pie with Avocado and Fried Eggs

Prep time: 10 mins | Cook time: 45 mins | Total time: 55 mins | Serves: 2

Ingredients

- 2 yukon gold potatoes, peeled, Blade C/D
- salt and pepper, to taste
- 1 teaspoon garlic powder
- 2 large eggs
- ½ avocado
- sriracha, to taste
- parsley, to garnish

Directions

1. Preheat the oven to 400 degrees. In a medium mixing bowl, add in the potato noodles, drizzle with olive oil and toss together with the salt, pepper and garlic powder. Spray a 9" diameter x 2" pie pan with cooking spray and pack with potato noodles. Bake for 45 minutes or until crispy

and golden brown. Once done, use a spatula to carefully remove the potato pie from the pan and set on a large dinner plate.

2. After 40 minutes, place a large skillet over medium-high heat. Once heated, add in the eggs and fry until egg whites are set. Meanwhile, slice the avocado.

3. At this point, you can divide the potato pie into two pieces for easier sharing or you can serve the pie as one and share.

4. After you divide or leave as one, top with avocado slices, fried eggs and drizzle with sriracha and garnish with parsley. Enjoy immediately.

Spiralized Tortilla Espanola with Chorizo

Prep Time: 10 m | Cook Time: 25 m | Total Time: 35 m | Servings: 4 large slices

Ingredients

- 1 tbsp olive oil
- 1 yellow onion, diced
- 2 small spicy chorizo links, small diced
- 2 310g white potatoes, peeled, Blade A
- salt and pepper, to taste
- 6 eggs + 5 egg whites, beaten
- 1 tbsp chopped parsley, to garnish

Directions

1. Preheat the oven to 375 degrees.
2. Place a large nonstick skillet over medium heat and add in the olive oil. Once the oil heats, add in the onion and chorizo and cook for 2 minutes or until the onions become translucent.
3. Then, add in the potato noodles, season with salt and pepper and toss with pasta tongs, careful not to break the noodles. Cook for about 5 minutes, tossing occasionally, until the potatoes are almost cooked completely.
4. Pour the egg mixture evenly over the potato noodles. If some potatoes stick out of the eggs, that's okay. Let cook for 1-2 minutes or until eggs set on the bottom of the skillet.
5. Bake in the oven for 15-17 minutes or until edges brown. Remove skillet from the oven, garnish with parsley and serve. Slice into 4 or 8 pieces.

Squash Zoodler Omelet

"Quick and healthy breakfast!"

Servings: *2* | ***Prep***: *10 m* | ***Cook***: *15 m* | ***Ready In***: *25 m*

Ingredients

- 1 yellow squash, ends trimmed
- 1 tablespoon butter
- 1/4 cup fresh spinach, or more to taste
- 2 tablespoons chopped fresh cilantro 2 eggs
- 1/4 cup milk
- 2 tablespoons shredded mozzarella cheese
- salt and ground black pepper to taste

Directions

1. Process the yellow squash through a zoodler (vegetable peeler that forms noodle-shape pieces) until squash zoodles form.
2. Heat butter in a skillet over medium heat; cook and stir squash zoodles, spinach, and cilantro until zoodles are tender, 5 to 7 minutes. Spread mixture evenly into the bottom of the skillet.
3. Whisk eggs and milk together in a bowl; pour over squash mixture. Cook until egg is firm, about 5 minutes. Sprinkle mozzarella cheese over egg mixture and cook until cheese is melted, about 5 minutes; season with salt and pepper.

Nutritional Information

- Calories:176 kcal 9%
- Fat: 12.7 g 20%
- Carbs: 6.2g 2%
- Protein: 10.2 g 20%
- Cholesterol: 208 mg 69%
- Sodium: 251 mg 10%

Sweet Potato Rice Breakfast Bowl with Avocado and Scallions

Prep time: 10 mins | Cook time: 15 mins | Total time: 25 mins | Serves: 2

Ingredients

- 1 tablespoon extra virgin olive oil
- 1 medium sweet potato, peeled, Blade D
- salt and pepper, to taste
- 2 eggs
- ½ avocado, pitted, peeled and sliced thinly
- 2 scallions, diced
- ¼ teaspoon red pepper flakes, to garnish

Directions

1. Place the sweet potato noodles in a food processor and pulse until rice-like.
2. Heat the oil in a large skillet over medium-high heat. Once oil is shimmering, add in the sweet potato rice. Stir and season with salt and pepper. Cover, reduce heat to medium-low and let cook for 7 minutes or until rice is softened. When done, divide into two bowls.
3. When rice is almost done, place a small skillet over medium-high heat and coat with cooking spray. Add in the eggs and let cook until egg whites set, about 5 minutes.
4. Top the rice bowls with the eggs and then add the sliced avocado and garnish with scallions and red pepper flak

Sweet Potato Rice Mexican Breakfast Skillet

Prep Time: 15 mins | Cook Time: 20 mins | Total Time: 35 mins | Servings: 2-3

Ingredients

- 1 (345g) medium sweet potato, peeled, Blade C
- 1 small ear of corn
- 1 large garlic clove, minced
- 1/3 cup chopped white onion
- 1/3-1/2 cup chopped green bell pepper
- 1 14oz can whole peeled tomatoes
- 1/2 tsp chili powder

- 1 avocado, peeled, insides cubed
- 1.5 tbsp chopped cilantro
- 1/2 cup black beans
- 1 egg (or 2)
- 2 tbsp crumbled cotija cheese

Directions

1. Place your sweet potato noodles into a food processor and pulse until rice-like. Set aside.
2. Place the corn into a saucepan and cover with water. Bring to a boil and cook for 2 minutes or until corn softens. Drain and set aside.
3. Heat a 8 or 10" skillet over medium heat and then add in the olive oil, garlic and onions. Cook for 1 minute and then add in the green peppers. Cook for 2-3 minutes or until onions are translucent.
4. Add in the sweet potato rice. Toss to combine and then add in two of the tomatoes in the can by crushing them with your hands over the skillet. Add in 2 tbsp of the juice from the can. Then, add in the chili powder, avocado, cilantro, black beans and shave off 3/4 of the corn kernels into the skillet. Toss to combine fully and then let cook, stirring occasionally, for 6-8 minutes or until sweet potato rice softens.
5. While the skillet cooks, fry an egg in another skillet.
6. When the sweet potato rice skillet is cooked, top it with the fried egg, sprinkle with cotija and serve.

Tofu Scramble with Broccoli Noodles

Prep Time: *10 m |* ***Cook Time:*** *15 m |* ***Total Time:*** *25 m |* ***Servings:*** *3*

Ingredients

- 2 broccoli stems, Blade C (florets saved for future use)
- 1 14oz block of extra-firm tofu
- 2 tablespoons extra virgin olive oil
- ½ onion, diced
- 2 cloves of garlic, minced
- 1 small red bell pepper, finely diced
- 1 teaspoon cumin
- 1 teaspoon turmeric
- 1 tablespoon nutritional yeast flakes (optional)
- salt and pepper, to taste

Directions

1. Bring a medium pot of water to a boil. Once boiling, add in the broccoli noodles and cook for 2-3 minutes or until broccoli noodles are al dente.
2. While the broccoli cooks, place the tofu on a plate lined with paper towels. Using a fork, smash the tofu until it crumbles. Blot the top with paper towels to remove as much excess moisture as possible. Set aside.
3. Heat a large skillet over medium heat and add in the olive oil. Once oil heats, add in the onion, garlic and peppers. Cook for 3-5 minutes or until vegetables soften. Add in the cumin, stir for 1 minute and then add in the tofu, broccoli noodles, turmeric and nutritional yeast flakes. Season with salt and pepper and cook for 2-3 minutes or until the tofu is heated through.
4. Serve warm.

Two-Ingredient Pancakes With Cinnamon Spiralized Apples

Prep time: 5 mins | Cook time: 10 mins | Total time: 15 mins | Serves: 12 mini pancakes (3 servings)

Ingredients

- 4 large eggs, beaten
- 2 medium ripe bananas
- 2 teaspoons coconut oil
- 1 apple, Blade D
- ¼ teaspoon cinnamon
- maple syrup, to serve

Directions

1. Place the bananas in a bowl and mash it with a fork until no big clumps remain. If you have the time, try using an electric mixer to really get those clumps out. Add in the eggs and mix together thoroughly to combine.
2. Heat a griddle or large skillet over medium-high heat. Once the pan is heated, coat with cooking spray and then ladle in the pancake mixture, 2 tablespoons at a time. Cook the pancakes for 1-2 minutes or until set on the bottom, then flip and cook another 2 minutes or until the pancakes are slightly browned and cooked through. They won't be fluffy, they'll be very

flat – but embrace this new texture! Repeat in batches until all the batter is used, transferring to a plate as they finish.

3. Once the pancakes are done, add in the coconut oil and swirl around to coat the pan. Add in the apple noodles and sprinkle with cinnamon. Cook the apple noodles for 2-3 minutes or until totally wilted.

4. Place 4 pancakes per plate and top with apples. Drizzle with maple syrup. Serve.

Chapter 3: Dessert

***

Apple-Cranberry Tart

"If you think spiralizers are just for making zucchini zoodles, you're in for a surprise. You can make thinly-sliced, half apple slices in no time using a spiralizer."

Servings: *4|* ***Prep:*** *30 m |* ***Cook:*** *38 m |* ***Ready In:*** *1 h 23 m*

Ingredients

- 1/4 cup dried cranberries cooking spray
- 2 Granny Smith apples, peeled
- 1 teaspoon lemon juice
- 1/2 teaspoon vanilla extract
- 2 tablespoons white sugar
- 1 tablespoon cornstarch
- 1/2 teaspoon ground cinnamon
- 1/2 teaspoon ground nutmeg
- 1/4 teaspoon salt
- 1 (9 inch) prepared pie crust
- 1 egg white, beaten
- 1 tablespoon turbinado sugar, or to taste

Directions

1. Place cranberries in a small bowl. Cover with boiling water. Let soak until plump, about 15 minutes. Drain.
2. Preheat oven to 350 degrees F (175 degrees C). Grease a baking sheet lightly with cooking spray.
3. Cut a deep vertical slice into both sides of each apple, being sure not to cut through to the core. Attach 1 apple to a spiralizer fitted with the straight-flat blade and cut into thin half-slices. Repeat with second apple.
4. Combine cranberries, apple slices, lemon juice, and vanilla extract in a bowl; toss to coat.
5. Mix white sugar, cornstarch, cinnamon, nutmeg, and salt together in a bowl. Stir into the apple mixture.
6. Roll pie crust out into a 10-inch round on a floured work surface. Transfer to the baking sheet.
7. Spoon apple mixture into the center of the crust, leaving a 2-inch border. Lift up edges of crust and fold around apple mixture. Brush edges with egg white. Sprinkle turbinado sugar all over tart.

8. Bake in the preheated oven until apples are tender and crust is golden brown, 38 to 40 minutes. Transfer to a serving plate and slice.

Nutritional Information

- Calories:333 kcal 17%
- Fat: 15.1 g 23%
- Carbs: 47g 15%
- Protein: 3.9 g 8%
- Cholesterol: 0 mg 0%
- Sodium: 395 mg 16%

Cacao Plantain Rice Balls with Pepitas

Prep Time: 10 m | Cook Time: 3 m | Total Time: 13 m | Servings: 5-6 balls

Ingredients

- 1 plantain, peeled, Blade C
- 5 medjool dates, pitted and roughly chopped
- 1 tsp cacao
- 2 tsp de-shelled roasted and salted pepitas
- 3 tsp coconut flakes

Instructions

1. Place your plantain noodles into a food processor and pulse until like rice. Place into a large skillet over medium-high heat and cook for 3 minutes, tossing frequently.
2. Place the plantain rice, medjools, cacao and coconut flakes into a food processor and pulse until sticky and smooth.
3. Place the mash into a bowl and add in the pepitas. Mix with hands to incorporate the pepitas. Then, form 5-6 balls with hands and place each onto a plate. Refrigerate for 15 minutes and then enjoy or enjoy immediately.

Coconut Plantain "Rice" Pudding

Prep Time: 5 minutes | Cook Time: 10 minutes | Total Time: 15 minutes | Servings: 1

Ingredients

- 1 1/3 cup vanilla almond milk
- 1 medium-ripe plantain, peeled, Blade C
- 1/8 tsp cinnamon
- 1/4 cup raisins
- 1-2 tsp coconut flakes

Instructions

1. Place your plantain noodles into a food processor and pulse until made into rice-like bits. Place into a medium saucepan, along with 1 cup of the almond milk.
2. Bring the contents of the saucepan to a boil. Once boiling, lower heat to a simmer. Simmer for 10 minutes. At around 5 minutes, the rice should have reduced. Whenever it does reduce (almost starts sticking to the bottom), add in the other 1/3 cup of milk. Let reduce, stirring occasionally until creamy.
3. Once done, remove from heat and add in the cinnamon, coconut flakes and raisins. Stir until the cinnamon dissolves into the pudding.
4. Pour into a bowl and enjoy!

Easy Apple Crisp with Peanut Butter Granola

Prep Time: 10 m | Cook Time: 20 m |Total Time: 30 m | Servings: 4

Ingredients

- 2 Granny Smith apples, Blade A
- 1 Braeburn or Honeycrisp apple, Blade A
- 1/4 cup maple syrup
- 1 tsp ground cinnamon
- 1 cup of KIND's Peanut Butter Whole Grain Clusters granola*

Instructions

1. Preheat the oven to 400 degrees.

2. Place the apple slices in a bowl, drizzle with half of the maple syrup. Mix to combine and lay into the bottom of a small cast-iron skillet.
3. Bake in the oven for 5 minutes and then remove, sprinkle over the granola to cover the apples and drizzle with remaining maple syrup.
4. Bake the crisp for 10-15 minutes or until the apples soften completely. Remove from the oven and enjoy!

Easy Apple Noodle & Rhubarb Crisps

Prep Time: *10 minutes* | **Cook Time:** *35 minutes* | **Total Time:** *45 minutes* | **Servings:** *4*

Ingredients

- 3 rhubarb stalks
- 3 apples (I used gala and honey crisp), Blade C
- honey, to drizzle
- 1/2 cup granola of choice (I used Udi's Gluten Free - vanilla granola)

Instructions

1. Preheat the oven to 350 degrees.
2. Take your rhubarb and slice lengthwise down the stalk. Then, cube. In a bowl, toss the rhubarb with the apple noodles.
3. Take out four ramekins. In each ramekin, pack in the apple-rhubarb mixture three-quarters of the way full (leave room at the top for the granola).
4. Lightly drizzle the tops of each ramekin with honey and then bake for 30 minutes. After 30 minutes, remove the ramekins, place 2 tbsp of granola on top per ramekin and bake for 5 more minutes.
5. Once done, serve.

Gluten-Free Chocolate Zucchini Noodle Donuts with Coconut-Chocolate Glaze

Prep time: *20 mins* | **Cook time:** *30 mins* | **Total time:** *50 mins* | **Serves:** *6 donuts*

Ingredients

- 1 medium zucchini
- ½ cup coconut flour
- ¼ cup tapioca flour
- ¾ teaspoon baking soda
- ¼ teaspoon salt
- 2 teaspoons cinnamon
- ½ teaspoon nutmeg
- 1.5 tablespoons cacao powder
- 3 eggs
- 3 tablespoons maple syrup
- 2 teaspoons vanilla extract
- 2 tablespoons almond milk
- 1 tablespoon coconut oil, melted and cooled to room temperature
- 1 ripe banana, mashed
- 2 tablespoons unsweetened shredded coconut

For the chocolate

- ¼ cup vegan chocolate chips (I like Enjoylife brand)

Instructions

1. Preheat the oven to 350 degrees.
2. Grease a donut tin with cooking spray. Set aside.
3. Slice the ends off of the zucchini and then slice it halfway lengthwise. Spiralize, using Blade D. In a medium bowl, add in the coconut flour, tapioca flour, baking soda, salt, cinnamon, nutmeg and cacao.
4. In another medium bowl, mix the eggs, maple syrup, vanilla extract, almond milk, coconut oil and banana together.
5. Add the dry ingredients to the wet and add in the zucchini and stir until the batter is smooth.
6. Pour the batter into the donut tins and bake for 30 minutes or until a toothpick comes out clean when you pierce the center of a donut and the donut is firm and hardened on the outside, like a donut!
7. Pop the donuts out carefully.
8. Place a small saucepan over medium-high heat and add in the chocolate chips. Let heat, stirring frequently, until fully melted.
9. Place the donuts on a piece of parchment paper and drizzle over with chocolate. Dust with coconut flakes. Enjoy immediately or let stand for 20 minutes for the chocolate to harden.

Spiralized Apple 'Spaghetti' with Cinnamon Dressing

"Cool and refreshing dessert with the crunch of walnuts."

Servings: 2| *Prep:* 10 m | *Ready In:* 10 m

Ingredients

- 1 Red Delicious apple
- 1 (6 ounce) container plain Greek yogurt
- 2 teaspoons honey, or more to taste
- 1/4 teaspoon ground cinnamon
- 1/4 teaspoon vanilla extract
- 1/4 cup chopped walnuts

Directions

1. Attach apple to a spiralizer and cut into ribbons.
2. Whisk Greek yogurt, honey, cinnamon, and vanilla extract together in a bowl until blended. Add apple; toss to coat. Garnish with walnuts.

Nutritional Information

- Calories:257 kcal 13%
- Fat: 18 g 28%
- Carbs: 19.1g 6%
- Protein: 7.4 g 15%
- Cholesterol: 19 mg6%
- Sodium: 56 mg 2%

Sweet Ricotta Pear Ribbons with Roasted Honey Walnuts and Figs

Prep Time: 5 minutes | *Cook Time:* 10 minutes | *Total Time:* 15 minutes | *Servings:* 2

Ingredients

- 2 pears, peeled, Blade A
- 6 black mission figs, halved
- 1/2 cup ricotta cheese*
- 1/3 tsp vanilla extract
- 1 tbsp honey
- 1/2 cup walnuts
- more honey to drizzle

Instructions

1. Preheat your oven to 375 degrees. Prepare two baking dishes lined with parchment paper. In one dish, place your figs. Dab the sliced sides lightly with honey, using your fingers. Place in the oven for 10 minutes.
2. In the other dish, place your walnuts. Drizze with honey and mix with your fingers to coat the walnuts evenly. Three minutes before the figs are done, add in the walnuts. Remove both from the oven when done and remove from parchment paper immediately and set aside on a plate or in a bowl.
3. While your nuts and figs are baking, pour the ricotta cheese into a food processor and pulse until whipped. Place in a bowl and add in the vanilla extract and honey. Taste and add more vanilla/honey to your preference.
4. Time to assemble the dessert! Arrange your pear ribbons on a plate as the base for this dessert. Create a circle using the figs and walnuts (save a few.) Top with sweet ricotta and remaining walnuts and figs.

White Chocolate Zucchini-Oat Cookies (Gluten Free)

Prep Time: *10 minutes* | **Cook Time:** *12 minutes* | **Total Time:** *22 minutes* | **Servings:** *24 cookies*

Ingredients

Dry:

- 1 cup gluten-free flour
- 1 teaspoon baking soda
- ½ teaspoon kosher salt
- ¾ teaspoon ground cinnamon

Wet:

- ¼ cup apple butter
- ¾ cup brown sugar
- 1 large egg
- 1 teaspoon vanilla extract
- 1 cup grated zucchini
- 2 cups gluten-free rolled oats
- ½ cup white mini chocolate chips

Instructions

1. Preheat the oven to 350 degrees F. Line a baking sheet with a silicone mat or parchment paper.
2. In a medium-size bowl, whisk together flour, baking soda, kosher salt, and cinnamon. Set aside.
3. In a large bowl, add apple butter and brown sugar; mix until the brown sugar melts into the apple butter and the mixture becomes smooth. Whisk in the egg and vanilla. Add the grated zucchini and whisk to combine.
4. Using a rubber spatula, slowly stir in the flour mixture until just combined. Fold in the oats and chocolate chips.
5. Scoop the dough using a 1-tablespoon cookie scoop onto your prepared pan, spacing the cookies 3 inches apart. Bake for 11-12 minutes, or until the edges are slightly golden brown. Allow the cookies to rest on the pan for 3-5 minutes before transferring to a wire rack to cool completely.

Chapter 4: Snack and Side Dish

***

Apple-Potato Latkes

"A nontraditional approach to a potato latke. The shredding is done using a spiralizer, and the apple and maple syrup give you just enough sweetness to make these different. Good topped with sour cream or applesauce.""

***Servings:** 4 | **Prep:** 15 m | **Cook:**5 m | **Ready In:** 20 m*

Ingredients

- 1 russet potato, peeled
- 1 firm apple, peeled
- 1 egg, lightly beaten
- 3 tablespoons all-purpose flour
- 1 teaspoon maple syrup
- 1/2 teaspoon sea salt
- 1 pinch ground nutmeg
- 2 tablespoons vegetable oil, or as needed

Directions

1. Make a deep vertical cut on each side of the potato and apple.
2. Attach potato to a spiralizer fitted with the small shredded blade and cut into thin shreds. Repeat with apple. Spread shredded potato and apple on several layers of paper towels; squeeze to release as much moisture as possible. Transfer to a bowl.
3. Mix egg, flour, maple syrup, salt, and nutmeg into the bowl.
4. Heat vegetable oil in a skillet over medium heat. Spoon 2 tablespoons of the potato mixture into the skillet; flatten slightly with a spatula. Cook until golden brown, 3 to 4 minutes per side. Drain on a plate lined with paper towels. Repeat with remaining mixture, adding more oil if needed.

Nutritional Information

- Calories:164 kcal 8%
- Fat: 8.3 g 13%
- Carbs: 19.9g 6%
- Protein: 3.4 g 7%
- Cholesterol: 46 mg 16%

- Sodium: 241 mg10%

Baked Mexican Chips on a Stick

"Forget about ripping open a bag of potato chips and make your own healthier baked potato chips on a stick. These chips have a subtle Mexican flavor, but get creative and use different seasonings that you like. Once you get used to threading the potato spirals onto skewers, these are not only fun, but easy!"

Servings: *6 |* **Prep:** *15 m |* **Cook:** *17 m |* **Ready In:** *32 m*

Ingredients

- nonfat cooking spray
- 2 russet potatoes, unpeeled
- 2 teaspoons taco seasoning mix, or to taste
- 6 bamboo skewers
- 2 teaspoons sriracha sauce, or to taste
- 1 pinch sea salt to taste

Directions

1. Preheat oven to 425 degrees F (220 degrees C). Line a baking sheet with aluminum foil and grease with cooking spray.
2. Slice each potato into long spirals using a spiralizer fitted with the straight-flat blade. Cut each spiral into 3 shorter pieces.
3. Thread a skewer through the middle of each potato spiral. Gently push down to fan out spiral.
4. Set skewers on the prepared baking sheet; spray generously with cooking spray. Sprinkle taco seasoning on top.
5. Roast in the preheated oven until browned and crisp, 17 to 18 minutes. Season with sriracha sauce and sea salt.

Nutritional Information

- Calories:59 kcal 3%
- Fat: 0.1 g < 1%
- Carbs: 13.3g 4%
- Protein: 1.4 g 3%
- Cholesterol: 0 mg 0%

- Sodium: 206 mg 8%

Crispy Baked Spiralized Fries

Prep time: 10 mins | Cook time: 30 mins | Total time: 40 mins | Serves: 4

Ingredients

- 3 russet potatoes, peeled, Blade C, noodles trimmed
- olive oil, to drizzle (1.5-2 tablespoons)
- Salt and pepper
- 1 teaspoon chili powder
- 1 teaspoon garlic powder
- 1 teaspoon paprika

Instructions

1. Preheat the oven to 425 degrees.
2. Place the potato noodles on a nonstick baking sheet and drizzle with olive oil and season generously with salt and pepper. Toss to coat with your fingers and then sprinkle over all of the seasonings, one by one. Toss again to coat with your fingers and cover the noodles in the spices. Place the noodles in the oven and let roast for 25-30 minutes.
3. At 25 minutes, if there are any pieces that are starting to turn brown, take them out and set them aside and then continue to cook the noodles until they crisp up, checking every 2 minutes for anymore pieces that are cooking more quickly than others. After 30 minutes, all noodles should be cooked and crisped through. Let cool for 5 minutes. Cooling allows the fries to crisp up a bit more. Serve.

Curried Potato Noodles with Kale

Prep time: 10 mins | Cook time: 15 mins | Total time: 25 mins | Serves: 4

Ingredients

- 1.5 tablespoon extra virgin olive oil

- 1 garlic clove, minced
- 1 shallot, minced
- 1 large russet potato (or 2 medium red potatoes), Blade C, noodles trimmed
- 2 cups diced kale, stems removed
- For the seasoning:
- 1 tablespoon vegetable broth
- 1 teaspoon country Dijon mustard
- 1 teaspoon curry powder
- ¼ teaspoon cayenne powder
- ¼ teaspoon turmeric
- ¼ teaspoon cumin powder
- salt and pepper, to taste

Instructions

1. In a small mixing bowl, add in all of the ingredients for the curry seasoning. Whisk together and set aside.
2. Place a large skillet over medium heat and add in 1 tablespoon of the olive oil. Once oil heats, add in the garlic and shallots and cook for 1 minute or until shallots soften. Add in the potato noodles, toss well and then pour over with the curry seasoning. Toss to combine thoroughly, making sure to coat all the noodles and then cover and cook for 10 minutes or until cooked through but al dente, uncovering occasionally to toss.
3. Once cooked, uncover and add in the kale, the last half tablespoon of olive oil, season with salt and pepper and toss to combine or until kale wilts, about 3 minutes.
4. Plate into a serving bowl and enjoy as a side!

Deep-Fried Zucchini Spirals

"We have always enjoyed fried zucchini so when I saw the clever way to spiral cut them, I thought why not deep fry them like onion strings. I did and they were a hit! Sprinkle with Old Bay® to make this a perfect side dish for seafood. They can also be served as an appetizer with your favorite dip. The zucchini may be cut into chips if you do not have a spiral slicer."

Servings: 2| **Prep**: 15 m | **Cook**: 5 m | **Ready In:** 20 m

Ingredients

- 3 cups vegetable oil
- 1 egg 1 tablespoon milk
- 1/2 cup all-purpose flour
- 1/4 cup cornstarch
- 1 zucchini, cut into spirals using a spiral slicer
- 1 teaspoon seafood seasoning (such as Old Bay®), or to taste

Directions

1. Heat oil in a deep-fryer or large saucepan to 350 degrees F (175 degrees C).
2. Whisk egg and milk together in a bowl; pour into a gallon-size resealable plastic bag. Whisk flour and cornstarch together in another bowl; pour into a separate gallon-size resealable plastic bag.
3. Place zucchini spirals into milk mixture, seal the bag, and turn to coat spirals completely. Transfer zucchini to flour mixture, seal the bag, and shake gently to coat completely. Remove spirals from flour mixture and shake gently to remove any excess flour.
4. Working in batches, cook zucchini spirals in the preheated oil until golden brown and cooked through, 2 to 4 minutes. Transfer zucchini to a paper towel-lined plate to drain. Sprinkle seafood season over cooked zucchini spirals.

Nutritional Information

- Calories:524 kcal 26%
- Fat: 36.2 g 56%
- Carbs: 42.6g 14%
- Protein: 7.9 g 16%
- Cholesterol: 94 mg 31%
- Sodium: 322 mg 13%

Dijon-Chive Spiralized Potatoes

Prep time: 20 mins | Cook time: 10 mins | Total time: 30 mins | Serves: 3

Ingredients

For the potatoes:

- 1 tablespoon olive oil
- ½ teaspoon garlic powder
- 1 pound red potatoes, Blade D, noodles trimmed
- salt and pepper, to taste

For the dressing:

- ½ tablespoon country dijon mustard
- 2 tablespoons olive oil
- 2 tablespoons chopped chives
- 1 teaspoon apple cider vinegar
- salt and pepper, to taste

Instructions

1. Place the olive oil into a large skillet and once heated, add in the potato noodles and season with garlic powder, salt and pepper. Cook for 10 minutes, tossing frequently, or until potato noodles cook through.
2. Meanwhile, whisk together the ingredients for the dressing into a small bowl. Set aside.
3. When potatoes are done, place into a large mixing bowl and pour over the dressing and toss thoroughly to combine. Serve immediately or refrigerate to chill.

Easy Cheddar-Rosemary Spiralized Potato Pancakes

Prep Time: 10 minutes | Cook Time: 25 minutes | Total Time: 35 minutes | Servings: 4 medium potato pancakes

Ingredients

- 1 tablespoon extra virgin olive oil
- 2 medium potatoes, peeled, Blade C (about 1-1.25 pounds)
- ¼ teaspoon garlic powder
- salt and pepper, to taste
- ½ tablespoon finely chopped fresh rosemary
- 2 eggs, beaten
- 1/2 cup grated Cabot Cheese White Oak Cheddar (or cheddar of choice)

Instructions

1. Heat the olive oil in a large skillet over medium heat. Flick water into the skillet and if it sizzles, it's ready. Add the potato noodles and season with garlic powder, salt, pepper and rosemary. Toss to combine and then cover and cook, uncovering occasionally to toss, or until potato noodles are cooked through, about 10 minutes.
2. Transfer the potato noodles to a large bowl and add in the eggs and cheddar. Toss to combine and set aside.
3. Heat the same large skillet back over medium heat and spray with cooking spray. Once heated, add in a large scoop (about 1 cup) of the potato mixture. Flatten the mixture out and let cook for 2-3 minutes or until it sets on the bottom. Flip the pancake over and cook another 2-3 minutes or until crispy, flattening with the back of a spatula. Repeat until all of the potato mixture is used, forming about 4 medium pancakes or 6 small ones.
4. Transfer the potato pancakes to a plate and serve immediately.

Easy Roasted Garlic-Parmesan Potato Noodles

Prep Time: 10 m | Cook Time: 20 m | Total Time: 30 m | Servings: 6

Ingredients

- 2 pounds red potatoes, Blade C, noodles trimmed
- 1 tablespoon extra virgin olive oil
- salt and pepper, to taste
- ½ teaspoon garlic powder
- 1.5 tablespoons freshly grated parmesan cheese
- 2 tablespoons minced parsley, to garnish

Instructions

1. Preheat the oven to 425 degrees.
2. Place the potato noodles in a large mixing bowl immediately after spiralizing and pour over olive oil. Toss gently with your fingers to combine and then lay out on a parchment-paper lined baking sheet. Season with salt, pepper and garlic powder and roast for 12-15 minutes or until they start to turn golden brown.

3. Remove the potato noodles from the oven and set it to broil. Sprinkle the potatoes with parmesan cheese and set back in the oven for 3-5 minutes or until golden brown, careful not to burn (a few burnt edges are okay.)
4. Remove from the oven, garnish with parsley and transfer to a serving bowl. Serve immediately.

Everything Bagel Bun Spiralized Chips

Prep time: 10 mins | *Cook time:* 25 mins | *Total time:* 35 mins | *Serves:* 60 chips

Ingredients

For the chips:

- 2 large russet potatoes, peeled
- 3 tablespoons olive oil
- Everything bagel seasoning:
- 1 teaspoon poppy seeds
- 1 teaspoon sesame seeds
- 1¼ teaspoons garlic powder
- 1 teaspoon onion powder
- ½ teaspoon coarse sea salt
- ¼ teaspoon freshly cracked black pepper

Instructions

1. Preheat the oven to 400 degrees F. Line a baking sheet with parchment paper.
2. In a bowl, mix together the ingredients for the everything bagel seasoning. Combine well and set aside.
3. Slice the potatoes halfway through lengthwise, careful not to pierce the center. Spiralize the potatoes on Blade A to make the chip slices.
4. Lay the spiralized potatoes out on the parchment paper. If needed, line another baking sheet to accommodate all the slices – do not overlap potatoes.
5. Place the olive oil in a small bowl and using a brush, brush the slices with three-quarters of the olive oil. Sprinkle over evenly with three-quarters of the every bagel seasoning.
6. Bake in the oven for 15 minutes, flip over, brush with remaining olive oil and season with remaining seasoning. Place the chips back into the oven and cook another 7-10 minutes, checking every 2-3 minutes to make sure

the chips don't burn. If they begin to burn, remove the ones that are burning and place the others back in the oven.

7. Let rest for 5 minutes to fully crisp up before serving.

Flaxseed Crusted Chicken Tenders with Sweet Potato Noodles

Prep time: 10 mins | *Cook time:* 20 mins | *Total time:* 30 mins | *Serves:* 4

Ingredients

- 1 large egg
- 8 boneless chicken tenders
- 1 tablespoon extra virgin olive oil
- 2 medium sweet potatoes, peeled, Blade D, noodles trimmed
- salt and pepper, to taste
- ¼ teaspoon chili powder
- To serve: dipping sauce of choice (honey mustard, marinara, ketchup, etc)

For the flaxseed crust:

- ½ cup almond meal
- ¼ cup flaxseed (I use Bob's Red Mill)
- ½ teaspoon garlic powder
- ¼ teaspoon onion powder
- 1 pinch paprika
- salt and pepper, to taste

Instructions

1. Preheat the oven to 400 degrees. Line a baking sheet with parchment paper and set aside. NOTE: If you want to skip the oven, then skip this step.
2. Place all of the ingredients for the flaxseed crust, into a medium mixing bowl and stir to combine. Pour the breadcrumbs into a shallow baking dish and set aside.
3. Beat the egg in a medium mixing bowl and set aside next to the breadcrumbs.
4. Dredge the chicken in the beaten egg then dip in the flaxseed crust mixture. Dip on both sides and pat the crust mixture into any crevices on the chicken. Place the chicken on the prepared baking sheets and put into the oven for 12-15 minutes or until no longer pink on the inside and juices

run clear. If you aren't oven-baking, cook the crusted tenders in a skillet with olive oil over medium-high heat until no longer pink on the inside.

5. Meanwhile, place a large skillet over medium-high heat and add in the olive oil. Once oil is shimmering, add the sweet potato noodles, season with salt, pepper, chili powder, and cook, tossing, for about 7 minutes or until cooked to your preference.

Grilled Tomatoes and Basil Zucchini Noodles with Balsamic Glaze

Prep Time: 10 m | Cook Time: 15 m | Total Time: 25 m | Servings: 4

Ingredients

- 1 cup balsamic vinegar
- 3 beefsteak tomatoes, cut into ½ inch slices
- salt and pepper, to taste
- 2 tablespoons extra virgin olive oil
- 3 medium zucchinis, Blade A
- 1 large chiffonade of basil

Instructions

1. Place a medium saucepan over high heat and add in the vinegar. Once boiling, reduce to a simmer and cook until reduced halfway.
2. While balsamic is cooking, heat a grill or grill pan over medium-high heat. Brush the tomatoes and zucchini with the olive oil and season both generously with salt and pepper.
3. Once the grill is heated, add in the tomatoes. Let cook for 2 minutes, flip over and cook another 2 minutes or until heated through and grill marks appear. Set aside.
4. Add the zucchini to the grill or grill pan and periodically use a the back of a spatula (if using a grill pan) to compress the noodles down to cook quickly. Cook for just 3-5 minutes or until cooked through. When done cooking, the zucchini will sweat out moisture, so lightly pat dry and lay out in a [insert measurements here] serving dish. Season the zucchini with extra pepper and toss with the basil.
5. Top the zucchini with the tomatoes and drizzle the balsamic on top. Garnish with extra basil and serve.

Indian Carrot Noodle Salad with Spiced Lamb

Prep time: 20 mins | *Cook time:* 15 mins | *Total time:* 35 mins | *Serves:* 2

Ingredients

- 1 pound ground lamb, lean
- 2 teaspoons garam masala
- salt, to taste
- 3 large carrots, peeled, Blade D, noodles trimmed
- ¼ cup fresh cilantro
- ¼ cup fresh mint
- For the dressing
- ½ teaspoon dried cumin
- 1 small red onion, peeled and sliced thinly
- juice of 1 lemon + its zest
- 1 teaspoon freshly grated ginger
- 4 tablespoons extra virgin olive oil

Instructions

1. Heat a large skillet over medium-high heat and once heated, add in the lamb, crumbling with a wooden spoon, until all the fat releases into the pan. Add the garam masala and season with salt and pepper. Cook the lamb until its crispy, about 7 minutes.
2. Combine all of the ingredients for the dressing into a bowl and whisk together. In a large mixing bowl, add in the carrot noodles, mint and cilantro. Pour over the dressing and toss to combine.
3. Divide the lamb mince between four plates and top with the carrot noodles.

Peas And Pesto Potato Noodles

Prep time: 20 mins | *Cook time:* 20 mins | *Total time:* 40 mins | *Serves:* 4

Ingredients

- 1 tablespoon extra virgin olive oil

- 1.5 pounds yukon gold potatoes, peeled, Blade D, noodles trimmed
- salt and pepper, to taste
- 1 cup frozen garden peas
- For the pesto:
- 2 tablespoons pine nuts
- 2 packed cups of basil
- 2 tablespoons parmesan cheese
- 3 tablespoons extra virgin olive oil
- 1 large garlic clove
- salt and pepper, to taste

Instructions

1. Place a large skillet over medium-high heat and add in the olive oil. Once oil heats, add in the potato noodles and season with salt and pepper. Toss and then cover and cook, uncovering occasionally to toss, for 7-10 minutes or until potato noodles are cooked through. Place in a large mixing bowl.
2. While the potatoes cook, in a food processor, place all of the ingredients for the pesto and pulse until creamy. Taste and adjust to your preferences, if necessary. Set aside. Also, cook your peas according to package directions.
3. Once potato noodles, peas and pesto are done, combine in a bowl and toss thoroughly to combine. Serve immediately or place in refrigerator and serve later, chilled.

Potato Noodle and Green Bean Salad with Chive-Dijon Vinaigrette

Prep Time: 10 m | Cook Time: 15 m | Total Time: 25 m | Servings: 4-6

Ingredients

- 1/2 pound fresh green beans, cut into 1" pieces
- 1 tablespoon extra virgin olive oil
- 2 large potatoes, Blade C
- salt and pepper, to taste
- ½ teaspoon garlic powder

For the dressing:

- 2.5 tablespoons white wine vinegar
- 1 tablespoon Dijon mustard
- 1 tablespoon chopped chives

- 2 teaspoons lemon juice
- 2 tablespoons extra virgin olive oil
- salt and pepper, to taste

Instructions

1. Bring a medium pot filled halfway with water to a boil. Once boiling, add in the green beans and cook for 5 minutes or until tender. Drain into a colander and place in a large mixing bowl.
2. While waiting for the water to boil, whisk all ingredients for the vinaigrette together and set aside in the refrigerator.
3. In a large skillet, place in the olive oil. Once oil heats, add in the potato noodles, season with salt, pepper and garlic powder. Cover and cook for 5-7 minutes or until cooked all the way through.
4. Once potatoes are cooked, add to the bowl with green beans and pour in vinaigrette. Toss to combine thoroughly and transfer to a serving bowl. Enjoy immediately or chill and enjoy later.

Prosciutto Wrapped Maple-Balsamic Sweet Potato Noodle Rolls

Prep time: 15 mins | **Cook time:** 5 mins | **Total time:** 20 mins | **Serves:** 12 halved rolls or 6 large rolls

Ingredients

- 1 large sweet potato, peeled, Blade C
- 12 slices of prosciutto, sliced in half
- 3 tablespoons goat cheese
- 6 dates, pitted and sliced thinly
- ½ cup chopped pecans
- For the maple-balsamic:
- ¼ cup maple syrup
- 3 tablespoons balsamic vinegar
- 2 teaspoons Dijon mustard

Instructions

1. Place a large skillet over medium heat and add in the olive oil. Once oil heats, add in the sweet potato noodles and season with salt and pepper.

Cover and cook for 5-7 minutes, uncovering to toss occasionally, until noodles soften and cook through.

2. While the sweet potato noodles cook, whisk together the syrup and vinegar in a small saucepan and then bring to a boil. Cook until reduced to ⅓ cup, about 3-5 minutes, stirring occasionally. Remove from heat and stir in the mustard. Set aside.

3. Lay out two pieces of prosciutto and smear with ½ tablespoon of goat cheese. Then, sprinkle with about 1 tablespoons of pecans and then sliced dates from about 1 date. Lay out a layer of sweet potato noodles. Roll the prosciutto to wrap everything up. Slice in half and secure with a toothpick. Repeat with remaining prosciutto, to create 6 in total. If you'd like to create larger appetizers, don't slice in half and only create 3.

4. Arrange rolls on a serving platter and drizzle each with some of the maple-balsamic. Serve immediately.

Roasted Carrot Mummies

*Prep time: 15 mins | **Cook time:** 40 mins | **Total time:** 55 mins | **Serves:** 3*

Ingredients

- 3 large carrots
- 2 large red potatoes
- 1 tablespoon extra virgin olive oil
- salt and pepper, to taste
- ½ teaspoon garlic powder
- 2 small black olives
- 1 teaspoon goat cheese, about

Instructions

1. Preheat the oven to 450 degrees. Line a baking tray with parchment paper.
2. Bake the carrot on the parchment paper for 10 minutes. Then, remove the carrot from the oven and let cool until you can touch it.
3. Wrap your carrot with the potato noodles, leaving a bit of room at the top for the eyeballs to peek out. Brush over with olive oil. Season with salt, pepper and garlic powder. Repeat until all the carrots are "mummified" and place them all on the parchment paper.
4. Bake for 30 minutes. While carrots bake, prepare the mummy eyes: cut the olives into thin slices. Set aside.

5. Once carrots have baked, remove from the oven and add on the eyes in the space left when wrapping them: place two dabs of goat cheese and top with two olive slices. Enjoy!

Roasted Sweet Potato and Yam Noodles with Fennel, Charred Tomatoes, Olives and Pecorino

Prep Time: 15 minutes | **Cook Time:** 55 minutes | **Total Time:** 1 hour 10 minutes | **Servings:** 6

Ingredients

1. 2 large bulbs fennel, quartered*
2. 1 medium sweet potato, peeled, Blade C
3. 1 medium yam, peeled, Blade C
4. 4 tablespoons extra-virgin olive oil
5. kosher salt and freshly ground pepper, to taste
6. ¼ cup freshly grated pecorino cheese
7. ½ teaspoon oregano
8. 4 plum tomatoes, thirded (is that even a word?)
9. 1/3 cup pitted kalamata olives, halved
10. 2 tablespoons chopped fresh flat-leaf parsley
11. *to prepare, slice the very ends off and then cut the stalks off the bulb so that little to no stalk remains on the bulb. Then quarter.

Instructions

1. Preheat the oven to 375 degrees F.
2. In a large bowl, toss together half of the olive oil and the potato noodles. Arrange the potato noodles into a skillet or baking dish so that it fits in one layer and season with salt and pepper. In the same bowl, add in the rest of the olive oil with the fennel. Toss lightly and arrange the seasoned fennel on top of the sweet potato noodles in an even layer. Dust with the oregano and season with salt and pepper.
3. Add half of the pecorino cheese on top, sprinkling all over to coat the fennel and sweet potatoes. Roast until the fennel is fork tender, about 50 minutes.
4. Remove the dish from the oven and turn to broil. Lay the tomatoes on top of the fennel and sweet potatoes, cut-side up. Return the dish to the oven and broil the tomatoes until slightly charred and warmed through, 6 to 8 minutes.

5. Remove the dish from the oven and immediately sprinkle over with the remaining pecorino cheese and the olives. Garnish with the parsley and serve immediately.

Sesame Salmon with Spiralized Slaw

Prep time: 15 mins | Cook time: 30 mins | Total time: 45 mins | Serves: 2

Ingredients

For the salmon and slaw:

- 2 (3-4oz) pieces skinless, boneless salmon
- 1 large zucchini, Blade D, noodles trimmed
- 1 large carrot, Blade D, noodles trimmed
- 1 red bell pepper, Blade A, noodles trimmed
- 2 tablespoons chopped cilantro

For the dressing:

- ¼ cup rice vinegar
- 2 tablespoons soy sauce
- 1 tablespoon sesame oil
- 1 teaspoon honey
- 1 tablespoon freshly grated ginger
- 1 garlic clove, pressed and minced
- 1 teaspoon sriracha or similar hot sauce
- 1 teaspoon sesame seeds + more for garnish
- 2 tablespoons tahini

Instructions

1. Preheat the oven to 400 degrees. Line a baking sheet with parchment paper and set aside.
2. In a large mixing bowl, whisk together all of the ingredients for the dressing, except for the sesame seeds and tahini. Remove 2 tablespoons of the dressing and pour over the salmon pieces. Bake the salmon for 15-20 minutes or until cooked to your preference (15 minutes for medium-rare, 20 minutes for well done.)

3. Meanwhile, add in the tahini and sesame seeds to the bowl with the leftover dressing and add in the spiralized veggies and cilantro and toss together well.
4. When salmon is ready, divide the slaw among plates and top with the cooked salmon. Garnish the salmon with sesame seeds and serve immediately.

Nutrition Information

- Serving size: 1
- Calories: 455
- Fat: 26 g
- Saturated fat: 4 g
- Carbohydrates: 44 g
- Sugar: 20 g
- Sodium: 1678 mg
- Fiber: 6 g
- Protein: 25 g
- Cholesterol: 34 mg

Spicy Garlic Potato Noodles, Chorizo, Parsley and White Bean

Prep Time: *15 minutes* | **Cook Time:** *15 minutes* | **Total Time:** *30 minutes* | **Servings:** *4*

Ingredients

- 2 chorizo links, decased, sliced into ½" thick chunks
- 1/2 tablespoon extra virgin olive oil
- 1 large garlic clove, sliced thinly
- 1 large potato, peeled, Blade C, noodles trimmed
- 1 pinch cayenne powder
- ¼ teaspoon smoked paprika
- ¼ teaspoon chili powder
- salt and pepper, to taste
- 1 cup white beans (cannellini, Great Northern)
- ¼ cup whole parsley leaves

Instructions

1. Place a large skillet over medium heat and coat with cooking spray. Once heated, add in the chorizo and cook for 5 minutes or until cooked through. Transfer to a plate and set aside.
2. Place the skillet back over medium heat and add in the olive oil, garlic and potato noodles. Season with cayenne, paprika, chili powder, salt, and pepper, toss and cover and cook, uncovering occasionally to toss, for 5-7 minutes or until noodles are cooked through.
3. Once cooked, add in the white beans, parsley, chorizo, toss and let cook uncovered for 1 minute or until beans are heated through.
4. Transfer to a serving platter.for 5-10 more minutes or until sweet potatoes are easily pierced with the fork.
5. Let cool for at least 5 minutes and then serve.

Spicy Old Bay® Skinny Fries

"Leave that bag of frozen French fries in the freezer because these fries are just about as easy to make. They just might become your new favorite fries. An ice-cold bottle of beer is the perfect side kick."

Servings: 4 | **Prep**: 15 m | **Cook**: 14 m | **Ready In**: 29 m

Ingredients

- nonfat cooking spray
- 2 tablespoons extra-virgin olive oil
- 1 1/2 tablespoons seafood seasoning (such as Old Bay®)
- 1 teaspoon onion powder
- 1/2 teaspoon hot sauce
- 1/2 teaspoon garlic powder
- 2 large russet potatoes
- 1 tablespoon malt vinegar, or to taste sea salt to taste

Directions

1. Preheat oven to 425 degrees F (220 degrees C). Line 2 baking sheets with aluminum foil; spray with cooking spray.
2. Mix oil, seafood seasoning, onion powder, hot sauce, and garlic powder together in a bowl.
3. Cut potatoes into spirals using a spiralizer fitted with a large shredder blade; snip long spirals into smaller lengths.

4. Place potatoes into a large bowl; drizzle with oil mixture. Toss until potatoes are evenly coated.
5. Spread coated potatoes in a single layer onto the baking sheets, leaving 1/4-inch of space between potato spirals.
6. Bake in the preheated oven until bottom of potatoes are browned, 8 to 9 minutes. Flip potatoes with a spatula. Bake until potatoes are browned and crisp on top, about 6 minutes.
7. Sprinkle malt vinegar and sea salt over potatoes.

Nutritional Information

- Calories:216 kcal 11%
- Fat: 7.1 g 11%
- Carbs: 35.1g 11%
- Protein: 4.3 g 9%
- Cholesterol: 0 mg 0%
- Sodium: 719 mg 29%

Spiralized Brown Butter Sage Sweet Potato

"Fabulous and simplistic dish for those who don't like 'sweet' sweet potatoes. You can easily substitute butternut squash in this dish. Makes 3 large helpings or 4 medium-sized helpings."

Servings: 4| Prep: 10 m | Cook: 9 m | Ready In: 19 m

Ingredients

- 1 large sweet potato, peeled and halved crosswise
- 1 tablespoon olive oil, or more as needed
- 1/4 cup butter
- 9 fresh sage leaves salt to taste

Directions

1. Cut sweet potato into spaghetti-like ribbons with a spiralizer.
2. Heat olive oil in a large nonstick skillet over medium heat. Add sweet potato ribbons; cook, stirring often and adding more oil to prevent sticking, until starting to soften, 6 to 7 minutes. Transfer to a plate.

3. Heat butter in the same skillet until melted and foaming, about 1 minute. Add sage leaves; swirl until butter is a rich caramel color and leaves are crisp and dark green, 2 to 3 minutes. Remove sage leaves from the butter. Add sweet potato; stir to coat well.
4. Season sweet potato with salt and garnish with crisp sage leaves.

Nutritional Information

- Calories:231 kcal 12%
- Fat: 15 g 23%
- Carbs: 23g 7%
- Protein: 1.9 g 4%
- Cholesterol: 31 mg 10%
- Sodium: 183 mg 7%

Spiralized Garlic-Paprika Sweet Potato "Fries"

Prep time: *5 mins* | **Cook time:** *20 mins* | **Total time:** *25 mins* | **Serves:** *2*

Ingredients

- 1 sweet potato, peeled, Blade D*
- 1 tablespoon extra virgin olive oil
- salt, to taste (make sure you're using a sea salt grinder - makes such a difference)
- 1 teaspoon paprika
- 1 teaspoon garlic powder

*If you don't have the Inspiralizer, use the smallest noodle blade on your version

Instructions

1. Preheat the oven to 400 degrees. Spread the noodles out on a large baking tray and drizzle with the olive oil. Toss the noodles together gently with your fingers, coating the noodles in the oil. Season with salt, paprika and garlic powder.
2. Roast for 20 minutes, tossing halfway through (gently - be careful not to break the tender noodles!)
3. After 15 minutes, make sure to check the noodles to prevent burning. If starting to burn, toss those pieces gently.

4. Serve, discarding any completely burnt pieces, with favorite dip or ketchup.

Spiralized Parsnip Latkes

Prep Time: 10 minutes | Cook Time: 30 minutes | Total Time: 40 minutes | Servings: 5-6

Ingredients

- 2 large eggs, beaten
- 3 tablespoons matzo meal
- salt and pepper, to taste
- 2 large parsnips, peeled, Blade C, noodles roughly trimmed
- 1 small onion, peeled, Blade A, noodles roughly trimmed
- ¼ cup extra virgin olive oil
- optional apple sauce, for serving

Instructions

1. Preheat the oven to 425 degrees. Take out two heavy non-stick rimmed baking sheets.
2. While the oven preheats, in a large mixing bowl, add in the eggs, matzoh meal, and season generously with salt and pepper. Mix together to combine and add in the parsnip and onion noodles.
3. Pour the oil into the baking sheets and place in the oven for 5-7 minutes to heat the oil. Remove from the oven and place the parsnip mixture in handfuls onto the oil. Flatten and contain the mixture using a spatula.
4. Bake for 15 minutes or until the bottoms are golden and crisp. Remove from the oven, flip the latkes over and bake for another 10 minutes or until crisp and golden on both sides.
5. When done, transfer the latkes to a paper towel lined sheet to drain. Serve immediately with apple sauce, if desired.

Spiralized Patatas Bravas

Prep time: 15 mins | Cook time: 35 mins | Total time: 50 mins | Serves: 6-8

Ingredients

For the potato noodles:

- 3 pounds russet potatoes, Blade C, noodles trimmed
- 1 tablespoon extra virgin olive oil
- salt and pepper, to taste
- ¼ teaspoon garlic powder

For the bravas sauce:

- 1 (15-ounce) can whole peeled tomatoes
- 1 tablespoon extra virgin olive oil
- 1 cup diced yellow onion
- 3 medium garlic cloves, minced
- 1 teaspoon smoked paprika
- ¼ teaspoon red pepper flakes
- ¼ cup water
- salt, to taste
- 1 bay leaf
- 2 teaspoons sherry vinegar
- ½ teaspoon hot sauce

Instructions

1. Place the tomatoes with their juices in a medium bowl and, using your hands, break into rough 1-inch pieces and set aside.
2. Place a large skillet over medium heat and add in the oil. Once oil heats, add in the onion and cook until softened, about 5 minutes. Add the garlic, paprika, and red pepper flakes, stir to combine, and cook until fragrant, about 1 minute.
3. Add in the tomatoes and their liquid along with the water, salt, bay leaf, and bring to a simmer. Cook until the sauce has thickened and has reduced by about half, about 15 minutes.
4. While the sauce cooks, place another large skillet over medium-high heat and add in the oil. Once oil heats, add in the potato noodles and season with salt, pepper and garlic powder. Let cook for 10 minutes or until potato noodles are cooked through. When done, set aside on a serving plate and cover.
5. Once sauce is done cooking, remove the bay leaf and transfer the mixture to a blender. Purée the sauce until smooth and then add in the vinegar and hot sauce and pulse again to combine. Taste and add more hot sauce, if needed.

6. Pour the sauce over the potato noodles and garnish with cilantro or parsley. Serve immediately.

Spiralized Red Cabbage Slaw with Vegan Chipotle-Lime Dressing

Prep time: *20 mins* | **Total time:** *20 mins* | **Serves**: *6-8 cups*

Ingredients

For the slaw:

- 1 small red cabbage, Blade A (yields 6-8 heaping cups)
- For the slaw dressing:
- 1 large ripe avocado, peeled, pitted and insides mashed
- 3 tablespoons Chipotle Fabanaise by Sir Kensington's
- ¼ cup freshly squeezed lime juice
- ½ teaspoon Dijon mustard
- salt and pepper, to season

Instructions

1. Place all of the ingredients for the slaw dressing into a food processor and pulse until creamy. If you don't mind a little chunkiness, combine all ingredients in a bowl and whisk together until smooth as possible. Taste and adjust to your preferences.
2. Toss the cabbage and dressing together in a large bowl until combined. Serve as preferred

Spiralized Roasted Vanilla Sweet Potatoes and Apples

"Vanilla olive oil imparts a fabulously creamy taste to these roasted beauties! Adjust the spices to your taste."

Servings: *4* | **Prep:** *15 m* | **Cook:** *20 m* | **Ready In:** *40 m*

Ingredients

- cooking spray
- 1/3 vanilla bean
- 1/4 cup olive oil
- 1 large sweet potato, peeled and halved
- 1 large Red Delicious apple, unpeeled
- 2 tablespoons brown sugar
- 1/2 teaspoon ground cinnamon
- 1/4 teaspoon salt
- 1 pinch ground nutmeg ground ginger

Directions

1. Preheat oven to 400 degrees F (200 degrees C). Line a baking sheet with aluminum foil; spray with nonstick spray.
2. Split vanilla bean lengthwise with the tip of a sharp knife. Holding the pod open, scrape seeds from each half using the flat side of your knife.
3. Combine vanilla bean, scraped seeds, and olive oil in a small saucepan over very low heat. Warm the oil until fragrant, about 5 minutes. Remove from heat and let cool, about 5 minutes.
4. Cut sweet potato and apple into noodles using a spiralizer. Place in a large bowl.
5. Whisk 2 tablespoons olive oil, brown sugar, cinnamon, salt, nutmeg, and ginger together in a small bowl. Drizzle over sweet potato and apple; toss well to coat.
6. Spread sweet potato and apple in an even layer on the prepared baking sheet.
7. Bake in the preheated oven, turning once, until golden, about 10 minutes. Increase oven temperature to 425 degrees F (218 degrees C). Roast until ends of sweet potato start to brown and toast, 5 to 10 minutes more.

Nutritional Information

- Calories:278 kcal 14%
- Fat: 13.8 g 21%
- Carbs: 38.5g 12%
- Protein: 2 g 4%
- Cholesterol: 0 mg 0%
- Sodium: 211 mg 8%

Spiralized Tzimmes for Rosh Hashanah

Prep Time: 15 minutes | Cook Time: 35 minutes | Total Time: 50 minutes | Servings: 4

Ingredients

- 3 large carrots, peeled and cubed
- 2 large sweet potatoes, peeled, Blade C
- 1/2 cup bite-sized dried pitted prunes, roughly chopped
- 1/2 cup dried apricots, roughly chopped
- salt, to taste

For the sauce:

- 2 tablespoons honey
- 1 teaspoon ground cinnamon
- 1/3 cup fresh orange juice
- 2 tablespoons fresh lemon juice
- zest from 1 orange

Instructions

1. Preheat the oven to 350 degrees.
2. Bring a medium pot filled halfway with water to a boil. Once boiling, add in the carrots and cook for 3 minutes or until more easily pierced with a fork, but still firm. Drain, pat dry and set aside.
3. While the carrots are cooking, place a large skillet over medium heat and add in the olive oil. Once oil is heated, toss in the sweet potato noodles and season with salt and pepper. Cover and cook for 5-7 minutes or until almost fully cooked.
4. In a small bowl, whisk together the ingredients for the sauce.
5. In a large bowl, add in the sweet potato noodles, carrots, prunes, apricots and pour over sauce. Toss to combine thoroughly and place in an 11 x 7 baking dish. Season lightly with salt.
6. Cover with foil, bake for 20 minutes, basting with pan juices after 15 minutes. Remove the dish from the oven and serve immediately.

Summer Farro Salad with Spiralized Zucchini, Onions, and Mozzarella

Prep time: 15 mins | Cook time: 5 mins | Total time: 20 mins | Serves: 3-4

Ingredients

For the dressing:

- 1.5 tablespoons extra virgin olive oil
- ½ tablespoon red wine vinegar
- ½ tablespoon freshly squeezed lemon juice
- salt and pepper, to taste

For the salad:

- 1 medium zucchini, Blade C, noodles trimmed
- 1 cup cooked farro
- ½ cup halved mozzarella balls
- ½ small red onion, Blade A, noodles trimmed
- 1 basil chiffonade (about 8 basil leaves chopped)
- ½ cup jarred roasted red peppers, drained and sliced into ¼" thick slivers

Instructions

1. Place a large skillet over medium-high heat. Once the skillet is heated, add in the zucchini noodles and cook until warmed through and slightly softened, about 2 minutes. Set aside and if needed, drain into a colander first (if there is excess moisture released).
2. Meanwhile, in a small mixing bowl, whisk together the red wine vinegar, olive oil, lemon juice, and season with salt and pepper.
3. In a large serving bowl, combine the farro, mozzarella, zucchini noodles, onion noodles, basil, and roasted peppers. Pour over the dressing and toss thoroughly to combine. Taste and adjust with more salt and pepper, if needed. Serve.

Sweet Hot Mustard Brussels Sprout and Apple-Almond Salad

Ingredients

For the sweet hot mustard:

- 2 tablespoons Dijon mustard
- 1 tablespoons whole-grain mustard
- 3/4 teaspoon apple cider vinegar
- 2 tablespoons honey
- 1/2 teaspoon sriracha sauce

For the salad:

- 4 shallots, sliced into thin rings
- 1 tablespoon sherry vinegar
- 3.5 tablespoons extra virgin olive oil
- salt and pepper, to taste
- 1 pound brussels sprouts, trimmed and cut into thirds or quarters
- ½ cup slivered almonds
- 2 Gala red apples, Blade C

Instructions

1. To make the sweet hot mustard, in a large bowl, whisk both mustards, apple cider vinegar, honey and sriracha sauce. Set aside.
2. Place a large skillet over medium heat and add in ½ tablespoon of the olive oil. Once oil heats, add in the shallots, season with salt and cover, letting cook for 3-5 minutes or until lightly caramelized, shaking the pan occasionally. Once done, remove the shallots with a slotted spoon and into a large bowl with the sherry vinegar, mustard mixture, 1 tablespoon of the olive oil and season with salt and pepper. Set aside.
3. Place the large skillet back over medium-high heat and heat the final two tablespoons of olive oil. Once heated, add the brussels sprouts and season with salt and pepper. Cover and cook, stirring occasionally, until the sprouts are just tender and lightly browned, about 8-10 minutes. Transfer to the bowl with the mustard-shallot mixture and add in the almonds and apple noodles and toss. Arrange on a platter and serve.

Vegan Spiralized Summer Spring Rolls

Prep time: 30 mins | Total time: 30 mins | Serves: 6 rolls

Ingredients

For the dipping sauce:

- 1 teaspoon sesame oil
- ¼ cup peanut oil
- ¼ cup tahini
- 3 tablespoons soy sauce
- 2 tablespoons red wine vinegar
- 2 teaspoons chili oil
- 1 teaspoon honey
- ½ teaspoon cayenne pepper

- 1 garlic clove, minced

For the spring rolls:

- 6 rice paper wrappers
- 1 large avocado, peeled, pitted and thinly sliced (1/8" thick)
- handful of fresh cilantro
- handful of fresh mint
- 1 large English seedless cucumber, Blade D, noodles trimmed
- about 2 medium carrots, peeled and julienned
- about 2 packed cups Boston or Bibb lettuce
- 1 large lime, quartered
- pepper, to season

Instructions

1. Make the dipping sauce. Combine all of the ingredients into a food processor and pulse until creamy. Reserve six tablespoons and save the rest in the refrigerator for future use (or freezer.)
2. Create an assembly line of the vegetables for the spring rolls (this just helps you keep organized).
3. Fill a shallow dish with warm water. One at a time, dip a rice wrapper sheet into the water for 5 to 10 seconds. Remove and place on a flat surface, like a cutting board or plate.
4. In the middle of one of the rice wrappers, lay 2 avocado slices (only do 1 if that's all can fit) down, 1 pinch of cilantro and 1 pinch of mint, cucumber noodles, carrots, and top with lettuce. Squeeze over with ½ lime wedge and season with pepper.
5. Fold the bottom half of the rice paper wrapper over the filling. Holding firmly in place, fold the sides of the wrapper in. Then, pressing firmly down to hold in place, roll the entire wrapper horizontally up from the bottom to the top. Turn the roll so that the seam faces down and the avocado faces up.
6. Continue with the remaining ingredients and rice wrappers to make four. Place on a plate and cover with plastic wrap and refrigerate, if not serving immediately.
7. Serve the spring rolls with the dipping sauce.

Vegan Sweet Potato and Brussels Sprout Gratin with Marcona Almond-Maple Cream Sauce

Prep Time: 20 minutes | *Cook Time:* 45 minutes | *Total Time:* 1 hour 5 minutes | *Servings:* 4

Ingredients

- 1 tablespoon extra virgin olive oil
- 3 tablespoons diced shallots
- 3 cups shredded brussels sprouts
- salt and pepper, to taste
- 1/3 cup raisins
- 2 medium sweet potatoes, peeled

For the almond cream sauce:

- 1 cup roasted, unsalted marcona almonds – without skin (if you can't find these, roasted and unsalted regular almonds will do)
- 1 cups low-sodium vegetable broth
- 1 tablespoon maple syrup
- 2 large garlic cloves, peeled and smashed

Instructions

1. Preheat the oven to 425 degrees. Grease a 10" cast-iron skillet with cooking spray and set aside.
2. In a large skillet, add in the olive oil. Once oil heats, add in the shallots and let cook for 1 minute or until fragrant. Add in the brussels sprouts and season with salt and pepper. Cook for 3 minutes or until almost cooked through, stirring frequently. When done, transfer to a medium bowl, add in the raisins, toss to combine and set aside.
3. While brussels sprouts cook, combine all of the ingredients for the dressing into a high-speed blender (I used my Nutribullet) until creamy, about 2 minutes. Set aside.
4. Slice the sweet potatoes halfway through lengthwise, careful not to pierce farther than the center. Spiralize the potatoes using Blade A.
5. In the bottom of the prepared cast iron skillet, add in a layer of the sweet potatoes. Top with a layer of the almond cream sauce and then top that with a layer of the brussels sprout-raisin mixture. Top that with another

layer of the sweet potatoes, then another layer of the almond cream sauce and then top with the rest of the brussels sprout-raisin mixture. Top the brussels with the remaining sweet potatoes and top with the remaining almond cream sauce.

6. Cover the skillet with tinfoil and bake for 40 minutes. Remove the foil and bake for 5-10 more minutes or until sweet potatoes are easily pierced with the fork.

7. Let cool for at least 5 minutes and then serve.

Vinaigrette Chicken and Vegetables

"Quick, healthy dinner. I made the vinaigrette the previous day using red wine vinegar, olive oil, and Dijon mustard."

Servings*: 2 |* ***Prep****: 20 m |* ***Cook****: 35 m |* ***Ready In****: 55 m*

Ingredients

- 4 skinless chicken thighs
- 1/4 cup onion, chopped
- 2 cloves garlic, minced
- 2 cups spiral-sliced zucchini
- 1 cup spiral-sliced carrots
- 1/2 chopped red bell pepper
- 1/4 cup vinaigrette salad dressing

Directions

1. Heat a nonstick skillet over medium heat, and cook chicken thighs until barely pink in the center, about 20 minutes, turning once; stir in onion and garlic, and cook and stir until onions are translucent, about 5 minutes.

2. Stir zucchini, carrots, and bell pepper into chicken mixture; cook and stir until vegetables are tender with a bite at the center and chicken is no longer pink at the center, about 5 minutes. An instant read thermometer inserted into the center of chicken thighs should read at least 165 degrees F (74 degrees C).

3. Stir vinaigrette into chicken mixture; cook until heated through, about 2 minutes.

Nutritional Information

- Calories:332 kcal 17%
- Fat: 15.3 g 24%
- Carbs: 20.4g 7%
- Protein: 28.7 g 57%
- Cholesterol: 94 mg 31%
- Sodium: 412 mg 16%

Chapter 5: Salad

***

Al Fresco Zucchini Pasta Salad

Prep time: *25 mins* | **Total time:** *25 mins* | **Serves:** *6*

Ingredients

- 3 medium zucchini, spiralized, noodles trimmed
- 1½ cups fresh broccoli flowerets
- 1 large carrot, spiralized using Blade C, noodles trimmed
- 1 medium yellow bell pepper, diced
- ¼ cup white wine vinegar
- 2 tablespoons extra virgin olive oil
- 1 teaspoon Italian seasoning
- 1 teaspoon Dijon mustard
- Salt and black pepper to taste
- ⅛ teaspoon garlic powder
- 1 (28 ounce) can Tuttorosso® Diced Tomatoes in rich tomato juice, drained

Instructions

1. Bring a large saucepan filled halfway with water and a pinch of salt to a boil. Add broccoli and carrots and cook for 3 minutes; drain and rinse with cold water to stop cooking.
2. Combine the vinegar, olive oil, Italian seasoning, mustard, salt, black pepper and garlic power in a screw top jar. Cover and shake well.
3. In a large bowl combine the zucchini noodles, broccoli, carrots, diced tomatoes and yellow bell pepper. Shake dressing and pour over zucchini pasta mixture; toss gently to coat.

Apple, Fennel and Celeriac Slaw with Apple Cider Vinaigrette

Prep time: *30 mins* | **Total time:** *30 mins* | **Serves:** *4*

Ingredients

For the slaw:

- 1 small celeriac, peeled, Blade C, noodles trimmed
- 1.5 tablespoons minced parsley
- 1 Granny Smith apples, Blade C
- 1 small fennel bulb, Blade D

For the dressing:

- 2 tablespoons apple cider vinegar
- 1 teaspoon honey
- 1 teaspoon dijon mustard
- 3 tablespoons extra virgin olive oil
- 1 tablespoon freshly squeezed lemon juice
- salt and pepper, to taste

Instructions

1. Whisk together all of the ingredients for the dressing into a small bowl. Set aside.
2. Rinse the celeriac in cold water and then pat dry. Add the celeriac to a large mixing bowl with the parsley, apple and fennel. Pour the dressing over and toss thoroughly to combine. Serve.

Autumn Kale and Quinoa Salad with Spiralized Apples

Prep time: 15 mins | Cook time: 25 mins |Total time: 40 mins | Serves: 4

Ingredients

- 2 teaspoons extra virgin olive oil
- 1.5 cups cubed butternut squash
- salt and pepper
- ½ cup uncooked quinoa
- 1.5 cups water + more as needed
- 6 cups chopped kale
- 2 apples (I like honey crisp!)
- ¼ cup pecans, to garnish
- ¼ cup crumbled goat cheese

For the dressing:

- 2 tablespoons extra virgin olive oil
- 1.5 tablespoons apple cider vinegar
- ½ teaspoon Dijon mustard
- 1.5 teaspoons honey
- salt and pepper

Instructions

1. Preheat the oven to 400 degrees. Line a baking sheet with parchment paper and spread out the butternut squash. Drizzle with the olive oil and season with salt and pepper. Let bake for 25 minutes or until fork tender.
2. While butternut squash cooks, cook the quinoa. Place the quinoa and water in a saucepot, bring to a boil, and then reduce to low and simmer for 15 minutes or until quinoa is cooked through, adding water if needed.
3. A few minutes before the squash is ready, prepare the dressing: place all ingredients into the bottom of a large mixing bowl and whisk together. Add in the kale, massage into the kale with fingertips for 15 seconds and then set aside.
4. Spiralize the apple with Blade C and add to the large bowl (with the dressed kale) along with the cooked butternut squash and quinoa. Toss well to combine and divide into plates. Top with goat cheese and pecans.

Nutrition Information

- Serving size: 4
- Calories: 360
- Fat: 19 g
- Saturated fat: 4 g
- Trans fat: 0 g
- Carbohydrates: 44 g
- Sugar: 14 g
- Sodium: 97 mg
- Fiber: 9 g
- Protein: 10 g
- Cholesterol: 5 mg

Avocado and Tomato Zucchini Noodle Salad with Basil Vinaigrette

Prep time: 20 mins | Total time: 20 mins | Serves: 4

Ingredients

For the vinaigrette:

- 1 ounce fresh basil
- 1 small garlic clove, peeled and chopped
- ¼ cup olive oil
- 2 tablespoons red wine vinegar
- ½ tablespoon water
- salt, to taste
- 1 small shallot, chopped
- 1 pinch red pepper flakes

For the salad:

- 2 medium zucchinis, Blade D, noodles trimmed
- 1 cup sun gold heirloom tomatoes (or cherry tomatoes), halved or sliced
- 1 large ripe avocado, peeled, pitted and sliced into eight slivers
- 1 cup defrosted cooked green peas
- pepper, to taste

Instructions

1. Place the ingredients for the vinaigrette into a high speed blender and pulse until creamy, about 30 seconds. Set aside.
2. Toss the zucchini noodles and tomatoes with three-quarters of the vinaigrette. Divide the noodle mixture into four bowls and top each with two avocado slices and sprinkle over with peas. Pour over the remaining vinaigrette and season generously with pepper.

Avocado-Tuna Salad with Cucumber Noodles

Prep time: *20 mins* | ***Total time:*** *20 mins* | ***Serves:*** *4*

Ingredients

- 1 ripe avocado, peeled and pitted
- 12oz canned white albacore tuna in water
- 1.5 teaspoon Dijon mustard
- 5 tablespoons Greek yogurt

- salt and pepper, to taste
- 2 seedless cucumbers, Blade B

Instructions

1. Place the avocado in a medium bowl and mash it with the back of a fork. Add in the tuna, Greek yogurt, Dijon mustard and season with salt and pepper. Add in the cucumber noodles and toss together. Save for later or serve immediately.

Baked Falafel and Cucumber Noodle Salad with Mint-Tahini Dressing

Prep Time: *10 minutes* | **Cook Time:** *30 minutes* | **Total Time:** *40 minutes* | **Servings:** *3*

Ingredients

For the falafel:

- 1 cup canned chickpeas, rinsed, drained and patted dry
- 1/3 cup chopped red onion
- 2 tablespoons chopped parsley
- 2 garlic cloves, minced
- 1/2 teaspoon ground cumin
- 1/2 teaspoon ground cayenne
- 1 teaspoon ground coriander
- salt and pepper, to taste
- 1 egg, beaten
- 3 tablespoons olive oil + more for coating a cast iron skillet

For the dressing:

- 3 tablespoons tahini
- zest and juice of 1 small lemon
- 1 garlic clove, finely minced
- 1 tablespoon freshly chopped mint
- 1/4 cup water
- 1 tablespoon red wine vinegar

For the salad:

- 1 cucumber, Blade C, noodles trimmed
- 3 packed cups baby arugula
- 6 cherry tomatoes, halved

Instructions

1. Preheat the oven to 400 degrees.
2. In a food processor, combine all of the ingredients for the falafel except for the additional oil for coating the cast iron skillet (later step). Process until no longer chunky, about 1 minute. Place into a mixing bowl and add in the egg. Toss to combine thoroughly.
3. Scoop out enough of the mixture to make 6 large golf ball sized falafel balls and then shape them into patties by setting them down and pressing down to slightly flatten. Set aside.
4. Place the falafel in a cast iron skillet coated lightly with olive oil (about 1 tablespoon.)
5. Bake for 12-15 minutes and then flip over and bake another 15 minutes or until the falafel is lightly browned on both sides.
6. While the falafel is baking, prepare the dressing and cucumber salad. Place all of the ingredients for the dressing into a bowl and whisk together. Set aside. For the salad, pat dry the cucumber noodles to remove all excess moisture and then combine in a large mixing bowl with the arugula. Toss to combine and divide onto two plates. Set aside.
7. When the falafel is done baking, divide equally among the salad plates and drizzle with dressing. Garnish with cherry tomatoes.

Beet Noodle, Pea and Arugula Salad with Lemon-Garlic Tahini Sauce

Prep time: 10 mins | Cook time: 10 mins | Total time: 20 mins | Serves: 2

Ingredients

For the dressing:

- 2 tablespoons tahini
- 2 tablespoons freshly squeezed lemon juice
- 2 teaspoons honey
- 1 garlic clove, minced
- 1 tablespoons extra virgin olive oil
- 1-2 tablespoons water
- salt & pepper, to taste

For the rest:

- 1.5 cups cooked peas
- 1 large beet (or 2 medium), peeled, Blade C
- 1 cup arugula

Instructions

1. Preheat the oven to 425 degrees.
2. Whisk together all of the ingredients – except for the water - in a medium bowl or pulse in a food processor until creamy. Add water as needed to make creamy. Taste and adjust to your preference.
3. Line a baking sheet with parchment paper and lay out the beet noodles. Drizzle with the olive oil and toss together to coat. Season with salt and pepper and roast for 10 minutes or until softened.
4. In a bowl, toss together the beets and peas. Transfer to a serving bowl or plate and drizzle with lemon-tahini sauce. Optional: serve atop a bed of greens. Serve with extra sauce

BLAT Salad with Zucchini Noodles

Prep time: 10 mins | Cook time: 15 mins | Total time: 25 mins | Serves: 2

Ingredients

- 4 strips of bacon, sliced into ½" pieces
- 2 romaine hearts, halved
- 1 medium zucchini, Blade D, noodles trimmed
- 1 small handful cilantro leaves
- 1 avocado, peeled, pitted and sliced thinly
- ¼ cup halved cherry tomatoes
- freshly cracked pepper, to garnish

For the dressing:

- 2 tablespoons extra virgin olive oil
- 1 teaspoon dijon mustard
- 1 teaspoon lemon juice
- 1 teaspoon red wine vinegar
- 2 teaspoons minced shallots
- salt and pepper, to taste

Instructions

1. Place the bacon in a large skillet over medium-high heat. Cook the bacon until crispy, about 5 minutes per side. Transfer to a paper towel lined plate when finished.
2. Meanwhile, prepare the dressing: combine everything into a small bowl and whisk until combined. Set aside.
3. Divide the romaine hearts onto plates and top with zucchini noodles,cilantro, avocado, and tomatoes. Top with bacon when finished and drizzle each with the dressing. Season with freshly cracked pepper.

Candy Cane Beet Noodle and Arugula Quinoa Salad with Parmesan-Garlic Vinaigrette

Prep Time: *10 minutes* | **Cook Time:** *15 minutes* | **Total Time:** *25 minutes* | **Servings:** *3*

Ingredients

- ¼ cup quinoa
- ½ cup water
- 1 large Chioggia Guardsmark beet, peeled, Blade C
- 2 cups baby arugula
- 1/3 cup quartered pitted green olives
- 2 tablespoons grated parmesan cheese

For the vinaigrette:

- 1 clove of garlic
- 2 tablespoons red wine vinegar
- salt and pepper, to taste
- 3 tablespoons extra virgin olive oil

Instructions

1. Place the quinoa and water in a small saucepan and bring to a boil. Once boiling, reduce to a simmer and cook for 15 minutes or until quinoa is fluffy. Add more water if needed.
2. While quinoa is cooking, prepare the vinaigrette. Add the garlic to a mortar (if you don't have a mortar, crush in a bowl) and lightly season with salt.

Grind into a puree and pour in the vinegar. Season with pepper and mix. Pour mixture into a bowl or dressing shaker and add in the olive oil. Mix to combine.

3. In a large mixing bowl, combine the beets, olives and arugula. Pour over the dressing, add in the cheese and toss to thoroughly combine. Let sit while the quinoa still cooks.

4. Once quinoa is done, add it to the mixing bowl and toss to combine. Serve.

Carrot Miso-Ginger Cucumber Noodles with Sunflower Seeds, Chickpeas, Kale, Avocado and Red Quinoa

Prep Time: *10 minutes* | **Cook Time:** *15 minutes* | **Total Time:** *25 minutes* | **Servings:** *2*

Ingredients

For the miso-ginger carrot dressing (makes 3/4 cups):

- 1/2 large carrot
- 1 medium shallot, minced
- 2 tsp minced ginger root
- 1 tbsp rice wine vinegar
- 1 tsp sesame oil
- 1/4 cup + 1 tsp canola oil
- 1/2 tsp soy sauce
- 1/2 tbsp white miso paste
- 1/2 tbsp water

For the rest:

- 1 large cucumber, Blade A
- 1/2 cup chickpeas
- 1 tbsp sunflower seeds
- 1 avocado, insides cubed
- 1/8 cup red quinoa
- 3 cups chopped kale

Instructions

1. Place 1/4 cup of water with 1/8 cup of red quinoa in a saucepan and bring to a boil. Once boiled, cook for about 10 minutes or until quinoa is fluffy when forked with a knife and water has fully absorbed into the quinoa.
2. Combine the ginger, shallots and carrots into a food processor and pulse until carrots are minced finely. Add in the rest of the ingredients and pulse until creamy. Set aside.
3. Place your cucumber noodles, quinoa, kale and 1/2 cup dressing into a bowl and toss to combine thoroughly.
4. Put the noodles and kale into a bowl and top with sunflower seeds, avocado, and chickpeas. Enjoy!

Chicken Waldorf Salad Cups with Spiralized Apples

Prep time: 15 mins | Cook time: 15 mins | Total time: 30 mins | Serves: 4

Ingredients

For the waldorf salad:

- 1 large chicken breast
- ½ cup walnuts
- 1 Gala apple or apple of choice, Blade C
- 1 cup grapes, halved (red or green – it's preference!)
- 1 celery stalk, diced
- 4 green lettuce leaves or 6 bibb lettuce cups

For the mayonnaise:

- ⅔ cup + 2 tablespoons nonfat plain Greek Yogurt
- 1 tablespoon Dijon mustard
- ½ teaspoon garlic powder
- 1 tablespoon lemon juice
- salt and pepper, to taste

Instructions

1. Place the chicken in a medium deep skillet and cover with water. Add a pinch of salt, cover, and bring to a simmer over medium-high heat. Once simmering, reduce heat to low and let simmer for 7-10 minutes or until chicken is cooked through and no longer pink inside. Transfer to a cutting

board and shred with two forks. Transfer the chicken to a plate and place in the refrigerator to chill for at least 15 minutes.

2. While chicken chills, place a small skillet over medium-high heat. Once skillet is heated, add in the walnuts and let toast for 5 minutes or until fragrant and starting to brown. When cool enough to handle, roughly chop and set aside.

3. Also, combine all of the ingredients for the fayonnaise together in the bottom of a large mixing bowl and whisk until combined. Set aside.

4. Add the apple, chicken, celery and walnuts to the large bowl with the fayonnaise. Toss to combine thoroughly.

5. Lay out your lettuce cups and fill with the waldorf mixture. Serve.

Chili-Lime Jicama And Corn Shrimp Salad

Time to prepare: 25 minute | Time to cook: 10 minutes | Serves: 3-4

Ingredients

For the shrimp:

- ½ tablespoon extra virgin olive oil
- 18 medium shrimp, defrosted, deveined, shelled
- ½ teaspoon paprika
- salt and pepper, to taste
- 1/4 teaspoon garlic powder

For the salad:

- 1 ear of corn, shucked
- 1 medium jicama (1 pound), peeled, Blade C, noodles trimmed
- 1 teaspoon chili powder
- 1 avocado, pitted, peeled and insides cubed
- 1 cup shredded purple cabbage
- 1 tablespoon chopped cilantro

For the dressing:

- juice of 2 limes
- 2 teaspoons red wine vinegar
- 1 tablespoon extra virgin olive oil
- salt and pepper, to taste

Directions

1. Place an ear of corn into a medium pot and cover with water. Bring to a boil, cook for 2 minutes or until corn is fork-tender and then drain into a colander and set aside.
2. Meanwhile, place a large skillet over medium-high heat and add the olive oil. Once oil heats, add in the shrimp and season with salt, pepper and garlic powder. Cook for 2 minutes and flip over, cooking another 1-2 minutes or until shrimp is opaque. Transfer shrimp to a plate.
3. In the large mixing bowl, toss together the corn (shave the kernels off the cob with a knife), jicama, chili powder, avocado, cabbage and cilantro. Pour over the dressing and toss thoroughly to combine.
4. Divide into bowls and top with shrimp.

Chilled Spring Cucumber-Dill Salad with Cashews and Quinoa

Prep time: *5 mins | **Cook time:** 20 mins | **Total time:** 25 mins | **Serves:** 4*

Ingredients

For the salad:

-   ½ cup dry quinoa
-   1 cup water
-   12 large asparagus spears
-   1 large cucumber
-   ¼ cup unsalted cashews

For the dressing:

-   ½ teaspoon lemon zest
-   2 tablespoons freshly squeezed lemon juice
-   1 teaspoon honey
-   ½ teaspoon country Dijon mustard
-   salt and pepper, to taste
-   3 tablespoons extra virgin olive oil
-   1 tablespoon freshly minced dill

Instructions

1. Place the quinoa and water in a small pot, cover and bring to a boil. Once boiling, reduce to a simmer and let cook for 15 minutes or until quinoa

fluffs up with a fork. If water evaporates completely, add more in tablespoons.

2. Once the quinoa is cooked, immediately transfer to a bowl, cover and chill in the refrigerator for at least 2 hours, preferably for 12 or more hours.

3. While quinoa chills, prepare the rest: peel the asparagus using a vegetable peeler and set aside. Then, spiralize the cucumbers with Blade B or C. Pat the noodles dry thoroughly, using paper towels. Roughly chop the cashews. Set the asparagus, cucumber noodles, asparagus and cashews aside in the refrigerator in a large mixing bowl.

4. Prepare the dressing: combine all ingredients in a medium bowl and whisk together. Set aside in the refrigerator.

5. Once the quinoa is done chilling, add it to the mixing bowl with the other ingredients, pour over the vinaigrette and toss to combine thoroughly.

6. Serve immediately or chill again in the refrigerator for future use.

Chilled Zucchini Noodle and Prosciutto Salad with Sunflower Seeds

Prep time: 20 mins | Total time: 20 mins | Serves: 1

Ingredients

For the vinaigrette:

- 1 tablespoon red wine vinegar
- ½ tablespoon minced shallot
- 1 tablespoon olive oil
- 1 teaspoon honey
- ½ teaspoon dijon mustard

For the pasta:

- 3 pieces of prosciutto, roughly sliced
- 1 medium zucchini, Blade C
- 1 teaspoon roasted and salted sunflower seeds
- 2 tablespoons deseeded, chopped tomatoes

Instructions

1. Whisk together all of the ingredients for the vinaigrette. Then, toss together the prosciutto, zucchini noodles, sunflower seeds, tomatoes and vinaigrette. Divide into bowls.

Coconut-Lime-Avocado Zucchini Noodle Salad with Quinoa, Peas, Asparagus, Scallions and Feta

Prep Time: 10 minutes | Cook Time: 15 minutes | Total Time: 25 minutes | Servings: 1

Ingredients

For the dressing:

- 1/2 avocado
- 2 tbsp coconut milk
- juice of 1/2 lime

For the rest:

- 1/3 cup cooked quinoa
- 2 tsp minced cilantro
- 1.5 tsp coconut flakes
- 3 asparagus stalks, chopped into 1" pieces
- 1/4 cup green peas
- 1 medium zucchini, Blade C
- 2-3 scallion stalks, diced
- 1/4 cup cubed feta

Instructions

1. In a food processor, place in all of the ingredients for the dressing. Pulse until creamy. set aside.
2. In a bowl, combine the quinoa, cilantro and coconut flakes. Toss to combine and set aside.
3. Bring a small saucepan filled halfway with water to a boil. Then, add in the asparagus. 1 minute later, add in the peas. Cook for 3-4 minutes or until vegetables are cooked and pour out into a colander.
4. Assemble your mason jar salad. First, put in dressing. Second, the zucchini noodles. Then, the quinoa. Then, the scallions. Then, the asparagus & peas. Then, the feta. Put the lid on the mason jar and refrigerate for later use.

Crusted Tuna with Sesame-Tahini Red Cabbage

Prep time: *25 mins |* *Cook time:* *5 mins |* *Total time:* *30 mins |* *Serves:* *3*

Ingredients

- 1 red cabbage, Blade A
- 1 tablespoon white sesame seeds
- 1 tablespoon black sesame seeds
- ¼ cup chopped scallions
- ½ tablespoon extra virgin olive oil
- 7.5-8oz 1 ahi tuna steak

For the dressing:

- 2 tablespoons tahini
- 1.5 tablespoon rice wine vinegar
- 1.5 teaspoon soy sauce
- 1.5 teaspoons honey
- 1 tablespoon sesame oil
- salt and pepper, to taste

Instructions

1. Measure out about 6 packed cups of the cabbage (or more, if you prefer) and place in a large mixing bowl and set aside.
2. Place all of the ingredients for the dressing into a bowl or food processor and mix until creamy. Taste and adjust, if necessary.
3. Place the cabbage and scallions in a large mixing bowl and drizzle with dressing. Toss to combine everything together and set aside.
4. Place the sesame seeds in a shallow dish or plate and toss to mix together. Set aside.
5. Place a large skillet over medium heat and add in the olive oil.
6. Meanwhile, press one side of the tuna steak down into the sesame seed mixture and then turn over and repeat.
7. Once oil is heated, add in the tuna steak, sesame seed side down. Sear for 1-2 minutes (depending on how well done you'd like it) and then flip over and cook another 1 minute. Remove the tuna and place on a cutting board. Slice thinly.
8. Divide the cabbage onto plates and top with the tuna steak slices.

Cucumber Noodle Cantaloupe Salad with Avocado and Feta

Prep Time: *10 minutes* | **Cook Time:** *5 minutes* | **Total Time:** *15 minutes* | **Servings:** *3*

Ingredients

- 2 medium cucumbers, Blade A
- 2 cups small-cubed cantaloupe
- 1/2 cup crumbled feta
- 1/2 cup diced very ripe avocado

For the dressing:

- 1 tbsp chopped mint
- 1 tbsp olive oil
- 2 tbsp water
- 2 tsp honey
- 2 tbsp white balsamic vinegar
- 2 tsp lime juice
- salt and pepper, to taste

Instructions

1. Pat dry your cucumber noodles until all excess moisture is removed. Place the noodles in a mixing bowl with the feta, avocado and cantaloupe.
2. Mix all of the ingredients for the dressing in a bowl and whisk together.
3. Pour the dressing over the salad and toss to combine thoroughly.
4. Pour the salad into a serving bowl and enjoy.

Cucumber Noodle Salad with Feta & Onions

Prep Time: *15 minutes* | **Servings:** *2*

Ingredients

For the vinaigrette:

- 2 tbsp olive oil
- ¼ cup red wine vinegar
- 1 tbsp lemon juice
- ½ tsp oregano
- salt and pepper, to taste
- 1 tsp honey (optional)

For the rest:

- 1 large cucumber, Blade A
- 1 cup packed baby arugula
- ½ onion, Blade C
- ¼ cup crumbled feta cheese

Instructions

1. Place all of the ingredients for the vinaigrette into a bowl and whisk together. Set aside.
2. Place the cucumber noodles on top of two sheets of paper towels. On top, place another two sheets. Lightly press down onto the noodles to absorb the moisture. Pat dry and then place in a bowl.
3. Add the baby arugula and onion to the cucumber noodles and toss to combine. Then, add in the vinaigrette and toss again to combine. Add in the feta, lightly toss and transfer to a serving bowl or platter.
4. Enjoy!

Cucumber, Scallion and Feta Salad with Cilantro-Lime Vinaigrette

Prep Time: *10 minutes* | **Total Time:** *10 minutes* | **Servings:** *4*

Ingredients

- 2 large seedless cucumbers, Blade A
- ½ cup chopped scallions
- 1/3 cup crumbled feta
- For the dressing:
- 1.5 tablespoon freshly squeezed lime juice
- 1.5 tablespoon white balsamic vinegar
- 2 teaspoons honey
- 1.5 tablespoon minced cilantro
- 1 tablespoon extra virgin olive oil

- pepper, to taste

Instructions

1. Pat the cucumber noodles try to remove excess moisture. Place the cucumber noodles and scallions in a serving bowl and set aside.
2. Place all of the ingredients for the dressing into a bowl and whisk together. Pour over the cucumber noodles and top with feta.

Curried Chicken Salad with Spiralized Cucumbers

Prep time: 5 mins | Cook time: 20 mins | Total time: 25 mins | Serves: 2

Ingredients

- 1 boneless, skinless chicken breast OR 1 cup cubed cooked chicken (if using pre-cooked chicken, skip the first part of this recipe's directions)
- salt
- ¼ cup Greek yogurt or vegan mayonnaise or mashed ripe avocado
- pepper (if using Greek yogurt, add in ½ teaspoon dijon mustard as well)
- ¼ heaping cup diced celery
- 1.5 teaspoons curry powder
- 1 tablespoon sliced almonds
- 1 tablespoon golden raisins
- ½ large English cucumber

Instructions

1. Place the chicken in a saucepan or wide skillet and add water to cover. Salt the water and set over high heat and bring to a roaring simmer. Once roaring, lower heat to medium-low and let cook for 12-15 minutes or until chicken is cooked through and skin is no longer pink. Drain and cut into bite-sized cubes.
2. While chicken cooks, prepare the curry mix: in the bottom of a medium mixing bowl, add the Greek yogurt (or vegan mayonnaise), salt, pepper, celery, curry powder, almonds, and raisins. Stir together well to combine. Set aside in the refrigerator while you wait for the chicken to finish.
3. Spiralize the cucumber with Blade A and trim the noodles. Divide into two bowls and set aside.

4. Once chicken is done, add it to the bowl with the curry seasoning and mix well to coat the chicken. Divide this prepared chicken mixture over the bowls with the cucumber noodles. Serve immediately.

Curried Kale and Spiralized Apple Salad with Dried Goji Berries and Shrimp

Prep time: 15 mins | Cook time: 5 mins | Total time: 20 mins | Serves: 2

Ingredients

For the dressing:

- 1 tablespoon freshly chopped shallot
- 1 teaspoon honey
- ½-1 teaspoons curry powder
- 2 tablespoons fresh lemon juice
- 2 tablespoons extra-virgin olive oil
- salt and pepper, to taste

For the salad:

- 2 cups finely chopped kale
- 1.5 tablespoons dried goji berries (or raisins/currants)
- 1 apple (I used Braeburn)
- 2 teaspoons extra virgin olive oil
- 8 medium sized shrimp, defrosted, peeled and deveined
- salt and pepper, to taste
- ¼ teaspoon chili powder

Instructions

1. Place all of the ingredients for the dressing into a small bowl and whisk together.
2. Place the kale and goji berries in a large mixing bowl and pour over the dressing. Toss to combine thoroughly.
3. Spiralize the apple with Blade C and add to the bowl with the kale. Toss to combine and divide onto plates.
4. Place a large skillet over medium-high heat and add in the olive oil. Season the shrimp with salt, pepper and chili powder. Once oil heats, add in the shrimp and cook about 2 minutes per side or until the shrimp turns

opaque and c-shaped. Divide the shrimp onto the salads. Serve immediately.

Deconstructed Greek Meatball Gyro Bowls with Spiralized Carrots

Prep time: *30 mins* | **Cook time:** *15 mins* | **Total time:** *45 mins* | **Serves:** *6*

Ingredients

For the meatballs:

- 1 pound ground lamb, lean
- 2 tablespoons freshly chopped flat leaf Italian parsley (or 1 tablespoon dried parsley)
- 1 tablespoon minced garlic
- 1 teaspoon ground cumin
- 1 teaspoon dried oregano
- salt and pepper (about ½ teaspoon of salt and ¼ teaspoon pepper)
- olive oil, to brush with (about 1 tablespoon)

For the salad:

- 2 large carrots, peeled, Blade D, noodles trimmed
- 1 large red onion, peeled and diced
- 5 medium vine tomatoes, seeded and chopped
- 6 packed cups spinach
- 1 tablespoon chopped mint, to garnish

For the tzatziki sauce:

- 1 cup plain nonfat Greek yogurt
- ¼ large seedless English cucumber, peeled and diced
- 2 minced garlic cloves
- 1 heaping tablespoon freshly chopped dill
- 1 tablespoon freshly squeezed lemon juice
- salt and pepper, to taste

Instructions

1. Preheat the oven to 425 degrees F. Line a baking tray with parchment paper and set aside.

2. Fill a large pot with water and bring to a boil. Once boiling, add the carrot noodles for just 2 minutes to lightly soften. If you'd like them softer, leave them for 3-5 minutes. Drain into a colander and set aside. Note: you can also serve the carrot noodles raw and skip the boiling step (it's personal preference.)
3. While waiting for the water to boil, prepare the meatballs. In a large mixing bowl, combine the ground lamb, parsley, oregano, garlic, cumin, salt and pepper. Mix well. Using your hands and about 2-3 tablespoons of meatball mixture at a time, form balls and set onto the parchment paper lined baking tray. Continue until 16-18 balls are formed. Brush each with the olive oil. Bake in the oven for about 12 minutes or until no longer pink inside.

4. Meanwhile, divide the carrot noodles evenly into six bowls. Chop the spinach and divide evenly into the bowls. Place the onions and tomatoes in a bowl and toss together. Sprinkle the spinach with the chopped onions and tomatoes. Set all aside.
5. Prepare the tzatziki. Put all of the ingredients for the tzatziki into a food processor and pulse until creamy. Taste and adjust if necessary.
6. Once the meatballs are done, finish assembling the bowls. Add three meatballs per bowl and drizzle with the tzatziki sauce. Garnish with mint and serve.

Easy Three Bean Zucchini "Macaroni" Salad

Prep time: 35 mins | Total time: 35 mins | Serves: 7 cups

Ingredients

For the salad:

- 1 large zucchini or 2 medium zucchinis
- 1 cup halved cherry tomatoes
- 1 orange bell pepper, deseeded and chopped
- ¼ cup finely chopped red onion
- ½ cup canned chickpeas, drained and rinsed
- ½ cup cannellini beans, drained and rinsed
- ½ cup red kidney beans, drained and rinsed
- 3 tablespoons fresh chives, finely chopped

For the dressing:

- 4 tablespoons extra virgin olive oil
- 2 tablespoons lemon juice
- 1 tablespoon balsamic vinegar
- 1 tablespoon dijon mustard
- 1 teaspoon garlic, minced
- pepper, to taste

Instructions

1. Slice the zucchinis lengthwise halfway through. Then, spiralize them with Blade C. Toss the zucchini and the rest of the ingredients for the salad into a large mixing bowl.
2. Combine all of the ingredients for the dressing in a bowl and whisk together. Pour over the zucchini salad and toss thoroughly to combine. Serve immediately or refrigerate for future use.

Fennel, Celery, and Pomegranate Salad

Prep Time: *15 minutes* | **Total Time:** *15 minutes* | **Servings:** *4*

Ingredients

- 1 fennel bulb, Blade C
- 3 celery stalks, thinly sliced on a diagonal
- 1.5 cups arugula
- 1 shallot, thinly sliced into rings
- ¼ cup fresh flat-leaf parsley, coarsely chopped
- ¼ cup pepitas
- 1/3 cup pomegranate seeds
- juice of 1 large lime
- 2 tablespoons extra virgin olive oil
- salt and pepper, to taste

Instructions

1. Softly toss the fennel, celery, arugula, shallot, parsley and half of the pepitas and pomegranates in a large bowl, along with the lemon juice and olive oil. Season with salt and pepper.
2. Serve topped with remaining pepitas and pomegranates.

Fig and Golden Beet Arugula Salad with Sunflower Seeds

Prep time: *20 mins* | **Cook time:** *10 mins* | **Total time:** *30 mins* | **Serves:** *2*

Ingredients

For the salad:

- 3 packed cups arugula
- 1 large golden beet, peeled, Blade D, noodles trimmed
- 3-4 figs, stems removed, quartered
- 1 tablespoon unsalted sunflower seeds
- For the dressing:
- 2 tablespoons extra virgin olive oil
- 1 tablespoon red wine vinegar
- 1 teaspoon honey
- ½ teaspoon dijon mustard
- 1 teaspoon freshly squeezed lemon juice
- salt and pepper, to taste

Instructions

1. In a small bowl, whisk together all of the ingredients for the dressing. Set aside.
2. In a large mixing bowl, add in the arugula and golden beet noodles. Pour in the dressing and toss to combine. Set aside in the refrigerator for 10 minutes. Remove, add in the figs and sunflower seeds and toss to combine again.
3. Divide the salad into two plates.

French Lentil and Arugula Salad with Herbed Cashew Cheese

Cook time: *30 mins* | **Total time:** *30 mins* | **Serves:** *4*

Ingredients

- 1/3 cup olive oil
- 1 small shallot, minced
- 1 teaspoon salt
- 2 tablespoons freshly squeezed lemon juice
- 1 tablespoon champagne vinegar (or apple cider vinegar)
- 1 teaspoon Dijon mustard
- 2 1/2 cups cooked lentils, drained well (preferably Le Puy green lentils)
- 2 cups firmly packed baby arugula leaves
- 1 cup spiralized radishes (Blade D) – or thinly sliced, if you can't find large enough radishes to spiralize
- 1 cup chopped endive
- 1 cup spiralized cucumber (Blade D)
- 1/4 cup chopped fresh dill
- 1/3 cup toasted walnuts, chopped
- Pepper
- For the Herbed Cashew Cheese - use ¼ cup (recipe instructions follows below)
- 1 1/2 cups cashew pieces or a combination of cashews and pine nuts, soaked in water for at least 3 hours and drained
- 2 tablespoons large-flake nutritional yeast
- 1 teaspoon salt
- 2 teaspoons herbes de Provence
- 1/4 teaspoon pepper
- 3 tablespoons freshly squeezed lemon juice
- 1 clove garlic, minced
- 4 tablespoons water

Instructions

1. In a small bowl or measuring cup, whisk together the olive oil, shallot, salt, lemon juice, vinegar, and mustard until evenly blended.
2. In a large bowl, stir together the lentils, arugula, radishes, endive, cucumber, and dill. Drizzle evenly with the dressing, then toss or stir until all the ingredients are evenly coated. Stir in the walnuts and season with black pepper to taste. Dot the top of the salad with small bits of the cashew cheese (about 1/2 teaspoon each).
3. Serve the salad right away, or store in an airtight container in the fridge for up to 3 days.
4. The Best Way to Cook Lentils
5. Good news: lentils are quicker to prepare from scratch than beans and add great texture and nutrition to dishes. To cook them, start with about 1 cup of red, brown, or Le Puy (green) lentils. Pick out any that are discolored or shriveled. Rinse the lentils under running water, then combine them in a

saucepan with 2 1/2 cups of water. Bring the water to a rapid simmer, then reduce to a gentle simmer. Add extra water as needed so that the lentils remain barely submerged. Simmer the lentils for 20 to 30 minutes, until they're tender but retain some chew. (Red lentils take less time to cook because they've been split, so they'll likely be tender in 20 to 25 minutes.) Drain them, then season with salt and pepper to taste. 1 cup of dry red, brown, or Le Puy lentils will make between 2 and 2 1/4 cups of cooked lentils.

6. Herbed Cashew Cheese
7. MAKES ABOUT 1 1/4 CUPS
8. Nut cheese can be made with almonds, Brazil nuts, macadamia nuts, or pine nuts, but cashews, with their buttery texture and mild taste, are perfectly suited to the task. This cashew cheese, which is soft and spreadable, is infused with herbs for a more complex flavor profile and nutritional yeast for a kick of umami. Spread it on crackers or toast or crumble it over a salad.
9. Put the cashews in a food processor or blender (preferably a high-speed blender). Add the nutritional yeast, salt, herbes de Provence, pepper, lemon juice, and garlic. Pulse a few times to break the cashews down until they have a wet, coarse, mealy texture.
10. With the motor running, drizzle in 2 tablespoons of the water. Now it's time for some kitchen intuition: keep adding water, stopping occasionally to scrape down the sides of the work bowl, until the mixture has a good consistency. It should be similar to thick hummus—a little coarse, but smooth and spreadable. You may not need all of the remaining 2 tablespoons of water. (If using a blender, start on a low speed and gradually increase to high speed as you add the water, using a plunger attachment the entire time to keep the mixture blending.)
11. Taste and adjust the seasonings as desired. Stored in a covered container in the fridge, the cheese will keep for about 5 days.

Ginger Tahini Cucumber Noodle and Carrot Salad

Prep time: 15 mins | Total time: 15 mins | Serves: 3-4

Ingredients

For the dressing:

- 3 tablespoons tahini
- 2 tablespoons rice vinegar
- 2 teaspoons grated ginger

- 2 tablespoons water + more for thinning
- salt and pepper

For the salad:

- 1 large cucumber, Blade A, noodles trimmed
- 1 large carrot, peeled and shaved into strips
- 1 teaspoon black sesame seeds

Instructions

1. Place the cucumber noodles and peeled carrots in a bowl and pour in the sauce. Toss to combine well.
2. Divide the noodles into bowls, top with sesame seeds and serve.

Goat Cheese Panzanella Salad with Spiralized Cucumbers

Prep time: 20 mins | Cook time: 10 mins | Total time: 30 mins | Serves: 4-6

Ingredients

For the bread:

- 1 teaspoon olive oil, to drizzle
- 3 pieces of whole wheat bread (I like Vermont Bread Company's Soft Whole Wheat) or a gluten-free bread of your choice
- salt and pepper, to taste

For the salad:

- 1 large seedless cucumber, Blade D, noodles trimmed
- 3 tablespoons chopped mint
- 4 basil leaves, sliced
- 1 cup halved cherry tomatoes
- 3oz crumbled goat cheese
- 1 garlic clove, finely minced
- ⅔ cup quartered pitted green olives
- 2 teaspoons red wine vinegar
- pinch of red pepper flakes
- 3 tablespoons extra virgin olive oil
- salt and pepper, to taste

Instructions

1. Heat a grill pan over medium-high heat and drizzle with olive oil. Once oil heats, add in the bread slices and cook for 3 minutes, flip over, season with salt and pepper and cook another 3-5 minutes until the bread has grill marks, is golden brown and is "toasted." When done, slice into cubes.
2. While the bread cooks, pat the cucumber noodles dry thoroughly to rid of excess moisture. Place into a large mixing bowl along with the mint, basil, tomatoes, goat cheese, garlic, olives, red wine vinegar, red pepper flakes, olive oil and season with salt and pepper.
3. Once the bread is done and cubed, add it into the bowl with the salad and toss thoroughly to combine until goat cheese coats all ingredients. Taste and adjust to your preference.

Goat Cheese, Beet Noodle and Cherry Salad

Prep time: *20 mins* | **Total time**: *20 mins* | **Serves**: *4*

Ingredients

For the salad:

- 2 medium beets, peeled, Blade D, noodles trimmed
- 1 box Kale Italia greens
- ½ pound pitted and halved cherries (bing or dark Hudson are best)
- ¼ cup roughly chopped walnuts
- ¼ cup crumbled goat cheese

For the dressing:

- ¼ cup fresh lemon juice
- 2 teaspoons Dijon mustard
- 2 teaspoons minced shallots
- 2 teaspoons honey
- ¼ cup extra-virgin olive oil
- salt and pepper, to taste

Instructions

1. Place all of the ingredients for the dressing into a bowl and whisk together. Taste and adjust to your preference, if needed.
2. Place the beet noodles, Kale Italia greens and cherries into a large mixing bowl and pour over the dressing and toss altogether to combine.
3. Plate the salad into bowls, top with goat cheese, walnuts and serve.

Golden Beet and Grapefruit Mint Salad with Crushed Walnuts

Prep time: 30 mins | *Cook time:* 5 mins | *Total time:* 35 mins | *Serves:* 4

Ingredients

For the salad:

- 2 golden beets, peeled, Blade A
- ¼ cup raw walnuts
- 1 ruby red grapefruit
- For the dressing:
- 2 teaspoons honey
- 1 tablespoon extra virgin olive oil
- 2 tablespoons chopped fresh mint leaves
- salt and pepper, to taste

Instructions

1. Bring a large pot filled ⅓ of the way with water to a boil. Once boiling, add the beet slices and cook for 7-10 minutes or until fork-tender. When done, drain into a colander and then rinse lightly with cold water until able to be handled.
2. Meanwhile, prepare the rest. Place the walnuts into a food processor and pulse until chunky-ground. Then, prepare the grapefruit: Cut a ¼-inch-thick slice from each end of grapefruit. Place, flat ends down, on your surface, and remove peel in strips, cutting from top to bottom following the sides of the grapefruit. Remove any remaining white flesh (the pith.) Hold the peeled grapefruit over a bowl and slice between membranes, and then gently remove whole segments and set aside. Reserve ¼ cup of the juice from the fruit and whisk it together with the other ingredients for the dressing and set aside.

3. Arrange the salad: lay down the golden beets, layer over with grapefruit slices and then drizzle with the dressing. Finish by dusting with the ground walnut. Serve fresh!

Golden Beet Chicken Pasta with Yogurt-Dill Sauce

Prep time: 15 mins | *Cook time:* 15 mins | *Total time:* 30 mins | *Serves:* 2

Ingredients

For the yogurt-dill sauce:

- ½ cup nonfat plain Greek yogurt
- 2 teaspoons lemon juice
- 1 teaspoon red wine vinegar
- ¼ teaspoon garlic powder
- salt and pepper, to taste
- 1 tablespoon chopped dill

For the salad:

- 1 cup cooked shredded chicken, chilled
- 2 medium candy cane (or other) beets, peeled, Blade D, noodles trimmed + beet greens, chopped (optional)

Instructions

1. Place a saucepot filled halfway with water to a boil and set a bowl nearby filled with ice. Once boiling, add in the beet noodles and greens (optional) and cook for 1-2 minutes or until slightly softened. Drain into a colander and immediately set over ice to stop the cooking process. Pat dry once cooled.
2. While the beets cool, place all of the ingredients for the yogurt-dill sauce into a bowl and whisk together. Set aside.
3. Place the chicken, beet noodles and beet greens (optional) into a large mixing bowl, add the yogurt-dill sauce and toss together to combine.
4. Plate the salad and garnish with any additional dill, if desired.

Golden Beet Noodles with Goat Cheese, Pepitas and Pomegranate

Prep time: 15 mins | Total time: 15 mins | Serves: 2

Ingredients

For the salad:

- 2 large golden beets, peeled, Blade D, noodles trimmed
- salt and pepper, to taste
- 1 tablespoon raw pepitas
- ¼ cup crumbled goat cheese
- ¼ cup pomegranate seeds

For the dressing:

- 1 teaspoon dijon mustard
- 2 tablespoons extra virgin olive oil
- 1 tablespoon apple cider vinegar
- 1 teaspoon honey
- salt and pepper, to taste

Instructions

1. Place all of the ingredients for the dressing into a small bowl and whisk together. Season with salt and pepper and adjust to your preferences, if necessary.
2. Place the beet noodles in a large mixing bowl and pour over the dressing. Toss together to combine and then add in the pepitas and half the goat cheese.
3. Transfer the noodles to a serving platter or divide onto two plates and garnish each with remaining goat cheese and pomegranate seeds.

Greek Zoodle Salad

"Zoodles (zucchini noodles) are all the rage and I keep looking for new ways to prepare *them. I decided to combine my love of Greek salad with the zoodles and came up with this recipe. A great alternative to high-carb pasta salads!"*

Servings: 4 | Prep: 10 m | Ready In: 25 m

Ingredients

- 2 zucchini
- 1/4 English cucumber, chopped
- 10 cherry tomatoes, halved, or more to taste
- 10 pitted kalamata olives, halved, or more to taste
- 1/4 cup thinly sliced red onion
- 2 ounces crumbled reduced-fat feta cheese
- 2 tablespoons extra-virgin olive oil
- 2 tablespoons fresh lemon juice
- 1 teaspoon dried oregano salt and ground black pepper to taste

Directions

1. Cut zucchini into noodle-shaped strands using a spiralizing tool. Place "zoodles" in a large bowl and top with cucumber, tomatoes, olives, red onion, and feta cheese.
2. Whisk olive oil, lemon juice, oregano, salt, and pepper together in a bowl until dressing is smooth; pour over "zoodle" mixture and toss to coat. Marinate salad in refrigerator for 10 to 15 minutes.

Nutritional Information

- Calories:147 kcal 7%
- Fat: 11.1 g 17%
- Carbs: 9.1g 3%
- Protein: 5 g 10%
- Cholesterol: 5 mg 2%
- Sodium: 391 mg 16%

Greek Zucchini "Orzo" Salad

Prep time: 30 mins | **Total time:** 30 mins | **Serves:** 3-4

Ingredients

For the salad:

- 1.5 cups seeded and chopped roma tomatoes
- ½ cup halved pitted kalamata olives
- ⅓ cup crumbled feta cheese
- 1 cup canned artichoke hearts, drained and quartered
- 1 cups baby spinach
- ¼ cup diced red onion

For the dressing:

- 1.5 tablespoons red wine vinegar
- 1 tablespoon extra virgin olive oil
- 1 teaspoon Dijon mustard
- 2 tablespoons lemon juice
- ¼ teaspoon dried oregano
- ¼ teaspoon dried parsley
- ¼ teaspoon dried basil
- pepper, to taste

For the orzo:

- 1.5-2 medium zucchinis, Blade C/D

Instructions

1. Place the zucchini noodles into a food processor and pulse until orzo-shaped (like a longer rice.) Be careful not to over-pulse, as zucchini is moist and will become mushy. Pat dry and set aside.
2. Combine all of the ingredients for the dressing into a bowl and whisk together. Taste and adjust to your preference.
3. Place all of the ingredients for the salad along with the zucchini in a large mixing bowl and pour over the dressing. Toss thoroughly to combine and serve or save in the refrigerator for up to 4 days for maximum freshness.

Grilled Romaine with Caramelized Onion Noodles, Blue Cheese and Greek Yogurt Balsamic Dressing

Prep Time: *15 minutes |* ***Cook Time:*** *20 minutes |* ***Total Time:*** *35 minutes |* ***Servings:***
4

Ingredients

- 2 romaine lettuce heads, rinsed, ends chopped off and cut in half lengthwise
- 2 tablespoon extra virgin olive oil
- salt and pepper, to taste
- 1 onion, peeled, Blade A
- 1/4 teaspoon garlic powder
- 1/2 cup crumbled blue cheese

For the dressing:

- ¼ cup nonfat plain Greek yogurt
- 3 tablespoon balsamic vinegar
- 2 teaspoons Dijon mustard
- 1 tablespoon honey
- salt and pepper, to taste

Instructions

1. Preheat the grill or grill pan to medium-high. Place half the olive oil in a bowl and while the grill is heating, brush the cut sides of the romaine lettuce with the olive oil. Season the cut side generously with pepper and lightly with salt.
2. Once grill pan is heated, place the sliced side down and let cook for about 5 minutes. Periodically, put medium pressure with a spatula on top to ensure the lettuce cooks. Repeat until all lettuce halves are cooked. Set aside.
3. After two lettuce halves have cooked, in another skillet, add in the rest of the olive oil. Once oil heats, add in the onion noodles and season with salt, pepper and garlic powder. Cook for 5-7 minutes or until caramelized and lightly browned.
4. Top the grilled lettuce with onions and blue cheese and drizzle with balsamic vinaigrette.

Indian-Spiced Cod and Garbanzo Bean Salad

Prep Time: *10 minutes* | **Cook Time:** *15 minutes* | **Total Time:** *25 minutes* | **Servings:** *4*

Ingredients

For the fish:

- 2 teaspoon cumin
- 1 teaspoon coriander
- 1/2 teaspoon ground ginger
- salt and pepper, to taste
- 4 tablespoons lemon juice
- 4 cod filets or other flaky white fish

For the salad:

- 1 large seedless cucumber
- 1 large carrot (about 1 lb)
- 1 small red onion
- 1 15-oz can garbanzo beans, rinsed and drained
- 1.5 cups quartered grape tomatoes
- 1 teaspoon lemon zest
- 2 tablespoons lemon juice
- 1.5 tablespoons extra virgin olive oil
- ½ teaspoon ground cumin
- ½ teaspoon curry powder
- ¼ teaspoon salt
- ground pepper, to taste

Instructions

1. Preheat the oven to 450 degrees.
2. In a small bowl, combine the cumin, coriander, ginger, salt, pepper and lemon juice. Place the fish in a shallow dish and pour over the spice mixture and toss around gently to coat. Bake the fish for 15 minutes or until fish flakes when forked.
3. Meanwhile, spiralize the cucumber (Blade C), carrot (Blade C) and onion (Blade A). Pat dry the cucumber noodles thoroughly. In a large bowl, combine the garbanzo beans, tomatoes, cucumber, carrots and onion.
4. In a screw-top jar or dressing shaker, combined the lemon zest, lemon juice, oil, cumin, curry powder, salt and pepper. Shake well.
5. Pour the dressing over the bean mixture and toss gently to coat. Refrigerate until ready to serve alongside fish.

Inspiralized Kale Waldorf Salad

Prep Time: 8 minutes | Cook Time: 10 minutes | Total Time: 18 minutes | Servings: 2

Ingredients

For the salad:

- 1 red apple, Blade C
- 4 cups of chopped kale
- 1/2 cup walnuts
- 5-7 green grapes, halved
- 1/2 cup celery, chopped
- 1 chicken breast, grilled/cooked and cut into strips

For the vinaigrette (makes 3/4 cup, only need 3 tbsp per serving)

- 2 tbsp red wine vinegar
- 1 tbsp sherry vinegar
- 1 tbsp minced shallot
- 3 tbsp olive oil
- 2 tbsp honey
- 3 tbsp ground dijon mustard (or less, if you don't like spicy)
- 1 tbsp water

Instructions

1. Place all of the ingredients for the vinaigrette into a container and shake until combined or place in a bowl and whisk. Set aside.
2. Place kale and celery in a bowl. Pour in vinaigrette and toss to combine. Divide onto plates and then top with walnuts, grapes, spiralized apple and chicken. Enjoy!

Israeli Couscous with Feta-Mint Zucchini Noodles

Prep Time: 15 minutes | Cook Time: 10 minutes | Total Time: 25 minutes | Servings: 2

Ingredients

- 1 cup water
- 1/2 cup uncooked, dry Israeli couscous

- 2 small zucchinis
- 2 tablespoons coarsely chopped fresh mint leaves
- ½ cup small cubed feta cheese

For the dressing:

- 2 tablespoons extra virgin olive oil
- 1 tablespoon apple cider vinegar
- 1 tablespoon fresh lemon juice
- 2 teaspoons honey
- 1/2 teaspoon grated lemon zest
- salt and pepper, to taste

Instructions

1. In a large saucepan, bring 1 cup of lightly salted water to a boil. Add in the couscous and cook for 10 minutes or according to package instructions, until tender. Drain and place in a large mixing bowl.
2. While couscous is cooking, spiralize the zucchinis, using Blade A. Trim the noodles and set aside.
3. Also, while couscous is cooking, in a small bowl, mix together the ingredients for the dressing and season with salt and pepper. Set aside.
4. Place a large skillet over medium heat and add in the zucchini noodles. Let cook for 2-3 minutes or until softened, heated and cooked to your preference. Pour the cooked zucchini into the large mixing bowl and add in the mint and feta. Pour in the dressing and toss to combine.
5. Serve immediately.

Israeli Cucumber Noodle Salad with Tuna

Prep time: *15 mins* | **Total time:** *15 mins* | **Serves:** *3-4*

Ingredients

- 1 seedless cucumber, Blade D, noodles trimmed
- 2.5 cups seeded and diced tomato
- 7oz canned tuna in water, drained
- 1.25 cup diced red onion
- 1 teaspoon ground cumin
- ¼ cup olive oil
- 3 tablespoons fresh lemon juice

- salt and pepper, to taste

Instructions

1. Pat the cucumber noodles dry and set aside in a large mixing bowl along with the tomato, tuna, onion, cumin, oil, lemon juice and season thoroughly with salt and pepper.
2. Toss to combine until all the ingredients are coated in the oil, and lemon juice. Serve.

Jalapeno-Citrus Golden Beet Noodle Salad with Crab, Avocado and Toasted Almonds

Prep time: 30 mins | Total time: 30 mins | Serves: 4

Ingredients

For the salad:

- ¼ cup slivered almonds
- 4 large golden beets, peeled, Blade C
- 2-3 cups watercress greens
- 1 cup lump crab meat
- 1 avocado, peeled, pitted and insides sliced thinly

For the dressing:

- ¾ tablespoon finely chopped shallot
- 2 tablespoons extra virgin olive oil
- 1.5 tablespoons apple cider vinegar
- ½ tablespoon fresh lemon juice
- ½ tablespoon fresh orange juice
- ⅛ teaspoon lemon zest
- ¾ teaspoon seeded and finely diced jalapeno
- 1 teaspoon honey
- salt and pepper, to taste

Instructions

1. Place a medium skillet over medium-high heat. Once heated, add in the almonds. Toast, stirring occasionally, until golden brown and fragrant, about 2 minutes.
2. Meanwhile, whisk together all of the ingredients for the dressing. Taste and adjust to your preferences. Then, in a large bowl, toss together the beets, watercress, crab and dressing. Divide into plates.
3. Garnish with avocado and toasted almonds.

Kohlrabi & Green Apple Noodle Arugula Salad with Goat Cheese, Dried Cranberries & Walnuts with a Honey-Dijon Dressing

Prep Time: 15 minutes | Total Time: 15 minutes | Servings: 1

Ingredients

- 1 kohlrabi, peeled, Blade C
- 1 green apple, Blade C
- 1/4 cup crumbled goat cheese
- 2 tbsp chopped walnuts
- 1 tbsp dried cranberries
- 1 handful baby arugula

For the dressing:

- 2 tbsp honey
- 1 tbsp red wine vinegar
- 3 tbsp olive oil
- 1 tbsp country dijon mustard
- salt and pepper, to taste

Instructions

1. Place all of the ingredients for the dressing in a bowl and whisk together. Taste and adjust to your preference.
2. Place the arugula and kohlrabi and green apple noodles in a bowl and pour over desired amount of dressing.
3. Top noodles with goat cheese, dried cranberries and walnuts. Enjoy!

Lemon-Garlic Celeriac Noodle Salad with Feta, Mint and Shaved Asparagus

Prep Time: *10 minutes* | **Cook Time**: *10 minutes* | **Total Time**: *20 minutes* | **Servings**: *3*

Ingredients

- 1 tbsp olive oil
- 1 garlic clove, minced
- 1 celeriac, peeled, Blade C
- 2 tbsp fresh lemon juice
- 2 tbsp slivered blanched almonds
- 12 asparagus stalks
- 1/4 cup feta cheese, cubed
- 3 tsp chopped mint (or use 6 mint leaves in the Microplane Herb Mill)

Instructions

1. Prepare your asparagus. Snap off the bottoms and then use a peeler to "shave" the asparagus. When done, chop off the tips and set aside.
2. Place a large skillet over medium-low heat and add in the olive oil. Then, add in the garlic and let cook for 30 seconds. Then, add in the celeriac noodles, asparagus tips and lemon juice. Cook for 5-7 minutes, tossing frequently. Add in the almonds, shaved asparagus and cook for 1 more minute.
3. When done, divide onto individual plates. Top each with equal amounts of feta and mint. Enjoy!

Lemon-Tahini Cucumber Noodles with Shrimp

Prep time: *20 mins* | **Cook time**: *5 mins* | **Total time**: *25 mins* | **Serves**: *2*

Ingredients

For the salad:

- 1 large English/seedless cucumber

- 2 roma tomatoes, seeded and diced
- 3 tablespoons minced mint
- 2 tablespoons minced parsley
- ⅓ cup diced red onion
- ⅓ cup pitted and halved kalamata olives
- ½ teaspoon sumac or paprika

For the shrimp:

- 8 large or 12 small shrimp, defrosted, peeled, deveined
- 2 teaspoons extra virgin olive oil
- ½ teaspoon garlic powder (or to taste)
- salt and pepper

For the dressing:

- 2 tablespoons tahini
- 2 tablespoons freshly squeezed lemon juice
- 1 teaspoon honey
- 1 small garlic clove, minced
- 2 tablespoons water, to thin
- salt & pepper, to taste

Instructions

1. Place all of the ingredients for the dressing into a food processor and pulse until creamy. Taste and adjust to your preference, if needed. Set aside.
2. Slice the cucumber halfway lengthwise and then spiralize it. Pat the noodles dry with paper towels and then place in a large mixing bowl, along with the tomato, mint, parsley and onion. Set aside.
3. Place a medium skillet over medium-high heat and add in the oil. Once oil heats, add in the shrimp and season with salt, pepper and garlic powder. Cook for 2 minutes, flip over and cook another 2 minutes or until shrimp are opaque and cooked through.
4. Transfer the cucumber mixture to a plate, top with dressing and then shrimp. Sprinkle over with sumac (or paprika) and enjoy.

Mango-Almond Jicama and Cabbage Salad

Prep time: 30 mins | Total time: 30 mins | Serves: 4

Ingredients

For the dressing:

- 1.5 cups diced mango (about 1 full mango)
- 1 tablespoon rice vinegar
- 2 tablespoons freshly squeezed lime juice
- ¼ cup unsweetened almond milk
- 1.5 tablespoon chopped cilantro
- ¼ teaspoon red pepper flakes
- salt, to taste

For the rest:

- 1 medium jicama, peeled, Blade C
- 1 cup diced scallions
- 1 cup cooked edamame
- 1 cup of spiralized red cabbage (using Blade A)

Instructions

1. Place all of the ingredients for the dressing into a blender and blend until smooth. Taste and adjust, if necessary.
2. Combine the jicama noodles, scallions, edamame and spiralized cabbage into a large mixing bowl and toss to combine. Drizzle with the dressing, toss again and set aside in the refrigerator. Let chill for 10 minutes, then toss together and plate. Garnish each bowl with avocado.

Mediterranean Zucchini Pasta Salad

Prep time: *30 mins* | **Total time:** *30 mins* | **Serves:** *6-8*

Ingredients

For the salad:

- 2 medium zucchinis
- 1 small red onion, peeled
- 14.5oz can quartered artichoke hearts, drained
- ½ cup halved pitted kalamata olives
- 1 cup drained and rinsed canned chickpeas
- ½ cup crumbled feta

- 14.5oz can diced tomatoes, drained

For the dressing:

- 4 tablespoons extra virgin olive oil
- 2 tablespoon red wine vinegar
- 1 tablespoon freshly squeezed lemon juice
- 1 teaspoon dried oregano
- ½ teaspoon dried parsley
- ½ teaspoon garlic powder
- 1 teaspoon Dijon mustard
- salt and pepper

Instructions

1. Place all of the ingredients for the dressing into a bowl and whisk together.
2. Slice the zucchinis halfway through lengthwise, careful not to pierce through the center. Spiralize the zucchinis with Blade C and add to a large mixing bowl. Grab the onion and again, slice halfway through lengthwise, careful not to pierce through the center. Spiralize the onion with Blade A and add half of the noodles to the bowl with the zucchini noodles and save the rest for future use. Then add in the artichokes, olives, chickpeas, feta, and diced tomatoes.
3. Pour the prepared dressing over the zucchini salad and toss well to combine. Serve or refrigerate for future use.

Mint-Ginger Kumquat, Bell Pepper and Cucumber Noodle Salad

Prep time: *20 mins* | **Total time:** *20 mins* | **Serves:** *2*

Ingredients

For the salad:

- 1 seedless cucumber, Blade A, noodles trimmed
- 1 green bell pepper, Blade A, noodles trimmed
- 1 tablespoon chopped mint
- ½ cup kumquats, thinly sliced
- 1 tablespoon slivered almonds
- ½ ripe avocado, thinly sliced

For the dressing:

- 1 tablespoon sesame oil
- 2 teaspoons honey
- juice from 1 small lime
- pepper, to taste
- 1 teaspoon minced ginger

Instructions

1. Add all of the ingredients for the dressing into a bowl and whisk together.
2. Pat the cucumber noodles dry thoroughly and add to a large mixing bowl along with the bell pepper noodles, mint and kumquats. Pour over the dressing and toss together.
3. Divide the salad onto two plates and top with almonds and avocado.

Mixed Greens and Quinoa Salad with Spiralized Cantaloupe

***Prep time:** 20 mins | **Total time:** 20 mins | **Serves:** 6*

Ingredients

For the salad:

- 1 medium cantaloupe, peeled, Blade B
- 10-12 cups mixed greens
- 1.5 cups cooked quinoa, preferably chilled
- ¾ cup crumbled feta
- ½ cup roughly chopped walnuts

For the dressing:

- ¼ cup olive oil
- 3 tablespoons apple cider vinegar
- 1 tablespoon honey
- 1.5 teaspoons dijon mustard
- salt and pepper, to taste

Instructions

1. Place all of the ingredients for the dressing together in a small bowl and whisk together. Taste and adjust to your preferences.
2. Toss the spiralized cantaloupe, greens, and quinoa together. Divide the salad mixture onto plates, sprinkle with feta cheese, walnuts and drizzle over with dressing.

Mozzarella and Cashew-Balsamic Zucchini Noodle Salad

Prep time: *20 mins* | **Cook time:** *10 mins* | **Total time:** *30 mins* | **Serves:** *2*

Ingredients

For the dressing:

- ¼ cup raw cashews, soaked in water for at least 2 hours
- 1 tablespoon balsamic vinegar
- 1 garlic clove, pressed
- ¼ cup cashew milk
- salt and pepper, to taste
- 1 teaspoon country Dijon mustard

For the salad:

- ½ cup mozzarella pearls (the "little ones")
- 1 cup cherry tomatoes, halved
- 1 orange or yellow bell pepper, Blade A, noodles trimmed
- 1 large zucchini, Blade B, noodles trimmed
- 1 tablespoon pine nuts

Instructions

1. Drain the cashews and then place them, along with the rest of the dressing ingredients into a food processor or blender and blend until creamy. Taste and adjust, if necessary. Set aside.
2. In a large mixing bowl, combine the mozzarella balls, cherry tomatoes, and bell pepper for the salad. Then, drizzle over the dressing and toss everything to mix well. Place in the refrigerator while you prepare the pine nuts.
3. Place a small skillet over medium heat. Once skillet is heated, add in the pine nuts and toast for 3-5 minutes or until golden brown and fragrant.

4. Divide the salad into bowls and top with pine nuts.

Mustard-Tarragon Zucchini Pasta Salad with Smoked Salmon and Peas

Prep Time: 10 minutes | *Cook Time:* 10 minute | *Total Time:* 20 minutes | *Servings:* 1

Ingredients

- 1 medium zucchini, Blade C
- 2-3oz smoked salmon, cut into 2" strips
- 3 tbsp cooked green peas

For the mustard-tarragon dressing:

- 1 tbsp olive oil
- 1 tbsp minced shallots
- 6 tarragon leaves, sliced thinly
- 2 tbsp country/grain Dijon mustard
- 1 tbsp vegetable broth
- 1 tbsp nonfat plain Greek yogurt
- salt and pepper, to taste

Instructions

1. Place a large skillet over medium heat and add in the oil. Once the oil heats, add in the shallots. Cook for about 2 minutes or until the shallots soften.
2. Add in the tarragon and vegetable broth. Cook until the broth reduces.
3. Add in the dijon mustard, stir to combine and then add in the Greek yogurt. Stir until creamy, season with salt and pepper, and add in the zucchini noodles.
4. Toss the noodles to combine and coat with the dressing. Add in the peas and smoked salmon, toss to combine and plate onto a dish. Enjoy!

No-Lettuce Lobster Cobb Salad with Zucchini Noodles

Prep time: 15 mins | *Cook time:* 30 mins | *Total time:* 45 mins | *Serves:* 2

Ingredients

- 2 raw lobster tails, about 10oz each (you could also buy this pre-cooked and skip the first step in this recipe, FYI)
- 2 strips of turkey bacon (I like Applegate!)
- 1 large zucchini
- 1 ear of corn, shucked
- ½ cup cherry tomatoes
- ½ avocado, pitted and peeled
- 1 boiled egg
- freshly cracked pepper, to garnish

For the dressing:

- 2 tablespoons extra virgin olive oil
- 1 tablespoon sherry vinegar
- 1 teaspoon country dijon mustard
- 3 tablespoons crumbled blue cheese
- 2 teaspoons freshly squeezed lemon juice
- 1 garlic clove, minced
- 1 pinch red pepper flakes
- salt and pepper, to taste

Instructions

1. Fill a pot halfway with water and bring to a boil. Once boiling, add in the lobster tails and cook for 8 minutes. Drain into a colander and remove the meat from the tails, chop, and set aside.
2. Meanwhile, on another burner, place a large skillet over medium-high heat and coat with cooking spray. Once heated, add in the bacon and cook until crispy, about 10 minutes. Transfer to a paper towel lined plate and set aside.
3. While the lobster and bacon cook, peel and spiralize the zucchinis with Blade D. Trim the noodles and set aside, dividing into two bowls (these will be what you eat the salad from, so pick a wide pasta or salad bowl.)
4. Once the lobster is done, refill the same pot halfway with water and place the corn and a pinch of salt. Place over high heat and bring to a boil. Once boiling, cook for 2-3 minutes or until the corn is fork-tender. Remove, drain into a colander and once cool enough to handle, shave the kernels off the cob and set aside.
5. While the corn cooks, prepare the rest: quarter the cherry tomatoes, crumble the cooked bacon, slice (or dice) the avocado, and quarter the boiled egg. Set everything aside.

6. Place all of the ingredients for the dressing into a food processor and pulse until creamy. Taste and adjust if necessary. Refrigerate until ready to use.
7. Now, it's time to assemble your salads! Top the zucchini noodle bowls evenly with cherry tomatoes, bacon, corn, avocado, boiled egg and lobster. Drizzle the bowls with the dressing and serve with freshly cracked pepper.

Packing Zucchini Pasta for Lunch

Prep Time: *10 minutes* | **Cook Time**: *10 minute* | **Total Time:** *20 minutes* | **Servings:** *2*

Ingredients

For the Vinaigrette

- 3 tbsp basil, chopped
- 1/2 cup feta
- 1 shallot, chopped
- 1 tbsp lemon juice
- salt and pepper to taste
- 2 tbsp olive oil
- 2 tbsp red wine vinegar
- 1 small garlic clove, minced

For the rest

- 10 Kalamata olives, pitted and halved
- 1 ear of corn
- 2.5 large cucumbers, Blade A
- 1 avocado, insides cubed
- 1/2 cup of walnuts
- 2 chicken breasts, grilled

Instructions

1. Place down a paper towel or two, put on the cucumber pasta, and press a paper towel on top until most of the moisture is absorbed.
2. Place a small saucepan on high heat and place in enough water to cover 1 ear of corn. Place in corn (halve first) and bring to a boil. Cook for about 3 minutes or until corn turns a brighter yellow and can pierce more easily

with a fork. Place in a colander to drain and then shave off kernels in a bowl, using a knife. Set aside.

3. In a food processor, combine all ingredients and pulse until creamy. Place the "dried" cucumber pasta in a bowl, add vinaigrette and mix thoroughly to combine. Plate onto two dishes.

4. Top with the rest of the ingredients, extra dressing and enjoy.

Pear Noodle, Mizuna Greens and Spiced Pecans with Parsley-Goat Cheese Vinaigrette

Prep Time: 15 minutes | **Cook Time:** 15 minutes | **Total Time:** 30 minutes | **Servings:** 3

Ingredients

- 1 tablespoon honey
- ¼ teaspoon cinnamon
- ¼ teaspoon cayenne
- salt, to taste
- ½ cup whole pecans
- 2 pears, Blade C, noodles trimmed
- 5 cups mizuna greens (or similar green, such as arugula)

For the dressing:

- 3 tablespoons extra virgin olive oil
- ¼ cup crumbled goat cheese
- 2 tablespoons lemon juice
- 1 tablespoon honey
- 1 tablespoon freshly minced parsley
- salt and pepper, to taste

Instructions

1. Preheat the oven to 325 degrees. While preheating, whisk together the honey with the cinnamon, cayenne and season lightly with salt. It should create a paste. Add the pecans into the mixture. Stir to combine thoroughly.

2. Lay the dressed pecans out on a parchment paper lined baking tray and bake for 10 minutes, flip over and bake another 5 minutes. Remove from the oven and set aside. Let the pecans cool for at least 5 minutes before

you use them in the rest of the recipe (they will become less sticky the longer they sit.)

3. While the pecans are baking, whisk together all of the ingredients for the dressing and mix until vinaigrette is creamy. Set aside.
4. When pecans are done, place the pear noodles, mizuna greens, and pecans in a large mixing bowl, pour over the dressing and toss to thoroughly combine. Serve.

Quick and Easy Asian Sesame Cucumber Salad

"A chilled sesame salad of spiralized cucumber. It reminds me of the seaweed salad you get at Japanese restaurants, but just cucumbers."

Servings: *4 |* ***Prep:*** *15 m |* ***Ready In:*** *45 m*

Ingredients

- 2 English cucumbers, peeled
- 1 teaspoon salt, divided, or to taste
- 2 tablespoons garlic-seasoned rice wine vinegar
- 1 tablespoon toasted sesame oil
- 1 tablespoon soy sauce
- 1 teaspoon white sugar
- 1/4 teaspoon toasted sesame seeds

Directions

1. Cut cucumbers into long, thin noodle shapes using a spiralizer set to the thinnest setting.
2. Place cucumber noodles in a fine-mesh strainer set over a bowl. Sprinkle with 1/2 teaspoon salt and toss until combined. Let cucumber stand until moisture is drawn out, about 30 minutes.
3. Whisk rice vinegar, sesame oil, soy sauce, and sugar together in a bowl until sugar is dissolved. Add cucumber; toss gently until coated. Season with remaining 1/2 teaspoon salt; sprinkle with sesame seeds.

Nutritional Information

- Calories:66 kcal 3%
- Fat: 3.7 g 6%
- Carbs: 8g 3%

- Protein: 1.2 g 2%
- Cholesterol: 0 mg 0%
- Sodium: 958 mg 38%

Rainbow Chard and Potato Noodle Salad with Crispy Pancetta, Quinoa and Parmesan-Oregano Vinaigrette

Prep time: 20 mins | *Cook time:* 20 mins | *Total time:* 40 mins | *Serves:* 2

Ingredients

For the salad:

- ½ cup diced pancetta
- 1 medium red potato
- salt and pepper, to taste
- ¼ teaspoon garlic powder
- 1 bunch rainbow chard, chopped (about 4 cups)
- ½ cup cooked quinoa

For the vinaigrette:

- 2 tablespoons extra virgin olive oil
- 1 tablespoon red wine vinegar
- 2 teaspoons grated parmesan cheese
- salt and pepper, to taste
- ⅛ teaspoon garlic powder
- ¼ teaspoon oregano flakes
- 1 teaspoon lemon juice
- 1 pinch red pepper flakes

Instructions

1. Place a large skillet over medium heat. Once heated, add in the pancetta and cook for 5 minutes or until pancetta is crispy and browned.
2. While pancetta cooks, spiralize the potato with Blade D and trim the noodles.
3. When pancetta is done, transfer with a slotted spoon or tongs to a paper towel lined plate and then immediately add in the potato noodles. Season the potatoes with salt, pepper and garlic powder and then cover and cook for 10 minutes or until al dente, uncovering occasionally to toss.

4. Meanwhile, prepare the vinaigrette. Combine all of the ingredients into a bowl and whisk together. Taste and adjust, if necessary. Set aside.
5. Then, combine the chard and quinoa in a large mixing bowl and set aside until the potato noodles are done. Once done, let the potato noodles cool for 5 minutes. Then, add them and the cooked pancetta to the bowl with the chard, pour in the dressing and toss to combine.
6. Divide onto plates.

Raw Beet Noodle and Rainbow Chard Salad with Avocado-Ranch Dressing

Prep Time: *30 minutes* | **Servings:** *6*

Ingredients

For the salad:

- 3 large beets, peeled, Blade C, noodles trimmed
- 5-6 cups chopped Rainbow Swiss Chard
- 6 packets of Nourish Snacks Ménage-a-Mix (or 1.5 cup mix of chickpeas, edamame and corn)

For the dressing:

- 1 ripe avocado
- 1 cup plain almond milk (or full-fat coconut milk)
- 3 tablespoons freshly squeezed lemon juice
- 2 teaspoons red wine vinegar
- 2 garlic cloves, minced
- 1.5 teaspoons freshly minced dill
- 2 teaspoons freshly minced parsley
- 1/2 teaspoon onion powder
- 1 teaspoon paprika
- salt to taste (about ¼ teaspoon)
- pepper to taste

Instructions

1. Combine all of the ingredients for the dressing into a high speed blender or food processor and pulse until creamy. Taste and adjust to your preferences. Set aside.

2. Toss the chard and beet noodles together in a large mixing bowl. Drizzle over with avocado-ranch dressing and let sit for 10 minutes to soften the beet and chard.
3. When ready to serve, divide into plates and top each with 1 packet of Nourish Snacks's Menage-a-Mix. If serving family-style, add the packets to a serving bowl with the beet and chard and toss together to combine.

Roasted Butternut Squash Salad with Maple Sesame Vinaigrette

Prep Time: *25 minutes* | **Cook Time**: *10 minutes* | **Servings:** *3*

Ingredients

- 1 medium butternut squash, peeled, Blade B, noodles trimmed
- salt and pepper, to taste
- 1 large asian pear
- 5 oz container of arugula
- ¾ cup pomegranate seeds
- 3/4 cup roughly chopped walnuts

For the vinaigrette:

- 1 tablespoon real maple syrup
- 1 tablespoon extra virgin olive oil
- 1 tablespoon sesame oil
- 2 tablespoons apple cider vinegar
- 1 teaspoon white sesame seeds
- 1 tablespoon soy sauce
- pepper, to taste
- 1 garlic clove, crushed and then minced

Instructions

1. Preheat the oven to 400 degrees. Line a baking sheet with parchment paper and lay out the butternut squash noodles. Coat lightly with cooking spray and season with salt and pepper and roast for 8-10 minutes or until cooked through but still al dente.
2. While the squash cooks, combine all of the ingredients for the vinaigrette and set aside.

3. Spiralize the pear and add to a large mixing bowl with the arugula and walnuts. Once butternut squash is done, add it to the large bowl, drizzle over the vinaigrette and toss thoroughly.
4. Serve immediately.

Roasted Peaches & Beet Noodles with Gorgonzola, Walnuts and Honey-Mint White Balsamic

*Prep Time: 15 minutes | **Cook Time**: 20 minutes | **Total Time**: 35 minutes | **Servings**: 2*

Ingredients

- 2 medium beets (350g each), peeled, Blade C
- 1 cup small-chopped white peaches
- 1/4 cup chopped walnuts
- 1/4 cup crumbled gorgonzola cheese

For the dressing:

- 1 tbsp chopped mint
- 1 tbsp olive oil
- 1 tbsp water
- 2 tsp honey
- 2 tbsp white balsamic vinegar
- 2 tsp lime juice
- salt and pepper, to taste

Instructions

1. Preheat the oven to 400 degrees.
2. Coat a baking tray with cooking spray and spread out your beet noodles. Season with salt and pepper.
3. In another baking tray, place down a piece of parchment paper, coat with cooking spray and then lay out your peaches.
4. Place the tray with the beets and tray with the peaches in the oven and bake for 15-20 minutes.
5. While the peaches are baking, place all of the ingredients for the dressing in a bowl and whisk. Set aside in the refrigerator.

6. When the noodles and peaches are done, mix together in a bowl with the walnuts. Divide the mixture into two bowls, top evenly with the gorgonzola cheese and drizzle evenly with the dressing.

Salmon Burgers with Kohlrabi Noodle and Flaxseed Caesar Salad

Prep time: 25 mins | Cook time: 10 mins | Total time: 35 mins | Serves: 2

Ingredients

For the burgers:

- ½ pound salmon filet, skinless, cut into cubes
- 2 teaspoons dijon mustard
- salt and pepper, to taste
- 1 small garlic clove, minced
- ¼ teaspoon grated lemon zest
- 1 tablespoon minced parsley
- 1 teaspoon lemon juice
- ¼ diced scallions

For the salad:

- 2 kohlrabis, peeled
- 1 tablespoon ground flax seeds (optional)
- For the dressing
- ¼ cup raw cashews, soaked for at least 30 minutes and drained
- ¼ cup unsweetened cashew (or almond) milk
- 1 garlic clove, chopped
- ½ tablespoon freshly squeezed lemon juice
- ½ teaspoon dijon mustard
- salt and pepper, to taste

Instructions

1. Place all of the ingredients for the dressing into a food processor or blender and pulse until creamy. Taste and adjust to your preferences.
2. Slice the kohlrabi halfway through (don't slice farther than the center) and then spiralize with Blade C.

3. In a medium mixing bowl, add in the kohlrabi noodles. Pour in ¾ of the dressing and toss to combine thoroughly. Set aside in the refrigerator, along with the rest of the dressing (place in a small bowl.)
4. Wipe out and clean the used food processor (or blender.) Then, place in all of the ingredients but the green onions for the salmon burgers. Pulse until the burger mix is formed (no large chunks of salmon left.) Don't overpulse and make the salmon pastey. Empty the salmon mix into a medium bowl and stir in the green onions. Form two patties.
5. Place a large skillet over medium-high heat and add in the olive oil. Once oil heats, add in the salmon burgers, season the tops with salt and pepper and let cook 2-3 minutes per side.
6. While salmon burgers cook, plate the kohlrabi noodles into two bowls and top each with flaxseed (optional).
7. When burgers are done, place atop the kohlrabi bowls and then drizzle each with leftover reserved Caesar dressing.

Scallop and Apple Noodle Spinach Salad with Spiced Walnuts

Prep time: 15 mins | Cook time: 10 mins | Total time: 25 mins | Serves: 3

Ingredients

For the walnuts:

- ½ tablespoon maple syrup
- ⅛ teaspoon cinnamon
- ⅛ teaspoon cayenne
- salt, to taste
- ¼ cup whole walnuts
- For the dressing:
- 2 tablespoons extra virgin olive oil
- 1 tablespoon freshly squeezed lemon juice
- salt and pepper, to taste
- ½ teaspoon dijon mustard

For the salad:

- 1 green apple
- 3oz baby spinach
- 1 tablespoon extra virgin olive oil
- 6 large scallops
- salt and pepper, to taste

- 2 tablespoons freshly squeezed lemon juice

Instructions

1. Preheat the oven to 425 degrees. In a medium bowl, whisk together the maple syrup with the cinnamon, cayenne and season lightly with salt. It should create a paste. Add the walnuts into the mixture. Stir to combine thoroughly.
2. Line a baking tray with parchment paper. Lay the dressed walnuts out on the parchment paper and bake for 5 minutes. Remove from the oven and set aside. Let the walnuts cool for at least 5 minutes before you use them in the rest of the recipe (they will become less sticky the longer they sit.)
3. While the walnuts cook, whisk together all of the ingredients for the dressing. Taste and adjust to your preferences. Set aside. Spiralize the apple with Blade C and place in a large mixing bowl along with the spinach. Set aside.
4. Once the walnuts are cooling out of the oven, place a large skillet over medium heat and add in the oil. While oil heats, season the scallops with salt and pepper. Once oil heats, add the scallops to the pan, cook for 1-2 minutes (or until golden brown on the bottom) and flip over, cooking another 1-2 minutes or until both sides are golden brown. Then, add the lemon juice to the pan, coating the scallops with the juice.
5. While scallops cook, pour the dressing over the greens and apple noodles. Toss together to combine and divide into two plates.
6. When scallops are done, divide onto plates and then garnish with walnuts. Serve immediately.

Shredded Chard, Apple Noodle and Tuna Salad with Lemon Dijon Vinaigrette

Prep Time: *10 minutes* | **Total Time:** *10 minutes* | **Servings:** *2*

Ingredients

- 6-7 large chard leaves
- 1 apple, stem removed, Blade C, noodles trimmed
- ¼ cup roughly chopped pecans
- 1 5oz can of tuna in water, drained
- freshly cracked pepper, to taste

For the dressing:

- 1 tablespoon apple cider vinegar
- 1 tablespoon water
- 1 teaspoon Dijon mustard
- 2 teaspoons lemon juice
- 1 teaspoon honey
- salt and pepper, to taste
- ½ tablespoon olive oil

Instructions

1. Place all of the ingredients for the dressing into a bowl and whisk until combined. Set aside.
2. Lay out the chard leaves. Cut out the thick stem and stack the leaves. Roll the stack up into a cigar and cut into thin ribbons to "shred" the chard.
3. Combine the chard, apple and pecans in a large mixing bowl. Add in the dressing, saving about two teaspoons. Toss to combine fully and then divide into two plates. Top the plates equally with tuna and drizzle the remaining vinaigrette onto the tuna. Season with cracked pepper.

Shredded Kale, Pear Noodle and Brussels Sprouts Salad

Prep time: 25 mins | Total time: 25 mins | Serves: 3-4

Ingredients

For the vinaigrette:

- 2 tablespoons extra virgin olive oil
- 1 tablespoon minced shallot
- salt and pepper, to taste
- 1 teaspoon honey
- 2 tablespoons apple cider vinegar
- ½ teaspoon Dijon mustard

For the salad:

- 6oz (about 2 cups) brussels sprouts, thinly sliced
- 1 pear, Blade D (any pear will do – I love Bosc or Anjou)
- 3 tablespoons sliced blanched almonds
- 1 cup finely chopped (aka shredded) kale

Instructions

1. Place a medium skillet over medium-high heat. Once heated, add in the sliced almonds and cook, shaking the pan frequently, until toasted and fragrant, about 3 minutes. Set almonds aside.
2. Whisk together all of the ingredients for the dressing. Taste and adjust to your preference, then set aside.
3. In a large mixing bowl, combine and toss the brussels sprouts, pear noodles, toasted almonds, and kale. Drizzle over with the vinaigrette and toss again. Serve.

Soy Ginger Chicken Spiralized Salad

Prep time: *25 mins* | **Cook time:** *20 mins* | **Total time:** *45 mins* | **Serves:** *3*

Ingredients

- 2 boneless chicken breasts
- ½ cup Tessemae's Soy Ginger Marinade (or use similar sauce like a sesame ginger or teriyaki)
- ½ napa cabbage head, chopped
- 2 large carrots, peeled
- ½ cup sliced scallions
- 3 tablespoons sliced raw almonds
- 1 red bell pepper
- ¼ cup chopped cilantro
- ½ tablespoon white sesame seeds + ½ tablespoon black sesame seeds, mixed

For the rest:

- 4 tablespoons Tessemae's Soy Ginger Marinade (or use similar sauce like a sesame ginger or teriyaki)
- 1 tablespoon smooth almond butter
- 1 pinch red pepper flakes

Instructions

1. Preheat the oven to 400 degrees. Line a baking sheet with parchment paper.

2. Place the chicken in a shallow baking dish or zip-tight bag and pour over the Soy Ginger marinade. Place in the refrigerator and let marinate for at least 20 minutes. Once marinated, transfer to the baking sheet and bake in the oven for 20 minutes or until juices run clear and no longer pink on the inside.
3. While the chicken marinates and then bakes, prepare the salad. Spiralize the carrots with Blade D and add to a large bowl along with the cabbage, along with the green onions, sliced almonds, bell peppers, and cilantro.
4. Prepare the dressing – whisk together the Soy Ginger marinade with the almond butter and red pepper flakes. Pour the dressing over the salad and toss together well.
5. For best results, let salad sit in the refrigerator for 20 minutes to soften the vegetables. If you'd like to enjoy immediately, divide onto plates, top with sesame seeds and sliced chicken

Spicy Tuna Salad with Cucumber Noodles

Prep time: *20 mins* | **Total time**: *20 mins* | **Serves**: *2*

Ingredients

- 1 large seedless English cucumber, Blade C, noodles trimmed

For the tuna:

- 6 ounces sushi grade ahi tuna
- 2 scallion stalks, diced
- 2.5 tablespoon sriracha sauce (or other hot sauce)
- 3 tablespoons greek yogurt

For the dressing:

- 2 teaspoons freshly squeezed lime juice
- ¼ teaspoon mashed and finely minced ginger
- 1 tablespoon rice vinegar
- 2 tablespoons extra virgin olive oil
- 1 teaspoon honey
- salt and pepper, to taste

Instructions

1. Pat dry the cucumbers thoroughly. Set aside.

2. Cut the tuna into small cubes and mash it with a fork. Set aside in a medium mixing bowl with the scallions.
3. Whisk together the ingredients for the dressing in a small bowl and set aside.
4. Whisk together the hot sauce and greek yogurt. Transfer to the bowl with the tuna and toss together until combined.
5. Divide the cucumber noodles into two bowls and drizzle with the dressing, then top with spicy tuna and drizzle again with the dressing

Spinach and Apple Noodle Salad with Pecans and Cranberries

Prep Time: 15 minutes | **Servings:** 3

Ingredients

For the salad:

- 5 cups of baby spinach
- 3 apples, Blade C
- ½ cup pecans
- 1/3 cup dried cranberries

For the dressing:

- 2 tablespoons extra virgin olive oil
- 1 tablespoon ground Dijon mustard
- salt and pepper, to taste
- 2 tablespoons balsamic vinegar
- 1 tablespoon honey

Instructions

1. Place the ingredients for the dressing into a bowl and whisk together until combined. Set aside.
2. Place all of the ingredients for the salad into a large serving or salad bowl and pour over the dressing. Toss to combine thoroughly and serve.

Spiralized Apple and Arugula Salad with Roasted Honey Glazed Acorn Squash

Prep time: 10 mins | *Cook time:* 40 mins | *Total time:* 50 mins | *Serves:* 4

Ingredients

For the salad:

- 1 acorn squash, seeded and halved and quartered (yield 8 slices)
- 3 teaspoons honey
- salt and pepper, to taste
- 1 large honey crisp or Gala apple (or favorite apple)
- 6 cups of baby arugula
- ⅓ cup roughly chopped pecans
- ½ cup crumbled feta

For the dressing:

- 3 tablespoons extra virgin olive oil
- 2 tablespoon apple cider vinegar
- 1 teaspoon honey
- 1 teaspoon dijon mustard
- salt and pepper, to taste

Instructions

1. Preheat the oven to 400 degrees F.
2. Assemble the acorn squash on a parchment paper lined baking sheet. Drizzle each slice with about ½ teaspoon of honey and season with salt and pepper. Roast for about 35-40 minutes or until squash is tender when pierced with a fork.
3. Fifteen minutes before the squash is done roasting, spiralize the apple with Blade D and add it to a large mixing bowl along with the arugula, pecans and half of the feta. Set aside.
4. Place all of the ingredients for the dressing into a small bowl and whisk together. Taste and adjust to your preference.
5. Once the squash is done, pour the dressing over the salad mixture and toss to combine thoroughly. Divide the salad onto four plates and top each with two squash slices and remaining feta.

Spiralized Apple Salad

"Let the spiralizer do all the work for you and then enjoy a fresh, crisp, crunchy apple salad with a mild vinaigrette dressing that comes together in minutes. You can use whatever apples you like just as long as they're fresh and have a firm texture. To keep the apples crisp, add the vinaigrette dressing right before serving."

***Servings**: 4| **Prep**: 15 m | **Cook**: 3 m | **Ready In:** 18 m*

Ingredient**s**

- 2 tablespoons extra-virgin olive oil
- 2 tablespoons white balsamic vinegar
- 1 tablespoon Dijon mustard
- 1 teaspoon honey, or more to taste
- 2 unpeeled Granny Smith apples
- 1 unpeeled Red Delicious apple
- 1/2 lime, juiced
- 1 tablespoon pine nuts

Directions

1. Whisk olive oil, white balsamic vinegar, Dijon mustard, and honey in a small bowl to make dressing.
2. Cut Granny Smith and Red Delicious apples into noodles using a spiralizer fitted with the large shredding blade.
3. Place apple noodles in a large bowl and toss with lime juice to keep them from turning brown. Pour in dressing; mix gently until salad is combined.
4. Place pine nuts in a small skillet over medium-low heat. Toast pine nuts, shaking often, until golden brown, about 5 minutes. Sprinkle pine nuts over salad.

Nutritional Information

- Calories:136 kcal 7%
- Fat: 7.9 g 12%
- Carbs: 17.1g 6%
- Protein: 0.8 g 2%
- Cholesterol: 0 mg 0%
- Sodium: 97 mg 4%

Spiralized Bell Pepper Antipasto

Prep time: 20 mins | *Cook time:* 20 mins | *Total time:* 40 mins | *Serves:* 4

Ingredients

For the bell peppers:

- 1 red bell pepper, Blade A
- 1 orange bell pepper, Blade A
- salt and pepper, to taste
- 1 teaspoon dried oregano

For the artichokes:

- 1.5 cups canned quartered artichokes, drained
- 1 teaspoon extra virgin olive oil
- salt and pepper, to taste
- ¼ teaspoon dried oregano

For the rest:

- ¼ cup small-cubed provolone cheese (about ¼" thick)
- ½ cup halved black olives
- 1 tablespoon chopped basil
- 2 packed cups mixed greens

Instructions

1. Preheat the oven to 450 degrees and line two large baking sheets with parchment paper. On one, lay out the bell pepper noodles and season with salt, pepper and oregano.
2. Place the artichokes in a medium mixing bowl with the olive oil and season with salt, pepper, and garlic powder. Toss to combine and spread out onto the other baking sheet.
3. Bake the artichokes and bell peppers for 20 minutes.
4. When the artichokes and peppers are done, place them into a large mixing bowl and add in the provolone cheese, olives and basil. Toss to combine thoroughly and then serve over the mixed greens.

Spiralized Carrot and Radish Salad with Peach Vinaigrette

"Fabulously raw carrot salad with sweetness from the carrots, peach vinegar, and coconut."

Servings: 1| Prep: 15 m | Ready In: 25 m

Ingredients

- 1 tablespoon Meyer lemon-infused olive oil
- 1 teaspoon peach-infused balsamic vinegar
- 1 pinch garlic powder
- salt and ground black pepper to taste
- 1 large carrot
- 1/3 daikon radish
- 1 tablespoon slivered almonds
- 1 tablespoon shredded coconut
- 1 teaspoon snipped fresh chives

Directions

1. Whisk lemon-infused olive oil, peach-infused vinegar, garlic powder, salt, and pepper together in a bowl to make vinaigrette.
2. Attach carrot to a spiralizer and cut into ribbons. Toss with vinaigrette in the bowl. Let stand until slightly softened, about 10 minutes.
3. Attach radish to the spiralizer and cut into ribbons. Toss with carrot mixture in the bowl. Garnish with almonds, coconut, and chives.

Nutritional Information

- Calories:256 kcal 13%
- Fat: 21 g 32%
- Carbs: 15.8g5%
- Protein: 3.4 g 7%
- Cholesterol: 0 mg 0%
- Sodium: 233 mg 9%

Spiralized Kani Salad

Prep time: 10 mins | *Total time:* 10 mins | *Serves:* 4 cups

Ingredients

- 5 kani sticks, sliced thinly into matchsticks
- 1 large seedless (English) cucumber, Blade D, noodles trimmed
- For the fayo:
- 5 tablespoons Greek yogurt
- 2 teaspoons rice vinegar

Instructions

1. Thoroughly pat-dry the cucumber noodles until excess moisture is blotted out. Set aside.
2. Whisk together all of the ingredients for the fayo together in the bottom of a large mixing bowl. Add in the kani, cucumber noodles and sesame seeds and toss thoroughly to combine.
3. Serve the salad over diced romaine lettuce, in Bibb lettuce cups or as is.

Spiralized Kohlrabi, Ruby Radish and Shaved Asparagus Salad with Lemon-Chive Dressing

Prep Time: 10 minutes | *Cook Time:* 10 minutes | *Total Time:* 20 minutes | *Servings:* 3

Ingredients

- 1 large kohlrabi, peeled
- 2 large red (cherry bomb) radishes, peeled, Blade C, noodles trimmed
- 3 large asparagus stalks, shaved (with a peeler)
- 1 tablespoon roasted and salted sunflower seeds

For the dressing:

- 2 tablespoons apple cider vinegar
- juice of half a large lemon
- salt and pepper, to taste
- 1 tablespoon olive oil
- 1 tablespoon freshly chopped chives

- 1 teaspoon honey

Instructions

1. Combine all ingredients for the dressing into a bowl and whisk. Set aside.
2. Cut the kohlrabi halfway through, careful not to cut through the center. Spiralize the kohlrabi, using Blade B. Place noodles in a bowl with the radish noodles and shaved asparagus.
3. Pour dressing over the noodles and toss to combine thoroughly. If possible, let sit for 30 minutes – 1 hour (longer is better) for flavors to infuse the kohlrabi and radishes. If not, immediately transfer to a serving platter or bowl and top with sunflower seeds.

Spiralized Roasted Beet Salad with Quince Vinaigrette

"Great salad for lunch or dinner! Spiralizing the beets makes for a quicker cooking time. Use any flavored vinegar of your choice - dark berry or fig vinegar make great options!"

Servings: 2 | **Prep:** 15 m | **Cook:**10 m | **Ready In:** 30 m

Ingredients

- cooking spray
- 2 beets, peeled
- 1/4 teaspoon salt
- 1/8 teaspoon ground black pepper
- 1/4 cup olive oil
- 3 tablespoons quince vinegar, or more to taste
- salt and ground black pepper to taste
- 1 (12 ounce) bag spring salad mix
- 2 ounces blue cheese, crumbled
- 2 ounces chopped walnuts
- 2 tablespoons fresh snipped chives

Directions

1. Preheat oven to 400 degrees F (200 degrees C). Line a baking sheet with aluminum foil and grease with nonstick cooking spray.
2. Cut beets into spirals using a spiralizer.

3. Place beet spirals in a bowl; add 1/4 teaspoon salt and 1/8 teaspoon black pepper and toss to combine. Spread out on the prepared baking sheet.
4. Bake in the preheated oven, stirring halfway, until softened, about 10 minutes. Let cool completely, 5 to 10 minutes.
5. Whisk olive oil, quince vinegar, salt, and pepper together in a small bowl to make dressing.
6. Divide spring salad mix between 2 plates. Top with cooled beet spirals. Scatter blue cheese, chopped walnuts, and chives over the beets. Drizzle dressing on top

Nutritional Information

- Calories:635 kcal 32%
- Fat: 54.4 g 84%
- Carbs: 28.1g 9%
- Protein: 14.6 g 29%
- Cholesterol: 21 mg 7%
- Sodium: 895 mg 36%

Spiralized Som Tam (Thai Papaya Salad)

Prep time: 20 mins | **Total time:** 20 mins | **Serves:** 4

Ingredients

- 1 green papaya, peeled and halved, seeds scooped out
- 6 Thai red chilis
- 4 clove of peeled garlic
- 1 cup green beans cut into 1" pieces
- 2 limes, juiced
- 4 tablespoon fish sauce
- 4 small vine tomatoes, chopped or sliced
- 4 tablespoons roasted peanuts

Instructions

1. Spiralize each papaya halve using Blade D. Set aside.
2. Using a mortar and pestle (or something similar), mash the garlic. Add chilli and mash together. Add the green beans and gently mash, just to

break the beans open. Add the peanuts and mash lightly again, just to crush the peanuts and break them up.

3. Add the fish sauce and the lime juice to the mortar and toss to combine using a spoon.
4. In a large bowl, add the spiralized papaya and tomatoes. Pour over the mixture from the mortar and pestle and toss to combine well. Lightly mash the papaya just to soften it and let the flavors absorb.
5. Serve.

Spiralized Tuna Nicoise Salad

Prep Time: 15 minutes | Cook Time: 20 minutes | Total Time: 35 minutes | Servings: 4

Ingredients

- 1/2 pound fresh green beans, cut into 1" pieces
- 1 cup halved heirloom cherry tomatoes
- 3/4 cup kalamata olives
- ½ small onion, thinly sliced
- 3 large eggs
- 1 tablespoon extra virgin olive oil
- 1 pound potatoes, peeled, Blade C, noodles trimmed
- salt and pepper, to taste
- ½ teaspoon garlic powder
- 8oz tuna steak

For the dressing:

- 2.5 tablespoons white balsamic vinegar
- 1 tablespoon Dijon mustard
- 1 tablespoon chopped parsley
- 2 teaspoons lemon juice
- 2 tablespoons extra virgin olive oil
- salt and pepper, to taste

Instructions

1. Bring a medium pot filled halfway with water to a boil. Once boiling, add in the green beans and cook for 5 minutes or until tender. Drain into a

colander and place in a large mixing bowl along with the tomatoes, olives, and onions. Set aside.

2. Meanwhile, place the eggs in a medium saucepan and cover with water and a pinch of salt. Cover and bring to a roaring boil. Once boiling, turn off the heat and let stand for 12-14 minutes to hard boil. When done, rinse under cold water until able to be handled. Peel the eggs and halve. Set aside.

3. While eggs and green beans cook, whisk all ingredients for the vinaigrette together and set aside.

4. In a large skillet, place in the olive oil. Once oil heats, add in the potato noodles, season with salt, pepper and garlic powder. Cover and cook for 5-7 minutes or until cooked all the way through, uncovering occasionally to toss.

5. Once potatoes are cooked, add to the bowl with the green beans and veggies and pour in the vinaigrette. Set aside.

6. Season both sides of the tuna steak with salt and pepper, pressing the pepper into the tuna. Pour the lemon juice over the tuna. Wipe down the large skillet and place it back over medium heat. Once heated, add in the seasoned tuna and sear for 1-2 minutes, flip over and sear another 1-2 minutes. If you prefer your tuna well done and not rare, cook for 3-4 minutes per side or until done to your preference.

7. Divide the potato noodle mixture into bowls and top each bowl with 1/3 of the tuna and 1 hard boiled egg. Garnish with freshly cracked black pepper and enjoy immediately.

Spiralized Yellow Squash with Basil and Mint

Prep time: 15 mins | Total time: 15 mins | Serves: 2

Ingredients

- 3 large yellow summer squash, cut into thin strands with a vegetable peeler or spiral slicer (spiralizer) or julienned
- 1 large celery stalk, thinly sliced
- 1 tablespoon finely chopped fresh basil
- 2 teaspoons extra-virgin olive oil
- 2 teaspoons freshly squeezed lemon juice
- 1 teaspoon finely chopped fresh mint
- 1/2 teaspoon freshly grated lemon zest
- 1/4 teaspoon ground cumin
- Pinch crushed red pepper flakes
- Sea salt and freshly ground black pepper, to taste

Instructions

- In a large bowl, combine all the ingredients, toss to coat, and serve.

Summer Chopped Chicken Salad with Spiralized Cucumbers and Salsa Verde

Prep time: 10 mins | Cook time: 20 mins | Total time: 30 mins | Serves: 4

Ingredients

- 8-10oz boneless, skinless chicken breast or 1.5 cups cubed cooked chicken
- salt
- 1 large ear of corn, kernels shaved off
- 1 teaspoon extra virgin olive oil
- ¼ teaspoon chili powder
- 1 English seedless cucumber
- ½ heaping cup diced tomatoes (I used cherry tomatoes)
- ½ red onion, diced
- 1 yellow bell pepper, seeded and diced
- 1 large handful of cilantro, lightly chopped
- 1 avocado, peeled, pitted, insides chopped
- ½ cup mild jarred salsa verde

Instructions

1. If you're NOT using pre-cooked chicken (if you are, skip this step): fill a large saucepan two-thirds full of water and bring to a boil over high heat. Salt it so that it tastes good, add the chicken breast, and remove the pot from the heat. Cover and let the chicken sit until cooked but very tender, about 15 minutes. Remove the chicken from the water and cut into it to check its doneness; if it's still a little pink, return it to the water for another minute or two. Remove the chicken to a plate and let it rest for 2 minutes and then slice into cubes.
2. While chicken cooks, cook the corn. Heat the oil in a medium skillet over medium-high heat. Once oil is shimmering, add in the corn and season with chili powder and salt. Cook until bright yellow and charred, 5-7 minutes.

3. Meanwhile, spiralize the cucumber with Blade A, applying light pressure so that the ribbons are thin. Pat the cucumber noodles dry with paper towels and trim the noodles with kitchen shears so that they are easier to manage.
4. In a large mixing bowl, combine the cucumbers, tomatoes, onions, bell peppers, cilantro, avocado, cooked corn and cubed cooked chicken. Pour in the salsa verde and toss well to combine.
5. Pour the mixture into the bowls and serve.

Tahini Kale Salad with Spiralized Butternut Squash and Feta

Prep time: 15 mins | Cook time: 15 mins | Total time: 30 mins | Serves: 4

Ingredients

- 1 large butternut squash, peeled, Blade C, noodles trimmed
- salt and pepper
- 1 large bushel of kale, chopped
- 4 whole eggs
- ¼ cup crumbled feta
- For the dressing:
- 2 tablespoons tahini
- 1 tablespoon freshly squeezed lemon juice
- 1 teaspoon honey
- ⅛ teaspoon garlic powder
- 2 tablespoons water, to thin + more as needed
- salt and pepper, to taste

Instructions

1. Preheat the oven to 400 degrees. Place the butternut squash noodles out on a parchment paper lined baking sheet. Spritz with cooking spray, season with salt and pepper, and bake for 7-10 minutes or until softened.
2. Meanwhile, prepare the tahini dressing. Place all of the ingredients in the bottom of a large mixing bowl and whisk together until creamy. Taste and adjust to your preferences, if necessary. Add the kale into the bowl. Toss and then massage dressing into kale leaves, massaging until softened, about 1 minute.
3. Place a large skillet over medium-high heat. Once pan is hot, crack in the eggs and fry until egg whites set, about 5 minutes.
4. While eggs cook, divide the butternut squash into plates and add the kale salad. Top with fried egg and garnish with feta.

Thai Quinoa and Zucchini Noodle Salad

Prep Time: 30 minutes | *Servings:* 4

Ingredients

For the salad:

- 2 medium zucchinis, peeled, Blade C, noodles trimmed
- 1 large carrot, peeled, Blade C, noodles trimmed (or julienned)
- 1 large bell pepper, sliced thinly
- 1/2 cup diced green onions
- 1 cup cooked quinoa (I used red)
- 2 tablespoons slivered raw almonds
- ¼ packed cup fresh cilantro

For the dressing:

- 1/4 cup almond butter
- 1.5 tablespoons lime juice
- 1 tablespoons rice wine vinegar
- 1 tablespoons soy sauce (or tamari, if gluten-free)
- 1/2 tablespoon sesame oil
- 1/2 tablespoons honey
- 1 teaspoons grated fresh ginger
- 1/2 tablespoon sriracha (or other Asian hot sauce)
- 2 tablespoons of water, to thin (or more as needed)

Instructions

1. Place all of the ingredients for the dressing into a food processor and pulse until creamy – or simply whisk together thoroughly. Taste and adjust, if necessary. Set aside.
2. Place the zucchini noodles in a large mixing bowl along with the carrot, bell pepper, green onions, quinoa, almonds and cilantro. Pour the dressing over the salad and toss together thoroughly.
3. Transfer the salad to a serving bowl and enjoy.

Vegan Kale and Sweet Potato Noodle Caesar Salad with Crispy Spiced Chickpeas

*Prep Time: 15 minutes | **Cook Time:** 40 minutes | **Total Time:** 55 minutes | **Servings:** 4*

Ingredients

For the salad:

- 1 tablespoon extra virgin olive oil
- 1 large sweet potato, peeled, Blade C
- salt and pepper, to taste
- ¼ teaspoon garlic powder
- 3 packed cups chopped kale

For the dressing:

- 1/4 cup raw cashews, soaked for at least 2 hours
- 1/4 cup unsweetened almond milk
- 1 large cloves garlic
- 1/2 tablespoons freshly squeezed lemon juice
- 1/2 teaspoon dijon mustard
- salt and pepper, to taste

For the chickpeas:

- 1 15-ounce can of chickpeas, drained, rinsed, patted dry
- 1/2 teaspoon ground cumin
- 1 teaspoon chili powder
- 1/4 teaspoon cayenne pepper
- ½ tablespoon extra virgin olive oil
- salt, to taste

Instructions

1. Preheat the oven to 400 degrees. In a small bowl, combine the cumin, chili powder, cayenne pepper and salt and whisk together. Add in the chickpeas, toss to coat, and then drizzle with the olive oil. Toss again to mix. Place the chickpeas out evenly over a parchment-paper lined baking sheet and bake 30-35 minutes or until crisp, shaking the pan half way through.

2. Twenty minutes into baking the chickpeas, place a large skillet over medium heat and add in the olive oil. Once oil heats, add in the sweet potato noodles and season with salt, pepper and garlic powder. Cover and cook, uncovering occasionally to toss, for 5-7 minutes or until sweet potato noodles are cooked through. Set aside in a large bowl when done.

3. While the sweet potato noodles cook, place all of the ingredients for the dressing into a high speed blender and pulse until creamy. Taste and adjust (more tang? more lemon! more spice? more pepper! more flavor? more dijon!) Set aside.

4. When sweet potato noodles are done, wipe the skillet clean. Coat with cooking spray and add in the kale. Sautee for 3 minutes or until the kale is warmed up and slightly wilted, seasoning lightly with pepper and add to the large bowl with the sweet potato noodles.

5. When the chickpeas are done roasting, prepare the salad. Pour the Caesar dressing over the kale and sweet potato noodles and toss to combine thoroughly. Portion onto four plates and top with spiced chickpeas. Serve immediately.

Vegetarian Hamburger Bowls with Spiralized Potatoes

Prep time: *25 mins* | **Cook time:** *15 mins* | **Total time:** *40 mins* | **Serves:** *4*

Ingredients

- 2 tablespoons extra virgin olive oil
- 1 russet potato, Blade D, noodles trimmed
- 1 pinch chili powder
- ¼ teaspoon garlic powder
- salt and pepper
- 8oz button mushrooms, sliced
- 4 cups chopped cauliflower florets
- ⅔ cups chopped raw walnuts
- 1 yellow onion, diced
- 1 garlic clove, sliced
- 1 tablespoon tomato paste
- ½ teaspoon paprika
- ¼ teaspoon cayenne pepper
- 1 tablespoon barbecue sauce
- 1 teaspoon liquid smoke
- 1 tablespoon soy sauce
- 2.5 cups shredded romaine lettuce
- ¾ cup shredded American or Cheddar cheese (optional)

- 1 cup quartered cherry tomatoes
- 4 butter pickles, sliced into rounds

For the dressing:

- 2 tablespoons nonfat plain Greek yogurt (or use vegan mayonnaise)
- ⅛ teaspoon garlic powder
- 1 teaspoon apple cider vinegar (or use 1 teaspoon of pickle juice)
- ½ teaspoon dijon mustard
- 1 teaspoon barbecue sauce
- pepper, to taste

Instructions

1. Heat half of the oil in a large skillet over medium-high heat. Once oil is shimmering, add the potato noodles and season with chili powder, garlic powder, salt, and pepper. Cook until wilted and browned, about 10 minutes. When done, set aside on a plate and tint with foil to keep warm.
2. Meanwhile, prepare the meat mixture. First, add the mushrooms to a food processor and pulse until finely chopped. Set aside in a bowl and then add in the cauliflower and pulse until ground to meat-size crumbles, do not overpulse or else it would be like couscous. Transfer to the bowl with the mushrooms and then add in the walnuts and pulse until ground, but not too much so that it's a powder. Transfer to the bowl with the pulsed vegetables.
3. Once potatoes are done cooking, heat the remaining oil in the same skillet used to cook the potatoes back over medium-high heat. Once oil is shimmering, add the garlic and onion and cook for 3 minutes or until softened.
4. Add the tomato paste and stir well to coat the mixture. Add in the pulsed vegetables (cauliflower, mushrooms) and pulsed walnuts. Season with paprika, cayenne, and salt and pepper. Stir well and then add the barbecue sauce, liquid smoke, and soy sauce. Stir again and let cook until browned and liquid has absorbed, about 5-10 minutes.
5. Meanwhile, prepare the dressing: add all the ingredients to a bowl and whisk well to combine. Taste and adjust to your preference.
6. Prepare the bowls: divide the potato noodles and hamburger meat mixture into four bowls. Top with lettuce, shredded cheese (if desired), pickles, and tomatoes.
7. Drizzle with dressing and serve.

Warm Balsamic & Roasted Grape Cucumber Noodles with Roasted Persimmons, Camembert and Pistachios

Prep Time: 15 minutes | *Cook Time:* 30 minutes | *Total Time:* 45 minutes | *Servings:* 1

Ingredients

- 1 cup red grapes
- olive oil to drizzle
- salt and pepper to taste
- 1 sprig of rosemary
- 1 persimmon, very ripe, sliced into 1/2 inch slices
- 1 medium cucumber, Blade A
- 2 tbsp balsamic vinegar
- 2 tbsp olive oil
- 1 pinch of oregano flakes
- (4) 1.5" slices of camembert cheese
- 1/4 cup pistachios, lightly roasted and deshelled

Instructions

1. Preheat the oven to 425 degrees. On a baking tray, pour in your red grapes. Drizzle lightly with olive oil and mix to coat. Sprinkle with salt, pepper and rosemary.
2. Bake the grapes in the oven for 25-30 minutes or until they are easily crushed with a fork.
3. 10 minutes before the grapes are done, lower the oven heat to 400, add the persimmon slices to a baking tray coated with cooking spray. Drizzle them lightly with olive oil and season with salt and pepper. Bake for 10 minutes.
4. While everything is roasting, prepare your balsamic. Add the balsamic vinegar, olive oil and oregano into a bowl and season with salt and pepper.
5. Place your cucumber noodles on a plate or bowl and set aside.
6. Once the grapes and persimmon slices are done, remove them from the oven.
7. Take about 5 grapes, crush them with a fork and put them in the balsamic vinegar bowl, including their juices. Whisk thoroughly.
8. Crush about half of the remaining roasted grapes. Place them on top of the cucumber noodles.
9. Top the cucumber noodles and grapes with the persimmon slices. Drizzle the salad with desired amount of balsamic vinegar and top with pistachios and camembert. Enjoy!

Zucchini & Kale Apple Slaw

Prep Time: *10 minutes |* ***Total Time:*** *10 minutes |* ***Servings****: 2*

Ingredients

- 1 cup finely chopped kale
- 1/2 cup half-moon apple slices (any apple preference)
- 1/2 cup half-moon zucchini slices
- 3 tbsp raisins
- 2 tbsp sliced almonds

For the vinaigrette:

- 2 tbsp olive oil
- 1 tbsp red wine vinegar
- 1 tbsp sherry vinegar
- 1 tbsp dijon vinaigrette
- 2 tbsp fresh lemon juice
- salt and pepper, to taste

Instructions

1. Toss all of the ingredients in the slaw together in a bowl and set aside.
2. Place all of the ingredients for the vinaigrette in a bowl and whisk together. Pour over the bowl of slaw and toss to combine.
3. Divide the slaw onto two plates and enjoy!

Chapter 6: Inspiralizer Rice

***

Beet Tabbouleh Salad with Egg and Chickpeas

Prep time: 35 mins | *Total time:* 35 mins | *Serves:* 6 cups

Ingredients

- 1 large beet (or 2 medium), peeled, Blade D
- ½ cups finely chopped fresh flat-leaf parsley
- ¼ cup finely chopped fresh mint
- ¾ cup diced tomatoes
- ¾ cup diced cucumbers
- 2 tablespoons freshly squeezed lemon juice
- 1 tablespoon apple cider vinegar (or red wine vinegar)
- 2 tablespoons extra virgin olive oil
- salt and pepper, to taste
- 1 cup chickpeas (drained and rinsed from a can)
- 3 hard-boiled eggs, halved

Instructions

1. Place the beet noodles into a food processor (in batches, if necessary) and pulse until rice-like. Place in a large mixing bowl and add in the parsley, mint, tomatoes and cucumber. Set aside.
2. Whisk together the lemon juice, vinegar, olive oil and season with salt and pepper. Pour over the bowl with the beet rice and then add in the chickpeas. Toss to combine.
3. Divide the beet mixture into two bowls and top each with a hard boiled egg.

Butternut Squash Rice, Sausage, Apple and Pecan Stuffing

Prep Time: 20 minutes | *Cook Time:* 35 minutes | *Total Time:* 55 minutes | *Servings:* 6

Ingredients

- 1 large butternut squash, peeled, Blade C
- 1 tablespoon extra virgin olive oil
- 3 garlic cloves, minced
- 3 celery ribs, diced
- ½ cup diced yellow or white onion
- 2 teaspoons dried thyme
- 3 sweet Italian sausage links, decased
- 3/4 cup roughly chopped pecans
- 1 Gala apple, Blade B
- 2 tablespoons chopped parsley
- salt and pepper, to taste
- ½ cup shredded parmesan cheese (optional)

Instructions

1. Preheat the oven to 400 degrees.
2. Place the butternut squash noodles into a food processor and pulse until rice-like. Set aside.
3. Place a large, deep skillet over medium heat and add in the olive oil. Once oil heats, add in the garlic, celery, onion, thyme and season with salt and pepper. Cook for 3-5 minutes or until the vegetables soften and then add in the sausage, breaking it up with a wooden spoon and cook until it's no longer pink, about 5 more minutes.
4. Add in the apples, butternut squash rice and parsley. Season with salt and pepper and stir to combine and cook for 2-3 minutes or until everything is heated through. Remove from heat and transfer to a large casserole dish. Fold in the pecans, stir once more and then top with the parmesan cheese (optional) and bake for 15-20 minutes or until butternut squash rice is no longer crunchy.

Carnitas and Avocado-Plantain Rice with Tomatillo Salsa Verde

Prep Time: *10 minutes* | **Cook Time:** *44 minutes* | **Servings:** *3*

Ingredients

For the pork:

- 1 pound pork (preferably shoulder), cut into cubes

- 1 tsp oregano
- 1 tsp cumin
- 1 tsp chili powder
- salt to taste (about 1/4 tsp)
- 3 tsp olive oil (optional)

For the rest:

- 1/2 white onion, chopped in half
- 2 bay leaves
- juice of 1 orange
- 2 garlic cloves, minced
- juice of 1/2 lime

For the rest:

- 3 green plantains
- 1 tbsp olive oil
- 1 garlic clove, minced
- 1.5 cups chicken broth
- 2 avocados, insides cubed

For the salsa verde:

- 2 medium tomatillos, leaves removed
- 1 tsp fresh lime juice
- salt, to taste
- 2 tsp diced jalapeno
- 2 tbsp chopped white onion
- 1/4 cup packed cilantro

Instructions

1. Place your pork in a bowl along with the oregano, cumin, chili powder and optional olive oil. Mix together to coat the pork pieces. When done, place them in a large saucepan.
2. Add the onions, bay leaves, lime juice, orange juice, and garlic cloves into the saucepan. Pour in enough water to cover the pork by 1". Bring mixture to a boil. Once boiling, cover loosely and cook for 20 minutes. Then, uncover and cook for another 20 minutes, giving a stir. If the liquid absorbs completely before the 40 minutes is up, add more water (about 1/2 cup at a time). When done, remove from heat and remove the bay leaves.
3. While the pork mixture is cooking, spiralize your plantains. Then, place the noodles into a food processor and pulse briefly until made into rice-like bits. Set aside.

4. Place the tomatillos into a medium saucepan and cover with water. Bring to a boil and then let simmer for about 10 minutes or until the tomatillos turn light green. Once done, pour into a colander. Then, place the tomatillos, lime juice, salt, jalapeno, onion and cilantro into a food processor and blend until a salsa. Taste and adjust to your preference with more salt, lime juice, etc. Set aside.
5. 10 minutes before your pork is done, place a large skillet over medium heat and add in the olive oil. Then, add in the garlic. Let cook for 30 seconds and then add in the plantain rice. Stir and pour in half of the chicken broth. Stir and let plantain rice reduce. Once reduced, add in the remaining chicken broth and let reduce again. Taste and if the consistency is right, stir in the avocado and cook for three more minutes. If not, add in more chicken broth and continue to reduce. When done, divide onto three plates.
6. Top the plantain-avocado rice with the carnitas and then top each with salsa verde. Enjoy!

Chicken Sausage and Peppers with Sweet Potato "Dirty Rice"

*Prep time: 25 mins | **Cook time:** 25 mins | **Total time:** 50 mins | **Serves:** 4*

Ingredients

- 1 tablespoon extra virgin olive oil
- 9-10 ounces (about 4 small links) chicken sausages, sliced into ½" chunks
- 1 yellow bell pepper, chopped into ½" chunks
- 1 red bell pepper, chopped into ½" chunks
- 2 medium sweet potatoes, peeled, Blade D
- 2 garlic cloves, minced
- 2 celery ribs, diced
- ½ cup chopped red onions
- 1 tablespoon + ½ cup chicken broth, low sodium + more if needed
- 2 tablespoons tomato paste
- 1 teaspoon dried oregano
- 1 teaspoon smoked paprika
- salt and pepper, to taste
- chopped parsley, to garnish

Instructions

1. Place a large skillet over medium heat and add in the olive oil. Once oil heats, add in the sausage, peppers and let cook for 5-7 minutes or until peppers soften and sausage is browned.
2. Meanwhile, place the sweet potato noodles into a food processor and pulse until rice-like and set aside.
3. Once the meat is browned, transfer to a plate with peppers and then let skillet cool down for 1 minute and then add in the garlic, celery and onions to the skillet. Let cook for 30 seconds and then add in the tablespoon of the chicken broth. Let vegetables cook for 2-3 minutes or until onions are translucent and then add in the tomato paste. Stir for 1 minute or until tomato paste coats the vegetables.
4. Then, add in the sweet potato "rice," oregano and paprika and season with salt and pepper. Stir to combine and let cook for 1 minute. Then, add in the chicken broth, stir again and let cook, covered, for 5 minutes, uncovering occasionally to stir. If the rice starts to stick to the bottom of the pan, add more chicken broth by the tablespoon. Then, add in the sausage and peppers and cook for another 2-3 minutes, or until sweet potato rice is cooked through.
5. Once done, add in the parsley, stir to mix and then transfer to a serving bowl or individual bowls and enjoy.

Crunchy Miso Beet Rice with Spinach and Egg

Prep Time: *20 minutes* | **Cook Time:** *10 minutes* | **Total Time:** *30 minutes* | **Servings:** *2*

Ingredients

For the miso dressing:

- 1 tablespoon miso
- 2 tablespoons rice vinegar
- ½ teaspoon grated fresh ginger
- 1 tablespoon sesame oil
- ½ tablespoon honey
- 1 tablespoon water

For the rice:

- 1 large beet, peeled, Blade C
- 2 cups spinach

- 2 scallions, diced
- ½ teaspoon sesame seeds, to garnish
- 2 eggs

Instructions

1. Combine all of the ingredients for the miso dressing into a small bowl and whisk until fully combined. Set aside.
2. Place the beet noodles into a food processor and pulse until rice-like. Set aside in a medium mixing bowl.
3. Place a large skillet over medium heat and add in the spinach. Cook for 5 minutes or until spinach wilts. Add the spinach and miso dressing to the bowl with the beet rice, and toss to combine. Divide the rice into two bowls and set aside.
4. In the same skillet, crack in the eggs. Let eggs cook until whites set and then top each bowl of rice with an egg and garnish with scallions and sesame seeds.

Daikon Chicken "Biryani"

Prep Time: 25 minutes | Cook Time: 20 minutes | Total Time: 45 minutes | Servings: 3

Ingredients

- 2 daikon radishes, peeled, Blade C
- 1 tablespoon extra virgin olive oil
- 4 shallots, chopped
- 1 small red onion, diced
- 2 garlic cloves, minced
- 1/2 jalapeno, seeded and minced (use the full jalapeno if you like spicy)
- 2 teaspoons grated ginger
- 2 chicken breasts, thinly sliced into strips
- 1 teaspoon ground cumin
- 2 teaspoons ground coriander
- ½ teaspoon ground cinnamon
- ½ teaspoon ground turmeric
- ¼ teaspoon nutmeg
- ½ cup plain nonfat Greek yogurt
- 1/2 cup golden raisins
- ¼ cup packed cilantro leaves

- 1 tablespoon chopped mint leaves

Instructions

1. Place your daikon radish noodles into a food processor and pulse until rice-like bits. Place in a bowl near a sink. Place another bowl next to the bowl of rice. Take large handfuls of the rice and squeeze out the excess water into the sink and then place in the empty bowl. Repeat this until you've squeezed out the excess moisture in all of the rice. Set aside.
2. Place a large skillet over medium heat and add in the olive oil. Once oil heats, add in the shallots, onions, garlic, chili, ginger and cook for 3-5 minutes or until onions are translucent.
3. Add in the chicken, season with salt and pepper, cover and cook for 5 minutes or until chicken is cooked through. Add in the cumin, coriander, cinnamon, turmeric and nutmeg, stir to combine and then add in the yogurt and raisins. Cover the pan, lower the heat to a simmer and cook for 5 minutes to let the flavors develop. Then, add in the daikon rice, cilantro and mint and stir and cook another 1-2 minutes or until rice heats through.
4. Serve immediately.

Daikon Radish "Rice" with Gochugaru and Fried Egg

Prep Time: 10 minutes | Cook Time: 10 minutes | Total Time: 20 minutes | Servings: 1

Ingredients

- 1 large daikon radish, peeled, Blade C
- 1 tbsp virgin coconut oil (or olive oil)
- 1/2 tsp peeled and minced ginger
- 1 small garlic clove, minced
- 1/4 cup diced scallions
- 1/4 tsp gochugaru (sub in a pinch of regular red pepper flakes here if you don't have gochugaru)
- 1 large whole egg
- pepper, to taste

Instructions

1. Place your diakon radish noodles into a food processor and pulse until rice-like bits. Place in a bowl near a sink. Place another bowl next to the bowl of rice. Take large handfuls of the rice and squeeze out the excess water into the sink and then place in the empty bowl. Repeat this until you've squeezed out the excess moisture in all of the rice. Set aside.
2. In a large skillet, place in the oil. Then, place in the garlic and ginger. Let cook for 30 seconds and then add in the scallions and daikon rice. Cook for 1 minute and then sprinkle over the gochugaru. Stir to combine and cook for 3-5 minutes, stirring frequently. Set aside when done, in a bowl.
3. In the same skillet, crack over the egg and let cook until the whites set. Once done, place on top of the bowl of rice and season with pepper.
4. Then, combine the brussel sprouts and chicken sausage in the skillet. Add in the rutabaga rice, stir to combine and season with salt, pepper, and oregano. Pour in 1/2 cup of chicken broth and let simmer, stirring occasionally, until all the broth is reduced. Then, add in 1/2 cup more and let cook until reduced again. Taste and if the rutabaga is still crunchy, continue to cook for 6-8 more minutes, stirring occasionally.
5. When done, plate into bowls and garnish with parsley.

Easy Post-Workout Salmon Dinner

Prep Time: 15 minutes | Cook Time: 20 minutes | Total Time: 35 minutes | Servings: 1

Ingredients

- 1 medium sweet potato
- 1 garlic clove
- salt and pepper, to taste
- handful of cilantro leaves
- 1 packed cup of baby spinach
- 1 4oz piece of skinless salmon
- 1/2 tablespoon extra virgin olive oil
- 1 lemon

Instructions

1. Preheat the oven to 415 degrees.
2. While the oven is preheating, peel and spiralize the sweet potato, using Blade C. Place the noodles into a food processor and pulse until rice-like.

Set aside 1 cup of rice into a mixing bowl and save the rest for future meals.

3. Mince the garlic clove, chop 2 teaspoons of cilantro (leaving a little extra to garnish) and add it to the mixing bowl and season with salt and pepper. Toss to combine.
4. In the middle of a piece of tinfoil about 10 x 10, add in the rice mixture. Top the rice mixture with the spinach and then top with the salmon and drizzle with the olive oil and rub in with fingertips or brush. Season generously with salt and pepper. Garnish with extra cilantro.
5. Slice the lemon in half and squeeze one half over the top of the mixture. Then, place one thinly sliced lemon piece (from the other half) on top of the salmon.
6. Fold the foil into a pouch over the mixture, securing at the top, leaving about 1" of room for the salmon to steam.
7. Bake for 20-25 minutes, depending on the thickness of the salmon.
8. Remove from oven and serve on a plate, eating directly out of the foil.

Fall Harvest Butternut Squash Rice and Lentil Pilaf

Prep Time: *10 minutes* | **Cook Time:** *35 minutes* | **Total Time:** *45 minutes* | **Servings:** *4*

Ingredients

For the pilaf:

- ½ cup dry lentils (any type works), rinsed
- 1 cup water
- 1 medium butternut squash, peeled, Blade C
- 1 tablespoon extra virgin olive oil
- 2 garlic cloves
- 1 teaspoon fresh chopped rosemary
- ½ sweet Vidalia onion
- 1 celery stalk
- 1 cup sliced leeks
- salt and pepper, to taste
- ½ cup chopped walnuts
- ½ cup dried cranberries (unsweetened – no sugar added)

Instructions

1. Place lentils and water in a medium saucepan and bring to a boil. Once boiling, lower to a simmer and cook uncovered for 30-35 minutes or until cooked through. Add more water to always slightly cover the lentils, as needed.
2. After lentils are cooked, place the butternut squash noodles in a food processor and pulse until rice-like. Set aside. Dice the Vidalia onion, celery and mince the garlic cloves. Set aside.
3. Place a large skillet over medium heat and add in the olive oil. Once heated, add in the garlic and rosemary and cook for 30 seconds or until fragrant. Add in the celery, onion and leeks, cook for 2-3 minutes or until onions are translucent and then add the butternut squash rice and season with salt and pepper.
4. Stir the butternut squash rice to combine and cover and cook for 5-8 minutes, shaking the pan occasionally, or until cooked through (taste.) If the squash is still crunchy, cover the skillet and cook for 2-3 more minutes.
5. When done, add in the lentils, walnuts, cranberries and stir to combine for 1-2 minutes to warm up the cranberries. Serve immediately.

Goat Cheese Stuffed Toasted Plantain Rice Balls

Prep Time: 10 minutes | *Cook Time:* 20 minutes | *Total Time:* 30 minutes | *Servings:* 5-6 rice balls

Ingredients

- 2 medium-ripe plantains, peeled, Blade C
- 1 piece of whole wheat toast
- 1 egg, beaten
- salt to taste
- 3 tsp coconut flakes
- 5-6 tsp goat cheese

Instructions

1. Preheat the oven to 400 degrees.
2. Place your spiralized plantain noodles into a food processor and pulse until made into rice-like "bits." Set aside.
3. Place your piece of bread into a food processor and pulse until made into breadcrumbs. Set aside.

4. Place a large skillet over medium heat and coat with cooking spray. Place your plantain rice in the skillet and toast until the plantain bits are a darker color and begin to slightly brown. When done, pour out into a mixing bowl.
5. In the bowl, add in 3 tbsp of the breadcrumbs, egg, salt, and coconut flakes. Mix to combine thoroughly.
6. Over a baking tray lined with parchment paper, mold plantain mixture into balls. Lay each down on the baking tray. Then, take a tsp of goat cheese, roll into a ball and stuff into the rice ball. At this point, you will have to re-mold the rice balls.
7. Repeat until all of the mixture is used.
8. Place the rice balls into the oven and cook for 13-15 minutes. Enjoy!

Honey Ginger Tofu and Carrot Rice with Bok Choy

Prep Time: *15 minutes* | **Cook Time:** *30 minutes* | **Total Time**: *45 minutes* | **Servings:** *2*

Ingredients

- 1 large carrot, peeled, Blade C
- 1 tablespoon extra virgin coconut oil
- 1 teaspoon peeled and minced ginger
- 1 small garlic clove, minced
- salt and pepper, to taste
- 2 teaspoons sesame oil
- 2 bunches baby bok choy (about 10oz), stiff bottom trimmed off
- salt and pepper, to taste

For the tofu:

- 3 tablespoon soy sauce
- 1 tablespoon honey (or omit, if strict vegan)
- 2 teaspoons shredded ginger (or very finely minced)
- 7oz extra firm tofu, moisture squeezed out, cubed

Instructions

1. Preheat the oven to 400 degrees. Whisk the soy sauce, ginger and honey together in a bowl until combined. Place the cubed tofu in the bowl with the dressing and set aside. Let stand for 5 minutes and then place on a

baking tray lined with parchment paper. Bake for 10 minutes, flip over and bake another 10 minutes.

2. After you flip the tofu over, place the carrot noodles in a food processor and pulse until rice-like. In a large skillet over medium heat, add in the coconut oil. Once oil heats, add in the garlic and ginger. Let cook for 30 seconds or until fragrant and then add in the carrot rice. Season with salt and pepper and cover and cook for 5 minutes or until carrot softens to a rice-like consistency.

3. While the rice is cooking, heat a large grill pan over medium heat. Brush the bok choy with the sesame oil and place onto the heated grill pan. Cook for 2 minutes, flip over and cook another 2-3 minutes or until bok choy is heated and cooked through.

4. Place the finished bok choy in a bowl and top with carrot rice, then tofu.

How to Spiralize a Plantain & Plantain "Rice" and Beans

Prep Time: 15 minutes | Cook Time: 19 minutes | Servings: 3-4

Ingredients

- 2 large plantains, peeled, Blade C
- 2 tbsp olive oil
- 2 cloves of garlic, minced
- 3/4 cup diced yellow onion
- salt and pepper, to taste
- 1/2 tsp Adobo seasoning
- 1 tsp chili powder
- 1 tsp cumin powder
- 1/2 cup low-sodium chicken broth
- 1 14oz can whole peeled plum tomatoes
- 1 14oz can of black beans, rinsed and pat-dried

Instructions

1. In batches, place your plantain noodles into a food processor and pulse until made into rice-like bits. Set aside.

2. Place a large skillet or saucepan over medium heat. Add in your olive oil. Once the oil heats, add in the garlic and red pepper flakes. Cook for 30 seconds and then add in the onion. Cook for 2 minutes and then add in the plantain rice. Season with salt, pepper, chili powder, Adobo and cumin.

3. Cook the plantains for about 2 minutes and then add in the chicken broth. Let fully reduce and then take the tomatoes from the can and crush them with your hands over the skillet and into the rice. Pour in half the juices from the can and discard the rest.
4. Add in the black beans and cook for another 2-3 minutes. When done, divide into bowls and enjoy!

Jalapeno and Chorizo Carrot Rice with Avocado

Prep Time: 10 minutes | *Cook Time:* 15 minutes | *Total Time:* 25 minutes | *Servings:* 2

Ingredients

- 1 large carrot, peeled, Blade C
- 1 tablespoon extra virgin olive oil
- 2 spicy chorizo links, decased and crumbled
- 1 tablespoon chopped cilantro
- juice of 1 lime
- 3 teaspoons finely diced jalapeno
- 1/2 cup chicken broth
- salt and pepper, to taste
- 1/2 teaspoon chili powder
- 1/2 avocado, insides cubed

Instructions

1. Place the carrot noodles in a food processor and pulse until rice-like. Set aside.
2. Place a large skillet over medium heat and add in the olive oil. Once oil heats, add in the chorizo and cook for about 3 minutes to slightly brown the meat.
3. Add in the carrot rice, jalapenos, cilantro, lime juice, chicken broth and chili powder. Season with salt and pepper and stir to combine. Cook for 5-7 minutes or until fully reduced, stirring occasionally.
4. Divide rice mixture into bowls and top with equal amounts of avocado.

Jalapeno Carrot Rice Salad with Charred Peppers, Pepitas & Avocado-Tomato Salsa

Prep Time: *15 minutes* | **Cook Time:** *10 minutes* | **Total Time:** *25 minutes* | **Servings:** *2*

Ingredients

- For the salsa:
- 2 plum tomatoes, seeds remove, chopped
- juice of 1 lime
- 1/4 cup diced red onion
- 2 tbsp chopped cilantro
- 1-2 avocados, insides cubed

For the pepper:

- 1 large red bell pepper
- For the carrot rice:
- 1 large carrot, peeled, Blade C
- 1 large clove of garlic, minced
- 1 small jalapeno, seeds removed, minced
- salt and pepper, to taste
- 1/4 cup vegetable broth
- 2 tbsp roasted salted pepitas

Instructions

1. In a bowl, place in all of the ingredients for the salsa. Toss to combine and set aside.
2. Place a red bell pepper on the stovetop with the heat on high. Char, rotating, until pepper skin is completely blackened. Place in a paper bag or plastic container, seal, and let steam for about 5 minutes. Then, peel off the skin of the pepper and slice into strips. Set aside.
3. Place your carrot noodles into a food processor and pulse until made into rice-like bits. Then, place a large skillet over medium heat and add in the olive oil. Then, add in the garlic and cook for 30 seconds. Then, add in the jalapenos and carrot rice and season with salt and pepper. Cook for 2 minutes and add in the vegetable broth. Cook for 5 more minutes or until carrot has softened.
4. In two bowls, divide the rice. Then, top with equal parts of the salsa and peppers. Finally, top each with 1 tbsp of pepitas. Enjoy!

Kohlrabi and Egyptian Spinach Creamy "Orzo" with Seared Lemon Scallops

Prep Time: 20 minutes | *Cook Time:* 15 minutes | *Total Time:* 35 minutes | *Servings:* 2

Ingredients

- 1 large kohlrabi, peeled, Blade C
- 1.5 tablespoons extra virgin olive oil
- 1 large clove of garlic, minced
- ½ cup white onion, minced
- 1.5 cups chopped Egyptian spinach (or arugula, if you can't find Egyptian)
- salt and pepper, to taste
- ¼ cup vegetable broth
- juice and zest of half a small lemon
- 6 jumbo diver scallops
- 3 tablespoons grated parmigiano reggiano cheese
- 1 tablespoon minced mint or parsley, to garnish

Instructions

1. Place the kohlrabi noodles into a food processor and roughly pulse or until shaped like orzo (not small like rice, slightly larger.) Set kohlrabi aside.
2. Place a large skillet over medium heat and add in 1 tablespoon of the olive oil. Once oil heats, add in the garlic and onions. Cook until onions are translucent, 2-3 minutes. Then, add in the Egyptian spinach and cook for 2 minutes or until mainly wilted. Then, add in the kohlrabi and season with salt and pepper and let cook for 1 minute, stirring frequently. Add in the vegetable broth and cook for about 5 minutes or until kohlrabi has orzo consistency – al dente. Remove from heat and stir in the parmigiano-reggiano and just the lemon zest.
3. Divide the kohlrabi "orzo" onto two plates, cover and set aside.
4. Wipe down the skillet used to cook the kohlrabi and set back over medium-high heat. Add in the remaining half tablespoon of olive oil. While oil heats, season scallops generously with salt and pepper. Once oil heats, add in the scallops in a single layer and sear for 2 minutes, flip over and sear another 2 minutes or until scallops are a deep golden brown and just firm and opaque. Then, pour on the lemon juice and take off the heat.

5. Uncover the dishes of "orzo" and top each plate with 3 scallops. Garnish with mint (or parsley) and enjoy!

One Pot Vegan Fajitas with Sweet Potato Rice

Prep time: *25 mins* | **Cook time:** *20 mins* | **Total time:** *45 mins* | *Serves: 4*

Ingredients

For the fajitas:

- 1 tablespoon extra virgin olive oil
- 1 garlic clove, minced
- 2 teaspoons seeded and minced jalapeno
- 1 tablespoon tomato paste
- 1 small yellow onion, peeled, Blade A, noodles trimmed
- 1 green bell pepper, Blade A, noodles trimmed
- 1 red bell pepper, Blade A, noodles trimmed
- 1 orange bell pepper, Blade A, noodles trimmed
- 2 medium sweet potatoes, peeled, Blade D
- ½ cup vegetable broth
- 1 avocado, peeled, pitted and insides sliced thinly
- 1 tablespoon chopped cilantro

For the fajita seasoning:

- ¼ teaspoon cayenne pepper
- 1 teaspoon chili powder
- ¼ teaspoon garlic powder
- ½ teaspoon paprika
- ½ teaspoon smoked paprika
- ½ teaspoon onion powder
- ¼ teaspoon cumin
- salt, to taste
- ¼ teaspoon oregano

Instructions

1. Place the sweet potato noodles into a food processor and pulse until rice-like.

2. Place a large, wide skillet over medium heat and add in the olive oil. Once oil heats, add in the jalapeno and garlic and let cook for 30 seconds or until fragrant. Stir in the tomato paste and stir frequently until vegetables are coated in the paste, about 30 seconds. Add in the onions, bell peppers and let cook for 5 minutes or until vegetables begin to soften.
3. Add in the sweet potato rice and add in the fajita seasoning ingredients and season with salt and pepper. Stir to combine thoroughly and then add the vegetable broth. Cover and let cook for 5 minutes and then uncover and let cook for another 5 minutes or until sweet potato rice softens and moisture is mostly evaporated.
4. Top with avocado slices and garnish with cilantro. Serve.

Pesto Broccoli Sweet Potato Rice Casserole – Two Ways!

Prep Time: 15 minutes | Cook Time: 40 minutes | Total Time: 55 minutes | Servings: 1 casserole

Ingredients

For the pesto:

- 2.5 cups basil leaves, packed
- 3 tbsp of pine nuts
- 1/4 cup of olive oil (if you like it thicker, less olive oil)
- 5 cranks of the sea salt grinder
- 5 cranks of the peppercorn grinder
- 1 large clove of garlic minced

For the rest:

- 2 cups small broccoli florets
- 1 large sweet potato (350g), peeled, Blade C
- pepper, to taste
- 1/3 cup low-sodium vegetable broth
- 1.5 cups shredded mozzarella (optional)

Instructions

1. Preheat the oven to 400 degrees.
2. Place all of the ingredients for the pesto into a food processor and pulse until smooth. Taste and just, if necessary. Pour half of the pesto out into a

bowl and add in the broccoli. Toss until broccoli is coated with the pesto. Set the broccoli and remaining pesto aside.

3. In the bottom of the casserole, spread out a thin layer of pesto. Then, spread out a layer of the sweet potato rice. Then, add the broccoli. Then, add the rest of the rice to cover the broccoli. Drizzle the remaining pesto over the rice. Then, pour over the vegetable broth. Season with pepper. If using mozzarella, spread over in an even layer over the rice to cover.

4. Cover the casserole with tinfoil and bake for 40 minutes.

Pesto Turkey & Beet Rice Lettuce Wraps

Prep Time: *15 minutes* | **Cook Time:** *15 minutes* | **Total Time:** *30 minutes* | **Servings:** *4*

Ingredients

For the pesto:

- 4 cups packed basil
- 1/4 cup pine nuts
- 2 tsp minced garlic
- 1/4 cup grated parmesan cheese
- salt and pepper, to taste
- 1/3 cup olive oil

For the rest:

- 1 very large beet, peeled, Blade C
- 2 tbsp olive oil
- 2 garlic cloves, minced
- pinch of red pepper flakes
- 1/2 cup diced red onion
- 1/2-1/3 pound lean ground turkey
- 1/4 cup chicken broth
- 1 tsp dried oregano flakes
- 2 heads of bibb lettuce

Instructions

1. Take your spiralized beet noodles and place them into a food processor. Pulse until made into rice-like bits. Set aside.

2. Place all of your ingredients for the pesto into a food processor and pulse until creamy. Taste and adjust to your preference.
3. Place a large skillet over medium heat and add in your olive oil. Once oil heats, add in your garlic and red pepper flakes. Cook for 30 seconds and then add in your red onion. Cook the onion for 2-3 minutes or until translucent and then add in your turkey meat, oregano and season with salt and pepper.
4. Cook the turkey meat until no longer pink, about 5 minutes. Then, add in the chicken broth and let reduce. Once reduced, add in the beet rice and toss to combine.
5. Let the beet rice cook, stirring frequently, for about 5 minutes. If watery (from the beet juice), pour the contents of the skillet into a colander, drain and put back into the skillet.
6. Next, fold in the pesto sauce. Stir to combine and cook for 1 minute. When done, spoon into lettuce wraps and enjoy!

Pesto Turnip and Broccoli Rice with Poached Egg

Prep Time: 20 minutes | Cook Time: 15 minutes | Total Time: 30 minutes | Servings: 3

Ingredients

- 2.5 cups small broccoli florets
- 2 large turnips, peeled, Blade C
- 1 tablespoon extra virgin olive oil
- 1 large garlic clove, minced
- 1 pinch red pepper flakes
- salt and pepper, to taste
- 3 large eggs

For the pesto:

- 1.5 cups basil leaves, packed
- 2 tablespoons pinenuts
- 1/4 cup olive oil
- ½ tsp grinded sea salt
- ¼ tsp grinded pepper
- 1 tablespoon grated parmesan cheese
- 1 large clove of garlic, minced

Instructions

1. Bring a medium saucepan filled halfway with water to a boil. Once boiling, add in the broccoli and cook for 2-3 minutes or until more easily pierced with a fork. Drain into a colander and pat dry thoroughly. Set aside.
2. While waiting for broccoli to cook, place the turnip noodles into a food processor and pulse until rice-like. Set aside the rice and wipe out the food processor and set aside for later use.
3. Place a large skillet over medium heat and add in the olive oil. Once heated, add in the garlic and red pepper flakes. Cook for 30 seconds or until fragrant and then add in the turnip rice and broccoli. Season with salt and pepper and cook, covered for about 5 minutes or until softened to a rice-like consistency.
4. While turnip rice is cooking, add all of the ingredients for the pesto into the food processor and pulse until creamy. Taste and adjust to your preference.
5. Once turnip rice is cooked through, transfer to a large mixing bowl and add in the pesto. Toss to combine and set aside.
6. After the pesto rice is made, fill a medium saucepan halfway with water and bring to a steady simmer. Crack the eggs individually into a ramekin or small bowl. Then, create a gentle whirlpool in the simmering water to help the egg white wrap around the yolk. Slowly tip the egg into the water. Let cook for three minutes. Remove with a slotted spoon and gently rest on a paper towel lined plate to drain.
7. Divide the pesto turnip rice onto plates and top with a drained poached egg. Serve immediately.

Poke Bowls with Kohlrabi Rice

Prep time: *20 mins* | **Total time:** *20 mins* | **Serves:** *4*

Ingredients

- 8 ounces sashimi grade ahi tuna steak, diced into bite-sized pieces
- 1 large kohlrabi (or 2 medium), peeled, Blade D
- 1 ripe avocado, peeled, insides cubed
- 1 tablespoon freshly squeezed lime juice
- pepper, to taste

For the poke dressing:

- 2 teaspoons toasted white sesame seeds
- 2 teaspoons sesame oil

- 3 tablespoons soy sauce (low-sodium)
- 1 teaspoon rice vinegar
- ¼ heaping cup finely diced scallions

Instructions

1. Place the tuna in a bowl with the poke dressing ingredients. Stir to combine and set aside to marinate.
2. Meanwhile, place the kohlrabi noodles into a food processor and pulse until rice-like. Add to a medium bowl with the avocado and lime, and stir to combine. Season lightly with pepper.
3. Divide the rice into 4 small bowls and top with equal amounts of the tuna poke. Serve.

Pomegranate Sweet Potato Rice Bowls with Roasted Maple Butternut Squash and Goat Cheese

Prep time: 20 mins | Cook time: 40 mins | Total time: 1 hour | Serves: 2

Ingredients

- 2 tablespoons extra virgin olive oil
- 1 tablespoon maple syrup
- 1 cup cubed butternut squash
- salt and pepper, to taste
- 1 pomegranate
- 1 large sweet potato
- ¼ cup crumbled goat cheese

Instructions

1. Preheat the oven to 400 degrees. Line a baking sheet with parchment paper.
2. Place the maple syrup and half of the olive oil in the bottom of a medium mixing bowl and whisk together. Place the butternut squash cubes in the bowl, season with salt and pepper and toss together to coat. Lay the butternut squash out on the prepared baking sheet and bake for 35 minutes or until baked through and soft, and slightly browned.

3. Meanwhile, remove the seeds from the pomegranate. Rinse the mixing bowl used to season the butternut squash and fill with water. Slice the pomegranate into quarters and submerge it under the water and carefully remove the seeds. The seeds will sink to the bottom and the white flesh will rise to the top. Scoop out the flesh with a slotted spoon and then drain the pomegranates into a colander and set aside. Save ¼ heaping cup of pomegranates and reserve the rest for future use.

4. Next, peel and spiralize the sweet potato, using Blade D. Place the noodles into a food processor and pulse until rice-like.

5. Place a large skillet over medium heat and add in the rest of the olive oil. Once oil heats, add in the sweet potato rice and season with salt and pepper. Stir and cook for 1 minute. Cover the sweet potato rice and cook for 5 minutes, uncovering to stir occasionally and then let cook for 3 more minutes, uncovered, or until sweet potato rice reaches your preferred rice-like consistency. Stir in the goat cheese, remove from heat and add in the butternut squash.

6. Divide the sweet potato into bowls and top pomegranates.

Pork Fried "Turnip" Rice

Prep Time: *2 hours, 15 min* | **Cook Time:** *1 hour 10 min* | **Total Time:** *3 hours 25 minutes* | **Servings:** *4-5*

Ingredients

For the pork:

- 1 pound pork shoulder/pork butt
- 1/2 tablespoon honey
- 1/2 teaspoon salt
- 1/4 teaspoon five spice powder
- 1/2 teaspoon paprika
- pinch of white pepper
- 1/2 tablespoon sherry
- 1/2 tablespoon soy sauce, low-sodium
- 1/4 teaspoon sesame oil
- 1 teaspoons hoisin sauce
- 1 teaspoons tomato paste
- 1/2 tablespoon extra virgin olive oil
- 2 cloves garlic, smashed and then minced
- 1/2 tablespoon hot water

For the rice*:

- 3 large turnips
- 2 large eggs
- 1/2 tablespoon extra virgin olive oil
- 1 small white onion
- 1 tablespoon low-sodium soy sauce
- white pepper, to taste
- 1 teaspoon sesame oil
- 4 scallions

Instructions

1. Whisk all of the ingredients for the marinade in a small bowl, reserve 2 tablespoons and place the rest in a large zip top bag.
2. Cut the pork into 3" long pieces and place in the zip top bag. Shake and place in the refrigerator for at least 2 hours, ideally overnight.
3. While meat is marinating, dice the white onion and scallions. Set aside in the refrigerator for later use.
4. Once the meat is marinated, preheat the oven to 475 degrees. Line a baking tray with tin foil and place a metal rack on top. Pour ¼ cup of water over the tin foil. Place the pork on the metal rack and roast for 25 minutes. After 25 minutes, baste the pork with the juices that collect in the tin foil and brush the pork with half of the reserved marinade. Bake for another 20 minutes and then switch to broil and cook for 1-2 minutes or until outside crisps (be careful not to let burn!)
5. Using the reserved tablespoons of marinade, brush the pork. Let the meat rest for 10 minutes and then cut into ½ inch chunks.
6. While the pork cools, peel and spiralize the turnips, using Blade C. Place the turnip noodles into a food processor and pulse until rice-like. Set aside.
7. Place a large skillet over medium-high heat and coat with cooking spray. Beat the eggs and then scramble. Set aside.
8. Wipe down the skillet used to scramble the eggs and add in the olive oil over medium heat. Once oil heats, add in the onion and cook 2-3 minutes or until translucent. Then, add in the cooked pork and turnip rice. Let cook for 3-5 minutes or until turnip is no longer crunchy and then add in the soy sauce, sesame oil, white pepper, scallions, eggs and cook for 1-2 minutes or until everything is heated through.

Pumpkin-Goat Cheese Sweet Potato "Risotto" with Maple-Pecan Crusted Pork

Prep Time: *15 minutes* | *Cook Time:* *20 minutes* | *Total Time:* *35 minutes* | *Servings:*
4

Ingredients

For the pork chops:

- 4 boneless pork chops
- Salt and pepper, to taste
- 2 tablespoons maple syrup
- 1 tablespoon Dijon mustard
- ½ cup pecans, crushed almost to a powder
- 1 teaspoons chili powder

For the risotto:

- 2 large sweet potatoes
- 1 tablespoon extra virgin olive oil
- 2 garlic cloves
- ¼ teaspoon red pepper flakes
- 1 shallot
- salt and pepper, to taste
- 1.25 cups canned pumpkin puree
- ½ cup chicken broth, low-sodium
- 1 teaspoon thyme flakes
- ½ cup crumbled goat cheese (about 3oz)
- 1 tablespoon freshly chopped parsley, to garnish

Instructions

1. Preheat the oven to 425 degrees.
2. Pat your pork chops dry and season with salt and pepper and place on a parchment-paper lined baking sheet. Place maple syrup, chili powder, mustard and pecans in a small bowl and whisk together until combined. Using a brunch, spread the maple mixture over both sides of the pork chops. Bake for 16-18 minutes or until cooked all the way through. Reserve pan juices.
3. While the pork chops are baking, peel and spiralize the sweet potatoes, using Blade C. Place the noodles into a food processor and pulse until rice-like. Mince the garlic cloves and shallot and set aside.
4. Place a large skillet over medium heat and add in the oil. Once oil is heated, add in the garlic, red pepper flakes and shallots. Cook for 1 minutes or until shallots are translucent. Add in the sweet potato rice and season with salt

and pepper. Cook, stirring often, for 2-3 minutes or until rice heats through and begins to soften.

5. Add in the pumpkin, thyme and broth and cook for 5 minutes or until sweet potato rice softens. Remove from heat, add in goat cheese and mix until goat cheese is evenly combined.

6. Portion the sweet potato risotto into bowls and top each with a pork chop and a drizzle of pan juices. Garnish with parsley.

Quinoa-Beet Rice Salad with Veggies and Feta

Prep Time: 15 minutes | *Cook Time:* 15 minutes | *Total Time:* 30 minutes | *Servings:* 2.5-3 cups

Ingredients

- salt, to taste
- 1 ear of corn
- 1/4 cup dry quinoa
- 1/2 cup water
- 2 medium beets, peeled, Blade C
- pepper, to taste
- 1/4 cup cilantro leaves
- 1/2 cup pinto beans
- 1/2 cup diced red bell pepper
- 1/3 cup pitted and halved green manzanilla olives
- 1/2 avocado, peeled, diced in small cubes
- 1/4 cup feta cheese
- 1 tbsp apple cider vinegar
- 2 tbsp fresh lime juice

Instructions

1. Cover your ear of corn with lightly salted water in a medium saucepan, bring to a boil and cook for 2 minutes or until corn is easily pierced with a fork. Drain into a colander and slice off kernels with a knife, into a bowl. Set aside.

2. In a small saucepan, place in the dry quinoa with the water. Bring to a boil and then simmer for 10-15 minutes or until quinoa is fluffy. Add more water by the tablespoon if quinoa sticks to the bottom before its done cooking. Set aside once done.

3. Place your beet noodles in a food processor and pulse until rice-like. Pour into a large mixing bowl with the cilantro, beans, bell pepper, olives, avocado, feta, apple cider vinegar and lime juice.
4. Season with salt and pepper and toss everything to combine thoroughly. Transfer to a serving bowl and enjoy!

Red Kale and Sweet Potato Rice Bowls with BBQ Chicken

Prep time: 5 mins | Cook time: 60 mins | Total time: 1 hour 5 mins | Serves: 4

Ingredients

- 2 tablespoons extra virgin olive oil
- 3 boneless chicken breasts (or thighs, if you like darker meat) – don't use thinly sliced
- 1 cup Tessemae's BBQ sauce
- 2 medium sweet potatoes
- 2 ripe avocados
- 1 large red onion
- 2 garlic cloves
- 1 large bunch of kale
- ½ cup low sodium chicken broth
- salt and pepper, to taste

Instructions

1. Preheat the oven to 400 degrees. Drizzle half of the olive oil on a rimmed baking sheet and spread around with a brush to coat the surface of the pan, where the chicken will be placed.
2. Place the chicken thighs (or breasts) skin down on the pan and roast for 25 minutes. Remove the pan from the oven and brush the BBQ sauce all over the tops of the chicken. Using a spatula, carefully flip the chicken (careful not to tear the skin) and then brush the sauce over the other side. Bake for 7 more minutes and then remove from the oven again, brush with more sauce and then bake another 7 minutes.
3. While the chicken cooks: peel and spiralize the sweet potato, using Blade C. Place the noodles into a food processor and pulse until rice-like and set aside. Then, cube the insides of the avocados. Then, thinly slice the onions. Then, mince the garlic. Then, chop the kale into at least 4 cups.
4. Remove from the oven again, brush with more sauce and then increase the oven temperature to 425 degrees. Roast for another 5 minutes or until

sauce beings to brown around the edges and chicken is cooked through (no longer pink on the inside.) Remove the chicken from the oven and let rest for 5 minutes and then slice into ½" strips.

5. Once you remove the chicken for the final time, place a large skillet over medium heat and add in the rest of the olive oil. Once oil heats, add in the onions and let cook 2-3 minutes or until translucent. Then, add in the garlic and let cook for 30 seconds or until fragrant. Then, add in the sweet potato rice and broth. Let cook, stirring occasionally, for 2-3 minutes and then add in the kale, season with salt and pepper and cook another 5 minutes, or until kale is wilted and sweet potato rice is cooked and softened but not mushy (taste test occasionally.) Stir in the avocado and let cook for about 2 minutes or until heated through.

6. Divide the rice into bowls and top with BBQ chicken slices.

Sausage and Brussel Sprout Rutabaga Rice

Prep Time: 10 minutes | Cook Time: 20 minutes | Total Time: 30 minutes | Servings: 4

Ingredients

- 1 medium rutabaga, peeled, Blade C
- 1 tbsp olive oil
- 1 minced garlic clove
- 1 pinch red pepper flakes
- 1 shallot, minced
- 1/2 cup sliced brussel sprouts
- 2 chicken sausage links, decased
- 1/2 tsp oregano flakes
- salt and pepper, to taste
- 1 cup low-sodium chicken broth
- freshly chopped parsley, to garnish

Instructions

1. Place your rutabaga noodles into a food processor and pulse until made into rice-like bits. You should be able to set aside two cups of "rice."
2. Place a large skillet over medium-low heat and add in the olive oil. Then, add in the garlic, red pepper flakes and shallots. Cook for 30 seconds and then add in the brussel sprouts.

3. Cook the brussel sprouts for 2 minutes and then push to the side. Add in the sausage, crumbling with your hands as you place it in the skillet. Use a wooden spoon to continue to crumble it as it cooks. Let the sausage cook through so that it is no longer pink.
4. Then, combine the brussel sprouts and chicken sausage in the skillet. Add in the rutabaga rice, stir to combine and season with salt, pepper, and oregano. Pour in 1/2 cup of chicken broth and let simmer, stirring occasionally, until all the broth is reduced. Then, add in 1/2 cup more and let cook until reduced again. Taste and if the rutabaga is still crunchy, continue to cook for 6-8 more minutes, stirring occasionally.
5. When done, plate into bowls and garnish with parsley.

Shredded Chicken and Broccoli with Daikon Fried Rice

Prep time: *20 mins* | **Cook time:** *10 mins* | **Total time:** *30 mins* | **Serves:** *2*

Ingredients

For the sauce:

- 2 scallions, diced, white and green parts divided
- 2 tablespoons low sodium soy sauce
- 1 tablespoon sesame oil
- ¼ teaspoon hot sauce (Frank's and Tessemae's are great options)
- ¼ teaspoon honey
- For the chicken and broccoli:
- 1.5 cups broccoli florets
- ¾ cup shredded chicken breast*

For the rice:

- 1 large daikon radish, peeled, Blade C
- 2 teaspoons virgin coconut oil
- 1 teaspoon peeled and minced ginger
- 1 small garlic clove, minced
- 1 large whole egg
- 1 teaspoon low sodium soy sauce
- pepper, to taste

*To shred chicken: place ½ pound boneless chicken breast into a small saucepan and pour in enough water to cover. Place over medium heat, bring to a boil, and simmer until the thickest part of the breast meat is no longer pink, 10 to 12 minutes.

Transfer the chicken to a bowl and then shred the chicken, using two forks.

Instructions

1. Bring a medium pot filled halfway with water to a boil. Once boiling, add in the broccoli and cook for 2-3 minutes and then drain into a colander. Set aside and wipe down pot and reserve aside for use later in the recipe.
2. Whisk together all of the ingredients for the sauce in a small mixing bowl (using green parts of scallions only) and set aside.
3. Place your daikon radish noodles into a food processor and pulse until rice-like bits. Place in a bowl near a sink. Place another bowl next to the bowl of rice. Take large handfuls of the rice and squeeze out the excess water into the sink and then place in the empty bowl. Repeat this until you've squeezed out the excess moisture in all of the rice. Set aside.
4. In a large skillet, place in the coconut oil. Then, place in the garlic, ginger and white parts of the scallions. Let cook for 30 seconds and then add in the daikon rice. Cook for 2 minutes, stirring frequently and then make a cavity in the center of the rice and crack in the egg. Scramble the egg and then once mostly scrambled, mix into the rice, soy sauce and season with pepper.
5. While daikon rice is cooking, place the pot used to boil the broccoli over medium-high heat and add in the chicken, broccoli and sauce. Bring to a boil and then reduce heat to low and keep warm as daikon rice finishes cooking.
6. Divide the daikon rice into bowls and top with chicken and broccoli. Serve immediately.

Slow Cooker Curry Cashew-Coconut Chicken with Ginger-Cilantro Turnip Rice

Prep time: 15 mins | Cook time: 3 hours | Total time: 3 hours 15 mins | Serves: 4

Ingredients

- 4 boneless skinless chicken breasts
- 1 red chile pepper, chopped
- 5oz green beans, trimmed
- 2 garlic cloves, minced
- ½ white or yellow onion, sliced
- 1 14-ounce can coconut milk (full-fat)

- 1 teaspoon turmeric
- 2 tablespoons curry powder
- salt and pepper, to taste
- ½ cup raw cashews

For the rice:

- 2 large turnips
- 2 teaspoons coconut oil
- 1 garlic clove, minced*
- 1 tablespoon minced ginger*
- salt and pepper, to taste
- ¼ cup chopped cilantro*

*Prepare these ingredients once you press start on the slow cooker.

Instructions

1. Add chicken pieces, red peppers, green beans, garlic and onions to the slow cooker.
2. In a medium bowl, whisk together the coconut milk, turmeric, curry powder, salt, and pepper. Pour mixture into slow cooker and stir to coat chicken and veggies. Cover and cook on high for 2.5-3 hours or on low 4.5-5 hours. Uncover, stir in the cashews, and cook another 15 minutes on low.
3. Once you add in the cashews, prepare the rice. Peel and spiralize the turnips, using Blade D. Transfer the noodles to a food processor and pulse until rice-like and set aside. You may have to do this in batches, depending on the size of your food processor.
4. Place a large skillet over medium-high heat and add in the oil. Once oil heats, add in the garlic and ginger. Let cook for 1 minute or until fragrant. Add in the turnip rice and season with salt and pepper. Let cook for 7 minutes or until turnip reaches your preferred rice-like consistency. When done, turn off the heat, fold in the cilantro, stir and divide into four bowls. Top each bowl with chicken, onions, green beans and ladle over with the sauce.

Spiced Chicken Kabobs over Moroccan Celeriac Rice

Prep Time: 30 minutes | Cook Time: 15 minutes | Total Time: 45 minutes | Servings: 3 cups of rice, 6 kabobs

Ingredients

- 1/2 tablespoon extra virgin olive oil
- 1.5 large shallots, peeled, minced
- 1 large garlic clove, minced
- 1 tablespoon pine nuts
- 1 large celeriac (or two medium), peeled, Blade C
- ½ teaspoon ground cumin
- ½ teaspoon ground coriander
- ¼ teaspoon paprika
- 1/3 cup diced dried apricots
- salt and pepper, to taste
- 1/3 cup low-sodium chicken broth
- 2 tablespoons freshly chopped parsley
- ¼ cup crumbled feta, to garnish (optional)

For the kabobs:

- 1 teaspoon ground cumin
- ½ teaspoon ground coriander
- 1 teaspoon paprika
- pinch of ground cinnamon
- pinch of ground ginger
- ¼ teaspoon cayenne pepper
- salt and pepper, to taste
- 1 large chicken breast, cut into 1" cubes (about 1 pound)
- ½ tablespoon extra virgin olive oil
- 2 teaspoons lemon juice
- 1 large bell pepper (any color)
- 1 medium red onion
- 1 dozen cherry tomatoes

Instructions

1. If you're using wooden skewers, make sure you soak them for at least 30 minutes – 1 hour to avoid burning in the oven. If you're using a metal skewer, you can skip this step.
2. Preheat the oven to 425 degrees. Place the kabob spices (cumin, coriander, paprika, cinnamon, ginger, cayenne) into a large bowl and mix together. Add in the chicken, olive oil and lemon juice and season with the salt and pepper. Toss to mix thoroughly. Let marinate in the refrigerator for 20 minutes.
3. While chicken marinates, place the celeriac noodles into a food processor and pulse until rice-like. Set aside. Then, chop the onion and bell peppers into 1" pieces.

4. Once the chicken is marinated, skewer the marinated chicken, bell peppers, onion sand tomatoes as you prefer (in any order.) You should be able to make 6 skewers, with 2-3 pieces of chicken per skewer.
5. Arrange the skewers on a large nonstick baking sheet in a single layer and bake until chicken is just cooked through and vegetables are tender, about 10 minutes.
6. Meanwhile, place a large skillet over medium heat and add in the oil. Add the shallot and cook for 1-2 minutes until translucent and fragrant. Add the garlic and pine nuts and cook, stirring frequently, until the nuts are lightly toasted, slightly golden brown. Add in the celeriac rice and stir in the spices and apricots and mix well. Season with salt and pepper, pour in the chicken broth, cover and cook for 5-7 minutes or until celeriac reaches a rice-like consistency and is no longer crunchy, uncovering the skillet to stir occasionally.
7. Stir in the parsley and divide into three plates, topping each plate each with 2 kabobs.

Spicy Chicken and Plantain Rice with Mango-Avocado Salsa

Prep Time: *20 minutes* | **Cook Time:** *20 minutes* | **Total Time:** *40 minutes* | **Servings:** *3-4*

Ingredients

For the Chicken:

- 1 tbsp olive oil
- 3 boneless skinless chicken breasts, cubed
- 1 tbsp chilli powder
- 1/2 tsp cumin
- 1 tsp coriander
- 1 tsp garlic powder
- 1/2 tsp onion powder
- 1 tsp paprika
- 1/4 tsp red chilli flakes
- salt and pepper to taste
- 1/2 cup chicken broth

For Salsa:

- 1 ripe mango (peeled and chopped)
- 1 avocado, chopped

- 1 jalapeno, seeds removed and finely minced
- zest and juice of one lime
- 2 tbsp chopped cilantro
- salt and pepper to taste

For Plantain Rice:

- 3 medium-ripe plantains
- 1 tbsp olive oil
- 1/2 a yellow onion, finely chopped
- 2 cloves garlic, minced
- 1/2 tsp cumin
- 1/2 tsp coriander
- 1/2 to 1 cup chicken broth
- salt and pepper to taste

Instructions

1. Combine all of your ingredients for the salsa into a bowl and toss to combine. Set aside in the refrigerator.
2. Peel the plantains and spiralize them, using Blade C. Place the noodles in a food processor and pulse until the noodles become rice-like. Set aside.
3. Mix all of your spices for the chicken in a bowl and stir to combine. Set aside. Place a large skillet over medium heat and add in the olive oil for the chicken. Cook until lightly browned and then add in the dry spice mixture and stir to coat the chicken. Then, add the chicken broth and turn down to a simmer, cooking for about 5 minutes. When done, plate into separate dishes for serving.
4. While the chicken is cooking, place another large skillet over medium heat and add in the olive oil for the plantain rice. Then, add in the onion and garlic. Cook for 2 minutes and then add in the plantain rice spices. Stir to combine and then add in the plantain rice, cook for 1 minute and then add in the chicken broth. Let reduce fully and add more broth if needed. Cook to your desired consistency, about 5 minutes.
5. Top the dishes that have chicken in them with the plantain rice and top with mango-jalapeno salsa. Enjoy!

Spiralized Golden Beet Arroz con Pollo

Prep time: *20 mins* | **Cook time:** *35 mins* | **Total time:** *55 mins* | **Serves:** *4*

Ingredients

For the chicken:

- 1.25 pounds bone-in chicken, combination of legs, breasts and thighs
- 1 teaspoon paprika
- ½ teaspoon onion powder
- ½ teaspoon garlic powder
- ½ teaspoon cumin
- 1 tablespoon extra virgin olive oil
- salt and pepper
- ¼ - ½ cup chicken broth, as needed

For the rice mixture:

- 4 golden beets, peeled, Blade D
- 1 medium yellow onion, diced
- 1 red bell pepper, seeded and diced
- 1 green bell pepper, seeded and diced
- 2 large garlic cloves, minced
- 1 14.5oz can diced tomatoes, drained but liquid reserved
- 1 teaspoon paprika
- ½ teaspoon cumin
- ¼ teaspoon chili powder
- salt and pepper
- ½ cup defrosted peas
- 1 avocado, peeled, pitted, insides sliced

Instructions

1. Place the chicken in a plastic bag along with the paprika, onion powder, garlic powder, and cumin. Shake the bag to coat the chicken.
2. Heat the oil in a large skillet over medium-high heat. Once oil is shimmering, add in the chicken and season with salt and pepper. Cook the chicken until browned on all sides and no pink is showing, about 5 minutes per side. Add the chicken broth as the pan dries and the chicken starts to stick. Using tongs, transfer the chicken to a plate and set aside.
3. While chicken cooks, place the beet noodles into a food processor and pulse until rice-like. You may have to do this in batches. Set aside.
4. Add the onions, bell peppers, and garlic to the pan and cook for 5 minutes or until vegetables soften. Add in the drained tomatoes, paprika, cumin, and chili powder and stir to coat the veggies in the seasonings.
5. Add in the golden beet rice and season with salt and pepper. Stir together to combine with the veggies. Nestle in the cooked chicken and pour over any juices left on the plate. Add in the liquid left from the can of tomatoes. Cover and let cook for 15 minutes or until the chicken is no longer pink

when sliced into its thickest part, adding the peas after about 10 minutes of cooking.

6. Divide the chicken and golden beet mixture into bowls and top with avocado.

Spiralized Mushroom Turnip Risotto with Dijon-Honey Salmon

Prep time: *20 mins* | **Cook time:** *15 mins* | **Total time:** *35 mins* | **Serves:** *3*

Ingredients

- (3) 3oz salmon filets, skinless
- 1 tablespoon country dijon mustard
- 1 teaspoon honey
- 2 medium turnips, peeled, Blade D
- 1 tablespoon extra virgin olive oil
- 5oz baby portobello mushrooms (or cremini), sliced
- salt and pepper
- 1 garlic clove, minced
- 1 tablespoon minced shallots
- 2 sprigs of fresh thyme
- ½ cup vegetable broth (or chicken, if not vegetarian)
- ¼ cup grated parmesan cheese
- 1.5 tablespoons freshly chopped parsley, to garnish

Instructions

1. Preheat the oven to 425 degrees and line a baking sheet with parchment paper. While the oven preheats, peel and spiralize the turnips. Place the turnip noodles (in batches) into a food processor and pulse until rice-like. Don't process too much or else the bits will be too small. Once done, set aside the rice into a bowl.
2. Once oven preheats, place the salmon filets down on the parchment paper. Mix the dijon mustard and honey in a small bowl and then spread on top of each salmon filet. Bake the salmon for 12-15 minutes or until cooked to your preference (12 for medium, 15 for well done.)
3. Place a large skillet over medium heat and add in the olive oil. Once oil heats, add in the mushrooms, garlic and shallots. Season with salt and pepper and let the mushrooms cook for 2-3 minutes or until slightly wilted and then add in the turnip rice, thyme, season with salt and pepper and stir to combine. Cook for 5 minutes or until turnip softens, stirring frequently.

4. Add in ½ cup of vegetable broth and let reduce, stirring frequently and let cook for another 5-7 minutes. If the turnip rice is still crunchy after that and needs to cook more, keep cooking. If it's cooked enough, add in the Parmesan cheese and half of the parsley, stir to combine and let cook for 30 seconds or until cheese melts fully into the turnip rice.
5. Divide into bowls and garnish with remaining parsley.

Strawberry Zucchini Salad with Poppy Seed Vinaigrette

Total Time: *15 minutes* | **Servings:** *2-3*

Ingredients

Dressing:

- ½ cup EVOO
- 3 tbsp. Apple Cider Vinegar
- 1 tbsp. Poppy Seeds
- 1 tbsp. Honey
- 1 tbsp. Dijon Mustard
- Salt and Pepper

Salad:

- 4 cups Fresh Baby Spinach
- 1 cup Sliced Strawberries
- 1 cup Blackberries
- 1 Avocado, Diced
- ¼ cup Chopped Walnuts
- 1 Zucchini, Spiralized on Blade C

Directions:

- Spiralize Zucchini using Ali's method to get half moons (slice the zucchini halfway, and spiralize.) Combine all ingredients in a bowl. Whisk all ingredients for the dressing in a bowl. Add to salad and enjoy!

Thai Pork & Peanut Coconut Red Curry with Sweet Potato Rice

Prep Time: 15 minutes | *Cook Time:* 20 minutes | *Total Time:* 34 minutes | *Servings:* 3

Ingredients

- 1 tbsp coconut oil (or vegetable oil)
- 1 garlic clove minced
- ¼ tsp minced ginger
- 1/3 cup minced green onions
- 1 red bell pepper, sliced into strips
- 2 boneless pork tenderloins, sliced into ½-inch strips
- ¼ cup peanut butter
- 1/4 cup Thai red curry paste
- 1 can coconut milk
- ¼ cup chicken broth
- 1 tbsp fresh cilantro leaves
- 2 cups sweet potato rice*

Instructions

1. Place a large skillet over medium heat and add in the oil. Add in the garlic and ginger and cook for 30 seconds. Then, add in the onions. Let cook for 1 minute and then add in the pork slices. Cook the pork for about 5 minutes until it starts to brown. Remove the pork and add in the red bell pepper slices. Let cook for 3 minutes and then put the pork back into the skillet.
2. Add in the peanut butter and curry paste. Stir to combine and then add in the coconut milk and chicken broth. Toss to combine, cover the skillet and let simmer for 10 minutes, stirring occasionally. After 10 minutes, uncover and let simmer for 5 more minutes.
3. Once done, remove the cover and stir in the cilantro. Remove from heat and transfer to a serving bowl. Serve alongside the sweet potato rice. Enjoy!

Thyme Beet Risotto with Walnuts

Prep Time: 10 minutes | *Cook Time:* 15 minutes | *Total Time:* 25 minutes | *Servings:* 2

Ingredients

- 2 large beets, peeled, Blade C
- 1 tablespoon extra virgin olive oil
- 1 clove of garlic, minced
- 2 tablespoons minced shallots
- salt and pepper, to taste
- 1 teaspoon fresh thyme leaves
- 1/4 cup vegetable broth
- 1/3 cup roughly chopped walnuts
- 1/4 cup grated parmesan cheese

Instructions

1. Place the beet noodles into a food processor and pulse until rice-like. Be careful not to over-pulse, so go slowly.
2. Heat the olive oil in a large skillet over medium-heat. Once heated, add in the garlic and shallots. Let cook for 30 seconds or until fragrant and then add in the beets. Season the beets with salt, pepper and add in the thyme.
3. Stir to combine and add in the vegetable broth. Bring to a boil and then lower to a simmer. Let cook for 5-7 minutes or until beets soften. Once softened, remove from heat, stir in the parmesan cheese and walnuts and stir until cheese melts into the risotto.
4. Serve immediately.

Chapter 7: Noodles

***

Ahi Tuna Poke Bowls with Avocado and Cucumber Noodles

Prep Time: 20 minutes | *Total Time:* 20 minutes | *Servings:* 3

Ingredients

- 1 large sashimi grade ahi tuna steak, diced into bite-sized pieces
- 1 very ripe avocado, peeled, insides cubed
- 1 small jalapeno, seeds removed, finely minced
- 1 tablespoon minced cilantro
- 1.5 tablespoons freshly squeezed lime juice
- salt and pepper, to taste
- 1.5-2 large seedless cucumbers, Blade C, noodles trimmed
- For the poke dressing:
- 2 teaspoons toasted white sesame seeds
- 2 teaspoons sesame oil
- ¼ cup soy sauce (low-sodium)
- 1 teaspoon rice vinegar
- ¼ heaping cup finely diced scallions

Instructions

1. Place the tuna in a bowl with the poke dressing ingredients. Stir to combine and set aside to marinade.
2. While the tuna marinades, combine the avocado, jalapeno, cilantro and lime juice in a medium sized mixing bowl and season with salt and pepper. Whisk together until creamy. Taste and adjust, if needed.
3. Thoroughly pat dry the cucumber noodles and add them to the mixing bowl and toss the noodles until they're completely coated in the avocado sauce.
4. Divide the cucumber noodles into three bowls and top with equal amounts of the tuna poke, using a slotted spoon to portion out the poke, to avoid extra liquid. Serve.

Asian Peanut Zucchini Noodles with Chicken

Prep Time: 20 minutes | *Cook Time:* 20 minutes | *Total Time:* 40 minutes | *Servings:*

3

Ingredients

For the peanut sauce:

- 1/3 cup lower sodium chicken broth
- 2 tablespoons peanut butter
- 3/4 tablespoon honey
- 3/4 tablespoon low sodium soy sauce
- 1/3 tablespoon sriracha sauce
- 1/3 tablespoon grated fresh ginger
- 1 small garlic clove, crushed

For the chicken and veggies:

- ½ pound boneless, skinless chicken breast, cut into thin strips
- salt and pepper, to taste
- ½ tablespoon sriracha sauce (or to taste)
- ½ tablespoon low sodium soy sauce
- juice of ¼ lime
- 2 garlic cloves, crushed
- ½ tablespoon grated fresh ginger
- ¼ tablespoon sesame oil
- ½ cup chopped scallions
- 2 medium carrots made into matchsticks (via julienne peeler)
- 1 large broccoli stem, Blade C, noodles trimmed
- 2 medium zucchinis, Blade C, noodles trimmed
- 1 tablespoon chopped unsalted roasted peanuts
- 3 lime wedges
- 3 springs of fresh cilantro, for garnish

Instructions

1. In a small saucepan, combine the chicken broth, peanut butter, honey, soy sauce, sriracha, ginger and garlic. Bring to a simmer over medium-low heat and cook, stirring occasionally, until the flavors blend and the sauce is slightly thickened, 8 to 10 minute
2. Season the chicken strips with salt and pepper and then transfer it to a large bowl and add the sriracha, soy sauce, lime juice, 1 of the garlic cloves and the ginger.
3. Heat a large nonstick skillet over high heat. Add the sesame oil, then add the chicken. Cook, stirring, until cooked through, 2-3 minutes. Transfer to a plate. Add the remaining 1 garlic clove, the scallions, carrots and broccoli

noodles and season with salt. Cook, stirring, until the vegetables are crisp-tender, 1-2 minutes. Transfer to a plate.

4. Add the zucchini noodles to the hot skillet and toss. Cook for 2-3 minutes or until noodles are al dente. Add the cooked veggies, chicken and peanut sauce and cook, tossing everything together, for 1 minute.

5. Divide the noodles and chicken evenly among 3 bowls. Top each with the peanuts and serve with a lime wedge and a sprig of cilantro, for garnish.

Asian Sesame Spiralized Carrots

Prep time: 10 mins | Total time: 10 mins | Serves: 2

Ingredients

- 1 large carrot, peeled, Blade D, noodles trimmed
- 2 teaspoons toasted sesame seeds
- 1.5 tablespoons rice vinegar
- 1 tablespoon sesame oil
- 1 heaping teaspoon fresh ginger, peeled and grated
- 1.5 teaspoons low-sodium soy sauce
- 2 scallions, diced
- freshly ground black pepper, to taste

Instructions

- Combine all of the ingredients into a large bowl and toss well. Let sit for 10 minutes in the refrigerator so that the carrots soften or serve immediately.

Avocado-Basil Zucchini Noodles with Chile-Lime Shrimp & Corn

Prep Time: 7 minutes | Cook Time: 5 minutes | Total Time: 12 minutes | Servings: 2

Ingredients

For the sauce:

- 5 tsp lime

- 8 cranks of the sea salt grinder
- 10 cranks of the peppercorn grinder
- 1 avocado
- 1/4 cup Chobani 0% plain Greek yogurt
- 12 basil leaves
- 1 medium clove of garlic, minced

For the rest:

- 2.5-3 zucchinis, Blade C
- salt and pepper to taste
- 2 tsp chili powder or more (to season shrimp)
- 8 medium shrimp
- 1 whole lime
- 1 ear of corn
- olive oil cooking spray

Instructions

1. Preheat the oven to 400 degrees.
2. Place your corn on a baking sheet and lightly spray with cooking spray. Season with salt and pepper. When oven preheats, bake for 10 minutes. When done cooking, scrape off kernels with a knife into a bowl and set aside.
3. Place all of the ingredients for the sauce into a food processor and pulse until creamy. Taste and adjust, if needed.
4. Place your zucchini noodles into a bowl, pour over the creamy sauce and mix to combine thoroughly. Add in the corn.
5. Plate the noodles into a bowl.
6. Season shrimp with salt, pepper and chile powder. Set aside.
7. Place a skillet over medium heat and spray with cooking spray. Once heated, add in the shrimp and squeeze the lime over the shrimp. Cook for about 2 minutes, flip over and cook for another 1-2 minutes or until shrimp is opaque and cooked through.
8. Top the zucchini noodles with the shrimp and enjoy!

Balsamic Roasted Spiralized Beets with Brussels Sprouts and Hummus Dressing

*Prep time: 15 mins | **Cook time:** 15 mins | **Total time:** 30 mins | **Serves:** 2*

Ingredients

For the brussels sprouts:

- 1 heaping cup halved brussels sprouts
- 2 teaspoons extra virgin olive oil
- 2 teaspoons soy sauce, low sodium
- pepper, to taste

For the beets:

- 1 medium beet, peeled, Blade C, noodles trimmed
- 1 tablespoon extra virgin olive oil
- 1 tablespoon balsamic vinegar
- ¼ teaspoon garlic powder
- salt and pepper, to taste

For the hummus dressing:

- ¼ cup hummus
- 1 tablespoon freshly squeezed lemon juice
- ½ tablespoon water
- salt and pepper, to taste

Instructions

1. Preheat the oven to 425 degrees. Line two baking sheets with parchment paper.
2. On one of the baking sheets, lay out the brussels sprouts. In a small bowl, whisk together the oil and soy sauce and drizzle over the sprouts. Toss the sprouts to combine and then season with pepper. Roast for 15 minutes.
3. Meanwhile, prepare the beets. In a small bowl, whisk together the olive oil, balsamic vinegar and garlic powder.
4. On the other baking sheet, lay out the beet noodles and drizzle with the balsamic mixture. Toss the noodles together until combined and season with salt and pepper. Roast for 7 minutes or until al dente.
5. While the beets and brussels sprouts roast, combine all of the ingredients for the dressing into a small bowl and whisk together to combine.
6. Divide the beet noodles and brussels into two bowls and top with hummus dressing.

Basque Chicken with Red Potato Noodles

Prep Time: *15 minutes* | ***Cook Time:*** *30 minutes* | ***Servings:*** *3*

Ingredients

- 1 lb skinless, boneless chicken thighs or breasts, cut into 2" pieces
- salt and pepper, to taste
- ½ tablespoon extra virgin olive oil
- ½ yellow onion, thinly sliced
- 1 small red bell pepper, thinly sliced into strips
- ¼ teaspoon paprika
- 1 garlic clove, minced
- 1 cup grape tomatoes, roughly chopped, seeds discarded
- 1 large red potato, Blade C
- ½ cup chicken broth, low sodium
- ¼ teaspoon red pepper flakes
- ½ teaspoon fresh thyme
- 1/2 cup small pimiento-stuffed olives (about 8)
- 1.5 tablespoons freshly minced parsley, to garnish

Instructions

1. Season the chicken with salt and pepper. In a large Dutch oven or deep skillet, heat the oil over medium-high. Add in the chicken and cook for about 5 minutes or until lightly browned, turning occasionally to evenly cook.
2. Add in the onion, pepper and paprika, cooking 2-3 minutes or until crisp-tender. Then, add in the garlic, tomatoes, broth, red pepper flakes, thyme and season with salt. Bring to a boil and then reduce heat to a simmer, cooking covered for 5 minutes and then uncover, add in the potato noodles, toss to combine evenly and then cook another 10 minutes or until chicken is tender and potato noodles are cooked through.
3. Stir in the olives, garnish with parsley and serve. I transferred mine to a cast-iron skillet for presentation, but you can divide immediately into plates or serve in the Dutch oven/pot.

Beet and Anjou Pear Noodles with Warm Bacon-Pistachio Dressing & Baked Goat Cheese

Prep Time: 25 minutes | *Cook Time:* 10 minutes | *Total Time:* 35 minutes | *Servings:* 1

Ingredients

- 1/2 whole wheat english muffin
- 1 tbsp + 1/4 tsp olive oil
- 2 tsp freshly chopped parsley
- salt and pepper, to taste
- 1/2 roll of goat cheese (about 2 oz)
- 1-2 slices of bacon
- 1 anjou pear, Blade C
- 1 large beet, peeled, Blade C

For the pistachio dressing:

- handful of roasted and salted pistachios (deshelled)
- 1 tsp honey
- 1/2 tsp dijon mustard
- pepper, to taste
- 1 tsp red wine vinegar

Instructions

1. Preheat the oven to 375 degrees.
2. Place the english muffin in a food processor and pulse until made into breadcrumbs. Place a medium skillet over medium heat and add in a 1/4 tsp of olive oil. Cook breadcrumbs, tossing occasionally, until toasted. Transfer breadcrumbs to a bowl, add in parsley, season with salt and pepper and set aside on a plate.
3. Take your goat cheese and roll it in the breadcrumb plate and roll it around until it's coated.
4. Place the goat cheese on a baking tray coated with cooking spray. Place the beet noodles on another baking tray coated with cooking spray.
5. Place the goat cheese and beet noodles in the oven. Cook both for 7 minutes.
6. While the goat cheese is cooking, place a large skillet over medium heat. Add in your slices of bacon. Cook until to your preferred level of crispiness and set aside on a paper-towel lined plate. Save 1 tbsp of the bacon grease and set aside in a bowl.
7. Prepare the pistachio dressing. Add all of the ingredients listed into a food processor and pulse until pistachios are pureed and no major chunks of nuts remain. Add to a bowl or dressing shaker and add in the bacon grease. Stir.
8. Place your beet and pear noodles into a bowl and drizzle with pistachio dressing. Toss to combine and then plate.
9. Top the dressed noodles with the baked goat cheese and then crumble the bacon on top. Enjoy!

Black Bean and Avocado-Jalapeno Turnip Noodle Bowl

Prep Time: 15 minutes | **Cook Time:** 15 minutes | **Total Time:** 30 minutes | **Servings:** 2

Ingredients

- 1/2 tablespoon extra virgin olive oil
- 1 garlic clove, finely minced
- 1 tablespoon finely diced jalapeno (seeded)
- 1 large red bell pepper, sliced thinly
- 1 half small yellow onion, sliced thinly
- ¼ tsp cayenne pepper
- 1/4 tsp smoked paprika
- ¼ tsp cumin
- ¼ tsp oregano
- salt and pepper, to taste
- 2 medium turnips, peeled, Blade C
- 3/4 cup canned black beans, drained, rinsed & patted dry
- ¼ cup vegetable broth
- For the avocado mash:
- Inside flesh of 1 ripe avocado, mashed
- 1 tablespoon roughly minced cilantro
- salt and pepper, to taste
- 1 tablespoon lime juice

Instructions

1. Place a large skillet over medium heat and add in the olive oil. Once oil heats, add in garlic, jalapeno, peppers and onions. Cook for 2-3 minutes or until vegetables begin to soften. Add in the cayenne, smoked paprika, cumin and oregano and season with salt and pepper.
2. Stir the mixture and then add in the turnip noodles, black beans, and vegetable broth and cook for another 5 minutes or until turnip noodles are cooked through.
3. While turnips are cooking, mix together the ingredients for the avocado mash and set aside.
4. When turnip noodles are cooked, serve into bowls and top with a dollop of avocado mash.

Cauliflower and Lentil Butternut Squash Noodle Bowl with Maple Tahini

Prep time: 10 mins | *Cook time:* 35 mins | *Total time:* 45 mins | *Serves:* 4

Ingredients

For the cauliflower and butternut squash:

- 3 cups cauliflower florets (about ½ a small head of cauliflower)
- salt and pepper, to taste
- 1 small butternut squash, peeled, Blade D, noodles trimmed
- For the lentils:
- ¼ cup dry lentils of choice
- 1 cup water

For the dressing:

- 1.5 tablespoons tahini
- 2 tablespoons apple cider vinegar
- 1 tablespoon maple syrup
- 1 tablespoon extra virgin olive oil
- salt and pepper, to taste
- 1 tablespoon water + more if needed to thin

Instructions

1. Preheat the oven to 400 degrees. Lay out the cauliflower on a parchment paper lined baking sheet and drizzle with the olive oil. Season with salt and pepper and roast for 35 minutes or until fork-tender.
2. Line another baking sheet with parchment paper and lay out the butternut squash noodles. Season with salt and pepper and 10 minutes before the cauliflower is done, add it to the oven and bake for 8-10 minutes or until cooked to your preference.
3. Meanwhile, bring the water and lentils to a boil in a small pot over high heat. Once boiling, reduce to a simmer and cook for 15 minutes or until lentils are soft but not mushy. Add water if needed. When done, drain into a colander.
4. Place all of the ingredients for the dressing into a food processor and blend until creamy. Set aside.
5. When cauliflower and butternut squash is done, divide into two bowls and top with lentils. Drizzle with tahini sauce.

Chicken Pad Thai with Daikon Noodles

Prep Time: 15 minutes | *Cook Time:* 20 minutes | *Total Time:* 35 minutes | *Servings:*
2

Ingredients

- 2 whole eggs
- 1/4 cup roasted unsalted peanuts
- 1 tablespoon peanut oil (or oil of choice)
- ½ pound thin chicken breast, sliced into strips
- salt and pepper, to taste
- 1 garlic clove, minced
- ½ cup diced scallions
- 1 tablespoon coconut flour
- 1 tablespoon roughly chopped cilantro + whole cilantro leaves to garnish
- 1 medium daikon radish, Blade C, noodles trimmed

For the sauce:

- 3 tablespoons freshly squeezed lime juice
- 2 tablespoon fish sauce
- 1 tablespoon soy sauce
- 1.5 tablespoon chili sauce (I used Thai chili garlic sauce)
- 1.5 tablespoon honey

Instructions

1. Scramble the eggs and set aside.
2. Place all of the ingredients for the sauce into a bowl, whisk together and set aside.
3. Place the peanuts into a food processor and pulse until lightly ground (no big peanuts should remain, but it shouldn't be powdery). Set aside.
4. Place a large skillet over medium heat. Add in half of the oil and let heat. Once heated, add in the chicken and season with salt and pepper. Cook for 5 minutes or until chicken is cooked through and no longer pink. Turn the heat down to low and set the chicken aside on a plate, using tongs or a slotted spoon. Immediately add in the daikon noodles, season with salt and pepper and toss to coat the noodles in the juices. Cook for 3-5 minutes or until daikon has softened.
5. Transfer the cooked daikon to a large bowl and add in the other ½ tablespoon of oil. Add the garlic and scallions into the pan, stirring constantly to avoid burning and cook for about 1 minute, until the scallions

begin to soften. Add in the sauce and then the flour, turn the heat back up to medium and whisk quickly so that the flour dissolves and the sauce thickens.

6. Once the sauce is thick, add back in the daikon noodles and toss to combine thoroughly, tossing until noodles are completely coated in the sauce.

7. Add in the cooked chicken (with any juices), scrambled eggs and half the ground peanuts. Cook for about 30 seconds, tossing to fully combine.

8. Plate onto dishes and garnish with cilantro leaves, the rest of the scallions and the rest of the ground peanuts. Serve with lime wedges.

Chicken Paillard and Asian Pear and Cashew Salad

Prep Time: 5 minutes | Cook Time: 15 minutes | Total Time: 20 minutes | Servings: 2

Ingredients

For the dressing:

- ½ teaspoon finely chopped jalapeno
- 3 tablespoons fresh lime juice
- 2 tablespoons rice vinegar
- 2 scallions, thinly sliced
- 2 teaspoons honey
- 1 teaspoon grated fresh ginger
- salt and pepper, to taste

For the rest:

- 1 tablespoon extra virgin olive oil
- 2 thin, boneless chicken breasts (or pound 1 chicken breast to ¼" thickness and slice in half)
- salt and pepper, to taste
- 1 medium Asian pear
- 2 celery stalks, very thinly sliced
- ¼ cup packed cilantro leaves
- 1/4 cup roasted cashews, roughly chopped

Instructions

1. Place all of the ingredients for the dressing in a bowl and toss to combine. Set aside.
2. Season both sides of the chicken breasts with salt and pepper. Place a large skillet over medium heat and add in half of the olive oil. Once oil heats, add in one of the chicken breasts and cook for 2-3 minutes, flip over and cook another 2-3 minutes or until chicken breast is cooked through and no longer pink. Repeat with the remaining olive oil and the other chicken breast.
3. Once chicken is done, spiralize the pear, using Blade C and place in a bowl with the celery and cilantro. Pour over the dressing and toss to combine.
4. Assemble the plates. Place a chicken breast in the middle of the plate and then top with pear salad. Top with cashews.

Chicken Pho with Daikon Noodles

Prep Time: 15 minutes | Cook Time: 45 minutes | Total Time: 1 hour | Servings: 4

Ingredients

- 1 tablespoon extra virgin olive oil
- 1 small yellow onion, diced
- 1" piece of peeled ginger, minced
- 8 cups low-sodium chicken broth
- 4 cups water
- 1 pound chicken breasts or thighs, bone-in
- 2 chicken drumsticks
- 1 large daikon radish
- 1 bunch scallions (about 6 stalks)
- 1 jalapeno
- 1 lime
- 1 tablespoon Asian fish sauce
- ¼ cup cilantro
- 1 cup mung bean sprouts

Instructions

1. Place a large pot over medium heat and add in the olive oil. Once oil heats, add in the onions and ginger. Let cook for 3-5 minutes or until onions are translucent. Add in the water, broth and chicken and bring to a boil. Once

boiling, reduce to a simmer and cook covered for 25 minutes or until chicken is cooked through.

2. While chicken cooks, peel and spiralize the daikon radish. Also, dice the scallions. Also, thinly slice the jalapeno. Also, quarter the lime.

3. Remove the chicken and drumsticks and discard the skin from the chicken breasts and drumsticks and shred the chicken from the breast. Leave the drumstick intact. Return the bones from the chicken breast back into the pot and cook another 10-15 minutes, along with the fish sauce.

4. Add the shredded chicken and drumsticks back to the pot along with the daikon noodles and let noodles cook for 2-3 minutes or until cooked to your preference.

5. Stir in the scallions and ladle soup into bowls. Garnish with jalapeno, cilantro, mung bean sprouts and serve with lime wedges.

Cinnamon-Rosemary Carrot and Parsnip Noodles with Roasted Hazelnuts and Ricotta

*Prep Time: 5 minutes | **Cook Time:** 15 minutes | **Total Time:** 20 minutes | **Servings:** 2*

Ingredients

- 1 large parsnip (at least 2" in diameter), peeled, Blade C
- 1 large carrot (at least 2" in diameter), peeled, Blade C
- 1/4 cup chopped roasted hazelnuts
- 1/2 cup ricotta cheese
- salt and pepper to taste
- 2 sprigs of rosemary
- 1 tsp ground cinnamon

Instructions

1. Preheat the oven to 350 degrees. Once heated, place the hazelnuts on a baking tray coated with cooking spray. Cook for about 6-8 minutes.

2. Once nuts are done roasting, take them out and peel off their skins. Since the nuts will be hot, you can wait for them to cool or use gloves or a paper towel to rub the skins off. Once all nuts are peeled, set aside.

3. Place a large skillet over medium-low heat and place in the tbsp of olive oil. Add in the carrot and parsnip noodles and season with salt, pepper, rosemary, and cinnamon.

4. Cook for about 6-8 minutes, stirring frequently, or until noodles soften and are no longer tough.
5. Plate the noodles into two dishes and top each evenly with a ¼ cup dollop of ricotta. Sprinkle on hazelnuts and enjoy!

Cold Spiralized Sesame Noodle Salad

Prep time: *35 mins* | **Total time:** *35 mins* | **Serves:** *4*

Ingredients

- 1 seedless English cucumber, Blade D, noodles trimmed
- 1 large carrot, peeled, Blade D, noodles trimmed
- 1 medium zucchini, Blade D, noodles trimmed
- ½ cup shelled frozen edamame, defrosted (or peas)
- 4-5 cups spinach, thinly sliced
- ½ cup roughly chopped roasted unsalted almonds

For the dressing:

- ¼ cup rice vinegar
- 2 tablespoons tahini or creamy almond butter
- 2 tablespoons tamari (or soy sauce)
- 1 tablespoons sesame oil
- 1 teaspoon honey
- 1 tablespoon freshly grated ginger
- 1 garlic clove, pressed and minced
- 1 tablespoons sesame seeds
- 1 teaspoon sriracha sauce (or chili garlic sauce or red pepper flakes)

Instructions

1. Pat dry the cucumber noodles to rid of excess moisture. Place into a large mixing bowl along with the carrot and zucchini noodles. Add in the edamame, spinach and almonds.
2. Whisk together all of the ingredients for the dressing until creamy. Taste and adjust if necessary.
3. Pour the dressing over the noodle salad and toss to combine thoroughly. Serve immediately or chill for future use, 1-2 days in the refrigerator for optimal freshness.

Corned Beef with Spiralized Carrots & Cabbage

Prep Time: 5 minutes | *Cook Time:* 2 hours | *Total Time:* 2 hours, 5 minutes |
Servings: 4

Ingredients

For the beef:

- 2 lb flat cut corned beef (with spice packet)
- 3 tbsp water
- For the rest:
- 1 large head of cabbage
- 3 large carrots, peeled
- 1 medium yellow onion
- 2 tbsp olive oil
- 2 garlic cloves, minced
- ¼ tsp red pepper flakes
- 3 cups chicken broth, low-sodium
- 2 cups water
- 1 tsp dried thyme flakes
- 1 tbsp freshly chopped parsley
- freshly cracked pepper, to taste (from a peppercorn grinder)
- country dijon mustard (or spicy honey Dijon), to serve

Instructions

1. Preheat the oven to 350 degrees.
2. Remove your corned beef from the package, set aside the spice packet and lightly pat the meat dry.
3. Place a piece of tinfoil underneath the beef (fat side up) and place on a baking tray or shallow dish. Pour in the water and pat the spices onto the meat.
4. Wrap the beef in the tinfoil, leaving at least an inch at the top when enclosing it. Bake for 2 hours. When done, open the foil on top and place back in the oven on broil for 2-3 minutes. Then, remove foil completely, saving the liquids from the pouch (reserve and set aside). Place the beef on a cutting board and let set for 5-10 minutes. Then, slice off the fat top (if preferred). Then, slice pieces on an angle (against the grain) and set aside

on a serving platter. Pour the reserved liquid from the baked beef on top of the slices.

5. While the beef is baking, prepare your vegetables. First, spiralize your cabbage and carrots. Using Blade A, spiralize the cabbage. Using Blade C, spiralize your carrots. Set aside. Then, dice your onion and set aside.

6. Fifteen minutes before the corned beef is done baking, place a large saucepan over medium heat and add in the olive oil. Then, add in the garlic and red pepper flakes. Let cook for 30 seconds and then add in the onions. Cook the onions for 2 minutes and then add in the vegetable broth and water. Add in the carrot noodles, thyme and parsley. Bring to a boil and then lower to a simmer add in the cabbage. Stir to combine and season with pepper. Stir for 2-3 minutes or until cabbage is softened. When done, use a slotted spoon to remove the cabbage and noodles and place into a serving dish. Pour half of the remaining liquid into the serving dish and discard the rest.

7. Serve the cabbage and noodles alongside the sliced corned beef. Serve with country Dijon mustard or spicy honey mustard. Enjoy!

Daikon Noodle Vegetable Lo-Mein

Prep time: 15 mins | *Cook time:* 15 mins | *Total time:* 30 mins | *Serves:* 2-3

Ingredients

- 2 tablespoons low sodium soy sauce
- ½ teaspoon grated fresh ginger
- ½ teaspoon Sriracha (or similar Asian hot sauce)
- 1 teaspoon sesame oil
- 1 teaspoon honey
- 1 tablespoon extra virgin olive oil
- 1 garlic clove, minced
- 4oz sliced shiitake mushrooms
- 3 scallions, diced
- 1 red bell pepper, sliced thinly (any color will do)
- 6 baby corns
- 1 small carrot, julienned
- 1 tablespoon dry sherry
- 1 large daikon radish, peeled, Blade C, noodles trimmed
- 1 cup chopped baby bok choy
- ½ teaspoon white sesame seeds, to garnish

Instructions

1. In a small bowl, combine the soy sauce, ginger, hot sauce, sesame oil and honey. Heat oil in a wok or large skillet over high heat and add the garlic, mushrooms, and the white parts of the scallions. Cook for 30 seconds and then add in the peppers, baby corn and carrots. Cook for about a minute and then add in the dry sherry and cook for another minute.
2. Add the sauce mixture, daikon noodles, remaining scallions and bok choy to the wok and cook for about 5 minutes or until daikon noodles are to your preference.
3. Portion into bowls and garnish with sesame seeds.

Daikon Noodles and Broccolini with Asian Pork Meatballs

Prep Time: 15 minutes | *Cook Time:* 20 minutes | *Total Time:* 35 minutes | *Servings:* 4

Ingredients

For the meatballs:

- 1 pound lean ground pork
- 1 teaspoon peeled and minced ginger
- 1/3 cup chopped scallions
- 1 tablespoon soy sauce (or tamari, if you're gluten free)
- 1 teaspoon finely minced garlic
- 3 teaspoons chopped cilantro
- salt and pepper, to taste

For the soup:

- 1 teaspoon sesame oil
- 1 tablespoon peeled and minced ginger
- 2 bunches broccolini, halved (make sure to cut off any rough ends on the stems)
- pepper, to taste
- 4 cups chicken broth
- 2 cups water
- 1 tablespoon soy sauce (or tamari, if you're gluten free)
- 1 tablespoon fish sauce
- 2 teaspoons chili sauce or sriracha
- 3 medium daikon radishes, peeled, Blade C, noodles trimmed
- ½ cup cilantro leaves

Instructions

1. Preheat the oven to 400 degrees and line a baking sheet with parchment paper.
2. Place all of the ingredients for the meatballs into a large bowl and mix together. Form 10-12 golf ball sized meatballs with hands and place on the parchment paper. Bake until cooked through, about 18 minutes.
3. Once you place the meatballs in the oven to bake, place a large saucepan over medium heat and add in the sesame oil. Once oil heats, add in the ginger, cooking for 30 seconds or until fragrant. Add in the broccolini, season with pepper and cook for 3-5 minutes or until it turns bright green. Add in the chicken broth, water, soy sauce, fish sauce and chili sauce. Cover and bring to a boil and then uncover, lower heat and simmer for 10 minutes until broccolini is crisp-tender. Then, add in the daikon noodles and cook for 3-5 minutes or until noodles are to your preference (if you like al dente, no more than 3 minutes, if you like softer, go up to 5 minutes.)
4. Portion the soup into bowls, top with 3 golf ball sized meatballs. Garnish with cilantro and serve immediately.

Easy Coconut Green Curry with Zucchini Noodles

Prep time: 15 mins | Cook time: 15 mins | Total time: 30 mins | Serves: 2

Ingredients

- 1 tablespoon coconut oil or extra virgin olive oil
- 2 garlic cloves, minced
- 2 teaspoons minced ginger
- 4 scallions, diced (white parts only – reserve the green parts for garnish)
- 1 tablespoon Thai green curry paste
- 1 13.5-ounce canned coconut milk
- 2 medium zucchinis, Blade C/D, noodles trimmed
- 4oz of snap peas
- handful of thai basil leaves or cilantro

Instructions

1. Heat the oil in a large pot over medium-high heat, and once oil heats, add the garlic, ginger and scallions. Cook for 30 seconds or until fragrant and

then add in the curry paste (be careful – the paste will fry, which is good, but can get on your clothes.)

2. Scoop the thickened coconut solids out of the top of the can of coconut milk, leaving the watery milk below. Add these solids to the skillet for about 2 minutes.

3. Add the rest of the coconut milk and then the zucchini noodles and snap peas. Reduce the heat to medium-low and simmer for 3-5 minutes, or until the zucchini noodles are softened.

4. Portion into bowls and garnish with scallions, cilantro or thai basil and serve.

Easy Sesame Cucumber Noodles

Prep Time: 20 minute s | Total Time: 20 minutes | Servings: 5-6

Ingredients

For the sauce:

- 2 tablespoons sesame oil
- 3.5 tablespoons soy sauce
- 2 tablespoons rice vinegar
- ¼ cup tahini or creamy peanut butter
- 1 tablespoon honey
- 1 tablespoon finely grated ginger
- 2 teaspoons minced garlic
- 2 teaspoons sriracha

For the rest:

- 3 teaspoons white sesame seeds
- 4-5 large English cucumbers, Blade C, noodles trimmed*
- 4 scallions, diced, to garnish

Instructions

1. In a medium bowl, whisk together the sesame oil, the soy sauce, rice vinegar, tahini (or peanut butter), honey, ginger, garlic and sriracha.

2. In a large bowl, toss the cucumber noodles with the sesame sauce. Transfer to a serving bowl and garnish with sesame seeds and scallions.

Garlic Broccoli Noodles with Toasted Pine Nuts

Prep Time: 10 minutes | Cook Time: 15 minutes | Total Time: 25 minutes | Servings: 2

Ingredients

- 1 large broccoli head with stem
- 2 tablespoons olive oil
- 1 pinch of red pepper flakes
- salt and pepper, to taste
- 1 tablespoon pine nuts
- 3 garlic cloves, thinly sliced
- 1 tablespoon fresh lemon juice
- 1 tablespoon grated pecorino romano cheese

Instructions

1. Slice off the head of the broccoli, leaving as little stem on the florets as possible. Set aside the broccoli florets. Slice the bottom end off the broccoli stem so that it is evenly flat. Spiralize the broccoli stem, using Blade C.
2. Place a large skillet over medium heat and add in the olive oil. Once the oil heats, add in the broccoli florets, stems, red pepper flakes and season with salt and pepper. Cover and cook for 3-5 minutes, shaking the skillet frequently, letting the broccoli cook.
3. While the broccoli is cooking, place your pine nuts in a small skillet over medium heat. Let toast until fragrant and the pine nuts slightly brown, about 5 minutes. Be careful not to burn the pine nuts – toss occasionally. When done, set aside.
4. Add in the garlic and lemon juice and cook for 3-5 more minutes (covered) or until broccoli is tender but more easily pierced with a fork. Transfer the broccoli to a serving bowl and top with pine nuts and pecorino romano cheese.

Ginger Garlic Salmon Carrot & Zucchini Noodle Bowl with Shiitake & Oyster Mushrooms

Prep Time: 10 minutes | Cook Time: 20 minutes | Total Time: 30 minutes | Servings: 2

Ingredients

- 1 carrot, peeled, Blade C (at least 1.5" in diameter)
- 1 large salmon filet, cut into 1" cubes
- 2 tbsp coconut aminos
- 1 tbsp water
- 1 tbsp sesame oil
- 2 eggs, beaten
- 1 tbsp olive oil
- 1/4 tsp freshly minced ginger
- 1 tsp minced garlic
- 3/4 cup shiitake mushrooms, stems removed
- 1/2 cup oyster mushrooms, stems removed
- pepper, to taste
- 2 medium zucchinis, Blade C

Instructions

1. Preheat the oven to 400 degrees. In a bowl, add the coconut aminos, salmon, and sesame oil. Let sit for 5 minutes to marinade and then place on a baking tray and bake for 10-15 minutes or until salmon is baked through. Set aside, once done.
2. While the salmon is marinading, place a medium skillet over medium-low heat and coat with cooking spray. Add in the egg and scramble. Set aside.
3. Boil a medium saucepan half-way full with water. Once boiling, add in the carrot noodles. Cook for about 3 minutes or until noodles soften. Set aside.
4. Place a large skillet over medium heat and add in the olive oil. Once the oil heats, add in the garlic and ginger. Let cook for 30 seconds and then add in the mushrooms. Season with pepper and cook for 5 minutes or until mushrooms have mainly wilted.
5. Add in the zucchini and carrot noodles. Toss and cook about 3 minutes or until zucchini noodles have softened.
6. Fold in the salmon and eggs, toss to combine and top with salmon. Enjoy!

Ginger Roasted Salmon and Sweet Potato Noodles with Miso-Maple Dressing

Prep time: *20 mins* | **Cook time:** *15 mins* | **Total time:** *35 mins* | **Serves:** *2*

Ingredients

For the salmon:

- (2) 3oz skinless salmon filets
- salt and pepper, to taste
- 1 teaspoon rice vinegar
- ½ teaspoon grated fresh ginger
- ½ teaspoon honey
- 1 teaspoon extra virgin olive oil

For the miso dressing:

- 1.5 teaspoons white miso
- 1.5 teaspoons tahini
- 1 teaspoon maple syrup
- 1 teaspoon sesame oil
- 1.5 teaspoons rice vinegar
- water, to thin

For the pasta:

- 1 large sweet potato (or 2 small sweet potatoes), peeled, Blade D, noodles trimmed
- 1 tablespoon extra virgin olive oil
- salt and pepper, to taste
- 2 large scallions, diced

Instructions

1. Preheat the oven to 425 degrees. Line a baking sheet with parchment paper and place the salmon on top and season with salt and pepper.
2. Prepare the salmon. Whisk together the vinegar, ginger, honey and oil. Pour half over each salmon filet. Roast for 15 minutes or until cooked through.
3. While salmon roasts, place all of the ingredients for the dressing into a bowl and whisk together until combined (or use a food processor.) If too thick, add water to thin out. Taste and adjust to your preference. Set aside.
4. Place a large skillet over medium-high heat and add in the olive oil. Once oil heats, add in the sweet potato noodles and season with salt and pepper. Cook for 10 minutes or until noodles are cooked through. Halfway through, add in half of the scallions. Gently toss while cooking to best avoid breaking the noodles (they will break as they soften, but don't worry – that's normal!)
5. Place the sweet potato noodles into two bowls and top with roasted salmon. Drizzle with miso dressing and garnish with remaining scallions.

Ginger-Miso Carrots with Watercress and Baked Tofu

Prep time: 15 mins | *Cook time:* 30 mins | *Total time:* 45 mins | *Serves:* 2

Ingredients

For the tofu:

- 6.5 oz extra-firm tofu
- ¼ cup low-sodium soy sauce
- 1 teaspoon sesame oil

For the salad:

- 2 large carrots
- 3 cups watercress
- ½ teaspoon black sesame seeds + ½ teaspoon white sesame seeds, mixed

For the dressing:

- 2 tablespoons extra virgin olive oil (or avocado oil, if you have it)
- 2 tablespoons rice vinegar
- 1 teaspoon white miso
- ½ tablespoon sesame oil
- ½ inch piece of ginger, grated
- 1 tablespoon of water
- salt and pepper, to taste

Instructions

1. Preheat the oven to 350 degrees. Line a baking sheet with parchment paper and set aside.
2. Press excess moisture out of the tofu by squeezing between two layers of paper towels (or other preferred method.) Repeat until moisture is absorbed.
3. Dice the tofu into cubes and place in a medium mixing bowl along with the other ingredients for the tofu. Let marinate for 10 minutes and then arrange on the prepared baking tray.
4. While the tofu marinates, combine all the ingredients for the dressing and whisk together until combined.

5. Bake the tofu for 30 minutes or until browned and stiffened, flipping the tofu pieces over halfway through.
6. While tofu bakes, peel and spiralize the carrots. Then, place the carrot noodles into a large mixing bowl and set aside. 10 minutes before the tofu is done cooking, drizzle the dressing over the carrot noodles and toss to combine. Place in the refrigerator until the tofu is done.
7. Once the tofu is done, add the watercress to the bowl with the carrots. Toss to combine and then plate the salad, top with tofu and garnish with sesame seed mix.

Gruyere and Asparagus Potato Noodle Casserole

Prep Time: 10 minutes | Cook Time: 27 minutes | Total Time: 37 minutes | Servings: 8

Ingredients

- 2 385g white potatoes, peeled, Blade C
- 2 cups grated gruyere cheese
- 10-12 asparagus spears, bottoms snapped off
- pepper to taste from peppercorn grinder
- 2 tsp grated parmigiano-reggiano cheese

Instructions

1. Preheat the oven to 400 degrees. In a 1.9 quart casserole dish, place in half of your spiralized potato noodles. On top, evenly spread one cup of the gruyere.
2. Next, lay the rest of the potato noodles on top of the layer of gruyere.
3. Then, sprinkle the other cup of gruyere over the noodles.
4. Lay down your asparagus over the gruyere, pressing down each time. Dust with freshly cracked pepper.
5. Finally, place into the oven and bake for 30 minutes. After 30 minutes, remove the casserole, set the oven to broil and sprinkle the top of the casserole with the parmigiano-reggiano cheese. Place the casserole back into the oven and broil for 2 minutes.
6. When done, slice into eight pieces and serve.

*Haris*sa *Zucchini Spaghetti Skillet with Kale, Chickpeas and Poached Eggs*

Prep Time: 10 minutes | Cook Time: 20 minutes | Total Time: 30 minutes | Servings: 2

Ingredients

- 1/2 tbsp olive oil
- 1 garlic clove, minced
- 1/4 cup diced shallots
- 1 cup diced tomatoes (or half a 14oz can of diced tomatoes)
- 2 tbsp Mina Harissa Spicy Red Pepper Sauce
- 1/2 tsp cumin
- 1 small pinch of saffron
- salt and pepper, to taste
- 1.5 cups chopped kale
- 3/4 cup chickpeas
- 2 medium zucchinis, Blade C
- 2 whole eggs
- feta and chopped parsley, to garnish

Instructions

1. Place a medium cast iron skillet over medium-low heat and add in the olive oil. Once the oil heats, add in garlic and shallots. Cook for 30 seconds and then add in the diced tomatoes, harissa sauce, cumin, saffron and season with salt and pepper. Stir to combine and let cook for 1 minute.
2. Add in the chopped kale, stir to combine and let cook until sauce is reduced. Once sauce is reduced, add in the zucchini noodles and chickpeas. Toss the noodles around until covered in the sauce.
3. Move the mixture around to create two pockets for the eggs. Crack one egg into each pocket. Cover the skillet and let cook for about 5 minutes or until egg whites have fully set.
4. Remove the cover, garnish with parsley and feta. Enjoy!

Inspiralized Vegetable Lo-Mein

Prep Time: 10 minutes | Cook Time: 15 minutes | Servings: 2

Ingredients

For the noodles

- 3 large yellow squashes, Blade C
- 2 tbsp canola oil
- 3 tsp garlic, minced
- 1.5 tsp ginger, minced
- 2 cups of broccoli florets
- 10 snap peas
- 1 medium red bell pepper, cut into 1/4 inch strips
- 1/2 cup of cooked edamame
- 2 heads of baby bok choy, white ends removed
- 3/4 cup chopped carrots, cut into 1/4 inch thick rounds
- 1/2 cup sliced water chestnuts
- 1.5-2 tsp sesame seeds, for garnish
- 1 tsp red pepper flakes
- salt and pepper

For the sauce

- 1 tbsp sesame oil
- 1/4 cup vegetable broth, low-sodium
- 2 tbsp soy sauce
- 2 tbsp hoisin sauce
- 2 tbsp corn starch*

Instructions

1. Place a medium saucepan on high heat, filled with enough water to cover the broccoli and carrots. Once boiling, add in the broccoli and carrots and cook for about 2-3 minutes or until broccoli and carrots begins to soften but cannot be easily forked. Pour vegetables into a colander, pat dry and set aside.
2. Next, combine all ingredients for the sauce and whisk together until cornstarch dissolves. Set aside.
3. Put a large skillet over medium heat and pour in canola oil. Once oil heats, add in red bell peppers. Cook for about 2-3 minutes or until vegetables begin to soften. Add in the garlic, ginger, red pepper flakes, water chestnuts, snap peas, carrots, broccoli and season with salt and pepper.
4. Cook for about 3 minutes and then add in squash noodles, bok choy, edamame and the sauce prepared earlier. Cook until squash noodles are covered with sauce and soften, about 3 minutes.

5. Once finished, plate onto dishes and garnish with sesame seeds. Enjoy with chopsticks!

Italian Zucchini Pasta Spring Rolls

Prep time: *30 mins |* ***Total time:*** *30 mins |* ***Serves:*** *6 spring rolls*

Ingredients

For the rolls:

- ½ cup thinly sliced jumbo black olives *
- 1 large zucchini, Blade C, noodles trimmed*
- ½ small red onion, sliced thinly*
- 3oz of ¼" thick matchstick slices of provolone cheese* (they'll break up into smaller cubes as you slice them, that's okay)
- 4oz of ¼" thick matchstick slices of salami*
- 2 tomatoes, deseeded and sliced into ¼" slivers from 28oz can of Tuttorosso Tomatoes Peeled Plum Tomatoes*
- 6 rice paper sheets

*don't prep until you are prompted to in the directions below

For the dressing:

- 3 tablespoon red wine vinegar
- 2 tablespoon extra virgin olive oil
- ¼ cup lemon juice
- ½ teaspoon dried oregano
- ½ teaspoon dried parsley
- ½ teaspoon dried basil
- ¼ teaspoon red pepper flakes
- salt and pepper, to taste

Instructions

1. Whisk all of the ingredients for the dressing together and set aside.
2. Toss together the zucchini noodles with half of the dressing in a large mixing bowl. Place in the refrigerator for at least 15 minutes to soften the zucchini (or up to overnight!)

3. While the zucchinis sit in the fridge, prep all of the ingredients with astericks (*).
4. Fill a bowl with warm water. Submerge 1 of the rice paper sheets for about 3-4 seconds and then lay on your surface. Let sit for 30 seconds or until pliable.
5. Lay the fillings on the edge of the rice paper closest to you. First, add in the olives and onions, then salami, provolone and tomato slice. Top with zucchini noodles.
6. Then, gently pull away the edge of the wrap from the work surface and roll over all the fillings. Roll away from you and tuck in your filling toward you, keeping the roll tight. Once you roll over your fillings one complete time, fold the edges in and then keep rolling, keeping the roll tight.
7. Slice the roll in half. Repeat until all rice paper sheets and fillings are used up.
8. Serve with the extra dressing for dipping!corn mixture. Sprinkle with cheese and drizzle the platter with the chipotle sauce and garnish with cilantro and jalapenos. Serve immediately with lime quarters.

Korean Beef Rice Bowls with Spiralized Cucumbers and Daikon Rice

Prep time: *15 mins* | **Cook time:** *20 mins* | **Total time:** *35 mins* | **Serves:** *4*

Ingredients

For the beef:

- 1 pound ground beef, lean
- 2 garlic cloves, minced
- ½ cup diced yellow onion
- 1 teaspoon freshly grated ginger
- 3-4 tablespoons low sodium soy sauce
- 1 teaspoon sesame oil
- ½ teaspoon red pepper flakes

For the bowls:

- 2 daikon radishes, peeled, Blade D, noodles trimmed
- 1 teaspoon coconut oil, room temperature
- 4 scallions, diced, white and green parts divided
- salt and pepper, to taste
- 2 tablespoons gochujang sauce or more, if desired
- sesame seeds, to garnish (about ½ tablespoon)

- 1 English seedless cucumber, Blade D, noodles trimmed

Instructions

1. Heat a large nonstick skillet over high heat. Once skillet is hot, spray with cooking spray and add the ground meat. Breaking the meat up with a wooden spoon, cook the meat until cooked through and browned, 5-7 minutes. Add in the garlic, onion, and ginger and season with salt and pepper, cooking for 1 minute or until fragrant.
2. Add the soy sauce, sesame oil and red pepper flakes to the skillet and stir well to combine. Cover the skillet and lower the heat to a simmer. Cook for 10 minutes to let the flavors develop.
3. Meanwhile, prepare the rice. Place the daikon noodles into a food processor and pulse until rice-like. Place a medium skillet over medium-high heat and add in the coconut oil. Once oil melts, add in the white parts of the scallions. Cook for 5 minutes or until scallions soften. Add in the daikon rice and season with salt and pepper. Cook for another 3 minutes or so just to heat the rice through and soften to your preference.
4. Divide the rice into bowls. Top with the beef and place a dollop of the gochujang sauce (about ½ tablespoon/bowl). Garnish the beef with sesame seeds. Top with cucumber noodles and serve.

Korean Bulgogi with Shiitaki Mushroom Turnip Rice

Prep time: 45 mins | *Cook time:* 10 mins | *Total time:* 55 mins | *Serves:* 4

Ingredients

For the marinade:

- 3 tablespoons tamari (or low sodium soy sauce, if not gluten-free)
- 2 tablespoons honey
- 1 tablespoon sesame oil
- ½ tablespoon toasted white sesame seeds
- 2 medium garlic cloves, finely minced
- 2 scallions, diced

For the rest:

- 1 pound sirloin steak, sliced thinly against the grain
- 1 small yellow onion, sliced into strips

- 3 medium turnips
- ½ tablespoon extra virgin olive oil
- 8-10oz shiitake mushrooms
- 1 garlic clove, minced
- 1 teaspoon minced ginger
- ¼ teaspoon red pepper flakes

Instructions

1. In a small bowl, whisk together all of the ingredients for the marinade and then place the marinade, steak and onions together in a zip-seal plastic bag and let marinade in refrigerator for 30 minutes, shaking the bag every 10 minutes (so 3 times total.)
2. Ten minutes after the steak is marinating, peel and spiralize the turnip, using Blade C. Place into a food processor and pulse until rice-like. Then, slice the shiitake mushrooms and set aside. Place a large skillet over medium heat and add in half of the olive oil and then, once heated, add in the garlic, ginger and red pepper flakes. Cook for 30 seconds and then add in the mushrooms, cooking for 2-3 minutes or until they begin to wilt. Add in the turnip rice, stir and cover for 5 minutes, uncovering occasionally to stir, or until rice texture is to your preference. Divide into four bowls and set aside, covered.
3. Place the large skillet back over medium heat. Remove the beef from the bag of marinade and set marinade aside. Add the beef in single layers to the pan, along with 1 tablespoon of the leftover marinade and cook for 3 minutes and then flip, cooking another 3 minutes or until beef is cooked. I like it browned, so I cooked a few minutes longer until dark brown.
4. Divide the beef atop the bowls of mushroom turnip rice, pouring any pan juices on top.

Kung Pao Chicken and Snap Peas with Spiralized Onions

Prep time: *20 mins* | **Cook time:** *20 mins* | **Total time:** *40 mins* | **Serves:** *4*

Ingredients

- 2 teaspoons coconut oil
- 1 pound boneless chicken breasts, cut into cubes
- 1 medium Vidalia onion, Blade A, trimmed
- salt and pepper, to taste
- 8 oz snow peas (or snap peas)

- 2 garlic cloves, minced
- 1 tablespoon minced ginger
- 4 dried red chiles, stems removed and then halved
- 3 scallions, diced, white and green parts separated
- 3 tablespoons chopped roasted unsalted cashews

For the kung pao sauce:

- 3 tablespoons light soy sauce
- 1 tablespoons rice vinegar
- 1 teaspoon honey
- 2 tablespoons sesame oil
- freshly ground pepper, to taste

Instructions

1. Whisk together the ingredients for the sauce and set aside.
2. Heat a wok or large skillet over medium-high heat and add in the coconut oil. Add the chicken, season with salt and pepper and cook for about 10 minutes until cooked through and golden brown. Immediately add in the onions and stir-fry until just wilted, about 1 minute. Add the snow peas, garlic, ginger, chiles and white scallions and stir-fry until snap peas are nearly crisp-tender, about 2 minutes more.
3. Add the prepared sauce and stir-fry to coat, about 1 minute.
4. Transfer to a platter or divided into bowls, sprinkle with the nuts, remaining scallions and serve.

Lime, Mint and Cucumber Noodle Ice Popsicles

Prep Time: *15 minutes* | **Total Time:** *15 minutes* | **Servings:** *6*

Ingredients

- 3/4 cup freshly squeeze lime juice
- 4 tablespoons chopped mint
- 6oz cucumber noodles
- water

Instructions

1. In each pop mold, place in 2 teaspoons of the mint and 2 tablespoons of the lime juice into the ice pop mold. Then, add in 1 oz of the cucumber noodles. Fill to the top of the mold with water and place the bottom on to secure.
2. Freeze for 4-6 hours, preferably overnight. To enjoy, run the pop mold under warm water first.

Mexican Street Corn Sweet Potatoes with Creamy Chipotle-Avocado Sauce

Prep time: 30 mins | *Cook time:* 15 mins | *Total time:* 45 mins | *Serves:* 4

Ingredients

- For the corn:
- 1 large ear of corn, shucked
- ½ tablespoon extra virgin olive oil
- ½ teaspoon chili powder
- salt, to taste

For the rest:

- 1 tablespoon extra virgin olive oil
- 1 garlic clove, minced
- 1 medium sweet potato, peeled, Blade C/D
- salt and pepper, to taste
- ¼ cup fresh cilantro leaves
- ¼ cup crumbled cotija cheese (or feta)
- 1 jalapeno, sliced thinly to garnish
- 1 lime, quartered

For the chipotle sauce:

- 1 chipotle pepper in adobo sauce with ½ teaspoon sauce
- ½ avocado, pitted and peeled
- salt, to taste
- ¼ teaspoon paprika
- 1 garlic clove
- juice of 1 lime
- 1 tablespoon of water

Instructions

1. Place the corn in a pot covered with water and a pinch of salt. Bring to a boil and then cook 2-3 minutes or until corn is easily pierced with a fork. Drain into a colander, pat dry completely and shave the kernels off the corn cob into a medium mixing bowl. Add in the olive oil, chili powder, cotija cheese (or queso blanco), season with salt and set aside.
2. Meanwhile, place a large skillet over medium heat. Add in the olive oil and once heated, add in garlic and cook for 30 seconds or until fragrant. Then, add in the sweet potato noodles, cover and cook for 5-7 minutes or until cooked through, uncovering occasionally to toss.
3. While corn and sweet potatoes cook, place all of the ingredients for the creamy chipotle into a food processor and pulse until creamy. Taste and adjust to your preference.
4. Plate the salad: lay out the sweet potato noodles on a platter and top with corn mixture. Sprinkle with cheese and drizzle the platter with the chipotle sauce and garnish with cilantro and jalapenos. Serve immediately with lime quarters.

Mini Cheese Plate with Warm Beet Noodles

Prep Time: 10 minutes | Cook Time: 15 minutes | Total Time: 25 minutes | Servings: 3

Ingredients

- 1 medium beet, peeled, Blade C, noodles trimmed
- ½ tablespoon extra virgin olive oil
- salt and pepper, to taste
- 5oz roll of goat cheese
- 1/4 cup whole pecans
- 2 tablespoons honey

Instructions

1. Preheat the oven to 425 degrees. Place the beet noodles out on a baking sheet and drizzle with the olive oil. Toss to combine and season with salt and pepper. Bake for 7-10 minutes or until softened. Remove from the oven and place in a medium bowl (I used a 6oz ramekin).
2. Assemble your cheese plate. Place the bowl of beets on one end of the cheese plate, with serving utensils.
3. Place on the goat cheese with a spreading knife.

4. Lightly crush the pecans using the back of a knife or spatula. Place them in a small bowl on the cheese board.
5. Place the honey in a small bowl with a serving spoon and onto the cheese board/plate.
6.   Serve and impress your guests!

Miso Roasted Tomatoes and Carrot Noodles

Prep Time: 10 minutes | Cook Time: 20 minutes | Total Time: 30 minutes | Servings: 4

Ingredients

- ¼ cup vegetable oil
- 3 tbsp rice vinegar
- 2 tbsp light yellow miso
- 1 tbsp peeled and minced ginger
- 1 tablespoon toasted sesame oil
- 1 tbsp honey
- 2 tsp lime zest
- 2 tbsp fresh lime juice
- salt, to taste
- 2 pints cherry tomatoes
- 3 large carrots, peeled, Blade C, noodles trimmed
- 4 scallion stalks, thinly sliced
- 2 tsp sesame seeds

Instructions

1. Preheat the oven to 425 degrees.
2. In a bowl, whisk the vegetable oil, vinegar, miso, ginger, seasame oil, honey, lime zest and lime juice until smooth. Season with salt.
3. On a baking sheet, toss the tomatoes with 3 tablespoons of the miso dressing and season with salt. Roast for 20 minutes, stirring, until the tomatoes are charred in spots. Scrape into a large bowl.
4. While the tomatoes are roasting, bring a medium saucepan with water to a boil. Once boiling, add in the carrot noodles and cook for 2-3 minutes or until al dente. Drain into a colander.
5. In a large mixing bowl, add in the carrot noodles, tomatoes, scallions and the dressing and toss well. Divide into bowls and top with sesame seeds.

Miso-Ginger Glazed Taro Noodles and Shrimp with Scallions and Pea Shoots

Prep Time: 10 minutes | Cook Time: 25 minutes | Total Time: 25 minutes | Servings: 2

Ingredients

For the miso-sauce:

- 2 tablespoons white miso paste
- 1 tablespoon low sodium soy sauce or tamari sauce
- 1.5 teaspoon freshly minced ginger
- 2 tablespoons rice wine vinegar
- 1.25 tablespoon honey
- 1.5 tablespoon water + more to thin if needed

For the rest:

- 1 tablespoon extra virgin olive oil
- 1 garlic clove, minced
- ½ cup diced scallions
- 2 medium taro roots, peeled, Blade C, noodles trimmed
- 12 medium shrimp, defrosted, deshelled, deveined
- 2 cups pea shoots (or watercress, if you can't find pea shoots)
- salt and pepper, to taste
- cilantro leaves, to garnish

Instructions

1. Fill a medium pot halfway with water and bring to a boil. Once boiling, add in the taro and cook for 5 minutes or until almost cooked fully. Drain and set aside.
2. Combine all of the ingredients for the miso-sauce into a food processor and pulse until creamy. Taste and adjust to your preferences. Set aside.
3. Season the shrimp with salt and pepper and set aside.
4. Place a large skillet over medium heat and add in the oil. Once oil heats, add in the garlic and scallions and let cook for 2-3 minutes or until scallions soften.

5. Add in the taro noodles, pour in the miso sauce, toss to combine and then add in the shrimp. Cover the skillet and cook for 3-5 minutes or until tarot noodles soften and the shrimp are opaque and cooked through.
6. Prepare your plates. Fill each plate with 1 cup of pea shoots and top with even amounts of the taro and shrimp noodles. Garnish with cilantro and serve.

Spiralized Cucumber Kimchi

Prep time: *30 mins* | **Total time:** *30 mins* | **Serves:** *6*

Ingredients

- 1 English seedless cucumber, Blade A, noodles trimmed
- 1 teaspoon kosher salt
- 2 garlic cloves, minced
- 2 scallions, white and light green parts only, finely chopped
- 1" piece fresh ginger, peeled and minced
- 2 tablespoons rice vinegar
- 1 tablespoon Korean chile powder (gochugaru)
- 2 teaspoons coconut sugar or honey
- ½ teaspoon fish sauce

Instructions

1. Add the cucumbers to a medium bowl along with the salt. Let stand for 30 minutes at room temperature.
2. Meanwhile, combine garlic, scallions, ginger, rice vinegar, chile powder, honey and fish sauce in a medium mixing bowl.
3. Drain the cucumbers and add them to the medium bowl with the vinegar mixture. Cover and refrigerate for at least 12 hours before serving. Lasts for up to 5 days in the refrigerator.

Spiralized Potato Noodle Kugel

Prep Time: *15 minutes* | **Cook Time:** *45 minute* | **Total Time:** *1 hour* | **Servings:** *8*

Ingredients

- ½ cup water
- 1 small yellow onion
- 3 large eggs + 1 large egg white, beaten
- 2 large Idaho potatoes, peeled, Blade C (about 2 pounds)
- 2.5 tablespoons gluten-free matzo meal
- salt and pepper
- ¼ teaspoon ground nutmeg
- 1 tablespoon extra virgin olive oil

Instructions

1. Preheat the oven to 450 degrees.
2. Bring one half cup of water to a boil in a small pot. While bringing to a boil, peel and spiralize the onion. Set aside in a large bowl with the eggs, potato noodles, onion, matzo meal, ground nutmeg and season generously with salt and pepper. Stir well and add in the boiling water.
3. Heat an 8 by 11.5" baking dish over high heat with the olive oil on the stovetop until the oil crackles when you flick water in it. Once heated, pour in the potato noodle mixture.
4. Transfer the baking dish to the oven and bake for 20 minutes. Lower the temperature to 375° and bake for 25-30 minutes longer, until golden and crisp on the sides.
5. Switch the oven to broil and broil the dish as close to the heat as possible for about 2 minutes or until the top browns and crisps. Let the potato kugel stand for at least 10 minutes before serving.

Spiralized Sesame Cucumber and Zucchini Bowl with Avocado

Prep time: 20 mins | Total time: 20 mins | Serves: 4

Ingredients

For the dressing:

- 2 tablespoons freshly squeezed lime juice
- ¼ cup rice vinegar
- 3 teaspoons sesame oil
- 2 tablespoons freshly grated ginger
- 1 garlic clove, pressed

- 2 teaspoons soy sauce low sodium
- 1 tablespoon smooth peanut or almond butter

For the noodles:

- 1 large cucumber, Blade C, noodles trimmed
- 1 medium zucchini, Blade C, noodles trimmed
- 1 green bell pepper, seeded, diced
- 1 avocado, peeled, pitted, and insides cubed
- 1 cup cooked edamame beans
- ¼ cup chopped cilantro
- To garnish: 2 teaspoons toasted white sesame seeds

Instructions

1. Place all of the ingredients for the dressing into a bowl and whisk together.
2. Pat the cucumber noodles dry with paper towels and place into a large mixing bowl along with the rest of the ingredients for the noodles. Pour over the dressing and toss to mix. Garnish with sesame seeds.

Spiralized Sushi Bowl with Salmon Sashimi and Ginger Miso Dressing

Prep Time: *25 minutes* | **Total Time:** *25 minutes* | **Servings:** *4*

Ingredients

- 1 large daikon radish, peeled, Blade C
- 1 large cucumber, Blade C, noodles trimmed
- 1 large carrot, Blade C, noodles trimmed
- 1 sheet nori (dried seaweed), thinly sliced
- 12oz salmon sashimi (or kani, or tofu, or anything you'd like!)
- 1 avocado, insides sliced
- 4 scallion stalks, chopped
- 4 teaspoons toasted white sesame seeds

For the dressing:

- 2 teaspoon grated ginger
- 4 tablespoons apple cider vinegar
- 2 teaspoon miso paste
- 1 tablespoon soy sauce, low sodium
- 2 teaspoons honey

- 2 tablespoon tahini

Instructions

1. Place the daikon noodles into a food processor and pulse until rice-like. If needed, squeeze the excess moisture out of the daikon "rice." Set aside.
2. In a medium bowl, whisk together all of the ingredients for the dressing until creamy. If needed, use a food processor.
3. To assemble, place even amounts of the daikon rice into bowls and top with even amounts of cucumber, carrot, salmon sashimi, avocado, scallions and sesame seeds. Top each with dressing and serve.

Spiralized Vegetable Tahini Bowl with Tofu, Edamame & Avocado

Prep Time: *10 minutes* | **Cook Time:** *25 minutes* | **Total Time:** *35 minutes* | **Servings:** *1*

Ingredients

- 1 whole carrot, julienned
- 1/4 cucumber, Blade C
- 1/2 zucchini, Blade C
- 1/4 block of extra firm tofu
- 1 tsp black sesame seeds
- 1 tsp white sesame seeds
- salt and pepper, to taste
- 1/2 avocado meat, cut into cubes
- 1/4 cup edamame beans, cooked
- 2 tbsp chopped scallions

For the tahini dressing:

- 1/4 cup tahini
- 1 tbsp ginger
- 1 small garlic clove, minced
- 1 tbsp + 3 tsp rice vinegar
- 2 tsp soy sauce
- 1 tsp sesame oil
- 1 tsp mirin (or honey, if you can't find mirin)

Instructions

1. Preheat your oven to 375 degrees.
2. Place all of your spiralized vegetables and julienned carrots into a bowl and toss together to combine.
3. Place your tofu block on a few sheets of paper towels. Place a few more paper towels over the tofu and place a heavy book or can on top, to squeeze out the water.
4. After a few minutes, cut the tofu into chunks and toss in a bowl with soy sauce and white sesame seeds. If you have the time, let sit for 15 minutes to absorb the flavor. If not, that's okay.
5. Coat a baking sheet with cooking spray and lay down the tofu chunks, season with salt and pepper and bake for 20-35 minutes, depending on your preference. I like my tofu a bit tough, so I bake it for 30 minutes. Make sure to flip the tofu halfway through. Once done, set aside.
6. While the tofu is cooking, place all of the dressing ingredients into a food processor and pulse until creamy. Pour over the bowl of vegetables and mix thoroughly to combine. Top with avocado, black sesame seeds, scallions and cooked tofu. Eat with chopsticks!

Spiralized Daikon Miso Noodles With Tofu

Ingredients

- 1 daikon radish, peeled
- 4 teaspoons miso paste
- 2 teaspoons chili paste (like Sriracha)
- ½ cup cubed tofu (drained and patted dry)
- ¼ cup sliced scallions
- ½ cup sliced shiitake mushrooms
- 1 bunch baby bok choy chopped with ends trimmed

Directions

1. Spiralize the daikon with Blade D. While spiralizing, apply light pressure to yield thinner noodles, something between a spaghetti and an angel hair pasta. When finished, trim the noodles with kitchen shears.
2. Build your cup: spread the miso and chili paste out on the bottom of the mason jar. Top with tofu, scallions, mushrooms, and bok choy. Top with spiralized veggies.
3. Refrigerate for up to 2 days for optimal freshness. When ready to serve, remove the top and then fill with boiling water. Using a large spoon, mix the paste on the bottom so it combines well. Seal and let steep for 2-3 minutes before enjoying.

Sweet Potato, Roasted Onion and Quinoa Bowl with Tahini-Maple Dressing

*Prep Time: 10 minutes | **Cook Time:** 30 minutes | **Total Time:** 40 minutes | **Servings:** 3-4*

Ingredients

- 1 small red onion, cut into 1" cube pieces
- 1 + 1/2 tablespoons of extra virgin olive oil (divided)
- salt and pepper
- 3/4 cup dry quinoa, rinsed
- 2 cups water
- 1 large sweet potato, peeled, Blade C
- ½ teaspoon garlic powder

For the dressing:

- 1.5 tablespoons tahini
- 3 tablespoons apple cider vinegar
- 1 tablespoon maple syrup
- 1 tablespoon extra virgin olive oil
- salt and pepper, to taste
- 1 tablespoon water + more if needed to thin

Instructions

1. Preheat the oven to 425 degrees. Place the onions a nonstick baking tray and drizzle with ½ tablespoon of the olive oil. Toss with hands to fully coat and season with salt and pepper. Roast for 20-25 minutes, tossing once.
2. While the onions are roasting, place the quinoa in a small saucepan with the water, cover, bring to a boil and then uncover and lower heat and let simmer for 15-20 minutes or until quinoa is fluffy.
3. Once you place quinoa on the stovetop, place a large skillet over medium heat and add in the rest of the olive oil. Once oil heats, add in the sweet potato noodles and season with salt, pepper and garlic powder. Cover and cook for 5-7 minutes, uncovering to toss occasionally, until sweet potatoes are cooked through.

4. While the sweet potatoes are cooking, combine all of the ingredients for the dressing into a bowl and whisk until combined. Add more water if needed to thin the dressing out to your preference.
5. Once onions, sweet potatoes and quinoa are done cooking, combine the quinoa, sweet potatoes and onions in a bowl and top with a drizzle of the dressing.

Szechuan Zucchini Noodles with Thai Ginger Steak

Prep time: 35 mins | Cook time: 20 mins | Total time: 55 mins | Serves: 4

Ingredients

For the dressing and steak:

- 2 large garlic cloves, minced
- 4 teaspoons minced ginger
- 3 tablespoons sesame oil
- 2 teaspoon rice wine vinegar
- 6 tablespoons soy sauce (low sodium)
- 2 teaspoons honey
- 1 teaspoon chili-garlic sauce (or Sriracha)
- ¼ cup tahini a
- ¾ pound skirt steak

For the rest:

- 3 large zucchinis
- 1 lime
- 4 scallions
- ¼ cup cashews
- 3 cups spiralized (or simply shredded) red cabbage
- salt and pepper, to taste
- 1 tablespoon freshly squeezed lime juice
- 1 cup cooked edamame beans

Instructions

1. Place all of the ingredients for the dressing EXCEPT for the tahini into a food processor and pulse until creamy. Pour half of the dressing out and into a zip-seal bag or shallow glass dish and keep the rest in the food

processor. In the bag or dish, add in the steak, toss to combine and refrigerate, letting marinate for at least 20 minutes. As for the tahini, add it into the food processor and pulse until creamy. Set aside and reserve.

2. While the steak marinates, spiralize the zucchini (Blade D) and set aside. Then, quarter the lime. Then, slice the scallions diagonally and set aside. Then, place a small skillet over medium-high heat. While it heats, roughly chop the cashews and once heated, add in the cashews and toast for about 5 minutes or until golden brown and fragrant and then set aside.

3. Heat a grill, cast iron skillet or grill pan to medium high - coat with cooking spray. Remove the steak from the marinade and shake off any excess and place the steak on the grill/skillet/pan. Season the steak with salt and pepper. Cook the steak for 2-4 minutes per side for medium rare (if the steak is thick, opt for 4 minutes, but if it's thin, opt for 2).

4. Transfer the steak to a cutting board and allow to rest for about 10 minutes. Slice the steak thinly against the grain.

5. While the steak rests, place a large skillet over medium-high heat and add in the olive oil. Once oil heats, add in the cabbage, and half of the scallions. Season with salt and pepper, lime juice and cook for 2 minutes or until cabbage begins to soften. Then, add in the zucchini noodles and half of the reserved dressing and the edamame. Cook for 3-5 minutes or until zucchini noodles are al dente. Pour in the remaining dressing, toss to warm and then divide into bowls.

6. Garnish each bowl with cashews and remaining scallions and top with steak. Serve with lime wedges.

Teriyaki Chicken, Bok Choy and Corn Zucchini Noodles

Prep Time: *10 minutes* | **Cook Time:** *15 minutes* | **Total Time:** *25 minutes* | **Servings:** *2*

Ingredients

- 3/4 cup cubed chicken breast
- 2-3 tbsp favorite teriyaki sauce (I use Annie Chun's)
- 1 ear of corn
- 1 large garlic clove, minced
- 1 pinch red pepper flakes
- 2 bunches of baby bok choy, bottom tough stems remove
- 1 tsp low-sodium soy sauce
- 1/2 cup chicken broth
- 2 medium zucchinis, Blade C

Instructions

1. Preheat the oven to 375 degrees. Place your chicken on a baking tray and pour over with teriyaki sauce. Mix together so that the chicken is covered. Let marinade while oven preheats. Once oven preheats, bake for 15-17 minutes or until chicken is cooked through.
2. While the chicken is marinading, cover your corn with water in a medium saucepan. Lightly salt the water and cover, bringing to a boil. Cook for another 2 minutes once boiled and then set aside to strain in a colander.
3. Place a large skillet over medium heat and coat with cooking spray. Once the skillet warms, add in the garlic and red pepper flakes. Let cook for 30 seconds and then add in the bok choy. Toss to combine and let cook for about 2 minutes or until bok choy begins to wilt. Then, shave off the kernels of the corn with a knife into the skillet. Then, add in the soy sauce and chicken broth.
4. Let reduce for about 3-5 minutes or until most of the liquid is gone. Then, add in the zucchini noodles. Toss to combine and let cook for 2-3 minutes, tossing frequently, or until noodles have softened to your preference. Remove from heat, place in the cooked chicken, toss to combine and then divide into bowls. Enjoy!

Teriyaki Pineapple Shrimp with Bell Pepper Noodles

Prep time: 30 mins | Cook time: 15 mins | Total time: 45 mins | Serves: 2

Ingredients

- ½ pound medium shrimp, defrosted, deveined, shells removed
- 2 medium red bell peppers
- salt and pepper, to taste
- ½ tablespoon extra virgin olive oil
- ½ tablespoon coconut oil
- 2 disc-shaped slices of pineapple about ¼ inch thick
- ½ cup diced scallions
- 1 teaspoon white sesame seeds, to garnish

For the teriyaki sauce:

- ¼ cup soy sauce (or coconut aminos or tamari)
- 1 tablespoon rice vinegar
- ½ tablespoon freshly grated ginger

- 1 garlic clove, pressed and minced
- 1 tablespoon sesame oil
- 1 tablespoon honey
- ¼ cup freshly squeezed orange juice
- 1 teaspoon sriracha/hot sauce or a pinch of red pepper flakes

Instructions

1. Mix together all of the ingredients for the teriyaki sauce into a medium mixing bowl and add in the shrimp. Cover and place in the refrigerator.
2. Spiralize the bell pepper, using Blade A. Trim the noodles with kitchen shears and set aside.
3. Place a large skillet over medium heat and add in the olive oil. Once oil heats, add in the bell peppers and season with salt and pepper. Cook, tossing occasionally, or until bell pepper noodles are softened and cooked to al dente or your preference. Set aside.
4. Place a grill pan over medium-high heat (or just use the same skillet, if you don't have a grill pan) and then add in the coconut oil. Let coconut oil melt and then add in the pineapple. Cook for 1 minute, flip over and cook another 1 minute or until pineapple is warmed through. Set aside on a cutting board.
5. Add in the marinated shrimp along with 1 tablespoon of extra marinade (leave the rest of the leftover marinade in the bowl) and cook for 2 minutes, flip and cook another 2-3 minutes or until opaque. When done cooking, pour over about 1 tablespoon of the marinade and let sizzle.
6. While shrimp cooks, slice the pineapple into bite-sized chunks.
7. When shrimp is done, set aside onto a plate and then add in the pineapple, bell pepper noodles, about 2 tablespoons of the leftover marinade and half of the scallions. Toss together to combine flavors.
8. Divide the bell peppers into bowls and top with shrimp and remaining scallions. Garnish with sesame seeds.

Teriyaki Zucchini "Fried" Noodles with Shrimp, Peppers, Onions and Broccoli

Prep Time: 15 minutes | Cook Time: 15 minutes | Total Time: 30 minutes | Servings: 1

Ingredients

- olive oil cooking spray

- 3/4 cup broccoli florets (about 5)
- 1 egg, beaten
- 3 tsp sesame oil
- 1/2 tsp freshly minced ginger
- 1 tsp minced garlic
- 1/2 red onion, sliced lengthwise into 1/2-inch thick "strips" (fajita-style)
- 1 small red bell pepper, sliced into 1/2-inch thick "strips" (fajita-style)
- salt and pepper, to taste
- 1/4 tsp (or one small pinch) of red pepper flakes
- 3 tbsp soy sauce
- 1 tsp honey
- 1 tsp rice vinegar
- 3-4 jump shrimp, defrosted, peeled and deveined
- 1.5 medium zucchini, Blade C
- 1/4 tsp white sesame seeds

Instructions

1. Place a large skillet (or wok) over medium heat and coat lightly with cooking spray. Add in the broccoli and cook for about 3-4 minutes, tossing frequently.
2. While the broccoli is cooking, place a small skillet over medium-low heat. Once the pan heats, add in the egg and scramble. Set aside.
3. Add in garlic, red onion, red bell pepper, ginger and 2 tsp of the sesame oil. Cook for about 2 minutes or until bell pepper begins to soften.
4. Season all the vegetables with salt, pepper and red pepper flakes. Toss to combine. While the mixture is cooking, combine the soy sauce, last tsp of sesame oil, rice vinegar and honey in a bowl and whisk to combine. Set aside.
5. Add the shrimp to the skillet and let cook for 2 minutes, flip over, and add in the soy sauce mixture, zucchini noodles and scrambled egg. Toss to combine and stir frequently for about 2 minutes, or until the shrimp are cooked through and the zucchini noodles have softened and absorb teriyaki sauce.
6. Pour out the stir fry mixture into a bowl or plate and top with white sesame seeds. Enjoy!

Teriyaki-Ginger Salmon with Sesame Zucchini Noodles

Prep time: 15 mins | Cook time: 15 mins | Total time: 30 mins | Serves: 1

Ingredients

- For the teriyaki marinade:
- 2 tablespoons soy sauce (or coconut aminos or tamari)
- ½ tablespoon rice vinegar
- ¼ teaspoon freshly grated ginger
- 1 small garlic clove, pressed and minced
- ½ tablespoon sesame oil
- ½ tablespoon honey
- ¼ teaspoon sriracha/hot sauce
- 2 tablespoons diced scallions

For the salmon:

- 3 oz salmon filet, skinless

For the pasta:

- 1 medium zucchini
- ½ tablespoon sesame oil
- 1 garlic clove, finely minced
- 1 teaspoon minced ginger
- 1 tablespoon diced scallions
- pinch of red pepper flakes
- 2 oz snow peas

Instructions

1. Preheat the oven to 425 degrees. Line a baking sheet with parchment paper.
2. Whisk together all of the ingredients for the teriyaki marinade and add to a zip-lock plastic bag or shallow dish. Add in the salmon, shake lightly to coat (or, if using a dish, flip over until all sides are coated) and place in the refrigerator for 15 minutes.
3. While salmon marinates, spiralize your zucchini with Blade C and set aside in the refrigerator. Prepare the rest of your ingredients.
4. Remove the salmon from the marinade and place on the prepared parchment paper and drizzle over with 1 tablespoon of leftover marinade. Bake the salmon for 15 minutes or until fish flakes easily with a fork.
5. After roasting the salmon for 10 minutes, place a large skillet over medium heat and add in the sesame oil. Once oil heats, add in the garlic, ginger, scallions and red pepper flakes. Let cook for 30 seconds or until fragrant and then add in the snap peas and zucchini noodles and cook for 3-5 minutes or until noodles soften to your preference.
6. Plate the zucchini noodles and serve alongside the baked salmon.

Thai Zucchini and Cucumber Noodle Collard Green Wraps with Almond Butter Sauce

*Prep Time: 20 minutes | **Servings:** 5 wraps*

Ingredients

For the wraps:

- 5 large collard green leaves, stems removed
- 1 large zucchini, Blade C, noodles trimmed
- 1 medium cucumber, Blade C, noodles trimmed
- 1/4 cup cilantro leaves
- 1 large bell pepper, sliced thinly (1/4" thick)
- 1/2 cup shredded red cabbage

For the peanut sauce:

- 1 teaspoon shredded ginger
- 1 garlic clove, mashed to a paste
- 1/2 cup creamy almond butter (I like Justin's)
- 1.5 tablespoon fresh lime juice
- 2 tablespoons soy sauce, low-sodium
- 1 teaspoon honey
- 2 tablespoons water

Instructions

1. In a food processor, blend all of the ingredients for the peanut sauce until creamy. Set aside.
2. Lay out a collard green leaf. Spread over with a heaping spoonful of the almond butter sauce and spread out, leaving 1" around the corners for rolling. On top, add the zucchini, cucumber, cilantro, bell pepper and cabbage. Carefully roll like a burrito and secure with toothpicks. Repeat with remaining collard green leaves and then slice both in half and serve with any remaining peanut sauce for dipping.

Tuna Zucchini Noodle Casserole

Prep Time: *15 minutes |* *Cook Time:* *40 minutes |* *Total Time:* *55 minutes |* *Servings:*
6

Ingredients

- 1.5 tablespoon extra virgin olive oil
- 2 garlic cloves, minced
- ¼ teaspoon red pepper flakes
- 1 small white onion, diced
- 3 celery stalks, diced
- 8oz chopped baby bella mushrooms
- ½ teaspoon dried thyme flakes
- ½ teaspoon dried oregano flakes
- salt and pepper, to taste
- 1/2 cup chicken broth
- 1/3 cup grated parmesan cheese
- 3 5-ounce cans of tuna in water, drained
- 3 medium zucchinis, Blade A

For the breadcrumbs:

- 1/2 cup almond meal
- 1 tablespoon water
- 1/4 teaspoon dried oregano flakes
- 1/4 teaspoon dried basil flakes
- 1/4 teaspoon dried parsley flakes
- 1/4 teaspoon garlic powder

Instructions

1. Preheat the oven to 375 degrees and coat a 4-quart casserole dish with cooking spray. Set aside.
2. Place a large pot over medium heat and add in the olive oil. Once the oil heats, add in the garlic and red pepper flakes and cook for 30 seconds or until fragrant.
3. Add in the onions and cook until translucent, about 2-3 minutes. Once translucent, add in the celery, mushrooms and season with thyme, oregano and salt and pepper.
4. Cook for 5-7 minutes, stirring occasionally. Halfway through, add in the chicken broth and cook until reduced halfway. Once reduced halfway, stir in the parmesan cheese.
5. While the mixture is cooking, place your ingredients for the breadcrumbs in a bowl. Season with salt and pepper generously and then toss to

combine and then add in the water. Using your fingers, roll like a dough until all of the meal is formed into dough. Set aside.

6. Add in the tuna and cook for 1 minute, just to heat up the fish. Pour the mixture into the prepared casserole dish.
7. Add the zucchini noodles to the dish and lightly toss around until the mixture evenly spreads throughout the noodles.
8. Take the almond meal "dough" and crumble into breadcrumbs over the casserole, evenly until all of the "dough" is used.
9. Cover the casserole with tin foil and bake for 20 minutes. Remove the tinfoil and bake 10 more minutes to get the breadcrumbs browned.
10. Remove the casserole from the oven, pour and excess water out into a sink and serve.

Vegan Red Coconut Curry with Brussels Sprouts, Edamame and Spiralized Rutabaga

Prep time: 15 mins | Cook time: 20 mins | Total time: 35 mins | Serves: 4

Ingredients

- 1 tablespoon coconut oil
- 12 oz sliced brussels sprouts
- 2 garlic cloves, minced
- 2 teaspoons minced ginger
- 3 scallions, diced (white and green parts divided)
- 3 teaspoons Thai red curry paste
- 1 13.5-ounce lite coconut milk
- 3 cups vegetable broth
- 1 medium to large rutabaga, Blade D, noodles trimmed
- 1 cup frozen edamame, thawed
- handful of thai basil leaves or cilantro

Instructions

1. Heat the oil in a large pot over medium-high heat, and once oil heats, add the brussels sprouts, garlic, ginger, and white part of the scallions. Cook for 2 minutes or until brussels sprouts turn bright green. Add in the curry paste (be careful – the paste will fry, which is good, but can get on your clothes. You may want to move the skillet off heat while you stir the paste to reduce heat.)

2.   Add in the coconut milk, vegetable broth, stir and bring to a boil. Once boiling, add in the rutabaga noodles and edamame. Reduce heat to a low simmer and cover and let cook for 7-10 minutes or until rutabaga is cooked to al dente.
3.   Portion into bowls and garnish with green scallions, cilantro or thai basil and serve.

Vegan Zucchini Noodle Japchae

Prep Time: *10 minutes* | **Cook Time:** *15 minutes* | **Total Time:** *23 minutes* | **Servings:** *2*

Ingredients

- 2.5 packed cups spinach
- 1 tablespoon extra virgin olive oil (or oil of choice)
- 1 carrot, peeled, cut into matchsticks and halved
- ½ white onion, thinly sliced
- 1 3.5oz container shiitake mushrooms, stems removed, tops sliced into ½" pieces
- 1 large zucchini (or 2 medium), Blade C
- toasted sesame seeds, to garnish (about ¼ tsp)

For the sauce:

- 1 tablespoon sesame oil
- 2 teaspoon honey
- 2 tablespoons soy sauce
- ½ teaspoon toasted sesame seeds

Instructions

1.   Bring a small pot to a boil. While waiting to boil, combine all ingredients for the sauce, whisk together and set aside. Once water boils, add in the spinach for 30 seconds or until wilted and then transfer with a slotted spoon to a plate and gently squeeze out excess water. Set aside.
2.   Heat a large skillet over medium-heat and once heated, add in the olive oil. Once oil heats, add in the onion, carrots and shiitake mushrooms and cover and cook for 5-7 minutes or until mushrooms are wilted and carrots have mostly softened.

3. Add in the zucchini noodles and toss for 2-3 minutes or until zucchini is cooked to al dente. Pour the noodle mixture into a colander and toss to let excess moisture drain out. Place the drained noodle mixture back into the skillet.
4. Add in the spinach and pour in the sauce. Toss to combine all the flavors and warm the sauce, about 1 minute. Transfer to plates and garnish with sesame seeds.

Vegetable and Tofu Coconut Red Curry Daikon Noodles

Prep Time: 25 minutes | Cook Time: 20 minutes | Total Time: 45 minutes | Servings: 4

Ingredients

- ½ tablespoon extra virgin olive oil
- 2 garlic cloves, minced
- 1 tablespoon freshly minced ginger
- 5 scallions, whites and greens separated and then sliced on an angle
- 2 tablespoons red curry paste
- ½ tablespoon curry powder
- 1 15oz can coconut milk (shaken)
- 1 red bell pepper, sliced into ¼" strips
- 1 yellow or orange bell pepper, sliced into ¼" strips
- 2 cups broccoli florets
- 12oz extra firm tofu
- 1 large daikon, peeled, Blade B (about 1 lb)
- sriracha, to taste (1 tablespoon or more)
- 1/4 cup roughly chopped cilantro

Instructions

1. Pour the contents of the coconut milk into a medium mixing bowl and whisk together with a fork until the oil and thick parts combine. Set aside.
2. Remove the tofu from its package. Place on top of two layers of paper towels. Place two more layers of paper towels on top and press firmly down to release extra moisture. Repeat until all excess moisture is released and then cut into ½" cubes. Pat dry and set aside.
3. Heat the oil in a large pot over medium-high heat. Add in the garlic, ginger, scallion whites, curry paste and curry powder. Cook, stirring often, until fragrant, about 1-2 minutes.

4. Add the peppers and broccoli and sauté for 3-5 minutes or until vegetables begin to soften. Add in the coconut milk and then raise heat to bring to a simmer. Once simmering, reduce heat to medium-low and add in the tofu.
5. Cook at a simmer until vegetables are crisp-tender, about 5 minutes and then add in the daikon noodles and cook for another 5 minutes or until al dente.
6. When ready, if desired, add in sriracha, stir in cilantro and serve, garnished with green scallions.

Vegetarian Zucchini Noodle Pad Thai

Prep Time: 10 minutes | *Cook Time:* 15 minutes | *Total Time:* 25 minutes | *Servings:* 2

Ingredients

- 2 whole eggs
- 1/4 cup roasted salted peanuts
- 1/2 tbsp peanut oil (or oil of choice)
- 1 garlic clove, minced
- 1 shallot, minced
- 1 tbsp coconut flour
- 1 tbsp roughly chopped cilantro + whole cilantro leaves to garnish
- 2 medium zucchinis, Blade C

For the sauce:

- 2 tbsp freshly squeezed lime juice
- 1 tbsp fish sauce (or hoisin sauce, if you're strict vegetarian)
- 1/2 tbsp soy sauce
- 1 tbsp chili sauce (I used Thai chili garlic sauce)
- 1 tsp honey

Instructions

1. Scramble the eggs and set aside.
2. Place all of the ingredients for the sauce into a bowl, whisk together and set aside.
3. Place the peanuts into a food processor and pulse until lightly ground (no big peanuts should remain, but it shouldn't be powdery). Set aside.

4. Place a large skillet over medium heat. Add in oil, garlic and shallots. Cook for about 1-2 minutes, stirring frequently, until the shallots begin to soften. Add in the sauce and whisk quickly so that the flour dissolves and the sauce thickens. Cook for 2-3 minutes or until sauce is reduced and thick.
5. Once the sauce is thick, add in the zucchini noodles and cilantro and stir to combine thoroughly.
6. Cook for about 2 minutes or until noodles soften and then add in the scrambled eggs and ground peanuts. Cook for about 30 seconds, tossing to fully combine.
7. Plate onto dishes and garnish with cilantro leaves. Serve with lime wedges.

Zucchini Noodle Collard Green Wrap

Prep Time: *10 minutes* | **Total Time:** *10 minutes* | **Servings: 1**

Ingredients

- 1 large collard green leaf
- 2 tablespoons hummus
- 4-5 thin slices of cucumber
- 4-5 thin slices of red onion
- 3-4 thin slices of avocado
- 1/4 cup alfalfa sprouts
- 1/2 cup zucchini noodles

Instructions

1. Lay down a collard green leaf. Slice the tough stem off the bottom and discard.
2. Spread out the hummus on the leaf with the back of a spoon or a knife. Top with cucumber slices, then onion slices and then avocado slices. Top with sprouts and then top with zucchini noodles.
3. Pinching in the sides as you go, roll the burrito tightly. Pierce with toothpicks, cut in half and enjoy.

Chapter 8: Pasta

***

"Leftovers" Zucchini Pasta (featuring Garlic Green Beans & Vegan Whole Wheat Stuffing)

Prep Time: *10 minutes* | **Cook Time:** *10 minutes* | **Total Time:** *20 minutes* | **Servings:** *4*

Ingredients

- 4 pieces of whole wheat toast, cubed
- 1 tbsp olive oil
- 1 garlic clove, minced
- 2 celery stalks, diced
- 1/2 yellow onion, diced
- 4 sprigs of thyme, petals removed
- 1.5 tbsp freshly chopped parsley
- 3/4 cup vegetable broth
- pepper, to taste

Directions

1. Place a large skillet over medium-low heat and add in the bread cubes. Cook for about 2 minutes and then flip over and cook another 2 minutes or until bread is toasted and browned. Set aside in a bowl.
2. In the same skillet, add in the olive oil. Once oil heats, add in the garlic and cook for 30 seconds. Then, add in the celery and onion and cook for 3-4 minutes or until vegetables soften.
3. Once the veggies soften, add in the thyme and parsley and stir to combine.
4. Add in the toasted bread cubes and vegetable broth and cook until bread becomes completely softened from absorbing the broth. If the bread still appears rough, add more vegetable broth.
5. Once done, plate into a serving bowl, season with pepper and enjoy!

Almond-Gouda Sweet Potato Pasta with Baked Chicken

Prep Time: *15 minutes* | **Cook Time:** *25 minutes* | **Total Time:** *40 minutes* | **Servings:** *1*

Ingredients

For the sauce:

- 1 tbsp vegan butter (I prefer Earth Balance)
- 1/4 tsp finely minced garlic
- 1 tbsp whole wheat flour
- 3/4-1 cup unsweetened almond milk
- salt and pepper, to taste
- 1/2 cup shredded gouda cheese

For the rest:

- olive oil cooking spray
- 1/2 chicken breast
- 1 tbsp olive oil
- salt and pepper, to taste
- 1 pinch oregano flakes
- 1 medium sweet potato, peeled, Blade C
- 1 tsp garlic powder

Directions

1. Preheat the oven to 350 degrees.
2. Coat a baking tray with cooking spray. Place the chicken breast on the tray and drizzle with half of the olive oil. Massage the oil into the chicken and season with salt, pepper and oregano.
3. Bake the chicken for 20-25 minutes. After 20 minutes, remove from oven and slice open to see if the meat is white. If it's still pink, cook for another 5 minutes. If it's white, remove from the oven and set aside. If you don't want a big slice through your chicken, take out at 25 minutes to be safe.
4. While the chicken is cooking, place a large skillet over medium heat, coat with cooking spray and add in the sweet potato noodles. Season with salt, pepper and garlic powder and cook for 5-10 minutes, tossing frequently, or until noodles have softened to your preference.
5. Once the noodles are done, place into a bowl or plate and cover with tin foil.
6. Place a small saucepan over medium heat. Once heated, add in the butter and garlic and let fully melt.
7. Add in the flour and blend completely with the vegan butter.
8. Add in the milk and stir constantly until mixture thickens. Season with salt and pepper.
9. Add in the cheese and keep stirring until it completely melts. Keep on the heat.

10. Top the sweet potato noodles with the chicken breast.
11. Give the sauce a quick stir and use a ladle or spoon to pour the sauce lightly over the noodles.
12. Enjoy!

Aloo Gobi with Potato Noodles

Prep Time: 20 minutes | Cook Time: 20 minutes | Total Time: 40 minutes | Servings: 4

Ingredients

- 1 cauliflower head, chopped into florets*
- 1/2 tablespoon extra virgin olive oil
- 1 small onion, finely chopped*
- 1 large garlic clove, minced*
- 1 tablespoon minced ginger*
- 20 raw cashews, soaked in water for at least 2 hours (a little less than 1/4 cup)
- 1 14oz can diced tomatoes
- 1 bay leaf
- 1/4 teaspoon chili powder
- 1/4 teaspoon turmeric powder
- ¼ teaspoon garam masala
- 1/2 teaspoon ground coriander
- 1/4 teaspoon ground cumin
- 1 cup vegetable broth
- 1 large red potato, Blade C, noodles trimmed*
- salt and pepper, to taste
- 1 tablespoon chopped parsley, to garnish

Directions

1. Fill a large pot half-way with water and a pinch of salt and bring to a boil. Once boiling, add in the cauliflower and cook until slightly softened, but still firm, about 3 minutes. Once cooked, drain into a colander and set aside.
2. Back in the same pot, add in the olive oil and once heated, add in the onion, garlic and ginger and cook until onions are translucent, about 3-5 minutes.
3. While onions cook, add the cashews to a high-speed blender and process until creamy and smooth. Set aside.

4. Then, add in the tomatoes, bay leaf and cook for about 3 minutes. Then, add in the cashew cream, chili, turmeric, garam masala, coriander and cumin. Stir well to combine and let cook for 2 minutes for flavors to develop. Then, add in broth, potatoes and cauliflower, season with salt and pepper, stir and cover, cooking for 10 minutes or until potato noodles are al dente.
5. When done, remove bay leaf and divide the mixture into bowls and serve, garnished with parsley.

Autumn Harvest Roasted Butternut Squash Pasta

Prep Time: *20 minutes |* **Cook Time:** *45 minutes |* **Total Time:** *1 hour 5 minutes |*
Servings: 4

Ingredients

- 1 acorn squash, halved, seeds scooped out/removed
- 1 butternut squash, peeled
- cooking spray
- 2 tbsp olive oil + more for drizzling
- 2 garlic cloves, minced
- 1 cup diced ham
- 1/2 cup crushed pecans
- 1 cup diced celery
- 1/3 cup dried cranberries
- 3/4 cup feta cheese
- 1 cup kohlrabi greens (or other types of greens)
- 3/4 cup chopped red onion
- salt and pepper, to taste

Directions

1. Preheat the oven to 400 degrees.
2. Drizzle the cut-side of the acorn squash with olive oil and rub in. Place the squash cut-side down onto a baking tray coated with cooking spray. Place in the oven and bake for 35-40 minutes or until easily pierced with a fork. When done, set aside to cool.
3. While acorn squash is roasting, take your peeled butternut squash and chop off the bulbous end. Spiralize the body, using Blade C.
4. Place the spiralized noodles in a bowl and drizzle with olive oil. Mix together to combine and spread out on a baking tray lined with tinfoil.

Season with salt and pepper and when the acorn squash is done cooking, place into the oven and roast for 5-7 minutes or until noodles soften. When done, take out and set aside.

5. When you place the butternut squash noodles into the oven, place a large saucepan over medium-low heat and add in the 2 tbsp of olive oil.

6. Once the oil heats, add in the garlic and cook for 30 seconds. Add in the red onion and celery. Cook for 2 minutes or until vegetables soften. Add in the kohlrabi greens, ham, and season with salt and pepper.

7. When the noodles are done, add them into the saucepan with the cranberries and stir to combine.

8. Plate the mixture into four separate bowls and top each evenly with feta and pecans.

9. Take your acorn squash and cut each half into four pieces, lengthwise. Top each bowl of pasta with two acorn squash pieces.

10. Enjoy!

Avocado Pesto with Zucchini Pasta

"This is a delicious low-carb alternative to your standard pesto pasta. Filled with vegetables, protein and healthy fat, it is sure to satisfy every craving!"

Servings: 2 | Prep: 25 m | Cook: 20 m | Ready In: 50 m

Ingredients

- 3 zucchini, trimmed
- 1 ripe avocado - peeled, halved, and pitted
- 5 tablespoons pesto, or more to taste
- 1 skinless, boneless chicken breast
- 1/2 teaspoon paprika
- 1 pinch salt and black pepper to taste olive oil, divided
- 2 tablespoons grated Parmesan cheese (optional)

Directions

- Make zucchini noodles using a spiralizer.
- Mash avocado in a small bowl and mix in pesto until smooth.
- Flatten chicken breast with a meat hammer. Season on both sides with paprika, salt, and black pepper.
- Heat 1 tablespoon olive oil in a large skillet over medium heat. Cook chicken until golden and an instant-read thermometer inserted into the

center reads at least 165 degrees F (74 degrees C), about 6 minutes per side. Cool until easily handled, about 5 minutes; dice into small pieces.
- Heat remaining 1 tablespoon olive oil in a large skillet over medium heat. Add zucchini noodles; cook and stir until softened, 5 to 7 minutes. Stir in avocado pesto mixture and diced chicken; cook until flavors combine, 3 to 5 minutes. Sprinkle Parmesan cheese on top before serving.

Nutritional Information
- Calories:609 kcal 30%
- Fat: 49.4 g 76%
- Carbs: 21.5g 7%
- Protein: 26.8 g 54%
- Cholesterol: 50 mg 17%
- Sodium: 518 mg 21%

Baked Chicken and Kale Zucchini Pasta

Prep Time: *10 minutes* | **Cook Time:** *20 minutes* | **Total Time:** *30 minutes* | **Servings:** *1*

Ingredients
- 1/2 one chicken breast (about 70-75 g), slivered into strips
- salt and pepper, to taste
- 1 tsp oregano flakes
- olive oil cooking spray
- 1 cup of chopped kale
- 1 large zucchini, Blade C
- 1 pinch red pepper flakes
- 1/2 tsp garlic powder
- 1 lemon wedge

Directions
1. Preheat the oven to 350 degrees.
2. Lightly coat a baking tray with the cooking spray and add in the chicken strips. Season with salt, pepper and oregano flakes. Bake for 15-20 minutes or until chicken is no longer pink on the inside. Once done, remove from oven and set aside.

3. After 10 minutes of cooking the chicken, add a large skillet over medium heat. Let the pan heat up and coat lightly with cooking spray. Add in the kale and cook for about 3 minutes or until mostly wilted.
4. Add in the zucchini noodles, red pepper flakes, garlic powder, juice from the lemon wedge and toss to combine. Cook, stirring frequently, for about 3 minutes or until zucchini noodles soften.
5. Add the chicken to the zucchini pasta, toss to combine and plate. Enjoy!

Baked Zucchini Pasta with Pancetta, Olives and Broccoli

Prep Time: 15 minutes | *Cook Time:* 45 minutes | *Total Time:* 1 hour | *Servings:* 6

Ingredients

- 1-1.5 pounds plum tomatoes, halved lengthwise
- 3 garlic cloves, crushed
- 2 thyme sprigs
- ½ cup torn basil leaves + 1 basil sprig
- 2 tbsp extra virgin olive oil
- salt and pepper
- 1-1.5 lb broccoli, cut into small florets
- 4oz finely diced pancetta
- ¼ tsp red pepper flakes
- 1 large red onion, finely chopped
- 1 cup pitted green olives
- 2 large zucchinis, Blade A, noodles trimmed
- 1 cup fresh ricotta cheese
- 1/2 cup parmigiano-reggiano cheese

Directions

1. Preheat the oven to 425 degrees and coat a 9 x 13 baking dish and fill with zucchini noodles. Set aside.
2. On a baking tray, toss the tomatoes, garlic, thyme and basil sprigs with 1 tablespoon of the olive oil and season with salt and pepper. Roast for 17-20 minutes, until softened and browned slightly. Set aside to cook once done.
3. While the tomatoes are roasting, place the broccoli in another baking sheet and lightly spray with olive oil cooking spray and season with salt and pepper. Roast for 15 minutes or until crisp-tender. Leave the oven on and set broccoli aside.
4. Once the tomatoes are done, place a large skillet over medium heat and add in the other tablespoon of olive oil. Once the oil heats, add in the

pancetta and onion and cook for 5 minutes or until pancetta browns and onions soften.

5. While the pancetta is cooking, roughly chop the tomatoes and garlic, reserving all juices.

6. Once the pancetta and onions are done, add in the olives, chopped tomatoes (with juices and garlic) and stir to combine. Set aside in a large mixing bowl with the torn basil, cooked broccoli, pancetta mixture, ricotta cheese and half of the parmigiano-reggiano cheese. Season with salt and pepper, toss to combine thoroughly and then transfer the mixture to the prepared baking dish with the zucchini noodles. Toss to combine so that all noodles are coated with the mixture.

7. Sprinkle the remaining parmigiano-reggiano cheese on top and bake for 15-20 minutes, until browned on top

Baked Zucchini Spaghetti

Prep Time: 6 minutes | Cook Time: 27 minutes | Total Time: 33 minutes | Servings: 3

Ingredients

- 1 mozzarella cheese ball, chopped into 1 cup of small "chunks" or 1 cup shredded mozzarella cheese
- All of the ingredients from Bikini Bolognese
- 3 baking bowls (pictured below)

Directions

1. Put the oven to broil.
2. Cook Bikini Bolognese, according to the recipe. Once the zucchini is cooked, divide Bikini Bolognese among the baking bowls.
3. Top each bowl with even amounts of mozzarella cheese.
4. Put in the oven for 3 minutes, monitoring to make sure the cheese melts but does not burn. If there is a faint browning, it's done!

Balsamic Roasted Pearl Onions, Asparagus & Toasted Pine Nuts with Zucchini Pasta

Prep Time: 10 minutes | Cook Time: 25 minutes | Total Time: 35 minutes | Servings: 2

Ingredients

- 6 asparagus stalks
- olive oil, to drizzle
- 8 white pearl onions, peeled*
- 1/4 cup balsamic vinegar
- 1/4 tsp dried rosemary
- 1/2 tsp dried thyme
- 1.5 tbsp pine nuts
- 1.5 tbsp olive oil
- 1 large garlic clove, minced
- 1/4 tsp red pepper flakes
- 3 zucchinis, Blade A
- 1 tbsp grated parmesan cheese
- 1 tbsp freshly chopped parsley

Directions

1. Preheat the oven to 375 degrees. Take your asparagus, snap off the bottoms and slice them into 2" pieces.
2. On a baking tray, place in your asparagus pieces and drizzle with olive oil. Mix together to coat and set aside.
3. Place the pearl onions and balsamic vinegar in a bowl and toss to combine. Place the pearl onions on the baking tray with the asparagus.
4. Season the asparagus and onions with salt, pepper, thyme and rosemary. Roast the vegetables in the oven for 25 minutes. Toss halfway through.
5. Place a small skillet over medium heat and add in the pine nuts. Let cook for a couple minutes. Once you can smell the pine nuts toasting, flip them over and cook another couple minutes or until lightly browned. Transfer to a bowl and set aside.
6. 20 minutes into roasting the vegetables, place a large skillet over medium heat and add in the olive oil. Then, add in the garlic, cook for 30 seconds and then add in the red pepper flakes and zucchini noodles. Toss the zucchini noodles for 2-3 minutes or until tender.
7. When done, divide the noodles into two bowls and top each with even amounts of asparagus and pearl onions. Top with 1/2 tbsp of parmesan cheese per bowl. Garnish each with parsley and pine nuts.

Basil Pomodoro Zucchini Pasta with Chicken

Prep Time: 10 minutes | Cook Time: 20 minutes | Total Time: 30 minutes | Servings: 2

Ingredients

- 1 tablespoon extra virgin olive oil
- 1/2 pound boneless chicken breasts, roughly cubed
- salt and pepper, to taste
- 1/4 teaspoon garlic powder
- 1 large clove of garlic, minced
- 1/3 cup diced white onions
- 1 14oz can diced tomatoes (or crushed tomatoes) with juices
- 1-1.5 tablespoon chopped basil
- 2 medium zucchinis, Blade C, noodles trimmed

Directions

1. Place a pot/saucepan over medium heat and add in the olive oil. Once the oil heats, add in the chicken. Season with salt, pepper and garlic powder. Cook for 3 minutes and then flip over, cooking another 3-5 minutes or until chicken is cooked through and no longer pink on the inside.
2. Then, add in the garlic and onions and cook for 2-3 minutes or until onions start to soften and become translucent. Then, add in the canned tomatoes and roughly crush the tomatoes with a potato masher or the back of a fork. Bring to a boil and then reduce heat and simmer. Season with salt and pepper and let cook for 5 minutes, add in the basil and cook for another 5-10 minutes or until most of the liquid has evaporated and it is thicker, suitable for cooking with zucchini noodles. Add in the zucchini noodles and toss for 2-3 minutes or until noodles are al dente.
3. Divide into bowls.

Basil Zucchini Spaghetti with Cheesy Broiled Tomatoes

Prep time: 15 mins | Cook time: 10 mins | Total time: 25 mins | Serves: 4

Ingredients

- 2 large beefsteak tomatoes, each cut into 4 thick slices
- 1 tablespoon olive oil, plus more for lining the baking sheet
- salt and pepper, to taste
- 4 ounces fresh mozzarella, grated
- 2 tablespoons grated Parmesan cheese, plus more for garnish (optional)
- 1 large garlic clove, minced
- ¼ teaspoon crushed red pepper
- 3 medium zucchinis, Blade C, noodles trimmed
- ⅓ cup sliced fresh basil leaves + more to garnish

Directions

1. Heat the broiler.
2. Meanwhile, arrange the tomato slices in a single layer on a lightly oiled rimmed baking sheet. Season the tomatoes with salt and pepper. Dividing evenly, sprinkle the slices with the mozzarella and Parmesan. Broil until the cheese is bubbly and golden, 3 to 5 minutes.
3. Meanwhile, place a large skillet over medium heat and add in the oil. Once oil heats, add in the garlic and red pepper, cooking for 30 seconds. Then, add in the zucchini noodles, basil and season with more pepper. Cook for 3 minutes or until al dente.
4. Divide the zucchini noodle mixture onto plates and top each with the broiled tomatoes and more cheese, if desired. Garnish with basil.

Basil-Lemon Mediterranean Zucchini Pasta

Prep Time: 10 minutes | *Cook Time*: 5 minutes | *Servings: 1*

Ingredients

- 1.5 zucchinis, Blade C
- 1/4 wedge of lemon
- 5 basil leaves, chopped
- 3 sundried tomatoes, chopped into slivers
- ½ cup chickpeas
- 1 tbsp capers
- 4 pitless kalamata olives, halved
- 3 artichoke hearts from a can, drained & patted dry
- 1 tbsp olive oil

- salt and pepper, to taste
- 1 tsp dried oregano flakes
- 1 pinch red pepper flakes
- 1 garlic clove, minced

Directions

1. Season artichokes with salt and pepper. Heat up a grill pan or George Forman grill and cook the 'chokes for about 5 minutes or until they are slightly browned.
2. Place a large skillet over medium-low heat and add the olive oil. Once the oil heats, add in the garlic and cook for 30 seconds, stirring frequently. Add in the red pepper flakes and cook for 30 seconds.
3. Add in the zucchini noodles, chickpeas, artichokes, oregano flakes, sundried tomatoes, capers, kalamata olives, and basil. Season with salt and pepper and cook for about 2-3 minutes, stirring frequently, until zucchini softens and heats through.
4. Pour into a bowl and squeeze lemon over the bowl. Enjoy!

BBQ Shredded Chicken and Squash Noodle Bowls with Avocado-Cilantro Mash

Prep time: 20 mins | Cook time: 20 mins | Total time: 40 mins | Serves: 2

Ingredients

For the chicken:

- ½ pound boneless skinless chicken breast
- ¼ cup favorite BBQ sauce (I use Tessemae's Matty's BBQ Sauce)
- For the pasta:
- ½ tablespoon extra virgin olive oil
- 1 garlic clove, minced
- 1 pinch red pepper flakes
- 2 medium yellow patty pan squashes, Blade D, noodles trimmed
- For the avocado mash:
- 1 avocado, peeled, pitted, insides cubed and lightly mashed with a fork
- 1 tablespoon chopped cilantro
- 1 tablespoon freshly squeezed lime juice
- Salt and pepper, to taste

Directions

1. Place the chicken breast into a medium saucepan and pour in enough water to cover. Place over medium heat, bring to a boil, and simmer until the thickest part of the breast meat is no longer pink, 10 to 12 minutes. Transfer the chicken to a bowl and then shred the chicken, using two forks. Transfer the shredded chicken to a medium mixing bowl.
2. While the chicken is cooking, combine all of the ingredients for the avocado mash into a bowl and mix together until avocado is chunky-smooth. Season with salt and pepper and set aside.
3. A few minutes before the chicken is done, place a small pot over medium heat and add in the BBQ sauce, cooking until heated through, about 2 minutes.
4. Pour the heated BBQ sauce into the bowl with the chicken and stir until chicken is coated in the sauce. Set aside.
5. Place a large skillet over medium-high heat and add in the olive oil. Once oil heats, add in the garlic and red pepper flakes and cook for 30 seconds or until fragrant. Then, add in the squash noodles and cook for 2-3 minutes or until al dente (or cooked to your preference.)
6. Plate the squash noodles into two bowls and top with chicken and avocado mash.

Beef Taco Zucchini Spaghetti

Prep Time: *10 minutes* | **Cook Time:** *20 minutes* | **Servings:** *2*

Ingredients

- 3 zucchinis, Blade C
- 1/2 pound of ground beef (the leaner the better!)
- 1 large garlic clove
- 1 pinch of crushed red pepper flakes
- 1 tsp dried oregano fakes
- 1 tbsp olive oil
- 1/3 cup red onion, chopped
- 1/4 cup chicken broth, low-sodium
- 2 medium tomatoes, seeds removed and chopped
- 1 avocado, insides cubed and removed
- 1/3 cup black beans
- 2 tbsp fresh cilantro, chopped
- 1/3 cup queso fresco, crumbled

- 1 ear of corn
- 1/2 cup black olives, quartered
- salt and pepper

Directions

1. Place a saucepan filled with enough water to cover the ear of corn. Bring to a boil and cook for about 2 minutes or until the corn is easily pierced with a fork. Remove and pour out over a colander and set aside.
2. Place a large skillet over medium-low heat. Add in olive oil. Once oil heats, add in garlic and cook for 1 minute. Add in red pepper flakes and onions and cook, stirring frequently, until onions begin to soften and turn translucent. Once done, push to the side and add in the beef and sprinkle with oregano.
3. Cook the beef until it's no longer pink and then mix with the onions and garlic. Cook for about 1 minute together and add in the chicken broth. Raise the heat to medium and cook until most of the liquid evaporates. Add in the tomatoes, season with salt and pepper and cook, stirring frequently for about 2 minutes.
4. Add in the cilantro, stir to combine and cook for 30 seconds.
5. Shave the kernels off the corn over the skillet (with a knife) and then add in the avocado, beans, olives and zucchini pasta. Cook for about 3 minutes or until zucchini pasta softens and heats through.
6. Plate onto dishes and top with queso fresco!

Beet Noodle Pumpkin Alfredo with Spiced Pecans

Prep Time: *20 minutes* | **Cook Time:** *20 minutes* | **Total Time:** *40 minutes* | **Servings:** *4-6*

Ingredients

For the spiced pecans:

- ½ cup whole pecans
- 1 tablespoon maple syrup
- ¼ teaspoon cinnamon
- ¼ teaspoon cayenne
- salt, to taste

For the alfredo pasta:

- 4 beets, peeled, Blade C, noodles trimmed
- salt and pepper, to taste
- ½ tablespoon extra virgin olive oil
- 4 sage leaves
- Pinch of red pepper flakes
- ¼ cup diced shallots
- 2 garlic cloves, minced
- ½ cup pumpkin puree
- ¼ teaspoon ground cinnamon
- 1 pinch of nutmeg, to taste
- ½ cup raw cashews, soaked for at least 2 hours and then drained
- ½ - 1 tablespoon nutritional yeast
- ½ cup low-sodium vegetable broth + more for thinning as needed
- freshly minced parsley, to garnish

Directions

1. Preheat the oven to 425 degrees. In a bowl, whisk together the maple syrup with the cinnamon, cayenne and season lightly with salt. It should create a paste. Add the pecans into the mixture. Stir to combine thoroughly.
2. Take out two baking sheets and line both with parchment paper. On one, lay the dressed pecans out on a parchment paper lined baking tray and bake for 5 minutes, flip over and bake another 5 minutes. Remove from the oven and set aside. Let the pecans cool for at least 5 minutes before you use them in the rest of the recipe (they will become less sticky the longer they sit.)
3. Five minutes after the pecans are in the oven, lay out the beet noodles on the other lined baking sheet. Coat with cooking spray and season with salt and pepper. Bake for 5-10 minutes (I kept mine in for 7) or until your desired al dente consistency.
4. After both the pecans and beets are in the oven, place a large skillet over medium heat and add in the olive oil. Once oil heats, add in the sage and cook until crispy. Remove with a slotted spoon and transfer to a small, paper-towel lined plate.
5. Place the red pepper flakes and shallots and garlic immediately into the skillet and cook for 2-3 minutes or until translucent, stirring constantly to avoid burning. Then, add in pumpkin puree, season with salt, pepper, nutmeg, cinnamon and crumble in the sage. Let cook for 1-2 minutes for flavors to develop, again stirring constantly.
6. In a high-speed blender, combine the pumpkin mixture, cashews, nutritional yeast (start with ½ tablespoon and add more to your preference) and vegetable broth. Pulse until creamy and add more vegetable broth, if needed. Taste and adjust (not cheesy enough? More nutritional yeast? Not salty enough? More salt.)

7. Divide the beet noodles into bowls and top with a scoop of the pumpkin alfredo sauce (about 1/3 – ½ cup). Top with parsley and pecans.

Beet Noodles with Tomatoes, Feta and Bacon

Prep time: 15 mins | Cook time: 20 mins | Total time: 35 mins | Serves: 2

Ingredients

- 3-4 strips of bacon of choice
- 1 large (or 2 medium) red beets, peeled, Blade C/D
- ½ cup cherry tomatoes
- 1 large garlic clove, finely minced
- salt and pepper, to taste
- 1 tablespoon chopped parsley, to garnish
- 2-3 tablespoons crumbled feta cheese

Directions

1. Place a large skillet over medium-high heat and coat with cooking spray. Once heated, add in the bacon strips and cook until crisp, about 7 minutes. Transfer to a paper towel lined plate.
2. Remove about half of the bacon fat from the skillet and set the skillet aside for 1-2 minutes to cool down and then place back over heat. Add in the beet noodles and toss for 1 minute or until the noodles begin to wilt. Then, add in the tomatoes, garlic, salt, pepper and cover and let cook for 5-7 minutes, uncovering occasionally to toss, or until beet noodles are wilted and cooked to al dente.
3. Once done, transfer the beet noodle mixture to a serving platter, crumble over with the bacon and garnish with parsley and feta. Serve immediately.

Bikini Bolognese

Prep Time: 10 minutes | Cook Time: 25 minutes | Total Time: 35 minutes | Servings: 2

Ingredients

- 2-2.5 large zucchinis, Blade C
- 1/2 lb ground turkey
- 2 tbsp olive oil
- 1/2 medium red onion, chopped (a little more than 1/3 of a cup)
- 1/2 of 1 celery stalk, diced
- 1/2 of 1 whole carrot, diced
- 1 tsp red hot pepper flakes (or more if you like it spicy!)
- 2 medium cloves of garlic, minced
- 1 14 oz can of crushed tomatoes (San Marzano is the best!)
- 3/4 tbsp tomato paste (about 3 tsp)
- salt and pepper to taste
- 1/4 cup chicken broth
- 1/3 cup chopped basil
- 1 tbsp oregano flakes
- shaved Parmesan cheese, for garnish

Directions

1. Add your carrots and celery to a food processor and pulse until chopped finely. There can still be chunks, just no big ones. The end mixture should be somewhere in between chunky and pureed.
2. Put a large skillet over medium heat and add in the olive oil and season with salt and pepper. Once oil heats, add in garlic and cook for 30 seconds. Add in red pepper flakes, cook for 30 seconds and then add in the onions. Cook onions for 1-2 minutes or until they begin to soften. Add in carrot/celery mixture and cook for 1 minute.
3. Push the veggie mixture to the side and add in the ground turkey, crumbling as you add. Crumble with a spatula or wooden spoon. Add a pinch of the oregano flakes. Cook turkey until the meat is no longer pink.
4. Combine the veggies with the turkey and season with another pinch of oregano flakes. Add in the chicken broth and cook until reduced (water evaporates).
5. Add in the crushed tomatoes, tomato paste and season generously with salt and pepper. Add in the remaining oregano flakes. Bring to a boil and then lower heat and let simmer for 15 minutes. 5 minutes before the sauce is reduced, add in the basil.
6. After 15 minutes, add in the zucchini pasta and mix thoroughly to combine. Plate onto dishes and garnish with Parmesan cheese.

Broccoli Rabe Pasta with Spicy Italian Sausage (Zucchini Noodles)

Prep Time: 5 minutes | Cook Time: 10 minutes | Total Time: 15 minutes | Servings: 2

Ingredients

- 2 zucchinis, Blade A
- 2 tbsp olive oil
- salt and pepper
- 2 cloves of garlic, minced
- 1 tsp red pepper flakes
- 2 spicy Italian sausage links (or chicken sausage!)
- 1/2 cup chicken broth
- 1/2 bunch broccoli rabe
- 1 tbsp juice from a lemon (optional)
- pinch of oregano flakes
- 1/2 cup Pecorino Romano cheese, grated

Directions

1. Prepare your broccoli rabe. Rinse the leafs and pat dry. Cut off most of the stems (the thickest parts). Pull off some skin of the stems, using a peeler. Peel until you hit the leaves. Set aside
2. Place a large skillet over medium heat and add in the olive oil. Slice the sausage into 1/2 inch chunks (or remove from caseing and crumble - whatever you prefer) and place into skillet along with the garlic and season with salt, pepper, and a pinch of oregano. Cook for about 3 minutes, flipping over to cook both sides.
3. Push the sausage to the side and add the broccoli rabe and red pepper flakes to the skillet. Stir and cook for about 1 minute and then add in the chicken broth, mixing the sausage and broccoli rabe together. Cook until reduced and broccoli rabe is mostly wilted. Then, add in zucchini noodles. Cook for about 2 minutes or until noodles begin to soften.Stir in Pecorino Romano cheese and lemon juice (optional) and combine thoroughly.
4. Plate onto dishes and enjoy!

Broccolini and Chickpea Zucchini Pasta with Gremolata Breadcrumbs

Prep Time: 10 minutes | Cook Time: 10 minutes | Total Time: 20 minutes | Servings: 1

Ingredients

For the pasta:

- 1 large zucchini, Blade C
- 4 pieces of broccolini (or more!)
- 1 tbsp olive oil
- 1/4 tsp red pepper flakes
- 1 garlic clove, minced
- salt and pepper, to taste
- 1/3 cup chickpeas
- 1/2 tbsp olive oil
- 3 tbsp grated Parmigiano-Reggiano cheese

For the breadcrumbs:

- 1/2 slice of whole wheat bread
- zest of 1 lemon
- 1 tbsp finely chopped fresh parsley
- 1 tbsp grated Parmigiano-Reggiano cheese
- salt and pepper, to taste
- 1/2 tbsp olive oil

Directions

1. Place the half slice of bread into a food processor. Pulse into breadcrumbs.
2. Place a skillet over medium heat, add in the 1/2 tbsp of olive oil and pour in the breadcrumbs. Cook, stirring frequently, until crumbs are toasted, about 3 minutes. Place in a bowl and add in the remaining ingredients. Toss to combine and set aside.
3. Place the same skillet over medium heat and add in the tbsp of olive oil. Once oil heats, add in the garlic and cook for 1 minute. Add in the red pepper flakes, cook for about 30 seconds, and then add in the broccolini and season with salt and pepper. Cook for about 5 minutes, or until broccolini turns a deeper green and is a bit easier to pierce with a fork.
4. Add in the last 1/2 tbsp of olive oil, chickpeas, and the zucchini noodles. Season lightly with pepper. Cook for about 2 minutes or until zucchini softens. Toss in the Parmigiano-Reggiano cheese and mix to combine, cooking another 30 seconds.
5. Pour everything into a bowl and top with gremolata breadcrumbs. Enjoy!

Brussels Sprouts and Butternut Squash Pasta with Parmesan and Cranberries

Prep time: 15 mins | Cook time: 15 mins | Total time: 30 mins | Serves: 2

Ingredients

- 1 small butternut squash, peeled, Blade D, noodles trimmed
- salt and pepper, to taste
- 2 tablespoons extra virgin olive oil
- 2 cups brussels sprouts, ends trimmed
- 1 garlic clove, minced
- 1 pinch (about ⅛ teaspoon) red pepper flakes
- 2 tablespoons dried cranberries
- ¼ cup grated parmesan cheese

Directions

1. Preheat the oven to 400 degrees. Line a baking sheet with parchment paper and lay out the butternut squash noodles. Season with salt and pepper and bake for 8-10 minutes or until cooked to your desired preference.
2. Meanwhile, place your brussels sprouts into a food processor and pulse until "shredded." There should still be some small chunks, but mainly just chopped up leaves. Set aside.
3. Place a large skillet over medium heat and add half of the olive oil. Once oil heats, add in the garlic, red pepper flakes and brussels sprouts, season with salt and pepper and cook for 5-7 minutes or until they begin to brown and leaves have turned a brighter green.
4. Once the butternut squash noodles are done, add them to the skillet with the brussels sprouts and add in the rest of the olive oil and the cranberries and stir and then fold in the parmesan cheese and remove the skillet from heat and keep stirring until the parmesan melts into the pasta.
5. Divide the pasta into bowls or plates.

Butternut Squash Carrot Noodles with Sausage & Kale

Prep Time: 10 minutes | Cook Time: 10 minutes | Total Time: 20 minutes | Servings: 1

Ingredients

- 1 large carrot, peeled, Blade C*
- 1 link chicken sausage
- 1 cup chopped kale
- 1/4 cup vegetable broth, low-sodium
- 1/2 cup Dave's Gourmet butternut squash
- cracked pepper

Directions

1. Boil a medium saucepan of water. Once boiled, add in the carrot noodles. Cook for 3 minutes. Drain in a strainer and set aside.
2. While the water is boiling, add a medium skillet over medium heat and add in the chicken sausage. Cook until no longer pink inside.
3. Once finished, add in the kale, vegetable broth, Dave's Gourmet sauce, and cook until sauce is boiling and kale is wilted.
4. Place the carrot noodles in a plate and top with sauce mixture. Season with cracked pepper. Enjoy!

Butternut Squash Mac and Cheese

Prep Time: 14 minutes | *Cook Time:* 15 minutes | *Total Time:* 29 minutes | *Servings:* 3

Ingredients

- 1 butternut squash, peeled, Blade B
- olive oil cooking spray
- 2 tbsp vegan butter
- 1 tbsp coconut flour
- 1/3 cup plain almond milk
- 1/2 cup grated sharp cheddar cheese
- 1/4 cup grated parmesan cheese

Directions

1. Preheat the oven to 400 degrees.

2. Take your spiralized butternut squash noodles and cut with a scissor, if they are not in half-moon shape. Lay the noodles on a baking tray coated in cooking spray. Bake in the oven for 5-7 minutes or until easily pierced with a fork. Set aside.
3. In a large saucepan, add in the vegan butter and let melt. Once melted, add in the coconut flour and whisk together until flour absorbs butter and becomes thick. Then, add in the almond milk and whisk together constantly until mixture thickens.
4. Once the mixture thickens, add in the baked butternut squash noodles and stir to combine. Once combined, add in the cheese and stir again to combine. If it is too thick, add in more almond milk. Once the cheeses have melted into the noodles and consistency is to your preference, divide into bowls and enjoy!!

Butternut Squash Noodle Turkey Bolognese Stuffed Acorn Squash with Melted Gruyere: Two Ways!

Prep Time: *20 minutes* | **Cook Time:** *35 minutes* | **Total Time:** *55 minutes* | **Servings:** *2*

Ingredients
- 1 acorn squash
- olive oil to drizzle
- 1 serving of my Bikini Bolognese*
- 1 cup butternut squash noodles, Blade C
- olive oil cooking spray
- salt and pepper to taste
- 1 cup shaved gruyere cheese

Directions
1. Preheat the oven to 400 degrees.
2. Cut the acorn squash in half. Scoop out all of the insides and make sure all seeds are removed. Drizzle lightly with olive oil and massage into squash flesh with fingers.
3. Place the acorn squashes cut-side down on a baking tray. Roast in the oven for 30 minutes or until easily pierced with a fork. Once done, remove from oven and flip over so that the cut side is up to cool. Set the oven to broil.
4. While the acorn squash is roasting, make the bikini bolognese.

5. Five minutes before the acorn squash is done roasting, add the butternut squash noodles onto a baking tray coated with cooking spray. Roast for those last 5 minutes and then add it to the skillet with the bolognese. Stir to combine and spoon half of the mixture into 1 of the acorn squash halves. Set aside.

6. For the other acorn squash, spoon out the flesh of the acorn squash and add it to the remaining bolognese mixture. Stir to combine thoroughly and add back into the acorn squash skin.

7. Sprinkle each acorn squash halve evenly with gruyere cheese and place in the oven to broil for 5 minutes, checking periodically to make sure the cheese is bubbling but does not burn.

8. Remove the acorn squash from the oven and enjoy!

Butternut Squash Noodles with Pancetta and Poached Egg

Prep time: 15 mins | Cook time: 15 mins | Total time: 30 mins | Serves: 2

Ingredients

- Olive oil spray (such as Bertolli) or a mister
- 20 ounces, spiralized butternut squash, made with the thick setting
- 2 teaspoons olive oil
- ½ teaspoon kosher salt
- Freshly ground black pepper
- 2 large eggs
- 2 ounces pancetta, chopped
- ¼ cup freshly grated Pecorino Romano cheese
- 1 tablespoon chopped fresh parsley

Directions

1. Preheat the oven to 400®F. Light mist 2 large baking sheets with oil.
2. Divide the butternut squash noodles between the prepared baking sheets and toss each 1 teaspoon oil, ¼ teaspoon salt, and pepper to taste. Roast until soft, 7 to 10 minutes.
3. Meanwhile, to poach the eggs, fill the large deep skillet with 1 ½ to 2 inches of water. Bring to a boil over high heat, then reduce the heat until it holds a simmer. Crack the eggs into individual bowls. One at a time, gently slide the eggs into the simmering water. Using a spoon, gently nudge the egg whites toward the yolks. Cook 2 to 3 minutes for a semi-soft yolk or 3

to 4 minutes for a firmer yolk. Using a slotted spoon or spatula, transfer the eggs one at a time to paper towels to drain.

4. In a large skillet, cook the pancetta over medium heat, stirring, until slightly browned, about 3 minutes. Remove the pan from the heat, add the roasted butternut squash noodles, and stir in the Romano and parsley.

5. To serve, divide the noodles between 2 plates and top each with a poached egg. Season with more pepper, if desired, and serve.

Nutrition Information

- Serving size: 2
- Calories: 342
- Fat: 20g
- Saturated fat: 7g
- Carbohydrates: 25g
- Sugar: 7g
- Sodium: 790mg
- Fiber: 4.5g
- Protein: 18g
- Cholesterol: 217mg

Butternut Squash Noodles with Shredded Brussels Sprouts, Walnuts and Caramelized Onions

Prep Time: *15 minutes* | **Cook Time:** *15 minutes* | **Total Time:** *30 minutes* | **Servings:** *3-4*

Ingredients

For the noodles:

- 1 medium butternut squash, peeled, Blade C
- ½ tablespoon extra virgin olive oil
- ¼ teaspoon garlic powder
- salt and pepper, to taste

For the rest:

- ½ cup roughly chopped walnuts
- 1 cup of brussels sprouts

- 2 tablespoons extra virgin olive oil
- 1 medium red onion, sliced thinly
- 1 large garlic clove, minced
- ¼ teaspoon red pepper flakes
- salt and pepper, to taste
- optional: ¼ cup grated parmesan cheese

Directions

1. Preheat the oven to 400 degrees. Spread the butternut squash noodles out on a baking sheet, drizzle with olive oil and season with garlic powder, salt and pepper. Line another baking tray with parchment paper and place the walnuts. Bake the butternut squash noodles alongside the walnuts, baking the walnuts for just 5 minutes and baking the noodles for 8-10 minutes or until al dente, tossing halfway through.
2. While the butternut squash is baking, shred the brussels sprouts. Chop the bottoms off and peel off the outer leaves, if tough and discolored. Slice them in half and then slice thinly lengthwise. Set aside.
3. Place a large skillet over medium heat and add in the olive oil. Once oil is shimmering, add in the garlic, red pepper flakes and onion and lower heat to medium-low and cook the onion, stirring occasionally, until onion is translucent and mainly wilted, about 3 minutes.
4. Add in the brussels sprouts and season with salt and pepper. Cover and cook the brussels sprouts, still on medium low heat, uncovering occasionally to stir, or until lightly browned and cooked (about 3-5 minutes). Take the skillet off the heat and add the parmesan (if adding) and then fold in the walnuts, stir, and pour into a large mixing bowl along with the butternut squash noodles.
5. Toss to combine and serve.

Butternut Squash Pasta with Spicy Garlicky Broccoli Rabe and White Beans

Prep Time: 15 minutes | Cook Time: 20 minutes | Total Time: 35 minutes | Servings: 4

Ingredients

- 1 medium butternut squash, peeled, Blade C, noodles trimmed
- olive oil cooking spray

- 1 tablespoon extra virgin olive oil
- 2 large garlic cloves, minced
- ¼ teaspoon red pepper flakes (or more, if you like it really spicy)
- 1 pound broccoli rabe, stems removed
- salt and pepper, to taste
- 1 cup low sodium chicken broth (or vegetable broth, if vegetarian)
- 1 can white beans (cannellini, Great Northern), drained, rinsed, patted dry
- 1 teaspoon oregano flakes
- 1/3 cup grated parmesan cheese

Directions

1. Preheat the oven to 400 degrees. Place the butternut squash noodles on a baking sheet and coat with cooking spray. Season with salt and pepper and bake for 8-10 minutes or until al dente. When done, divide noodles into bowls and set aside.
2. While the butternut squash is cooking, place a large skillet over medium heat and add in the olive oil. Once oil heats, add in the garlic, red pepper flakes and broccoli rabe. Season with salt and pepper and cook for 3-5 minutes, tossing occasionally, or until broccoli rabe is wilted. You can do this in batches.
3. Once the broccoli rabe is cooked, pour the chicken broth into the skillet and add the beans and oregano. Let cook for 5-10 minutes or until liquid is reduced by half.
4. Remove the skillet from the heat, stir in the parmesan cheese and toss to combine. Divide the broccoli rabe mixture equally over the bowls of butternut squash noodles. Serve immediately.

Butternut Squash Zucchini Pasta with Honey Roasted Walnuts and Goat Cheese

Prep Time: 7 minutes | Cook Time: 45 minutes | Total Time: 52 minutes | Servings: 2

Ingredients

- 1.5 zucchinis, Blade A
- 2.5 cups butternut squash cubes (if you buy the butternut squash whole, peel it thoroughly and chop into chunks)
- 1 medium shallot, minced

- 2 medium garlic cloves, minced
- 2 tsp Earth Balance vegan butter spread (optional)
- salt and pepper
- olive oil
- 1/3 cup 2% Greek Yogurt
- 1/3 cup Parmesan Reggiano cheese (optional)
- 1/3 cup vegetable broth (preferably low-sodium)
- 4 sage leaves, thinly sliced
- 1/2 - 3/4 cup lightly chopped walnuts
- 1/3 cup crumbed goat cheese (or more if you like more!)
- honey to drizzle
- 2 tsp cinnamon

Directions

1. Preheat the oven to 405 degrees. Toss your butternut squash lightly in olive oil and season with salt, pepper and a light dusting of cinnamon (very light - if you use too much, your sauce will become too sweet and cinnamony). Place in the oven for 30 minutes, tossing halfway through.
2. While your squash is cooking, spray the bottom of a baking sheet to coat. Pour your crumbled walnuts on top and drizzle lightly with honey. Mix together with your fingers until all walnuts are coated. 5 minutes before the squash is done cooking, place in the walnuts for 5 minutes, tossing half way through. When done, pour into a bowl and set aside.
3. Once the squash is done, place a handful of cubes at a time into a food processor. Pulse until no chunks are left. Continue until all squash is pureed. Place into a bowl and set aside.
4. Place a large saucepan over medium heat and add in 2-3 glugs of olive oil. Season lightly with salt and pepper. Once oil heats, add in garlic. After 1 minute, add in shallots and cook for 2 minutes or until shallots begin to soften. Add in sage leaves, stir for 30 seconds and then pour in vegetable broth.
5. After 30 seconds, stir in squash puree and season with salt and pepper. Stir for about 2 minutes or until squash absorbs the vegetable broth and becomes thicker.
6. Add in Greek yogurt and Parmesan Reggiano cheese. The cheese is optional and if you're watching your waistline, leave it out. The cheese gives the sauce a thicker consistency and a cheesy savory flavor, but the sauce tastes great without it! Lower heat a bit and stir for about 1-2 minutes to absorb the cheese and yogurt.
7. Add in the zucchini pasta ribbons and stir to combine thoroughly.
8. Once done, transfer to a bowl. Plate onto dishes and top with goat cheese and walnuts!

Cacio e Pepe with bacon (Zucchini Noodles)

Prep Time: *10 minutes* | **Cook Time:** *10 minutes* | **Total Time:** *20 minutes* | **Servings:**
2

Ingredients

- 3 strips of bacon
- 1 large garlic clove, minced
- 1 pinch of red pepper flakes
- 3 medium zucchinis, Blade C
- freshly cracked black pepper, from a grinder
- 1/4 cup grated pecorino romano cheese
- 1/4 cup grated parmigiano reggiano cheese + more to garnish

Directions

1. Place a large skillet over medium heat and coat lightly with cooking spray. Add in the bacon and cook for 3-5 minutes and then flip over, cooking for another 2-3 minutes. Once done, remove and place on a paper-towel lined plate.
2. Remove all of the oil from the bacon except for 2 tbsp. Add in the garlic and red pepper flakes and cook for 30 seconds. Then, add in the zucchini noodles and toss to cook, for about 2-3 minutes.
3. Season the zucchini with about 5 cracks of the pepper and add in the cheeses. Toss to combine thoroughly and then plate into two bowls. Top each bowl with a few more cranks of black pepper and crumble over a piece and a half of bacon in each bowl. Garnish with additional parmigiano reggiano cheese.

Cacio e Pepe with Coconut Bacon

Prep time: *15 mins* | **Cook time:** *20 mins* | **Total time:** *35 mins* | **Serves:** *2*

Ingredients

For the coconut bacon:

- 1 cup unsweetened coconut flakes (not shredded)
- 1 tablespoon liquid smoke (I used hickory flavor, but you can use anyone you'd prefer)
- 1 tablespoon reduced sodium tamari or soy sauce
- ½ tablespoon maple syrup
- salt, to taste

For the pasta:

- 1 tablespoon extra virgin olive oil
- 1 large garlic clove, minced
- 1 pinch of red pepper flakes
- 2 medium zucchinis, Blade D, noodles trimmed
- freshly cracked black pepper, from a grinder
- ¼ cup grated Pecorino Romano cheese
- ¼ cup grated Parmigiano Reggiano cheese + more to garnish

Directions

1. Preheat the oven to 350 degrees. Line a baking tray with parchment paper and set aside.
2. In a small bowl, whisk together the ingredients for the bacon, except for the coconut. Then, add in the coconut and toss together gently to mix well until all the coconut flakes are covered in the bacon dressing.
3. Spread the flakes out into an even layer on the prepared baking tray and season with salt. Bake for 10-12 minutes, flipping halfway, until flakes are mostly dry and turning golden on the edges. Keep in mind that the flakes will crisp as they cool, so don't worry if your flakes aren't crispy after 10-12 minutes.
4. Remove the "bacon" from the oven and set aside to cool.
5. While the bacon cools, place a large skillet over medium-high heat and add in the olive oil. Once oil heats, add in the garlic and red pepper flakes and cook for 30 seconds. Then, add in the zucchini noodles and toss to cook, for about 2-3 minutes.
6. Season the zucchini with a generous amount of freshly cracked pepper and add in the cheeses. Remove from heat, toss to combine thoroughly and then plate into two bowls. Top each bowl with a few more cranks of black pepper and 1 tablespoon of coconut bacon onto each plate. Garnish with additional Parmigiano Reggiano cheese, if desired.

California Bounty Beef and Vegetable Noodles

"Living in California one can get fresh vegetables year-round. Spiralized vegetables are

fun and creative for that special main or side spiced up with some California-made sriracha sauce. This recipe is easily adapted with other vegetables."

Servings: *2* | **Prep:** *30 m* | **Cook:***16 m* | **Ready In:** *51 m*

Ingredients

- 1/2 pound beef sirloin steak
- 1/2 teaspoon garlic salt
- 1/2 teaspoon freshly ground black pepper
- 3 tablespoons olive oil, divided
- 2 Mexican squash
- 1/3 large carrot
- 2 radishes
- 1/2 avocado, diced
- 1/2 cup grape tomatoes, halved
- 1/4 cup chopped cilantro
- 1/2 cup sour cream (optional)
- 1 tablespoon sriracha sauce (optional)

Directions

1. Season steak with garlic salt and black pepper.
2. Heat 1 tablespoon olive oil in a large skillet over medium-high heat. Add steak; cook until browned, 4 to 5 minutes per side. Transfer steak to a cutting board and let rest, about 5 minutes. Slice into thin strips.
3. Cut Mexican squash, carrot, and radishes into noodles using a spiralizer.
4. Heat remaining 2 tablespoons oil in the skillet over medium heat. Add carrot noodles; cook and stir until lightly browned, about 3 minutes. Add squash noodles; cook, stirring constantly, until tender, about 5 minutes.
5. Divide carrot and squash noodle mixture between 2 serving plates. Top with sliced steak. Garnish with radish noodles, avocado, grape tomatoes, and cilantro.
6. Whisk sour cream and sriracha sauce together in a small bowl. Drizzle over serving plates.

Nutritional Information

- Calories:589 kcal 29%
- Fat: 49.6 g 76%
- Carbs: 15.3g 5%
- Protein: 23.8 g 48%
- Cholesterol: 86 mg 29%

- Sodium: 877 mg 35%

Caramelized Onion and Bacon Kohlrabi Spaghetti with Shaved Parmesan

Prep time: 10 mins | Cook time: 20 mins | Total time: 30 mins | Serves: 4

Ingredients

- 5 strips of bacon
- 1 large red onion, Blade A
- salt and pepper
- 2 teaspoons extra virgin olive oil + more for drizzle
- 2 large kohlrabis, peeled, Blade C, noodles trimmed
- ¼ cup shaved parmesan to garnish

Directions

1. Place a large skillet over medium-high heat. Once the pan is heated, add in the bacon strips and cook until crispy, 7-10 minutes, tossing halfway through. When bacon is done, set aside (using pasta tongs) on a paper towel lined plate.
2. Pour out half of the bacon grease and then immediately add in the onion and season with salt and pepper. Cook the onions until caramelized, 10-15 minutes. If the onions stick to the bottom of the pan, add splashes of chicken broth if needed.
3. Once the onions are done, wipe down the skillet carefully. Then, add in the olive oil and then kohlrabi noodles. Season with salt and pepper and cook for 5-7 minutes or until kohlrabi wilts down and is cooked to your preference. Add the onions and crumble in the bacon and toss well to combine.
4. Divide the pasta into four bowls and garnish with an extra drizzle of olive oil (if desired) and shaved parmesan.

Carrot Noodles with Mushrooms and Sausage in a Cashew Cream Sauce

Prep Time: 25 minutes | Cook Time: 20 minutes | Total Time: 45 minutes | Servings:

4

Ingredients

For the pasta:

- 2 large carrots, peeled, Blade C, noodles trimmed
- 1 tablespoon extra virgin olive oil
- 3 cups sliced baby portobello mushrooms
- salt and pepper, to taste
- 4 sweet Italian sausage links, sliced into ½" thick rounds
- 1 tablespoon freshly minced parsley, to garnish

For the sauce:

- ¼ cup diced sweet Vidalia onion
- ½ cup raw cashews, soaked for at least 2 hours and then drained
- 2 garlic cloves, minced
- 1 tablespoon nutritional yeast
- 1 tablespoon lemon juice
- ¼ cup + 2 tablespoons of low-sodium vegetable broth + more for thinning as needed
- salt and pepper, to taste

Directions

1. Place a medium saucepan filled halfway with water and a pinch of salt over high heat and bring to a boil. Once boiling, add in the carrot noodles and cook for 2-3 minutes or until al dente. Once cooked, drain into a colander and set aside.
2. While the carrots are cooking, place a large nonstick skillet over medium heat and add in the olive oil. Once oil heats, add in the onions and cook until onions softened, about 3 minutes. Transfer with a slotted spoon to a plate and set aside, keeping the skillet over medium heat.
3. In the skillet, add in the mushrooms, season with salt and pepper and cover and cook for 5-7 minutes or until wilted. Transfer the mushrooms to a plate and set aside. In the same skillet, add in the sausage and cook 5-7 minutes or until browned and cooked through. Transfer to the plate with the mushrooms and set aside. Wipe down the skillet and keep off heat on the stovetop, for later use.
4. Place the cooked onions into a high-speed blender along with the cashews, garlic cloves, nutritional yeast, lemon juice, broth and season with salt and pepper. Taste and adjust to your preference or thin out with more broth, if too thick.

5. Place the same large skillet back over medium heat and add in the mushrooms and sausage, carrot noodles and toss. Pour in the cashew cream sauce. Toss to combine thoroughly until the cashew sauce is heated through. Portion into bowls and garnish with parsley.

Cheese and Vegetable Noodle Medley

"Don't throw those broccoli stems away! Broccoli stems have plenty of flavor and spiralize easily along with other vegetables. With the addition of cheese this makes for the perfect side dish."

Servings: 2 | Prep: 20 m | Cook: 8 m | Ready In: 28 m

Ingredients

- 2 tablespoons garlic-infused olive oil
- 1 Mexican squash, cut into noodle shapes
- 1 yellow squash, cut into noodle shapes
- 3 broccoli stems, cut into 3-inch noodle shapes
- 1 pinch garlic salt, or to taste ground black pepper to taste
- 1 cup shredded sharp Cheddar cheese
- 2 Fresno chile peppers, sliced into rounds

Directions

1. Heat oil in a skillet over medium heat; add Mexican squash, yellow squash, broccoli stems, garlic salt, and pepper. Cook, stirring constantly, until vegetables are tender but still firm to the bite, about 5 minutes.
2. Mix in Cheddar cheese; cook and stir until melted, 3 to 5 minutes. Transfer to a serving plate; garnish with Fresno chile peppers.

Nutritional Information

- Calories:529 kcal 26%
- Fat: 37.9 g 58%
- Carbs: 27.5g 9%
- Protein: 26.6 g 53%
- Cholesterol: 72 mg 24%
- Sodium: 676 mg 27%

Cheesy Gorgonzola Zucchini Pasta with Toasted Walnuts and Baked Anjou Pears

Prep Time: 5 minutes | *Cook Time:* 25 minutes | *Total Time:* 30 minutes | *Servings:* 1

Ingredients

- 1 large zucchini, Blade C
- 1/2 tbsp olive oil + more for drizzling
- 1/4 cup gorgonzola cheese + more for garnish
- salt and pepper
- 1 small garlic clove, minced
- 1 anjou pear
- 1/4 cup walnuts

Directions

1. Preheat the oven to 425 degrees.
2. Prepare your pears by slicing them into eight pieces, making sure to remove all seeds. Lay the slices down on a baking tray and drizzle with olive oil and season with salt and pepper. Bake for 20-25 minutes, tossing the pears halfway through. Five minutes before the pears are done baking, throw the walnuts into the tray. When done, set aside.
3. Once you add the walnuts to the baking tray, place a large skillet over medium heat and add in the 1/2 tbsp of olive oil. Once the oil heats, add in the garlic and cook for 1 minute. Add in the zucchini noodles, season with pepper and cook for about 1 minute or until they are heated through and start to soften.
4. Add in the gorgonzola cheese and cook for 1 minute, tossing to combine thoroughly. The cheese should fully melt into the noodles.
5. When the cheese is melted, place the noodles into a bowl. Top with pears, walnuts and extra gorgonzola. Enjoy!

Chia-Chimichurri Steak with Turnip-Chard Pasta

Prep Time: 20 minutes | *Cook Time:* 20 minutes | *Total Time:* 40 minutes | *Servings:*

4

Ingredients

For the pasta:

- 2 large turnips, peeled, Blade B, noodles trimmed
- salt and pepper, to taste
- ¼ teaspoon garlic powder
- 3 packed cups chopped swiss chard

For the steak:

- 2 bone-in ribeye steak
- salt and pepper, to taste
- 1 tablespoon extra virgin olive oil
- For the chimichurri:
- 1 cup packed fresh Italian parsley
- 1 teaspoon dried oregano
- 1 cup packed fresh cilantro
- 1 tablespoon chia seeds
- 3 garlic cloves, chopped
- 1 seeded jalapeno pepper (if you don't like spicy, use a small jalapeno)
- ¼ cup diced white onion
- 3 tablespoons red wine vinegar
- 3 tablespoons olive oil
- salt and pepper, to taste

Directions

1. Season the steak generously with salt and pepper. Add a large skillet over medium-high heat and add in the olive oil. Once oil heats, add in the steaks and sear for 5-7 minutes on each side, for medium-rare/medium. Remove the steaks with tongs and allow it to rest for 10 minutes before slicing thinly into strips, against the grain.
2. While steak cooks, place all of the ingredients for the chia-chimichurri into a food processor and blend until smooth. Taste and adjust to your preferences. Set aside.
3. Once steak is resting, place the large skillet back over medium heat and add in the turnip noodles, tossing to coat in the pan juices. Season the turnips with salt, pepper and garlic powder and cover and cook for 5-7 minutes or until turnip noodles cook to your preference (I like al dente.) Uncover, add in the chard and toss quickly to warm the greens.

4. Divide the pasta onto two plates, top with sliced steak and drizzle over with chia-chimichurri.

Chicken and Broccoli Butternut Squash Pasta

Prep time: 15 mins | Cook time: 20 mins | Total time: 35 mins | Serves: 4

Ingredients

For the pasta:

- 1 large butternut squash, peeled, Blade C, noodles trimmed
- salt and pepper
- 1 tablespoon extra virgin olive oil
- 2 boneless and skinless chicken breasts, cubed
- 3 cups broccoli florets
- red pepper flakes
- chopped parsley, to garnish
- For the sauce:
- 1 garlic clove, minced
- 1 tablespoon minced shallots
- ¾ cup raw cashews, soaked in water for at least 2 hours (up to 24), drained and rinsed
- ½ cup vegetable broth or more as needed to thin
- 2 tablespoons nutritional yeast
- ½ teaspoon salt
- 2 teaspoons lemon juice (freshly squeezed)
- pepper, to taste

Directions

1. Preheat the oven to 400 degrees. Lay the butternut squash noodles out on a parchment paper lined baking sheet, season with salt and pepper, and cook for 10-12 minutes or until cooked through but slightly al dente (or cooked to your preference.)
2. Meanwhile, prepare the chicken and broccoli. Heat the oil in a large skillet over medium-high heat. Once oil is shimmering, add in the chicken and season generously with salt and pepper. Let cook on all sides until browned on the outside, about 7 minutes. Add the broccoli, season with salt and pepper, and cook for about 5 minutes or until broccoli is tender.

3. Meanwhile, prepare the sauce. Place all ingredients into a food processor and pulse until creamy. Taste and adjust, if necessary.
4. When chicken and broccoli is done, add the butternut squash noodles to the pan along with the sauce and red pepper flakes. Toss well to combine.
5. Divide mixture onto four plates and garnish with parsley.

Chicken and Chickpea Broccoli Noodle Pasta

Prep Time: 15 minutes | Cook Time: 20 minutes | Total Time: 35 minutes | Servings: 3

Ingredients

- .5 tablespoon extra virgin olive oil
- 1 boneless chicken breast (about .75 lb)
- salt and pepper, to taste
- ¼ teaspoon dried oregano flakes
- 2 broccoli stems, Blade C
- 1/2 cup canned chickpeas, drained and rinsed
- ½ cup cooked green peas
- 1/2 cup thinly sliced leeks
- For the dressing:
- 2 tablespoons basil, chopped
- 1/3 cup feta
- 1/2 shallot, chopped
- 1 tablespoon lemon juice
- salt and pepper to taste
- 1 tablespoons olive oil
- 1 tablespoons red wine vinegar
- 1 small garlic clove, minced

Directions

1. Place a large skillet over medium heat and add in the olive oil. Meanwhile, season chicken with salt, pepper and oregano on both sides. Once oil is shimmering, add in the chicken and cook until no longer pink. Set aside.
2. Place a medium pot filled halfway with water over high heat and bring to a boil. Once boiling, add in the broccoli noodles and peas and cook for 2-3 minutes or until the broccoli noodles are softened and cooked to al dente and the peas are bright green. Drain and set aside.

3. While broccoli noodles are chilling, place all of the ingredients for the feta dressing into a food processor and pulse until creamy. Place the broccoli noodles, chickpeas, peas, leeks and dressing in a large bowl and toss to combine.
4. Serve immediately.

Chicken and Okra with Basil Feta Pesto Zucchini Pasta

Prep Time: 15 minutes | Cook Time: 15 minutes | Total Time: 30 minutes | Servings: 2

Ingredients

- 1 tablespoon extra virgin olive oil
- 1 large boneless skinless chicken breast, cubed
- salt and pepper, to taste
- 8 pieces of okra, sliced into ½" pieces
- salt and pepper, to taste
- 1 clove of garlic, minced
- 1 large zucchini, Blade B, noodles trimmed
- For the basil pesto:
- 3 tablespoons pine nuts
- 2 packed cups of basil
- ¼ cup feta cheese
- 3 tablespoons extra virgin olive oil
- salt to taste
- ¼ teaspoon grinded pepper

Directions

1. Combine all of the ingredients for the pesto into a food processor and blend until creamy. Set aside.
2. Place a large skillet over medium heat and add in the olive oil. Once oil heats, add in the chicken. Cook for 2-3 minutes or until almost cooked through and then add in the okra and garlic. Season with salt and pepper and cover and cook for 5-7 minutes or until chicken is fully cooked through, shaking the pan to prevent the garlic from burning.
3. While mixture is cooking, combine the zucchini noodles and pesto into a mixing bowl and toss to combine thoroughly, until all noodles are coated in pesto. Set aside.

4. When mixture is done cooking, pour into the bowl with the dressed zucchini noodles and toss to coat thoroughly. Divide into plates and serve

Chicken and Pesto Zucchini Fettuccine with Tomatoes

Prep time: 15 mins | *Cook time:* 20 mins | *Total time:* 35 mins | *Serves:* 4

Ingredients

For the chicken and pasta:

- 1 pound boneless chicken breast, cubed
- Salt and pepper, to taste
- ½ teaspoon garlic powder
- ¼ teaspoon dried oregano
- pinch of red pepper flakes
- 1 cup cherry tomatoes, halved
- 5-6 medium zucchinis, Blade B*

*This is specific to the Inspiralizer. If you don't have the Inspiralizer, use a thicker noodle blade.

For the pesto:

- 2 tablespoons pine nuts
- 2 packed cups of basil
- 2 tablespoons parmesan cheese
- 3 tablespoons extra virgin olive oil
- 1 large garlic clove
- salt and pepper, to taste

Directions

1. Place a large skillet over medium heat and add in the olive oil. Once oil heats, add in the chicken and season with salt, pepper, garlic powder, oregano and red pepper flakes. Cover and cook until chicken is cooked through and no longer pink on the inside, about 5-7 minutes. Halfway through, add in the tomatoes.
2. While the chicken is cooking, prepare the pesto: add all ingredients into a food processor and pulse until creamy.

292 | P a g e

3. Transfer the chicken to a plate when finished, leaving the juices in the pan. Immediately add in the zucchini noodles and toss for 3-5 minutes or until cooked to your preference.
4. Drain the zucchini noodles in a colander and then add to a mixing bowl and add in the pesto, chicken and tomatoes. Toss together to combine and transfer to a serving bowl or divide into ind.

Chicken Sausage and Broccoli Zucchini Pasta with Parmesan

Prep time: 10 mins | Cook time: 20 mins | Total time: 30 mins | Serves: 2

Ingredients

- 2 chicken sausage links, decased
- 2 garlic cloves, minced
- 1 cup chopped broccoli florets
- salt and pepper, to taste
- ½ teaspoon red pepper flakes
- ½ cup chicken broth, low sodium
- 2 medium zucchinis, Blade C, noodles trimmed
- ¼ cup grated parmesan cheese

Directions

1. Place a large skillet over medium-high heat. Once skillet is heated, add in the chicken sausage, crumbling with a wooden spoon. Cook for 5 minutes or until browned on the outside and then add in the garlic and broccoli. Season with salt, pepper, and red pepper flakes and stir well. Add in the chicken broth and cook, covered, for 5-7 minutes or until broccoli is fork tender and chicken sausage is cooked all the way through.
2. Once the broccoli and sausage is almost fully cooked, add in the zucchini noodles and toss well to combine. Cook for 3-5 minutes or until zucchini is al dente. Add in the parmesan cheese and toss well, off heat, until combined.
3. Divide the pasta into bowls and serve

Chicken Tetrazzini with Zucchini Noodles

Prep Time: *10 minutes* | **Cook Time:** *40 minutes* | **Total Time:** *50 minutes* | **Servings:** *4-5*

Ingredients

- 3 medium zucchinis, Blade C
- 3 tbsp olive oil
- 1 pound chicken breast, cut into strips/tenderloins
- salt and pepper, to taste
- 1 cup almond meal
- 2 tbsp chicken broth
- 1 tsp dried oregano flakes
- 1/2 tsp dried basil flakes
- 1/2 tsp dried parsley flakes
- 1/2 tsp garlic powder
- pinch of red pepper flakes
- 2 cloves garlic, minced
- 3/4 cup diced red onion
- 1.5 cups sliced portobello mushrooms
- 1/2 cup frozen green peas
- 1 tsp thyme
- 3/4 cup chicken broth
- 3 tsp coconut flour
- 2 tbsp freshly chopped parsley

Directions

1. Preheat the oven to 400 degrees.
2. Place a large skillet over medium heat and add in 1 tbsp of the olive oil. Add in your chicken and season with salt and pepper. Cook for 3-5 minutes on each side or until the chicken is no longer pink on the inside. Remove skillet from heat and remove chicken with tongs or a slotted spoon and cut into cubes, and set aside.
3. While the chicken is cooking, place your zucchini noodles into a roughly 10 x 10 casserole or baking dish. Set aside.
4. Also while the chicken is cooking, place your almond meal and basil, oregano, parsley, and garlic powder in a bowl. Season with salt and pepper generously and then toss to combine and then add in the chicken broth.

Using your fingers, roll like a dough until all of the meal is formed into dough. Set aside.

5. Place the skillet back over medium heat and add in the rest of the olive oil. Let heat and add in the garlic and red pepper flakes. Cook for 30 seconds and then add in the onions, thyme, mushrooms and peas. Season with salt and pepper and cook for 3-5 minutes or until mushrooms wilt.

6. Add in the chicken broth and let reduce for about 1 minute. Then, push vegetables to the side and add in the flour. Whisk immediately until creamy and then push the vegetables back in and stir to combine. Cook until the chicken broth is reduced.

7. Pour the mixture evenly over the noodles, add in the cooked chicken and toss in the baking tray to combine. Once combined, evenly spread the mixture in the baking tray. If the mixture seems to try, evenly pour over 1/2 cup of chicken broth.

8. Take the almond meal "dough" and crumble into breadcrumbs over the casserole, evenly until all of the "dough" is used.

9. Sprinkle over the casserole with the fresh parsley and bake 20-25 minutes.

Chicken Tikka Masala with Butternut Squash Fettucine

Prep Time: 25 minutes | **Cook Time**: 20 minutes | **Total Time**: 45 minutes | **Servings**: 4

Ingredients

For the pasta:

- 1 large butternut squash (or 2 medium), peeled, Blade B, noodles trimmed
- olive oil cooking spray
- salt and pepper, to taste
- ½ teaspoon garlic powder
- For the tikka masala:
- 1 tablespoon virgin, unrefined coconut oil (or extra virgin olive oil)
- 1 cup diced white onion
- 2 large garlic cloves, minced
- 1 tablespoon peeled and grated fresh ginger
- 1½ teaspoons garam masala
- 1½ teaspoons ground coriander
- 2 teaspoons cumin
- ½ teaspoon ground turmeric
- ¼ teaspoon cayenne pepper
- salt, to taste

- 1.5 cups canned tomato puree
- 1 tablespoon freshly squeezed lemon juice
- 1/4 cup nonfat Greek yogurt
- 1 ½ tablespoons chopped cilantro

For the chicken:

- ½ tablespoon extra virgin olive oil
- 1 pound boneless chicken breasts, cut into thin strips or 1" cubes
- salt and pepper, to taste

Directions

1. Preheat the oven to 400 degrees. Line a baking sheet with parchment paper and lay out the butternut squash noodles. Spray with cooking spray and season with salt, pepper and garlic powder. Roast for 8-10 minutes or until al dente.
2. In a large saucepan, heat the oil over medium heat. When the heats, add in the onion, garlic, and ginger. Cook for 2-3 minutes or until onion turns translucent. Add in the garam masala, coriander, cumin, turmeric, and cayenne pepper. Season with salt and add the tomato puree and lemon juice to the saucepan. Raise the heat to high and bring to a boil. Reduce the heat to low and cook at a simmer for about 10 minutes for the flavors to develop.
3. Once the sauce is simmering, cook the chicken: in a large skillet, add in the olive oil. Once oil heats, add in the chicken, season with salt and pepper and then cover to quick cookly, 5-10 minutes or until chicken is cooked through.
4. Once sauce is done, remove from heat, stir in the Greek yogurt and cilantro and then add in the chicken. Stir to combine.
5. Divide the butternut squash noodles into bowls and top with chicken tikka masala

Chickpea-Bacon Carbonara with Spiralized Sweet Potatoes

Prep time: 10 mins | Cook time: 10 mins | Total time: 20 mins | Serves: 2

Ingredients

- 4 slices bacon
- 2 tablespoons minced shallots

- 1 pinch red pepper flakes
- 2 garlic cloves, minced
- 1 large sweet potato or 2 small sweet potatoes
- salt and pepper
- ½ cup drained and rinsed canned chickpeas
- ¼ teaspoon onion powder
- ¼ teaspoon chili powder
- ¼ teaspoon paprika
- 2 whole large eggs
- ⅓ cup grated parmesan cheese
- chopped parsley, to garnish

Directions

1. Heat a large skillet over medium-high heat. Once pan is hot, add the bacon and cook until crispy, flipping halfway through.
2. Remove half of the bacon grease and reserve in a small cup or bowl. Then, add in the shallots and red pepper flakes to the skillet. Cook the shallots for 1 minute or until softened. Add the garlic and cook for 30 seconds or until fragrant. Then, add in the sweet potato noodles, season with salt and pepper and toss. Cook, stirring often, until cooked through, about 7 minutes.
3. Meanwhile, blot the chickpeas with a paper towel to remove excess moisture and then add to a medium mixing bowl with the onion powder, chili powder, paprika, and salt and pepper. Mix well.
4. Once noodles are done cooking, set the noodles aside and wipe down the skillet carefully, scrubbing off any browned bits. Add in the reserved bacon grease add in the chickpeas. Cook for 5-7 minutes or until browned and crisping up.
5. While the chickpeas are cooking, combine the eggs and parmesan cheese in a bowl and whisk together until not very clumpy. Season with the salt and pepper and set aside.
6. Once chickpeas are done cooking, add back in the sweet potato noodles and crumble in the bacon, then toss to combine. Remove from heat and slowly pour in the prepared parmesan sauce, stirring constantly, over the noodles. It's important to do this slowly and stir constantly so that the eggs cook while they heat up in the noodles. Use as much sauce as you want until the pasta has enough sauce for your preference.
7. Divide the pasta into bowls, top with parsley, and serve.

Chunky Lamb Ragu with Celeriac Noodles

Prep Time: *15 minutes* | ***Cook Time:*** *45 minutes* | ***Total Time:*** *60 minutes* | ***Servings:*** *3*

Ingredients

- ¾ - 1 pound ground lamb, lean
- 1 large garlic clove, minced
- 1 teaspoon ground cumin
- ½ teaspoon chopped rosemary
- ½ teaspoon chopped thyme
- salt and pepper, to taste
- ½ carrot, finely diced
- ¼ teaspoon red pepper flakes
- ½ small yellow onion, finely diced
- ½ celery rib, finely diced
- ½ tablespoon tomato paste
- 14.5oz can crushed tomatoes
- ½ cup low sodium chicken broth
- 1 medium celeriac (celery root)
- ½ tablespoon extra virgin olive oil
- 1 tablespoon chopped mint

Directions

1. In a medium pot over medium heat, add in the lamb, garlic, cumin, rosemary, thyme and season with salt and pepper. Break up the lamb with a wooden spoon and cook until browned. Then, add in the carrot, red pepper flakes, onion and celery and cook until vegetable soften and liquid mainly evaporates, about 5 minutes.
2. Stir in the tomato paste to combine thoroughly and then add in the tomatoes and stock and bring to a boil. Cover partially and simmer over low heat until sauce thickens, 20 to 25 minutes.
3. While sauce cooks, peel and spiralize the celeriac with Blade B and trim the noodles. Place a large skillet over medium heat and add in the olive oil. Once oil heats, add in the celeriac noodles, cover and let cook for 5-10 minutes or until celeriac is cooked to al dente, uncovering occasionally to toss. If celeriac noodles start to stick to the pan, add in drops of chicken broth.
4. Divide the celeriac noodles into bowls. Top the celeriac noodles with sauce and serve warm, garnished with mint.

Chunky Lentil Bolognese with Spiralized Sweet Potatoes

Prep time: 15 mins | Cook time: 50 mins | Total time: 1 hour 5 mins | Serves: 4

Ingredients

- 2 tablespoons extra virgin olive oil
- 1 red or yellow onion, peeled and diced
- 2 carrots, peeled, diced
- 2 celery stalks, diced
- 2 garlic cloves, minced
- ½ teaspoon red pepper flakes
- 1 tablespoon tomato paste
- 1 (28oz) can diced tomatoes
- ½ teaspoon dried basil
- 1 teaspoon dried oregano
- salt and pepper, to taste
- 1 cup dry green lentils, rinsed
- 3 cups vegetable broth
- 2 bay leaves
- 3 medium sweet potatoes, peeled, Blade D, noodles trimmed
- chopped parsley, to garnish

Directions

1. Heat half the oil in a medium saucepot over medium high heat. Once oil is shimmering, add in the onions, carrots, and celery and cook for 5 minutes or until vegetables soften and onions are translucent. Add in the garlic and red pepper flakes, and cook for 30 seconds or until fragrant.
2. Add the tomato paste and stir to combine. Add in the tomatoes and season with basil, oregano, salt and pepper and stir again. Add the lentils, stock and bay leaves and bring to a boil. Once boiling, reduce to a medium simmer (over medium-low heat) and cook for 30-40 minutes or until lentils are tender. Add more broth if the sauce dries out as the lentils are still cooking.
3. While lentil Bolognese cooks, place a large skillet over medium-high heat and add in the remaining oil. Once heated, add in the sweet potato noodles, season with salt and pepper and cook for 7 minutes or until al dente or to your preference. Divide into bowls and tent with foil or similar to keep warm while the lentils finish cooking.

4. When lentil Bolognese is done, taste and adjust with more salt, if needed. Divide the Bolognese over the sweet potato noodles and garnish with parsley.

Chunky Lentil Potato Noodle Bolognese

Prep Time: 15 minutes | *Cook Time:* 20 minutes | *Total Time:* 35 minutes | *Servings:* 2

Ingredients

- 1/2 cup dry Petite French Green Lentils from Bob's Red Mill
- 1 tbsp olive oil
- 1 garlic clove minced
- 1/2 cup diced celery
- 1/2 cup diced red onion
- 1/2 cup peeled and diced carrot
- 1 14oz can of diced tomatoes
- 1 tsp dried oregano
- 1/2 tsp dried basil
- salt and pepper, to taste
- 1-2 large Yukon Gold potatoes, peeled, Blade C

Directions

1. Boil 1 1/4 cups of water with 1/2 cup of lentils. Once brought to a boil, lower to a simmer and cook 15-20 minutes or until lentils are cooked and have softened, but do not break apart. Set aside.
2. While the water is boiling, place a large skillet over medium-low heat and add in the olive oil. Once the oil heats, add in the garlic. Cook for 30 seconds and then add in the celery, red onion and diced carrot. Cook for 3-4 minutes or until vegetables begin to soften.
3. Add in the diced tomatoes and crush most with the back of a fork or a potato masher. Season with salt, pepper, basil and oregano.
4. Reduce sauce for 10 minutes or until most of the liquid has absorbed.
5. While sauce is reducing, place another large skillet over medium heat and coat with cooking spray. Add in the potato noodles, season with salt and pepper and cook, tossing frequently, for 5 minutes or until noodles wilt and are cooked through. When done, set aside in two bowls.
6. Once sauce is finished, fold in cooked lentils and stir to combine. Top each bowl of potato noodles with equal parts of the bolognese sauce. Enjoy!

Crab Zucchini Pasta with Spicy Avocado Sauce

Prep time: 20 mins | *Total time:* 20 mins | *Serves:* 3

Ingredients

- 1.5 cups jumbo lump crab meat
- 3 zucchinis, peeled, Blade D, noodles trimmed
- For the sauce:
- 1 avocado, peeled and pitted
- ¼ teaspoon grinded sea salt
- pepper, to taste
- 1 small jalapeno, sliced (seeds included)
- 1 lime, juiced
- 1 garlic clove, minced
- 1.5 tablespoons chopped cilantro + more to garnish
- 2 teaspoons extra virgin olive oil

Directions

1. Place all of the sauce ingredients into a food processor. Pulse until creamy. Taste and adjust if necessary.
2. Place the zucchini noodles into a medium mixing bowl along with the avocado sauce and toss until combined. Add in the crab and toss again.
3. Divide into bowls and garnish with cilantro.

Creamy BLT Zucchini Pasta

Prep Time: 10 minutes | *Cook Time:* 20 minutes | *Total Time*: 30 minutes | *Servings:* 2

Ingredients

- 4 pieces of bacon
- 1 tablespoon extra virgin olive oil
- 1 garlic clove, minced

- ¼ teaspoon red pepper flakes
- 1 14.5oz can of crushed tomatoes
- 1 teaspoon tomato paste
- 1/2 teaspoon dried oregano flakes
- salt and pepper, to taste
- 2 medium zucchinis, Blade C, noodles trimmed
- 2.5-3 cups arugula
- ¼ cup grated parmigiano-reggiano cheese

Directions

1. Place a large skillet over medium-high heat and coat with cooking spray. Once heated, add in the bacon slices and cook for 2-3 minutes, flip over and cook another 3-5 minutes or until crispy. Set aside on a paper-towel lined plate.
2. Wipe down the skillet and place it back over medium-high heat. Add in the olive oil and once heated, add in the garlic and red pepper flakes and cook until fragrant, about 30 seconds. Then, add in the tomatoes and tomato paste. Season with salt and pepper and oregano and let cook for 10 minutes or until sauce is fully reduced.
3. Once reduced, add in the arugula and zucchini noodles. Cook, tossing frequently, for 2-3 minutes or until noodles wilt and cook through. Remove from heat and stir in the parmigiano-reggiano cheese. Toss noodle mixture until cheese melts and then crumble in the bacon and give another toss to combine.
4. Serve immediately.

Creamy Cajun Zucchini Pasta with Kale and Andouille Sausage

Prep Time: *10 minutes* | **Cook Time:** *15 minutes* | **Total Time:** *25 minutes* | **Servings:** *1*

Ingredients

For the sauce:

- 1 tsp chili powder
- 1 tbsp Chobani 0% plain Greek yogurt
- 1/2 tbsp Cajun seasoning
- 1/2 tbsp smoked paprika
- 5 tbsp chicken broth

- 1 small garlic clove, minced
- 1/3 cup chopped red onion

For the rest:

- 1.5 zucchinis, Blade C
- 1 Andouille sausage link
- 1 tbsp olive oil
- 1 small garlic clove, minced
- 1 cup chopped kale
- chopped parsley to garnish (optional)
- salt and pepper to taste

Directions

1. Place a large skillet over medium-high heat and spray with olive oil cooking spray. Add in the chopped kale and cook until kale is wilted. Set aside.
2. In the same skillet, place in the andouille sausage. Cook for 2 minutes and then flip over, add in the garlic and cook for another 2-3 minutes. When done, pour out garlic and sausage onto a plate and set aside.
3. In the same skillet, place in the olive oil. Once oil heats, add in the onions and garlic. Cook for about 2 minutes or until onions become translucent and begin to soften. Add in the paprika, chili powder, and Cajun seasoning and stir around with onions to combine thoroughly.
4. Add in the chicken stock and cook until reduced (no more liquid left!) Then, add in the Chobani Greek yogurt and stir to combine.
5. Add the zucchini pasta, cooked sausage, and cooked kale into the skillet. Season with salt and pepper. Cook the zucchini for about 2-3 minutes or until noodles soften and are heated completely.
6. Plate and enjoy! Garnish with fresh chopped parsley (optional).

Creamy Corn Kohlrabi Pasta

*Prep time: 10 mins | **Cook time:** 15 mins | **Total time:** 25 mins | **Serves:** 2*

Ingredients

- 1 tablespoon extra virgin olive oil
- 1 garlic clove, minced
- pinch red pepper flakes

- 1 tablespoon minced shallots
- 1 cups corn kernels
- salt and pepper
- ¼ cup vegetable broth + more as needed
- 2 medium kohlrabis, peeled, Blade C, noodles trimmed
- chopped parsley, to garnish

Directions

1. Heat half the oil in a large skillet over medium heat. Once oil is shimmering, add the garlic, red pepper flakes and shallots. Cook until shallots soften, about 2 minutes. Add in the corn, season with salt and pepper and let cook for 5 minutes or until corn softens.
2. Transfer all but ¼ cup of the corn mixture and vegetable broth into a blender or food processor and process until smooth, adding more broth if needed – it should be a thick sauce consistency. Transfer the ¼ cup of corn to a bowl and set aside.
3. Add the kohlrabi noodles to the skillet and place back over medium-high heat. Drizzle with remaining olive oil and season with salt and pepper. Let cook, tossing occasionally, until the kohlrabi wilts to your preference, about 5-7 minutes.
4. Once kohlrabi is cooked, add back in the pureed corn and reserved corn and toss well to combine.
5. Divide the mixture to two bowls and garnish with parsley.

Creamy Okinawa Sweet Potato Pasta with Leeks and Pancetta

Prep Time: *20 minutes* | **Cook Time:** *25 minutes* | **Total Time:** *45 minutes* | **Servings:** *4*

Ingredients

For the cauliflower sauce:

- Florets from 1 small head of cauliflower (about 4-5 cups)
- 1 small shallot, minced
- 1 large clove of garlic, minced
- 1 pinch red pepper flakes
- 1 cup chicken broth, low-sodium
- 1 tablespoon nutritional yeast flakes
- salt, to taste

For the rest:

- 1 tablespoon extra virgin olive oil
- 8oz cubed pancetta
- 2-3 cups chopped leeks
- 2 large (or 3 medium) Japanese Sweet Potatoes, peeled, Blade C, noodles trimmed
- salt and pepper, to taste
- 1 tablespoon freshly chopped parsley, to garnish

Directions

1. Bring a medium pot filled halfway with water and a pinch of salt to a boil. Once boiling, add in the cauliflower. Cook the cauliflower until tender and easily pierced with a fork, about 7 minutes. Drain into a colander.
2. While cauliflower cooks, place a large nonstick skillet over medium heat and in the pancetta. Cook the pancetta for 5-7 minutes or until browned. Reserve 1 tablespoon with a slotted spoon and set the rest aside.
3. Place the large skillet back over medium heat and add in the shallots, garlic and red pepper flakes and cook for 2 minutes or until shallots are softened. If needed, add in a drizzle of olive oil to keep the vegetables from sticking to the pan.
4. Transfer both the drained cauliflower and cooked shallot mixture into a high speed blender along with the chicken broth, nutritional yeast, season with salt and pulse until creamy. Taste and adjust to your preference. Set aside.
5. Place the large skillet back over medium heat and add in the olive oil. Add in the leeks and sweet potato noodles, season with salt and pepper and then cover, letting cook for 7-10 minutes, uncovering to toss occasionally, until noodles are al dente.
6. When noodles and leeks are cooked, pour in the cauliflower sauce, toss to combine and let cook for about 1 minute to heat the sauce back up (if needed.) Plate the pasta into bowls and top with reserved pancetta and parsley, to garnish.

Creamy Spiralized Rutabaga with Burst Cherry Tomatoes

Prep time: *10 mins* | **Cook time:** *20 mins* | **Total time:** *30 mins* | **Serves:** *4*

Ingredients

For the sauce:

- 1 garlic clove, minced
- 1 tablespoon minced shallots
- ¾ cup raw cashews, soaked in water for at least 2 hours (up to 24), drained and rinsed
- ½ cup vegetable broth
- 2 tablespoons nutritional yeast
- ½ teaspoon salt
- 2 teaspoons lemon juice (freshly squeezed)
- pepper, to taste

For the pasta:

- 1 cup cherry tomatoes
- 5 teaspoons olive oil
- salt and pepper
- ¼ teaspoon garlic powder
- 2 medium rutabagas (or 3 small), peeled, Blade C, noodles trimmed

Directions

1. Preheat the oven to 400 degrees. Line a baking sheet with parchment paper and lay out the tomatoes. Drizzle with 2 teaspoons of the olive oil and season with salt, pepper, and garlic powder.
2. On another baking sheet, line it with parchment paper and lay out the rutabaga noodles. Drizzle with the rest of the olive oil and salt and pepper.
3. Roast both the tomatoes and rutabaga in the oven for 15-20 minutes or until rutabaga is cooked through to al dente and tomatoes are browned and burst when pierced with a fork.
4. While the tomatoes and rutabaga bake, prepare the sauce. Place everything into a high speed blender and pulse until creamy. Taste and adjust to your preference with more nutritional yeast or salt.
5. Toss the rutabaga with the cheese sauce and divide onto plates. Top with the burst tomatoes. Serve as is or top with your favorite protein.

Creamy Tomato Zucchini Pasta with Salmon and Asparagus

Prep Time: 5 *minutes* | **Cook Time:** *25 minutes* | **Total Time:** *3 minutes* | **Servings:** *2*

Ingredients

- 2 large zucchinis, Blade A
- 1/2 medium onion, diced
- 1 tbsp olive oil
- salt and pepper
- 3/4 tsp red pepper flakes
- 2 medium cloves of garlic, minced
- 1.75 cans of (14oz) diced tomatoes
- 3 tsp dried oregano flakes
- 12 small asparagus stalks
- 4-5 oz salmon filet, cut into 1 inch chunks
- 3 tsp garlic powder
- 1/3 cup of 2% plain Greek Yogurt
- olive oil cooking spray

Directions

1. Preheat the oven to 410 degrees. In a baking dish, place in your asparagus stalks and salmon chunks. Spray over with cooking spray and season all with salt, pepper and garlic powder. Set aside.
2. Place a large skillet over medium heat and pour in olive oil. Season with salt and pepper. Once oil heats, add in garlic. Cook for 1 minute and then add in the red pepper flakes. Cook for 30 seconds and then add in the onions, tomatoes, oregano and season with more salt and pepper. I like my tomatoes crushed, so I took a potato smasher and smashed the tomato chunks – you can do this with a fork! Let the mixture cook for 5 minutes and then add the asparagus and salmon in the oven. Cook for 12-15 minutes, depending on the thickness of your salmon. Once done, take out and set aside.
3. Let the tomato skillet mixture cook for about 15-20 minutes or until the sauce reduces and most of the juices are gone. Add in the Greek Yogurt and mix to combine, until sauce lightens to a medium pink.
4. Next, add in the zucchini pasta, salmon and asparagus. Mix to combine thoroughly. Cook for about 2-3 minutes or until zucchini pasta softens.
5. Plate onto dishes and enjoy.

Crockpot Cauliflower Bolognese with Zucchini Noodles

Prep Time: 10 mins | Cook Time: 3 hours, 30 mina | Total Time: 3 hours 40 mins | Servings: 5-6

Ingredients

For the Bolognese:

- 1 head of cauliflower, cut up into florets
- 3/4 cup diced red onion
- 2 small garlic cloves, minced
- 2 tsp dried oregano flakes
- 1 tsp dried basil flakes
- 2 14oz cans diced tomatoes, no salt added
- 1/2 cup vegetable broth, low-sodium
- 1/4 tsp red pepper flakes
- salt and pepper, to taste
- For the pasta:
- 5 large zucchinis, Blade A

Directions

1. Place all of the ingredients for the bolognese into a crockpot. Place the crockpot on high and let cook for 3.5 hours.
2. When done, smash the cauliflower with a potato masher or fork until the florets break up to create a "bolognese."
3. Spoon the bolognese over bowls of zucchini noodles.

Deconstructed Manicotti Skillet with Zucchini Noodles

Prep Time: *10 minutes |* **Cook Time:** *40 minutes |* **Total Time:** *50 minutes |* **Servings:**
2

Ingredients

- 1/2 tbsp olive oil
- 1 large garlic clove, minced
- pinch of red pepper flakes
- 1/2 cup diced red onion
- 1 14oz can diced tomatoes, no salt added
- salt and pepper, to taste
- 5 basil leaves, chopped
- 3 cups baby spinach
- 2 zucchinis, Blade A
- 2 tbsp shredded mozzarella cheese

For the filling:

- 1/4 cup parmesan cheese
- 7.5oz of ricotta cheese
- 1/4 cup shredded mozzarella cheese
- 1 small egg

Directions

1. Preheat the oven to 375 degrees.
2. Place a large castiron or nonstick skillet over medium heat and add in the olive oil. Add in the garlic, red pepper flakes and onions and cook for 2-3 minutes or until onions are translucent.
3. Add in the canned tomatoes and season with salt and pepper. Stir and let cook for 10 minutes or until your sauce is reduced fully. Five minutes in, add the basil.
4. While the sauce is cooking, mix together all of the ingredients for the "filling." Season with salt and pepper. Set aside.
5. Then, place a large skillet over medium heat and coat with cooking spray. Once the skillet heats, add in your baby spinach and toss until wilted. Fold the spinach into the cheese mixture and set aside.
6. When the sauce is done cooking, remove half of the sauce and set aside. Make sure that the sauce is spread evenly on the bottom of the skillet and then top with the zucchini noodles. Top with the remaining sauce.
7. Next, make two pockets in the zucchini noodles on either side of the skillet and fill each with a dollop of the cheese "filling." Sprinkle over the skillet with the 2 tbsp of mozzarella. Season the top of the skillet with pepper.
8. Cover the skillet with tin foil and bake for 20-25 minutes or until the noodles soften and the cheese is completely melted.
9. Serve for two!

Dill-Zucchini Pasta with Cannellini Beans, Hearts of Palm and Feta

Prep Time: 10 minutes | Cook Time: 5 minutes | Servings: 1

Ingredients

- 1 tbsp olive oil
- 1 small garlic clove, thinly sliced
- 1-2 medium zucchinis, Blade C
- 1 tbsp chopped dill (or more)

- 1.5 tbsp lemon juice (fresh)
- 1/2 cup cannellini beans
- 1 heart of palm from a can of hearts of palm, chopped into 1/4" slices
- pepper, to taste
- 2 tbsp crumbled feta

Directions

1. Place a large skillet over medium heat. Add in the olive oil and then the garlic. Cook for 30 seconds and then add in the zucchini pasta, dill, lemon juice, beans and hearts of palm. Season with pepper and cook, tossing frequently, for about 3 minutes or until zucchini noodles reach your preference of doneness.
2. Plate into a bowl, top with feta and enjoy!

Easy Bacon Shrimp "Zucchini Noodle" Scampi

Prep Time: 10 minutes | Cook Time: 15 minutes | Total Time: 25 minutes | Servings: 2

Ingredients

- 2 piece of bacon
- 1 garlic clove, minced
- 1 pinch red pepper flakes
- 1/4 cup minced shallots
- 12 shrimps, defrosted, deveined and shells removed
- salt and pepper, to taste
- 4 tbsp freshly squeezed lemon juice
- 2-3 medium zucchinis, peeled, Blade C
- 2 tsp lemon zest
- 2 tbsp freshly chopped parsley

Directions

1. Place a large skillet over medium heat and add in the bacon. Cook bacon for 3 minutes on each side or until cooked to your crunchy preference. Remove with a slotted spoon and transfer to a plate lined with paper towel.

2. Leave only 1 tbsp of bacon fat in the skillet and add in the garlic. Cook the garlic for 30 seconds and then add in the red pepper flakes, shallots and shrimp. Season with salt and pepper and let shrimp cook for about 2 minutes, flip over, add in the lemon juice and zest and cook an additional two minutes. Remove the shrimps with a slotted spoon and set aside.
3. In the same skillet, add in the zucchini noodles and toss to combine, for about 2 minutes and then add in the shrimp and crumble in the bacon. Toss to combine. Divide onto two plates and garnish with chopped parsley

Easy Pomodoro Sauce

Prep Time: 10 minutes | Cook Time: 15 minutes | Total Time: 25 minutes | Servings: 1 cup

Ingredients

- 1 tbsp olive oil
- 1/2 tbsp minced garlic
- 1/2 heaping cup diced white onion
- 1 14oz can crushed San Marzano tomatoes
- salt, to taste
- 1.5-2 tbsp chopped basil

Directions

1. Place a large skillet over medium heat and add in the olive oil. Once the oil heats, add in the garlic and cook for 30 seconds or until fragrant.
2. Add in the onions and cook for 2 minutes or until onions are translucent.
3. Add in the crushed tomatoes and season with salt. Lower to a simmer, cook for 5 minutes and then add in the basil.
4. Let the sauce cook for another 5-10 minutes or until most of the liquid has evaporated and it is thicker, suitable for cooking with zucchini noodles.
5. Use with zucchini noodles or freeze to store for future use.

Easy Turkey Taco Celeriac Pasta

Prep Time: 15 minutes | Cook Time: 20 minutes | Total Time: 35 minutes | Servings: 3

Ingredients

- 1 large celeriac
- ½ tablespoon extra virgin olive oil
- 1 garlic clove, finely minced
- ½ cup diced white onion
- ½ diced red bell pepper
- ½ jalapeno, seeded, diced
- ½ pound lean ground turkey meat
- salt and pepper, to taste
- 1 14.5oz can diced tomatoes, drained
- ½ cup quartered olives
- 1/2 cup chicken broth, low sodium
- ½ cup organic cheddar cheese
- 1 tablespoon minced cilantro, to garnish
- ½ avocado, sliced into strips
- For the taco spices:
- ¼ tsp cayenne pepper
- 1 tsp chili powder
- ¼ tsp garlic powder
- ½ tsp paprika
- ½ tsp smoked paprika
- ½ tsp onion powder
- ¼ tsp cumin
- ¼ tsp oregano
- salt, to taste

Directions

1. Bring a large saucepan filled halfway with water to a boil.
2. While waiting for water to boil, peel and spiralize the celeriac, using Blade B. Trim the noodles.
3. Once boiling, add in the celeriac noodles and cook for 2-3 minutes or until al dente. Drain and set aside.
4. Place a large skillet over medium heat and add in the olive oil. Once oil heats, add in the garlic, onions, bell pepper, and jalapenos, cooking for 3-5 minutes or until onions turn translucent. Then, push the mixture to the side of the pan and add in the ground turkey.
5. Cook the turkey until it's completely browned, about 5-7 minutes. Then, mix veggies and turkey together in the skillet and season with taco spices and salt and pepper. Add in the tomatoes, olives and stir for 1 minute. Then, add in the chicken broth and cook for 5 minutes or until most of the broth reduces.

6. Stir in the cheddar cheese and keep stirring until cheese melts. Remove from heat. Divide to celeriac into two bowls and top with equal amounts of the sauce. Garnish with cilantro and serve with avocado slices.

Eggplant Noodles

Prep Time: 5 minutes | Cook Time: 10 minutes | Total Time: 15 minutes | Servings: 1

Ingredients

- 1 eggplant, Blade C
- 1 tbsp olive oil
- 1 tsp minced garlic
- 1 pinch red pepper flakes
- salt and pepper to taste
- 1/4 tsp oregano flakes
- 3 sundried tomatoes, sliced thinly
- 1/4 cup chickpeas
- 1 tbsp raisins

Directions

1. Place a large skillet over medium heat.
2. Add the olive oil into the pan. Once the oil heats, add in the garlic and cook for 1 minute. Add in the red pepper flakes, cook for 30 seconds and then add in the eggplant noodles.
3. Stir the noodles and season with salt, pepper and oregano. Add in the chickpeas, sundried tomatoes and raisins. Cook for about 5 minutes or until eggplant begins to darken in color.
4. Plate into a bowl and enjoy!

Fire Roasted Tomato Zucchini Pasta with Turkey Meatballs

Prep Time: *10 minutes |* **Cook Time:** *25 minutes |* **Total Time:** *35 minutes |* **Servings:**
2

Ingredients

For the meatballs:

- 1 garlic clove, minced
- 1/2 cup breadcrumbs
- 1 egg
- 1/4 cup grated parmigiano-reggiano cheese
- salt and pepper, to taste
- 2 tbsp warm water
- 1/2-3/4 lb lean ground turkey
- 1/2 tsp dried oregano flakes
- 2 tbsp freshly chopped parsley
- cooking spray

For the rest:

- 1 tbsp olive oil
- 1 garlic clove, minced
- 1/4 tsp red pepper flakes
- 1/4 cup diced red onion
- 1 14oz can Muir Glen Fire Roasted Diced Tomatoes
- 1/2 tsp dried oregano flakes
- 4-5 medium zucchinis, Blade C

Directions

1. Preheat the oven to 375 degrees.
2. In a large saucepan, add in the olive oil. Once the oil heats, add in the garlic. Let garlic cook for 30 seconds and add in the red pepper flakes and onions. Let cook for 2 minutes or until onions begin to soften. Add in the fire roasted tomatoes and crush with a potato masher or back of a fork. Season with pepper and oregano.
3. Cook the sauce until it is reduced fully and no moisture remains, about 10 minutes. Once reduced, add in the zucchini noodles and toss until noodles soften and sauce becomes the proper consistency, about 3 minutes.

4. While the sauce is reducing, place all of your ingredients for the meatballs into a bowl and mix together. Using your hands, mold into slightly larger than golfball sized meatballs. Arrange on a baking tray that's lightly coated in cooking spray. Cook for 10-12 minutes, flipping the meatballs over after 5 minutes.
5. Plate the noodles onto a plate or bowl and top with 3 meatballs! Enjoy.

Foil-Pouch Sweet Potato Noodle Chicken Fajitas

Prep Time: 15 minutes | *Cook Time:* 25 minutes | *Total Time:* 40 minutes | *Servings:* 3

Ingredients

For fajita mix*:

- ¼ tsp cayenne pepper
- 1 tsp chili powder
- ¼ tsp garlic powder
- ½ tsp paprika
- ½ tsp smoked paprika
- ½ tsp onion powder
- ¼ tsp cumin
- 1/2 tsp salt
- ¼ tsp oregano

For the rest:

- 8 chicken breast tenderloins (or 2 chicken breasts, cut into 8 tenderloin strips)
- 1 yellow bell pepper, sliced
- 1 green bell pepper, sliced
- ½ large red or white onion, sliced into ½ inch strips
- 2 tbsp olive oil
- juice of 1 lime
- 1 avocado, insides cubed
- 1 large (350g+) sweet potato, peeled, Blade C

Directions

1. Preheat the oven to 375 degrees.

2. Place a large skillet over medium heat and coat with cooking spray. Add in the chicken and cook for 2 minutes, flip and cook another 2 minutes. Set aside the cooked chicken on a plate.
3. In a bowl, combine all of the ingredients for the fajita mix. Set aside.
4. In another bowl, place in the bell peppers, cooked chicken, avocado, olive oil and lime juice. Toss to combine. Add 1 tbsp of the fajita mix seasonings to the bowl and toss to combine. Set aside.
5. Take out a large piece of tinfoil and place the sweet potato noodles in the center. Then, top with the fajita contents. Close the contents by folding the tinfoil into a pouch-like packet. Leave about 1 inch on the top, when enclosing (for the warm air to circulate and steam the contents).
6. Place the foil pouch on a baking tray and bake in the oven for 20-25 minutes. Serve in pouches or pour out onto plates. Enjoy!

Football Season & Pepperoni Pizza Zucchini Spaghetti

Prep Time: *5 minutes* | **Cook Time:** *25 minutes* | **Total Time:** *30 minutes* | **Servings:** *2*

Ingredients

For the pasta:

- 1.5 zucchinis, Blade C
- 1/3 cup chunkily-chopped mozzarella
- 10 pepperoni slices
- 1-2 slices of crusty whole grain bread (optional, for dipping)
- For the pizza sauce:
- 1 (14oz) can of crushed tomatoes
- 1/3 cup chopped red onions
- 1 garlic clove, minced
- 1 tbsp olive oil
- salt and pepper, to taste
- 1/4 tsp red pepper flakes (or less, if you don't like spice)
- 1 tsp dried oregano flakes
- 1/2 tsp dried basil flakes
- 1 tsp tomato paste

Directions

1. Place a large skillet over medium-low heat and add in the olive oil.

2. Once the oil heats, add in the garlic. Cook garlic for 1 minute and add in the red pepper flakes. Cook for 30 seconds and then add in the chopped onion. Stir and cook for about 2 minutes or until onions begin to soften.
3. Add in the crushed tomatoes, season generously with salt and pepper and add in the oregano and basil flakes. Stir to combine.
4. Let cook, stirring occasionally, for about 15 minutes or until the sauce fully reduces.
5. Once the sauce reduces, add in the zucchini pasta and pepperoni. Cook for about 2 minutes or until zucchini begins to soften and is heated through.
6. Add in the mozzarella cheese, cook for another 30 seconds, and then pour into a bowl and enjoy!

Garlic Mushroom and Leek Turnip Noodles

*Prep time: 20 mins | **Cook time:** 15 mins | **Total time:** 35 mins | **Serves:** 2*

Ingredients

- 1.5 tablespoon extra virgin olive oil
- ¼ cup diced sweet onions
- 2 garlic cloves, minced
- 1 pinch red pepper flakes
- 1 cup sliced leeks
- 2 cups sliced baby portobello mushrooms (or button mushrooms)
- 2 medium turnips, peeled, Blade C, noodles trimmed
- salt and pepper, to taste
- 1 tablespoon chopped parsley + more to garnish (optional)
- ¼ cup grated or shaved parmesan cheese, to garnish

Directions

1. Place a large skillet over medium heat and add in ½ tablespoon of the olive oil. Once oil heats, add the onions, garlic and red pepper flakes. Let cook for 2 minutes or until onions begin to soften.
2. Add in the leeks and mushrooms and cook for 3-5 minutes or until mushrooms begin to wilt. Transfer the veggies to a plate and set aside. Then, add in the rest of the olive oil and then the turnip noodles. Season with salt and pepper and cook for 5-7 minutes or until turnip noodles are al dente or cooked to your preference. When done, add in the mushrooms and leek mixture, parsley and toss to combine.

3. Divide the pasta into bowls and top with parmesan cheese and garnish with parsley, if desired.

Garlic Sweet Potato Noodles with Pancetta and Baby Spinach

Prep Time: 10 minutes | Cook Time: 15 minutes | Total Time: 25 minutes | Servings: 2

Ingredients

- 1 tbsp olive oil
- 1 large garlic clove, minced (about 1.5 tsp)
- 1/2 cup diced white onions
- 1 pinch red pepper flakes
- 1/2 cup cubed pancetta
- 1 large (350g+) sweet potato, peeled, Blade C
- 1/4 cup chicken broth
- 4 large basil leaves, chopped
- 3-4 packed cups of spinach

Directions

1. Place a large skillet over medium heat and add in the olive oil. Once the oil heats, add in the garlic, red pepper flakes and onions and cook for about 2 minutes or until onions are translucent.
2. Add in the sweet potato noodles and pancetta and season with salt and pepper. Toss to combine and let cook for a few minutes (about 2) and then add in the chicken broth and basil. Let fully reduce and then cook for 2-3 minutes or until sweet potato noodles are cooked through (taste to test.) Towards the end, add in the baby spinach and let cook for about 2 minutes or until spinach is wilted.
3. When done, divide evenly into bowls.

Garlic Zucchini Spaghetti with Italian Chicken Sausage, Tomatoes, Basil and Roasted Potatoes

Prep Time: 7 minutes | Cook Time: 30 minutes | Total Time: 37 minutes | Servings: 2

Ingredients

- 1.5 zucchinis, Blade C
- 1/2 whole tomato, chopped
- 1/2 cup chopped basil (and a bit extra for garnish)
- 1 tsp red pepper flakes (or more, if you like it spicy!)
- salt and pepper
- 2 small red potatoes, quartered
- olive oil
- 1 tbsp garlic powder
- 2-3 links, chicken sausage, caseings removed and cut into chunks
- 1/3-1/2 cup, Parmesan Cheese (optional!)
- 2 large garlic cloves, minced

Directions

1. Preheat oven to 425 degrees. In a bowl, place in red potatoes and pour in two glugs of olive oil. Spray a baking sheet with olive oil cooking spray. Place in potatoes and season with salt, pepper and garlic powder. Once preheated, add in potatoes. Halfway through, toss around. Once done, set aside.
2. Add 3-4 glugs of olive oil in a large skillet and season with salt and pepper. Once oil heats, add in garlic and cook for 1 minute, stirring frequently. Then, add red pepper flakes, stir for 30 seconds and then add in chicken sausage.
3. Cook the sausage for about 2 minutes and then flip and cook for another 2-3 minutes or until sausage is no longer pink. Add in tomatoes and cook for 1 minute.
4. Add in zucchini pasta, another glug (or two!) of olive oil and season with salt and pepper. Stir to combine. Add in roasted potatoes. Cook for 2-3 minutes or until zucchini softens.
5. Add in Parmesan cheese (of course, optional). Stir thoroughly to combine. Pour into serving bowl, plate onto dishes and serve garnished with any leftover chopped basil.

Garlic-Lemon Turnip Pasta with String Beans and Edamame

Prep time: 15 mins | Cook time: 15 mins | Total time: 30 mins | Serves: 2

Ingredients

- 1.25 pounds string beans, ends trimmed
- 2 tablespoons extra virgin olive oil
- 2 garlic cloves, minced
- 1 small shallot, minced
- ¼ teaspoon red pepper flakes
- 2 turnips, peeled, Blade B
- salt and pepper, to taste
- ½ teaspoon fresh lemon zest
- ½ cup cooked edamame beans
- 1 tablespoon freshly grated parmesan cheese, to garnish

Directions

1. Bring a medium pot filled halfway with water to a boil. Once boiling, add in the string beans and cook for about 5 minutes or until the beans are string-tender. Drain into a colander and set aside.
2. Once water starts boiling, place a large skillet over medium heat and add in the olive oil. Once oil heats, add in the garlic, shallots and red pepper flakes and cook for 2 minutes or until shallots are translucent.
3. Add in the turnip noodles and toss thoroughly to combine. Season with salt and pepper and cover, cooking for 5 minutes or until turnip noodles are al dente, uncovering occasionally to toss. Once cooked, add in the lemon zest, string beans and edamame and toss. Let cook for 2 minutes to let the edamame warm and flavors combine.
4. Divide pasta into bowls, garnish with parmesan and serve.

Garlic-Parmesan Zucchini Noodles and Spaghetti Pasta

*Prep Time: 15 minutes | **Cook Time:** 10 minutes | **Total Time:** 25 minutes | **Servings:***
2

Ingredients

- 2 ounces of spaghetti
- pinch of salt
- 3 medium garlic cloves
- 3 tablespoons extra virgin olive oil
- ¼ teaspoon red pepper flakes
- 1 medium zucchini

- 3 tablespoons grated parmesan cheese
- salt and pepper, to taste

Directions

1. Bring a large pot of water and a pinch of salt to a boil. Once boiling, drop in the spaghetti and cook until al dente, per package directions (typically 10 minutes.)
2. While the pasta is cooking, thinly slice the garlic and spiralize your zucchini using Blade C. Trim the noodles using a scissor. Set both aside.
3. When the pasta is ready, drain it and set aside, discarding the pasta water.
4. Place a large skillet on medium heat and pour in the oil. Add the garlic and chili flakes and cook for 30 seconds or until garlic is fragrant. Add in the zucchini noodles and toss for 2-3 minutes or until al dente. Then, add in the "real" spaghetti and season generously with salt and pepper.
5. Remove the skillet from the heat and add in the parmesan cheese. Toss until cheese is melted into the pasta. Serve immediately.

Gluten-Free Breaded Lemon Sole with Tomato Basil Chayote Pasta

Prep time: 15 mins | Cook time: 15 mins | Total time: 30 mins | Serves: 1

Ingredients

- ½ cup canned healthy tomato basil sauce (I like Rao's)
- 1 whole egg
- 2 tablespoons almond meal
- salt and pepper, to taste
- ¼ teaspoon garlic powder
- 3oz lemon sole (or other white fish)
- ½ tablespoon extra virgin olive oil
- 1 large lemon wedge
- 1 small chayote, Blade D, noodles trimmed

Directions

1. Place two shallow dishes side by side. In one, crack in the egg and whisk. In the other, add in the almond meal, season with salt, pepper and garlic powder and mix thoroughly. Spread the almond meal in an even layer in the baking dish.

2. Dip one sole filet in the egg and coat. Then, dip in the almond meal mixture, flipping over to coat all sides. Set aside on a plate.
3. Turn two burners on to medium-high heat. On one burner, place a medium skillet (for the fish.) On the other burner, place a larger skillet (for the chayote noodles.)
4. Place the olive oil in the medium skillet and let heat. Once heated, add in the fish and cook for 3 minutes, flip over and cook another 2-3 minutes or until the fish easily flakes with a fork and is opaque white and breading is golden brown. Once you flip over, squeeze the lemon over the fish.
5. Meanwhile, in the large skillet, add in the chayote noodles and cook for 3-5 minutes or until al dente. Once almost cooked, add in the tomato basil sauce and toss together, cooking another minute for the chayote to finish cooking and the sauce to heat.
6. Serve the chayote noodles with the lemon sole.

Gluten-Free Caesar Zucchini Noodles with Grilled Lemon Chicken, Tomatoes and Breadcrumbs

Prep time: 20 mins | *Cook time:* 20 mins | *Total time:* 40 mins | *Serves:* 3

Ingredients

For the dressing:

- ½ cup raw cashews, soaked for at least 30 minutes and drained
- ½ cup unsweetened almond milk
- 1 large cloves garlic
- 1tablespoons freshly squeezed lemon juice
- 1 teaspoon dijon mustard
- salt and pepper, to taste
- For the salad:
- 1 slice of gluten-free bread, cut into cubes
- 3 medium zucchinis
- 1 cup halved cherry tomatoes

For the chicken:

- 2 boneless, skinless chicken breasts (thin cut)
- ¼ cup lemon juice
- 1 teaspoon dried parsley
- ½ teaspoon garlic powder
- 1 tablespoon extra virgin olive oil

- salt and pepper, to taste

Directions

1. In a medium bowl, add in the lemon juice, parsley, garlic powder and season with salt and pepper. Set aside.
2. Meanwhile, place a large skillet over medium-high heat and add in the olive oil and let heat. While the oil heats, dip the chicken breasts in the marinade. Once the oil heats, add in the chicken breasts and cook for 2-3 minutes on one side and then flip over, cook another 3-5 minutes or until chicken is cooked through and juices run clear. When done, transfer to a cutting board. Slice the chicken into pieces.
3. Meanwhile, place the slice of gluten-free bread into a toaster and toast to crispy. Once crispy, slice into cubes and set aside. Also, slice the zucchinis halfway lengthwise and then spiralize them, using Blade D. Place the zucchini noodles into a large mixing bowl with the tomatoes and bread cubes and set aside.
4. Place all of the ingredients for the dressing into a food processor or high-speed blender and pulse until creamy. Taste and adjust to your preference, if necessary. Set aside.
5. Once chicken is cooked and sliced, pour the dressing over the zucchini noodle mixture and toss to combine.
6. Divide the noodles onto plates and top each with chicken breast slices. Drizzle with any remaining dressing.

Gluten-Free Zucchini Spaghetti Fried Eggs

Prep time: *15 mins* | **Cook time:** *10 mins* | **Total time:** *25 mins* | **Serves:** *2*

Ingredients

For the pasta:

- 2 medium zucchinis, Blade C/D
- 1 tablespoon extra virgin olive oil
- 1 large garlic clove, minced
- 1 small pinch red pepper flakes
- 2 large eggs
- For the breadcrumbs:
- 2 tablespoons almond meal
- ⅛ teaspoon dried oregano flakes

- ⅛ teaspoon dried basil flakes
- ⅛ teaspoon dried parsley flakes
- ⅛ teaspoon garlic powder
- salt and pepper, to taste
- 1 teaspoon water

Directions

1. Place a medium skillet over medium heat and coat with cooking spray. Meanwhile, in a small bowl, combine all of the ingredients but the water for the breadcrumbs and whisk together. Add in the water and use your hands to form a dough – it should end up in a ball.
2. Crumble the dough ball into the heated skillet and continually break up with a wooden spoon. Cook for 2-3 minutes or until breadcrumbs break up, harden and become "toasted." Set aside in a bowl and set the heated skillet to the side.
3. Place a large skillet over medium-high heat and add in the olive oil. Once oil heats, add in the garlic and red pepper flakes and cook 30 seconds or until fragrant. Add in the zucchini noodles and toss for 3-5 minutes or until noodles have reached your desired consistency preference (about 3 for al dente.)
4. Meanwhile, place the medium skillet back over medium-high heat and coat with cooking spray. Once heated (flick water into the pan and it should sizzle), add in the eggs and cook for 3-5 minutes or until egg whites set.
5. Plate the zucchini noodles, top with fried egg and sprinkle over breadcrumbs.

Golden Beet Pasta with Grilled Asparagus, Lentils and Roasted Garlic-Parmesan Dressing

*Prep time: 15 mins | **Cook time**: 40 mins | **Total time**: 55 mins*

Ingredients

For the garlic dressing:

- 1 head of garlic
- extra virgin olive oil, to drizzle (use about ½ teaspoon)
- 3 tablespoons extra virgin olive oil
- 1 tablespoon freshly grated parmesan cheese
- ½ tablespoons red wine vinegar

- salt and pepper, to taste
- For the lentils:
- ½ cup lentils of choice
- 1 cup water
- For the rest:
- 5 oz asparagus, ends trimmed
- 2 teaspoons extra virgin olive oil
- salt and pepper
- 2 medium golden beets, peeled, Blade D, noodles trimmed

Directions

1. Preheat the oven to 400 degrees. Peel the garlic to remove all the papery outer layers, leaving intact only the single layer around the individual cloves. Cut about ½ inch of the top of the head, exposing the individual cloves. Place on a baking tray or a muffin tin and drizzle with olive oil.
2. Cover the top of the garlic with aluminum foil and bake for 35-40 minutes or until garlic is soft and easily pierced with a fork. Remove the garlic from the oven and let cool until cool enough to handle. Peel away the papery skin and place 6 of the cloves in a food processor along with the olive oil, parmesan, red wine vinegar and season with salt and pepper and pulse until no large chunks of garlic remain. Set aside.
3. While the garlic is cooking, cook the lentils. Rinse the lentils under cold water. Place the lentils in a medium saucepan along with the water and bring to a rapid simmer. Once simmering, reduce to a low simmer and cook 20-30 minutes, adding water if needed (always keep lentils "barely covered.") Lentils are cooked once they are tender but not mushy. Set aside.
4. While lentils and garlic cook, place a large grill pan over medium-high heat. Add the asparagus to a bowl with the olive oil, season with salt and pepper and toss to combine. Once the pain is heated, add in the asparagus and season with salt and pepper. Cook for 3 minutes, flip over and cook another 3-5 minutes or until asparagus is grilled and fork-tender. Set aside and add in the beet noodles. Cook the beet noodles for 7-10 minutes, tossing occasionally, or until wilted and al dente.
5. Divide the beet noodles into bowls and top with asparagus and lentils. Drizzle each with roasted garlic

Greek Inspired Zucchini Pasta – Feta Turkey Meatballs!

Prep Time: *10 minutes* | **Cook Time:** *23 minutes* | **Total Time:** *33 minutes* | **Servings:** *2*

Ingredients

For the meatballs and pasta

- 2 zucchinis, Blade C
- 1 shallot, minced
- 1/2 piece of whole wheat bread, for breadcrumbs
- 1/2 lb ground turkey, 93% lean
- 1/2 tsp oregano
- 3 tbsp finely chopped fresh parsley
- 1/4 cup crumbled feta cheese
- salt and pepper to taste
- 1 garlic clove, minced
- 2 tablespoons of warm water

For the kale pesto

- 3 cups of chopped kale
- 3 tbsp pine nuts
- 1 clove of garlic, minced
- 1.5 tbsp of lemon juice (from a fresh lemon)
- 3 tbsp Parmesan cheese
- 8 cranks of a sea salt grinder
- 6 cranks of a peppercorn grinder
- 3-4 tbsp olive oil (or more, if you like it creamier)
- 3 tbsp water

Directions

1. Preheat the oven to 400 degrees. Spray a large baking sheet with cooking spray. Set aside. Add the bread to the food processor and pulse to make breadcrumbs. Set aside.
2. In a large mixing bowl, add the shallots, water, breadcrumbs, garlic, turkey, oregano, parsley, feta, garlic, salt and pepper. Mix with your fingers thoroughly. Grab a small handful of mixture and mold it in your hands into a golfball-sized meatball. Add to the baking sheet. Continue until all of the mixture is used, makes about six.
3. Add the meatballs to the oven and set the timer for 20 minutes. After 10 minutes, take out and flip the meatballs over. Cook for another 10-12 minutes or until the edges begin to brown.
4. While meatballs are cooking, combine all of the ingredients for the pesto into a food processor and pulse until creamy.

5. Pour the kale pesto on top of the zucchini noodles and mix thoroughly to combine. Divide the zucchini pasta onto the plates. When the meatballs are ready, add to the pasta and enjoy!

Greek Paleo Turkey Meatballs and Tomato Beet Spaghetti

Prep Time: 25 minute | Cook Time: 30 minutes | Total Time: 55 minutes | Servings: 4-6

Ingredients

For the meatballs and pasta

- 2 shallots, minced
- 2 garlic cloves, minced
- 1 pound ground turkey, at least 93% lean
- 1 teaspoon oregano
- ¼ cup finely chopped fresh parsley + more to garnish
- 1/2 cup crumbled feta cheese
- kosher salt and ground pepper to taste
- 4 beets, peeled, Blade C, noodles trimmed

For the sauce:

- 1 tablespoon extra virgin olive oil
- 1 28oz can crushed tomatoes
- 2 garlic cloves, minced
- ½ cup diced red onion
- ¼ cup capers
- 1/3 cup pitted and halved kalamata olives
- 2 teaspoons oregano
- freshly ground pepper, to taste

Directions

1. Preheat the oven to 400 degrees. Spray two large baking sheets with cooking spray. Set aside.
2. In a large mixing bowl, add the shallots, garlic, turkey, oregano, parsley, feta, garlic, salt and pepper. Mix with your fingers thoroughly. Grab a small handful of mixture and mold it in your hands into a golfball-sized meatball.

Add to one of the prepared baking sheets. Continue until all of the mixture is used, makes about 10-12. Set aside.

3. Place a large skillet over medium heat and add in the olive oil. Once oil heats, add in the garlic and onion. Let cook for 3-5 minutes or until onions are translucent. Add in the crushed tomatoes, capers, olives and season with oregano and pepper. Let cook at a medium simmer for 15 minutes or until sauce thickens.

4. Once you begin to simmer the sauce, place the meatballs in the oven for 15 minutes or until no longer pink on the inside. Also, spread the beet noodles out on the second prepared baking tray and roast for 10 minutes or until to your al dente preference.

5. Divide the beet noodles into bowls and top with pasta sauce and 2-3 meatballs.

6. Garnish with parsley and serve.

Grilled Ricotta Spaghetti & Brussel Sprouts with Butter Beans and Sundried Tomatoes

Prep Time: 7 minutes | Cook Time: 15 minutes | Total Time: 22 minutes | Servings: 2

Ingredients

- 2 zucchinis, Blade C
- 8-10 brussel sprouts
- 3 sundried tomatoes
- 1/2 cup ricotta cheese
- 1/2 cup butter beans
- 1 tsp olive oil
- 1 tsp red pepper flakes
- 1 large clove of garlic, minced
- salt and pepper, to taste
- pinch of garlic powder
- olive oil cooking spray

Directions

1. Turn on and heat up a George Forman grill. If you don't have one, skip this step (we will use a grill pan later).

2. Prepare your brussel sprouts by removing any tough outer leaves, slicing off the bottoms and halving them. Prepare your sundried tomatoes by cutting them into 1/4 inch strips. Set all aside.

3. Bring a small saucepan with enough water to cover the brussel sprouts to a boil. When ready, add in the brussel sprouts for about 3-4 minutes or until they are halfway done and almost able to be forked easily. Pour into a colander to drain and then pat dry thoroughly. When done, season brussel sprouts with salt, pepper and a pinch of garlic powder.

4. Spray both sides of the George Forman grill with olive oil cooking spray (or heat up a grill plan on the stovetop on medium-high heat). Place the brussel sprouts cut-side down onto the grill/grill pan and let cook for about 3-4 minutes or until sprouts have grill marks and are more easily pierced with a fork. When done, set aside.

5. Wipe down grill/grill pan and spray again with cooking spray. Place in zucchini noodles and cook for about 1-2 minutes. When done, set aside.

6. While noodles are cooking, place a large skillet over medium heat. Add in olive oil. Once oil heats, add in garlic, cook for about 30 seconds and then add in red pepper flakes. Cook for 30 seconds and then add in butter beans, brussel sprouts and sundried tomatoes. Cook for about 1 minute and then add in zucchini pasta and ricotta cheese. Stir to combine thoroughly for about 1 minute. Serve hot!

Grilled Shrimp over Zucchini Noodles

"A great alternative to pasta!"

Prep: *10 m* | **Cook:** *5 m* | **Ready In:** *15 m*

Ingredients

- 2 cups thinly sliced fresh basil
- 9 tablespoons olive oil, divided
- 1/3 cup toasted sliced almonds, divided
- 1 tablespoon red wine vinegar
- 1 shallot, coarsely chopped
- 2 cloves garlic, coarsely chopped
- 1 lemon, zested
- 1/4 teaspoon red pepper flakes
- 1 pound shrimp, peeled and deveined
- 5 zucchini kosher salt and freshly ground black pepper to taste

Directions

1. Blend basil, 1/2 cup olive oil, 1/4 cup almonds, vinegar, shallot, garlic, lemon zest, and red pepper flakes in a blender until lemon basil dressing is smooth.
2. Heat 1 tablespoon olive oil in a skillet over medium-high heat; saute shrimp until cooked through and pink, 2 to 4 minutes. Remove skillet from heat and mix shrimp with 2 tablespoons dressing in a bowl.
3. Run zucchini through a spiralizer to create spaghetti-size noodle shapes. Add to skillet; cook and stir over medium heat until zucchini noodles are tender, 1 to 2 minutes. Add 2 tablespoons lemon basil dressing and toss to coat. Remove skillet from heat.
4. Arrange shrimp on top of zucchini noodles; season with salt and black pepper. Top with remaining almonds.

Nutritional Information

- Calories:356 kcal 18%
- Fat: 28.6 g 44%
- Carbs: 8.1g 3%
- Protein: 18.4 g 37%
- Cholesterol: 138 mg 46%
- Sodium: 253 mg 10%

Healthy Kids' Halloween Party Idea: Spooky Green Monster Zucchini Noodles

Prep Time: 10 minutes | **Cook Time**: 25 minutes | **Total Time**: 35 minutes | **Servings**: 3

Ingredients

For the pesto:

- 3 cups packed with basil
- 3 tbsp pine nuts
- 2 garlic cloves, minced
- salt and pepper to taste
- 1/3 to 1/2 cup olive oil
- For the rest:
- 2 medium zucchinis, Blade C

- 3 medium-sized mozzarella balls, halved
- 3 jumbo black olives
- 1 large red bell pepper

Directions

1. Preheat the oven to 400 degrees. Line a baking tray with aluminum foil. Line the aluminum foil with wax paper. Cut the bell pepper in half, remove the seeds and top, and place on the wax paper, sliced side down. Roast for 22-23 minutes.
2. While the pepper is roasting, prepare your pesto. Place all ingredients (only use half of the olive oil) into a food processor and pulse. Add more olive oil until it is at your desired consistency.
3. Pour the pesto over the zucchini noodles and mix to combine. Plate the pesto noodles into a bowl. Top with eyeballs (mozzarella ball halves). Set aside.
4. Prepare the rest of the eyeballs. Take an olive and slice off the very ends. Then, halve the remaining olive to create the two "pupils." Place in the center of the mozzarella. Repeat for each dish and set aside.
5. When the peppers are done roasting, place in a ziplock bag to let cool. Once it is cool enough to handle, cut into 3 strips for "tongues." Place onto the dish and serve!

Healthy Zucchini Pasta Carbonara

Prep Time: 10 minutes | Cook Time: 10 minutes | Total Time: 20 minutes | Servings:
2

Ingredients

- 1 tbsp olive oil
- 1 large garlic clove, minced
- 1/4 tsp red pepper flakes
- 1/4 cup diced red onion
- 1/2 cup cubed pancetta
- 2 whole large eggs
- 3 medium zucchinis, Blade C
- pepper, to taste
- 1/3 cup grated parmesan cheese

Directions

1. Place a large skillet over medium heat and add in the olive oil. Once the oil heats, add in the garlic and red pepper flakes. Cook the garlic for 30 seconds, add in the onion and cook for 2-3 minutes or until the onion softens. Then, add in the pancetta cubes. Cook, stirring often, until cooked through, about 5 minutes.
2. Once the pancetta is done cooking, add a medium skillet over medium heat and crack over two eggs. Let them cook until the egg whites set.
3. While your eggs are cooking, add the zucchini noodles to the pancetta, season with pepper and toss to combine. Stirring frequently, let cook for about 2-3 minutes and then add in the parmesan cheese. Toss the noodles with the cheese and then plate into bowls. Top each bowl with one of the eggs. Enjoy!

Herbed Ricotta Butternut Squash Noodles with Walnuts, Chickpeas and Cumin-Roasted Carrots and Cauliflower

Prep Time: 15 minutes | *Cook Time:* 30 minutes | *Total Time:* 45 minutes | *Servings:* 1

Ingredients

- 1/4 butternut squash (the non-hollow part)*
- 1 tbsp olive oil + more for drizzling
- 2 tbsp walnuts
- salt and pepper, to taste
- 1 small garlic clove, minced
- 1/2 tsp cumin
- 1/4 cup ricotta cheese
- 1 tbsp finely chopped fresh parsley + extra for garnish
- 1/4 cup chickpeas
- 1 cup cauliflower florets
- 1/2 whole carrot, cut into 1.5" rectangular pieces

Directions

1. Preheat the oven to 400 degrees.
2. Place the carrots and cauliflower in a baking tray and drizzle lightly with olive oil. Add the cumin and season with salt and pepper. Mix to combine thoroughly. Place in the oven for 25-30 minutes. Once cauliflower is lightly browned, the veggies are done.
3. While the vegetables are roasting, prepare the butternut squash. Cut off about 1/4 of the vegetable, peel it, and spiralize it, using Blade C. Set aside.
4. Next, prepare your herbed ricotta. Place the ricotta and finely chopped parsley into a bowl and mix to combine. Set aside.
5. About 10 minutes before the veggies are done roasting, add in the olive oil to a large skillet over medium heat. Once the oil heats, add in the garlic. Cook garlic for 1 minute and add in the butternut squash noodles. Cook for about 5-7 minutes or until the squash softens.
6. Once the squash softens, add in the herbed ricotta and cook, tossing to combine thoroughly. Once the noodles are coated in the warmed sauce, plate in a dish and top with roasted vegetables and chickpeas.
7. Top with walnuts and garnish with additional parsley and enjoy!

Homemade Gluten-Free Gnocchi with Pomodoro Zucchini Pasta

Prep time: 10 mins | *Cook time:* 35 mins | *Total time:* 45 mins | *Serves:* 4

Ingredients

For the gnocchi:*

- 1 pound sweet potato (about 1 large sweet potato or 3 cups cubed sweet potato)
- ¾ cup almond flour
- ½ cup tapioca flour
- ¼ cup coconut flour
- 1 egg
- ¼ teaspoon salt
- For the rest:
- 1 cup pomodoro sauce (I use Victoria's Pomodoro Sauce)
- 3-4 teaspoons extra virgin olive oil
- 1 large zucchini
- ¼ cup grated parmesan cheese or more to garnish

*If you don't want to make your own gnocchi, buy your favorite brand in the store – 4 servings worth to complete this recipe.

Directions

1. Bring a medium pot filled halfway with water and a pinch of salt to a boil. While waiting for the water to boil, peel the sweet potatoes and chop them into cubes. Once boiling, add the sweet potatoes and cook until soft (when easily pierced with a fork like butter, they're ready.) Drain into a colander and then transfer to a large bowl.
2. With the back of a fork or potato masher, mash the sweet potatoes. Add in the almond, tapioca, and coconut flour and egg and salt. Mix well to combine.
3. Bring water to a boil in the same medium pot again. Meanwhile, place a shallow baking dish or piece of parchment paper near your workspace. Roll the dough into balls (about 1 inch) and then shape into mini-logs and place on the parchment paper and baking dish. Using your fork, make that gnocchi indent! You can also make long logs out of the mixture and separate into 1" pieces with a knife and then make the indent.

4. Place the tomato basil sauce in a medium pot over medium-high heat and bring to a simmer. Once simmering, reduce heat to low and keep warm until ready to use at the end of the recipe.
5. Once water is boiling, drop the gnocchi bites into the water. The gnocchi is done once it floats to the top and stays there, which takes about 2 minutes. Remove with a slotted spoon and set aside on a plate or on the same parchment paper or baking dish. Work in batches until all the gnocchi is cooked. Freeze what you're not going to use (for this recipe, 24 gnocchis) and place what you are going to use in the refrigerator to cool for 5 minutes
6. Heat 1 teaspoon of the oil in a large skillet over medium heat and once the oil is shimmering, add in the gnocchi and cook for 2 minutes on the top and bottom. Cook in batches until all 24 gnocchis are cooked.
7. While gnocchi cooks, spiralize the zucchini with Blade D. Trim the noodles with kitchen shears.
8. Place half of the tomato sauce in a large bowl and toss with the zucchini noodles. Pour the rest of the tomato sauce on top of the plates with the gnocchi and then top each with the dressed zucchini noodles. Top with parmesan cheese to garnish. Serve immediately.

Italian Turkey Zoodles

"This is an easy low-carb pasta with tomato meat sauce that is so yummy, and has a mild kick."

***Servings**: 4 | **Prep**: 15 m | **Cook**: 38 m | **Ready In**: 1h18 m*

Ingredients

- 3 zucchini
- 1 tablespoon salt, or more as needed
- 1 pound ground turkey
- 1/2 teaspoon garlic salt
- 1/2 teaspoon garlic powder
- 1/2 teaspoon onion powder
- 1/4 teaspoon cayenne pepper
- 1/4 teaspoon red pepper flakes
- 1 teaspoon olive oil
- 1 teaspoon minced garlic
- 1 (14.5 ounce) can diced tomatoes
- 1 (3 ounce) can tomato paste
- 2 tablespoons balsamic vinegar

- 2 teaspoons dried parsley
- 1 teaspoon dried basil
- 1/2 teaspoon Italian seasoning
- 1/2 teaspoon salt
- 1/4 teaspoon ground black pepper
- 1 cup small-curd cottage cheese
- 1 cup shredded mozzarella cheese

Directions

1. Make zucchini noodles using a spiralizer or julienne peeler. Place noodles in a colander and cover liberally with 1 tablespoon salt. Let sit until noodles release some moisture, about 20 minutes. Rinse noodles and pat dry.
2. Place ground turkey, garlic salt, garlic powder, onion powder, cayenne pepper, and red pepper flakes in a large oven-safe skillet over medium heat. Cook and stir until turkey is browned and juices run clear, about 5 minutes. Drain grease.
3. Push turkey to the sides of the skillet to make an empty space in the center. Add olive oil and minced garlic; cook until garlic is fragrant, about 1 minute.
4. Preheat oven to 400 degrees F (200 degrees C).
5. Stir diced tomatoes, tomato paste, balsamic vinegar, parsley, basil, Italian seasoning, 1/2 teaspoon salt, and black pepper into the skillet. Bring to a boil; cook until sauce thickens, about 15 minutes. Stir in noodles. Cover with cottage cheese. Sprinkle mozzarella cheese evenly on top.
6. Bake in the preheated oven until cheese is melted, about 15 minutes. Turn on broiler and broil until cheese is golden brown, about 2 minutes. Remove from oven and let sit for 5 to 10 minutes before serving.

Nutritional Information

- Calories:380 kcal 19%
- Fat: 17.2 g 27%
- Carbs: 17.1g 6%
- Protein: 40.2 g 80%
- Cholesterol: 110 mg 37%
- Sodium: 3074 mg 123%

Kohlrabi Spaghetti alla Foriana

Prep Time: 15 minutes | *Cook Time:* 10 minutes | *Total Time:* 25 minutes | *Servings:* 2-3

Ingredients

- ½ cup walnuts
- ½ cup pine nuts
- 5 cloves of garlic, sliced thinly
- 1.5 tablespoons extra virgin olive oil
- 2 medium kohlrabi bulbs, peeled, Blade C, noodles trimmed
- 1.5 teaspoons dried oregano
- ¼ cup golden raisins
- salt and pepper, to taste

Directions

1. Place the walnuts, pine nuts and garlic in a food processor and pulse until finely chopped.
2. Place a large skillet over medium heat and add in the olive oil. Once oil heats, add in the kohlrabi noodles and cook for 2 minutes or until they begin to soften. Then, add in the oregano, pulsed nut mixture, raisins and season with salt and pepper. Cook for 3-5 minutes, stirring constantly to avoid burning the nuts but just enough to fully cook the kohlrabi.
3. Serve into bowls.

Kohlrabi Spaghetti and Kale-Mushroom Bolognese

Prep time: 20 mins | *Cook time:* 1 hour | *Total time:* 1 hour 20 mins | *Serves:* 3

Ingredients

- 2 tablespoons extra virgin olive oil
- ½ yellow onion, finely diced
- 1 celery stalk, finely diced
- 1 carrot, peeled, finely diced
- ½ cup cremini mushrooms, finely diced
- 1 garlic clove, minced
- 1 tablespoon tomato paste
- 2 tablespoons fabulous red wine (Cabernet works perfectly)

- ½ pound 80 percent lean ground beef
- 1 14.5 ounce can organic crushed tomatoes
- ½ teaspoon sea salt
- ½ cup finely chopped kale leaves
- 2 medium kohlrabis, Blade C, noodles trimmed
- salt and pepper, to taste
- 2 basil leaves, sliced thinly (for garnish)

Directions

1. In a large stockpot over medium heat, warm the olive oil. Add the onion and cook for about 5 minutes, or until soft. Add the celery and carrot and cook for an additional 5 minutes. Add the mushrooms and garlic cook for 5 minutes more, or until all the liquid has evaporated.
2. Add the tomato paste, and stir to coat all the vegetables. Saute for an additional 5 minutes to deepen and develop the flavor. Add the meat, stirring frequently with a wooden spoon to break up any large pieces, and sauté for about 10 minutes, until the meat is cooked through.
3. Increase the heat to medium-high, add the red wine and deglaze the pan. Cook until all the alcohol has evaporated and the brown bits have released from the bottom of the pan, 2 to 3 minutes.
4. Add the crushed tomatoes and the sea salt. Reduce the heat to low and cook for 35 minutes, stirring occasionally.
5. Five minutes before the sauce is ready, add the kale to the sauce and then also place a large skillet over medium-high heat and spray with cooking spray. Once heated, add in the kohlrabi noodles, season with salt and pepper and cook for 3-5 minutes for al dente or longer for your preference. Note that you may need to cook the kohlrabi noodles in batches (or use a wok for extra room.)
6. Divide the kohlrabi noodles into bowls and top with the finished sauce and garnish with basil.

Lemon Garlic Broccoli Zucchini Pasta with Prosciutto and Toasted Breadcrumbs

Prep Time: *15 minutes* | **Cook Time:** *20 minutes* | **Total Time:** *35 minutes* | **Servings:** *1*

Ingredients

1. 1/2 slice of bread

2. olive oil cooking spray
3. 1 tbsp olive oil
4. 4-5 large broccoli florets
5. salt and pepper
6. 3 tsp minced garlic
7. 1.5 medium zucchinis, Blade C
8. juice from 1/2 a lemon
9. 1 pinch of red pepper flakes
10. 4 pieces of thinly sliced prosciutto, rolled

Directions

1. Place the bread into a food processor and pulse until chopped into breadcrumbs.
2. Place a medium skillet over medium heat, coat with cook spray, and add in the breadcrumbs. Cook, stirring frequently, for about 3 minutes or until the bread is toasted and crispy. Set aside.
3. Add a large skillet over medium-low heat and add in half of the olive oil.
4. Add in the broccoli, season with salt and pepper and cook for about 3 minutes, tossing frequently.
5. Add in 2 tsp of the garlic, the rest of the olive oil, and cook for another 3-5 minutes, tossing frequently. When done, remove broccoli with a slotted spoon to a bowl. Scrape the browned garlic out of the pan (and into the garbage) and then place the same pan over medium heat.
6. Add in the zucchini noodles, lemon juice, and red pepper flakes. Cook for about 2 minutes or until zucchini softens.
7. When done, add to the bowl with the broccoli and toss to combine.
8. Place the pasta mixture into a bowl and top with breadcrumbs and rolled prosciutto. Enjoy!

Lemon Herb Chicken with Zucchini Pasta and Ricotta

"A light yet flavorful dish. Perfect way to help use up your summer harvest"

Servings: *4|* **Prep:** *30 m |* **Cook:** *15 m |* **Ready In:** *3h45 m*

Ingredients

- 4 skinless, boneless chicken breast halves - cut into strips
- 4 cloves garlic, minced lemon, zested
- 1 tablespoon chopped fresh chives

- 1 teaspoon fresh thyme
- 1 teaspoon fresh oregano
- 1/2 teaspoon salt
- 1/4 teaspoon ground black pepper
- 1/4 cup olive oil, plus more for pan
- 4 zucchini squash, cut into 'noodles' using a spiral slicer or vegetable peeler
- 1 pinch red pepper flakes salt and ground black pepper to taste
- 1 1/2 cups ricotta cheese
- 4 fresh basil leaves, chopped
- lemon, juiced
- 2 fresh tomatoes, diced

Directions

1. Place chicken, garlic, lemon zest, chives, thyme, oregano, 1/2 teaspoon salt, 1/4 teaspoon pepper, and 1/4 cup olive oil in a resealable plastic bag; toss to coat chicken and refrigerate for 3 hours or up to overnight.
2. Heat a large skillet over medium heat; cook and stir chicken with marinade until chicken is no longer pink at the center and juices run clear, about 8 minutes. An instant-read thermometer inserted into the center should read at least 165 degrees F (74 degrees C). Remove chicken from pan; set aside to keep warm.
3. Drizzle about 1 teaspoon oil into the same skillet over medium-high heat; stir in zucchini and red pepper flakes and cook until zucchini is warm, about 3 minutes; season with salt and pepper. Stir ricotta cheese and basil into zucchini; cook until heated through, about 2 minutes.
4. Return chicken to pan with zucchini mixture; stir to combine. Remove pan from heat, squeeze lemon juice over entire dish, and garnish with diced tomatoes.

Nutritional Information

- Calories:425 kcal 21%
- Fat: 24.1 g 37%
- Carbs: 16.2g 5%
- Protein: 37.4 g 75%
- Cholesterol: 93 mg 31%
- Sodium: 525 mg 21%

Lemon Ricotta Zucchini Pasta with Kalamata Olives

Prep Time: 10 minutes | *Cook Time:* 10 minutes | *Total Time:* 20 minutes | *Servings:*
2

Ingredients

- 1½ cup ricotta cheese
- zest of 1 small lemon + 1 tsp of juice
- pepper, to taste
- ½ tablespoon extra virgin olive oil
- 1 garlic clove minced
- 1 pinch red pepper flakes
- 2 medium zucchinis, Blade A
- 1/3 cup halved kalamata olives

Directions

1. Place the ricotta cheese and olives in a large mixing bowl with the lemon zest and juice. Season with pepper and set aside.
2. In a large skillet, add in the olive oil. Once oil heats, add in the garlic and red pepper flakes and cook for 30 seconds or until fragrant. Then, add in the zucchini noodles and toss for 3 minutes or until al dente. Using pasta tongs to let excess moisture drip dry, transfer the zucchini noodles into the bowl with the ricotta sauce and kalamata olives. Toss to combine and then transfer to the pasta bowls using tongs, letting excess moisture drip off.
3. Serve immediately.

Lemon Zucchini Pasta with Roasted Artichokes

Prep time: 5 min | *Cook time:* 25 mins | *Total time:* 30 mins | *Serves:* 3

Ingredients

For the artichokes:

- 1 (13.75) can halved artichokes, drained, patted thoroughly dry
- 1 tablespoon extra virgin olive oil
- salt and pepper, to taste
- ½ teaspoon garlic powder
- For the pasta:
- 3 medium zucchinis

- 1 tablespoon extra virgin olive oil
- 2 garlic cloves, minced
- ¼ teaspoon red pepper flakes
- pepper, to taste
- ½ lemon, juiced
- ¼ cup grated parmesan cheese

Directions

1. Preheat the oven to 425 degrees. Line a baking sheet with parchment paper and set aside.
2. In a medium mixing bowl, toss together the artichokes, olive oil, salt, pepper and garlic powder. Lay the artichokes out on the baking sheet and bake for 20 minutes, tossing halfway through or until browned.
3. While the artichokes bake, spiralize the zucchini and mince the garlic. Set aside.
4. Ten minutes before the artichokes are done, place a large skillet over medium-high heat. Add in the olive oil and once heated, add in the garlic and red pepper flakes and let cook for 30 seconds or until fragrant. Add in the zucchini noodles, season with pepper and toss until cooked, about 5 minutes. When done, add in the cooked artichokes, lemon and parmesan cheese and remove from heat, tossing constantly to coat the noodles in the parmesan sauce.
5. Divide onto plates and serve.

Lemon-Dill Zucchini Pasta with Shrimp and Capers

Prep Time: 10 minutes | Cook Time: 10 minutes | Total Time: 20 minutes | Servings: 2

Ingredients

- 1 tablespoon extra virgin olive oil
- 1 garlic clove, minced
- 3 roma tomatoes, seeds removed, chopped
- 12 shrimp, deshelled, deveined
- juice of 1 lemon
- salt and pepper, to taste
- 2 zucchinis, Blade C
- 1.5 tablespoon freshly chopped dill
- 1 tablespoon capers

Directions

1. Place a large skillet over medium heat and add in the olive oil. Once the oil heats, add in the garlic and cook for 30 seconds or until fragrant. Then, add in the tomatoes, shrimp, lemon juice and season with salt and pepper. Let cook for about 5 minutes or until the shrimp are cooked through and opaque.
2. Add in the zucchini noodles, dill and capers and toss to combine. Cook for 2-3 minutes or until zucchini is al dente.
3. Divide into bowls and serve.

Lemon-Garlic Broccoli Noodles with White Beans and Parmesan

Prep time: 10 mins | *Cook time:* 15 mins | *Total time:* 25 mins | *Serves:* 2

Ingredients

-   1 large broccoli head with stem
-   ½ cup white beans
-   2 tablespoons olive oil
-   1 pinch of red pepper flakes
-   salt and pepper, to taste
-   1 tablespoon pine nuts
-   2-3 garlic cloves, thinly sliced
-   1 tablespoon fresh lemon juice
-   1 tablespoon grated parmesan cheese

Directions

1. Slice off the head of the broccoli, leaving as little stem on the florets as possible. Set aside the broccoli florets. Slice the bottom end off the broccoli stem so that it is evenly flat. Spiralize the broccoli stem, using Blade C.
2. Place a large skillet over medium heat and add in the olive oil. Once the oil heats, add in the broccoli florets, stems, red pepper flakes and season with salt and pepper. Cover and cook for 3-5 minutes, shaking the skillet frequently, letting the broccoli cook.
3. While the broccoli is cooking, place your pine nuts in a small skillet over medium heat. Let toast until fragrant and the pine nuts slightly brown, about 5 minutes. Be careful not to burn the pine nuts – toss occasionally. When done, set aside.

4. Add in the garlic and lemon juice and cook for 3-5 more minutes (covered) or until broccoli is tender but more easily pierced with a fork.
5. Add beans. Warm for 1 minute.
6. Transfer the broccoli to a serving bowl and top with pine nuts and parmesan cheese.

Lemon-Oregano Salmon and Leek Parsnip Pasta

Prep Time: 5 minutes | Cook Time: 30 minutes | Total Time: 35 minutes | Servings: 1

Ingredients

- 4oz skinless salmon filet
- extra virgin olive oil, to drizzle (optional)
- 1 tablespoon freshly squeezed lemon juice
- 1 pinch dried oregano flakes
- salt and pepper, to taste
- 2 medium parsnips
- 1 leek stalk
- 1 small garlic clove
- 2 teaspoons extra virgin olive oil
- 1 pinch red pepper flakes
- salt and pepper, to taste
- 2 tablespoons vegetable broth
- 2 teaspoons freshly chopped parsley, to garnish
- 1 lemon wedge, for serving

Directions

1. Preheat the oven to 425 degrees. Line a baking sheet with parchment paper and place salmon in the middle. Drizzle with olive oil (optional) and then splash over the lemon juice. Season with oregano, salt and pepper and bake for 20-25 minutes or until salmon flakes easily with a fork.
2. While salmon is baking, spiralize your parsnip with Blade C and set aside. Slice the leek thinly and set aside. Mince the garlic and set aside.
3. Ten minutes before salmon is done, place a large skillet over medium heat and add in the olive oil. Once oil heats, add in the garlic, leeks and red pepper flakes. Let cook for 1-2 minutes or until leeks soften. Add in the parsnip pasta, vegetable broth and cover and cook for 5-7 minutes or until parsnips are cooked through.

4. Once salmon is done, flake with a fork to break into pieces. Add to the skillet with the parsnip noodles, toss and transfer to a plate. Serve with lemon wedge.

Lentil and Broccoli Rabe with Turnip Spaghetti

Prep time: 20 mins | *Cook time:* 40 mins | *Total time:* 1 hour | *Serves:* 4

Ingredients

- 1 bunch broccoli rabe
- 1 tablespoon extra virgin olive oil
- 1 large garlic clove, minced
- 1 pinch red pepper flakes
- salt and pepper, to taste
- ½ onion, finely chopped
- 1 carrot, finely chopped
- 1 celery stick, finely chopped
- ¾ cup dry lentils
- 1.5 cups vegetable broth
- 1 14.5oz can diced tomatoes (with liquid)
- 1 cup tomato sauce
- ¾ teaspoon dried oregano
- ½ teaspoon dried thyme
- 1 bay leaf
- 4 medium turnips, peeled, Blade C, noodles trimmed
- 1 tablespoon freshly chopped parsley, to garnish

Directions

1. Bring a large pot filled halfway with water to a boil. While you wait for it to reach a boil, prepare the rabe: remove any tough or damaged outer leaves of the broccoli rabe and then peel the thick lower stems from the broccoli rabe (this takes out some of the bitterness.) Rinse and pat dry to remove any excess dirt.
2. Once the water is boiling, add in the broccoli rabe. Let cook for 1 minute and then remove with a slotted spoon or tongs and set aside. Bring the water back to a boil and add in the turnip noodles and let cook 2 minutes or until al dente. Drain into a colander and set aside, divided into two bowls and covered to keep warm.
3. Pat dry the broccoli rabe and chop into 1" pieces and set aside.

4. Place the large pot back over medium heat and add in half of the olive oil. Once oil heats, add in the garlic and red pepper flakes. Cook for 30 seconds or until aromatic and then add in the broccoli rabe. Season with salt and pepper and cook for 2-3 minutes to let the rabe absorb some flavor. Set aside and immediately add in the onions, celery and carrots. Cook for 5 minutes or until vegetables begin to soften and onions are translucent. Stir in the lentils, broth, tomatoes, tomato sauce, oregano, thyme and bay leaf and let cook, covered, for 15 minutes and then uncover and cook for another 15 minutes or until lentils are cooked through. Once lentils are cooked, remove the bay leaf and stir in the broccoli rabe, season with salt and pepper and let cook for another minute to warm the rabe.
5. Portion into bowls and serve, garnished with parsley.

Lime-Jalapeno Tilapia with Cilantro-Manchego-Pepita Pesto Zucchini Pasta

Prep Time: *10 minutes* | **Cook Time:** *12 minutes* | **Total Time**: *22 minutes* | **Servings**: *2*

Ingredients

For the pesto:

- 3/4 cup grated Manchego cheese
- 1/3 packed cup of cilantro leaves
- 1/4 tsp salt (or less)
- 2 tbsp deshelled roasted pepitas
- 1 garlic clove, minced
- 3 tbsp extra virgin olive oil
- pepper to taste

For the rest:

- 2 tilapia filets
- 1 lime
- salt and pepper, to taste
- 6 thin slices of a jalapeno
- 3 medium zucchinis, Blade A

Directions

1. Preheat the oven to 400 degrees. Place the tilapia filets on a baking tray lightly coated with cooking spray. Slice the lime in half and squeeze one half over one filet and the other half over the other filet. Season lightly with salt and pepper. Bake in the oven for 7 minutes. Then, take out, place 3 jalapeno slices on top of each filet and bake for another 3-5 minutes, or until tilapia is opaque and cooked through.
2. While the tilapia is roasting, place all of the ingredients for your pesto into a food processor. Pulse until creamy. Taste and adjust, if necessary.
3. In a large bowl, pour the pesto over the zucchini noodles and toss to combine thoroughly. Divide the noodles evenly onto two plates.
4. When the tilapia is done, top each bed of zucchini pasta with one filet. Enjoy!

Lobster Tail Fra Diavolo with Zucchini Noodles

Prep Time: 15 minutes | **Cook Time:** 30 minutes | **Total Time:** 45 minutes | **Servings:** 2

Ingredients

- 1.5 tablespoon extra virgin olive oil
- 2 4-oz lobster tails, deshelled and cut into chunks
- 1 tablespoon minced shallots
- 2 cloves of garlic, minced
- ¼ teaspoon red pepper flakes (or more, if you like it spicy)
- 1 14.5oz can San Marzano crushed tomatoes
- salt and pepper, to taste
- 2 medium zucchinis, Blade C, noodles trimmed
- 1 tablespoon freshly chopped parsley

Directions

1. Heat one tablespoon of oil in a large pot over medium heat. Once oil heats, add in the lobster. Cook until meat is cooked and opaque, about 5-7 minutes. Once cooked, transfer to a plate and set aside.
2. Add in the rest of the olive oil, the shallots, garlic and red pepper flakes to the pot. Cook until onions turn translucent, about 2-3 minutes. Add in the tomatoes, season with salt and pepper and bring to a boil. Reduce heat and simmer until reduced and thickened, about 15-20 minutes.

3. Return lobster to the skillet along with the zucchini noodles and cook for another 5 minutes to heat the lobster and cook the noodles to al dente.
4. Once done, serve the noodles into bowls with even amounts of lobster meat and sprinkle evenly with parsley

Low Carb Zucchini Pasta

"If you are a pasta lover and need a low-carb version closer to the real thing than spaghetti squash, you have found your match! This is a great recipe for one; super-quick and super-versatile. Serve with your favorite sauce."

Servings: 1 | **Prep**: 10 m | **Cook**: 5 m | **Ready In**: 15 m

Ingredients

- 2 zucchinis, peeled
- 1 tablespoon olive oil
- 1/4 cup water
- salt and ground black pepper to taste

Directions

1. Cut lengthwise slices from zucchini using a vegetable peeler, stopping when the seeds are reached. Turn zucchini over and continue 'peeling' until all the zucchini is in long strips; discard seeds. Slice the zucchini into thinner strips resembling spaghetti.
2. Heat olive oil in a skillet over medium heat; cook and stir zucchini in the hot oil for 1 minute. Add water and cook until zucchini is softened, 5 to 7 minutes. Season with salt and pepper.

Nutritional Information

- Calories:157 kcal 8%
- Fat: 13.9 g 21%
- Carbs: 7.9g 3%
- Protein: 2.9 g 6%
- Cholesterol: 0 mg 0%
- Sodium: 181 mg 7%

Maple Roasted Delicata Squash & Chickpea Zucchini Pasta with Toasted Pumpkin Gremolata Breadcrumbs

Prep Time: 20 minutes | *Cook Time:* 20 minutes | *Total Time:* 40 minutes | *Servings:* 2

Ingredients

For the breadcrumbs:

- 1/4 tsp crushed coarse sea salt
- 1/4 tsp ground pepper
- 1.5 tbsp finely chopped fresh parsley
- 1 piece of whole wheat bread
- zest of 1 lemon
- 1/4 tbsp olive oil
- 2 tbsp shelled pumpkin seeds
- 1 tsp chili powder
- 1/2 tsp cumin
- olive oil cooking spray

For the rest:

- 1 delicata squash
- maple syrup to drizzle
- salt and pepper, to taste
- 3 medium zucchinis, Blade C
- 1 tbsp olive oil
- 1 tbsp minced garlic
- 1/4 tsp red pepper flakes
- 1/2 cup chickpeas
- 1/4 cup freshly grated parmigiano-reggiano cheese + 1 tbsp extra for garnish

Directions

1. Preheat the oven to 400 degrees.
2. Take the delicata squash and cut it length wise. Scoop out the inside seeds and cut into 1" thick pieces. Place in a baking tray, coated with cooking spray.
3. Drizzle maple syrup over the squash very lightly. Rub in with fingertips or cooking brush and season with salt and pepper. Roast for 25-30 minutes,

flipping over twice throughout cooking to ensure that both sides brown evenly.

4. While the squash is roasting, place the pumpkin seeds in a baking tray and coat seeds with cooking spray. Season evenly with cumin, chili powder and salt and pepper. Bake in the oven for 3 minutes. Remove from the oven and place into a food processor. Chop roughly. Place into a bowl and set aside.

5. Place the bread into the food processor and pulse until made into breadcrumbs.

6. Place a medium skillet over medium heat and add in the 1/4 tbsp of olive oil. Once the oil heats, add in the breadcrumbs. Toast for about 2-3 minutes or until they just start to become crunchy. Add them into the bowl with the pumpkin seeds and add in the lemon zest, parsley, and salt and pepper. Set aside.

7. In a large skillet, place in the tbsp of olive oil. Once the oil heats, add in the garlic and cook for 1 minute. Add in the red pepper flakes, cook for 30 seconds and then add in the zucchini noodles and chickpeas. Cook the zucchini noodles for 2 minutes and then add in the cheese, stir to combine thoroughly, and plate into a dish.

8. Top the zucchini noodles with 4-5 pieces of delicata squash, 2 tbsp of the breadcrumbs and top with extra cheese, if desired.

9. Enjoy!

Mediterranean Chicken and Carrot Noodle Bowl with Tahini

Prep time: 25 mins | Cook time: 20 mins | Total time: 45 mins | Serves: 2

Ingredients

- 1 large carrot, peeled, Blade D, noodles trimmed
- pinch of salt
- ½ pound boneless chicken breast
- ½ tablespoon extra virgin olive oil
- ½ small onion, Blade A, noodles trimmed (or sliced thinly)
- salt and pepper, to taste
- 2 tablespoons crushed cashews
- For the tahini dressing:
- 2 tablespoons tahini
- 1 tablespoon freshly squeezed lemon juice
- 2 teaspoons honey
- 1 garlic clove, minced
- 1 tablespoon extra virgin olive oil
- 1-2 tablespoons water, to thin

- salt and pepper, to taste

Directions

1. Place a medium pot filled halfway with water and a pinch of salt to a boil, over high heat. Once boiling, add in the carrot noodles and cook for 1-2 minutes or until cooked to your preference. Drain into a colander, pat dry and set aside in a medium mixing bowl.
2. Meanwhile, place the chicken breast into a medium saucepan and pour in enough water to cover. Place over medium heat, bring to a boil, and simmer until the thickest part of the breast meat is no longer pink, 10 to 12 minutes. Transfer the chicken to a bowl and then shred the chicken, using two forks.
3. Place a large skillet over medium heat and add in the olive oil. Once oil heats, add in the onions. Season with salt and pepper and cover, cooking the onions until caramelized, 5 to 7 minutes.
4. While onions cook, prepare the tahini dressing: place all ingredients into a food processor and pulse until creamy. Taste and adjust if necessary.
5. Once onions are done, add in 1 tablespoon of the tahini dressing, the chicken and toss for 30 seconds to combine.
6. Drizzle the rest of the dressing into the bowl with the carrot noodles and toss together to combine. Plate the noodles into bowls and top with onions and chicken. Sprinkle with cashews.

Mexican "Sweet Potato Fideos" Soup with Avocado

Prep Time: 15 minutes | Cook Time: 15 minutes | Total Time: 30 minutes | Servings: 2

Ingredients

- 1 tbsp olive oil
- 1 garlic clove, minced
- 1/2 yellow onion, diced
- 1 14oz can diced tomatoes
- 1/2 tsp cumin
- 1 tbsp chili powder
- 3 cups vegetable broth, low-sodium*
- 1 large (320g+) sweet potato, peeled, Blade C**
- 1.5 tbsp chopped cilantro
- 1 avocado, insides cubed

Directions

1. Place a large saucepan over medium heat and add in the olive oil. Once the oil heats, add in the garlic and let cook for 30 seconds. Then, add in the diced onion and let cook for 2 minutes. Then, add in the diced tomatoes, cumin, chili powder and season with salt and pepper.
2. Let the tomatoes cook for 2-3 minutes to absorb the flavors of the seasonings and then add in the chicken broth. Cover, bring to a boil, add in the sweet potato "fideo" and reduce to a simmer. Let cook for 5-7 minutes or until the sweet potato "fideo" reaches your desired consistency. Half-way through cooking, toss in the chopped cilantro.
3. Once the soup is done, fold in the avocado. Portion into bowls and garnish with remaining chopped cilantro!

Mexican Squoodles with Creamy Fire-Roasted Green Chile Sauce

"Mexican squash is spiralized into noodles, also known as squoodles, for this dish with a creamy green chile sauce and Mexicorn®."

***Servings:** 4 | **Prep:** 15 m | **Cook:** 12 m | **Ready In:** 27 m*

Ingredients

- 1 tablespoon olive oil
- 1/2 onion, cut into noodle shapes
- 3 cloves garlic, crushed
- 4 Mexican squash, cut into noodle shapes
- 1 (11 ounce) can Mexican-style corn (such as Green Giant® Mexicorn®), drained
- 4 ounces Neufchatel cheese, softened
- 1 (4 ounce) can fire-roasted diced green chile peppers
- 1/4 cup milk

Directions

1. Heat oil in a skillet over medium heat. Add onion and garlic; cook and stir until onion is translucent, about 5 minutes. Stir in squash and corn; cook, stirring frequently, until squash is softened, about 5 minutes. Transfer to individual serving plates.

2. Combine Neufchatel cheese, chile peppers, and milk in a blender; blend until sauce is smooth.
3. Heat sauce in a saucepan over medium heat until warmed through, 2 to 4 minutes; pour over squash mixture.

Nutritional Information

- Calories:216 kcal 11%
- Fat: 10.7 g 16%
- Carbs: 25.4g 8%
- Protein: 8.2 g 16%
- Cholesterol: 23 mg 8%
- Sodium: 877 mg 35%

Mint Pesto Zucchini Pasta with Goat Cheese

Prep Time: *15 minutes* | **Servings:** *2*

Ingredients

- 2 medium zucchinis, Blade C
- ½ cup snow peas
- 1/2 cup diced scallions
- ¼ cup crumbled goat cheese (2-3oz)
- For the pesto:
- 2 tablespoon minced mint leaves
- 1/2 small avocado, peeled, insides cubed
- 1/2-1 teaspoon minced garlic
- zest of 1 small lemon
- 2 tablespoons freshly squeezed lemon juice
- 2 tablespoons slivered blanched almonds
- 3 tablespoons extra virgin olive oil
- salt and pepper, to taste

Directions

1. Place all of the ingredients for the pesto into a food processor and pulse until creamy. Taste and adjust, if necessary.

2. In a large mixing bowl, place in the zucchini noodles, snap peas and scallions. Pour the dressing over the mixture and toss to combine thoroughly.
3. Divide the noodle mixture into two bowls and top each equally with goat cheese.

Moroccan Chicken and Roasted Red Pepper Zucchini Pasta

Prep time: *15 mins* | **Cook time:** *60 mins* | **Total time:** *1 hour 15 mins* | **Serves:** *4*

Ingredients

- ¾-1 pound boneless chicken breasts or thighs
- 2 red bell peppers
- 1.5 cups golden yellow cherry tomatoes
- 3 kohlrabis (or turnips)
- 1 garlic clove, minced
- ¼ teaspoon red pepper flakes
- 1 medium red onion
- 1 tablespoon extra virgin olive oil
- salt and pepper, to taste
- ¼ cup crumbled feta cheese
- 1 tablespoon minced parsley, to garnish

For the Moroccan spice mix:

- 2 tablespoons extra virgin olive oil
- 2 teaspoon honey
- salt, to taste
- 1 large garlic clove, minced
- 2 teaspoons paprika
- 1 teaspoon ground cumin
- ½ teaspoon ground coriander
- ¼ teaspoon ground ginger
- ¼ teaspoon turmeric
- ¼ teaspoon cinnamon
- 1 pinch cayenne pepper

Directions

1. Preheat the oven to 400 degrees. Slice the tops off the peppers, deseed them and slice them in half. Line a baking sheet with parchment paper and lay out the bell peppers. Cook for 20 minutes and then, using tongs, flip over and cook another 20 minutes or until the peppers are evenly charred. Immediately transfer to a sealable glass container or paper bag and seal. Let sit for 5 minutes and then slice thinly.

2. While the peppers cook, whisk together all of the ingredients for the spice mix in a small bowl. Place the chicken in a zip-seal plastic bag and shake to coat. Let marinade for at least 15 minutes in the refrigerator. Once you flip the peppers after the first 20 minutes, add the marinated chicken and tomatoes to another baking sheet, lined with parchment paper. Roast for 15 minutes or until chicken is cooked through and is no longer pink inside. Remove from the oven and slice thinly, leaving the tomatoes on the baking tray.

3. While chicken cooks, peel and spiralize the kohlrabi (or turnip) using Blade B, trim the noodles and set aside. Then, mince the garlic. Then, thinly slice the red onion.

4. Once the chicken and peppers are finished, place a large skillet over medium heat. Once oil heats, add in the onions, garlic and red pepper flakes and cook for 3-5 minutes or until onions begin to wilt. Add in the kohlrabi (or turnip) noodles and toss. Cover and cook for 5-7 minutes or until cooked to your preference, uncovering occasionally to toss. Add in the cooked tomatoes, along with any juices from the baking tray.

5. When done, add in the roasted peppers and toss to combine and then remove from heat, sprinkle in the feta, toss to combine again and then divide into bowls and top with sliced chicken and garnish with parsley.

Mushroom, Pancetta & Lentil Zucchini Pasta with Toasted Almonds

Prep Time: 5 minutes | **Cook Time:** 35 minutes | **Total Time:** 40 minutes | **Servings:** 2

Ingredients

- 2.5-3 medium zucchinis, peeled, Blade C
- 1/4 cup dried lentils
- 1 tbsp olive oil
- 1 medium clove of garlic, minced
- 6 slices of pancetta
- 2 shallots, minced
- 3 cups of chopped portobello mushrooms

- 1/4 cup vegetable broth, low-sodium
- 2 tsp chopped fresh parsley
- 1 tbsp sliced almonds
- salt and pepper, to taste
- cooking spray

Directions

1. Prepare your lentils, according to package directions. Allot about 20-35 minutes for this. When done, set aside.
2. While lentils are cooking, cook the pancetta. Spray a large skillet with cooking spray and lay in the pancetta. Cook about 2 minutes per side or until pancetta is to your crispy preference. When done, transfer with a slotted spoon to a paper towel lined plate. Set aside.
3. Ten minutes before the lentils are done, place a large skillet over medium-low heat and add in the olive oil. Add in the garlic, cook for 30 seconds, and then add in the shallots. Cook for 30 seconds and then add in the mushrooms and season with salt and pepper.
4. Cook the mushrooms, shallots and garlic until the mushrooms wilt down and brown, about 6-8 minutes.
5. Halfway through cooking the mushrooms, add in the vegetable broth and reduce. If the broth isn't boiling, raise heat slightly.
6. While broth is reducing, place a skillet over medium heat and add in the almonds. Cook the almonds, about 1-3 minutes or until you can smell their nutty flavor. Be careful not to burn! Set aside once done.
7. After reducing, add in the pancetta and zucchini noodles. Cook for about 2 minutes, stirring frequently until the noodles are softened and heated through.
8. Add in the lentils, toss with freshly chopped parsley, and plate onto dishes.
9. Top with toasted almonds and enjoy!

Mussels and Sausage Zucchini Pasta

Prep Time: 25 minutes | **Cook Time:** 20 minutes | **Total Time:** 45 minutes | **Servings:** 4

Ingredients

- 1 tablespoon extra virgin olive oil
- 3 Italian sweet sausage links, decased
- 2 celery ribs, chopped

- 1 cup diced white onion
- ¼ teaspoon red pepper flakes
- 2 cloves of minced garlic
- 1 pint cherry tomatoes, halved
- salt and pepper, to taste
- 2 tablespoons chopped basil
- 2 dozen mussels
- 3 medium zucchinis, Blade C

Directions

1. Scrub each mussel individually, trying to remove as many of the stringy pieces that cling to the outside as possible. Then, look at the crack where the two shells meet on the mussel and pinch the strands that look like threads of brown seaweed, tugging to remove. Repeat with all mussels and set aside.
2. Heat the olive oil over medium heat in a large non-stick skillet. Once oil heats, crumble in the sausage and cook until browned, about 5 minutes. Then, add in the celery, onion, red pepper flakes and garlic and cook until vegetables soften, 3-5 minutes.
3. Raise the heat to medium-high and add in the tomatoes, season with salt and pepper and cover, cooking another 5 minutes.
4. Lower the heat and add in the basil and mussels. Cover the pan again and cook until the mussels open, about 2 minutes. Discard any that do not open.
5. Add the zucchini noodles into a large serving bowl and then pour over the mussel mixture and toss to combine. As the sauce sits over the noodles, it will soften them. Let sit for 2 minutes for the flavors to absorb and then serve.

Oil-Free Walnut Pesto Zucchini Noodles

Prep time: *30 mins* | **Total time:** *30 mins* | **Serves:** *4-6*

Ingredients

- PESTO
- 1 cup diced zucchini
- 1 cup fresh basil leaves, tightly packed
- 3 cloves garlic, minced
- 1/2 cup raw walnut halves

- 1/4 cup water
- 2 tablespoons freshly squeezed lemon juice
- 1/2 teaspoon sea salt

For the rest:

- 4 to 6 large zucchini, Blade C or D
- 1 teaspoon coconut oil (optional)
- 1 cup cherry tomatoes, halved
- Raw pine nuts, for garnish (optional)

Directions

1. Prepare the pesto: Combine all of the pesto ingredients in a high-speed blender and blend until completely smooth. For a chunkier texture, instead use the pulse function on your blender or food processor to gently mix the ingredients together.
2. Use a spiralizer or vegetable peeler to create "noodles" out of the peeled zucchini. For a warm dish, melt the coconut oil in a large skillet over medium heat and sauté the zucchini "noodles" and tomatoes until tender, 8 to 10 minutes. Add in the pesto and stir quickly, just enough to warm the sauce, about 1 minute. Serve warm, with a sprinkle of pine nuts. For a cold dish, simply toss the raw zucchini "noodles" with the prepared pesto and top with the tomatoes and pine nuts.

Paleo Cauliflower Alfredo with Gluten-Free Chicken Meatballs and Sweet Potato Noodles

Prep time: 20 mins | Cook time: 30 mins | Total time: 50 mins | Serves: 4

Ingredients

For the meatballs:

- 1 pound lean ground chicken
- 1 teaspoon garlic powder
- ½ teaspoon dried basil
- ½ teaspoon dried oregano
- 1 tablespoon freshly chopped parsley
- salt and pepper, to taste

For the alfredo:

- Half the florets from medium cauliflower
- 1 teaspoon extra virgin olive oil
- 1 medium garlic clove, minced
- 1 tablespoon minced shallots
- 1 cup chicken broth
- ¾ tablespoons nutritional yeast
- ¼ teaspoon Dijon mustard
- 2 teaspoons fresh lemon juice
- salt and pepper

For the pasta:

- 1 tablespoon extra virgin olive oil
- 3 large sweet potatoes, peeled, Blade D, noodles trimmed
- salt and pepper to taste
- 2 tablespoons minced parsley, to garnish

Directions

1. Preheat the oven to 450 degrees and line a baking sheet with parchment paper.
2. Make the meatballs: combine all of the meatball ingredients into a large mixing bowl and stir together. Then, shape the meat mixture into golf ball sized meatballs, about 8. Place on the baking sheet and bake for 15-18 minutes or until juices run clear and meat is cooked through.
3. Meanwhile, make the sauce: Place the cauliflower florets in a large pot and cover with salted water. Bring to a boil over high heat, then lower the heat to medium and cook for five to seven minutes or until easily pierced with a fork. Remove the cauliflower with a slotted spoon.
4. Heat the one teaspoon of olive oil in a medium nonstick skillet over medium heat. When the oil is shimmering, add one garlic clove and cook for 30 seconds or until fragrant. Add the shallots and cook for two to three minutes or until translucent. Transfer to a high-speed blender or large food processor, and add the cauliflower, the broth, nutritional yeast, mustard and lemon juice. Generously season with salt and pepper and blend the sauce until creamy, about one minute. Set aside.
5. Prepare the pasta: place a large skillet over medium heat and add in the olive oil. Season with salt and pepper and cook for 7 minutes or until cooked to your preference.
6. While pasta cooks, place a small pot over heat and pour in the cauliflower alfredo. Cook until heated and then let simmer until sweet potato noodles are ready.

7. When pasta and meatballs are done, transfer the sweet potato noodles to a serving bowl, top with meatballs and pour over the cauliflower alfredo. Garnish with parsley.

Paleo Chicken Piccata with Butternut Squash Noodles

Prep time: 20 mins | **Cook time:** 20 mins | **Total time:** 40 mins | **Serves:** 4

Ingredients

For the butternut squash:

- 1 medium butternut squash, peeled, Blade D, noodles trimmed
- olive oil, to drizzle
- 1 teaspoon garlic powder
- salt and pepper, to taste
- For the chicken:
- 1 egg, beaten
- 2 skinless and boneless chicken breasts, butterflied and then cut in half
- salt and pepper, to taste
- ⅓ cup freshly squeezed lemon juice
- ½ cup chicken stock, low sodium
- ¼ cup capers, rinsed
- ¼ cup freshly chopped parsley

For the breading:

- ¾ cup almond meal
- ½ teaspoon garlic powder
- salt and pepper, to taste
- ½ teaspoon dried parsley flakes
- ½ teaspoon dried oregano flakes
- ¼ teaspoon onion powder

Directions

1. Preheat the oven to 400 degrees. Meanwhile, spread the butternut squash noodles out on a baking sheet, drizzle with (optional) olive oil and season with garlic powder, salt and pepper. Bake the noodles for 8-10 minutes or until al dente, tossing halfway through.

2. While the butternut squash cooks, place the egg into a shallow dish and then combine all of the ingredients for the breading into another shallow dish, making sure to mix thoroughly.
3. Dip each chicken portion into the egg and then dip both sides into the breading mixture to coat. Set aside on a clean plate and season with salt and pepper.
4. Place a large skillet over medium-high heat and add in the olive oil. Once oil heats, add in the chicken and cook for 3 minutes, flip and cook for another 3-5 minutes or until cooked all the way through. Remove and transfer to a plate, leaving in all the juices.
5. Immediately add in the lemon juice, stock and capers. Bring to a boil and scraupe up the brown bits from the pan. Add the chicken back to the pan and simmer for 5 minutes. Remove the chicken and transfer to a platter. Stir in the parsley to the sauce and remove the pan from heat.
6. Divide the finished butternut squash noodles into four plates or bowls and top with chicken. Pour over extra sauce from the pan. Serve immediately.

Parchment Pouch Zucchini Spaghetti With Clams

Prep time: 15 mins | Cook time: 20 mins | Total time: 35 mins | Serves: 2

Ingredients

- 2 tablespoons olive oil
- 1 shallot, minced
- 2 cloves garlic
- 1 pounds small clams, scrubbed and rinsed
- 2 tablespoons dry white wine (or vegetable broth)
- ¼ teaspoon red pepper flakes
- salt and pepper, to taste
- ½ cup minced curly parsley
- 2 medium zucchinis, Blade D, noodles trimmed
- 2 lemon wedges, for serving

Directions

1. Preheat oven to 450 degrees. Prepare 2 sheets of parchment paper, each 2 feet long.
2. Place a large lidded skillet over medium heat and add 1 tablespoon of oil. Once oil heats, add the shallots and garlic. Cook until shallots soften, about

2 minutes. Then, add in the clams, wine (or broth) and red pepper flakes. Cover and steam until clams just open, about 3 minutes.

3. Remove the skillet from the stovetop and discard the garlic. Remove half of the clams from their shells and discard the shells. Season the juice in the pan with salt and pepper, to taste.

4. Return the skillet to medium heat. Once simmering, add in the zucchini noodles, remaining oil and parsley. Cook, tossing vigorously, until sauce reduces and becomes thicker, about 3 minutes. Season with pepper to taste.

5. Place a half of the zucchini pasta mixture in the center of each prepared sheet of paper. Drizzle each with some of the pan juices. Then, draw the long ends of the paper over the zucchini pasta so the edges meet. Fold edges over and continue folding to form a tight seal on top of each packet. Repeat with remaining mixture to make another pouch.

6. Transfer the packets to a baking sheet and bake until paper browns slightly, about 3 minutes. Place the packets on plates and serve with lemon wedges.

Parmesan Zucchini Pasta with Quinoa, Kale and Fried Egg

Prep time: 10 mins | Cook time: 10 mins | Total time: 20 mins | Serves: 2

Ingredients

- 1 tablespoon extra virgin olive oil
- 1 large garlic clove, minced
- 1 pinch of red pepper flakes
- 2 cups chopped kale
- salt and pepper, to taste
- 2 medium zucchinis, Blade D, noodles trimmed
- 1 cup vegetable broth
- 3 tablespoons grated parmesan cheese + more to garnish (optional)
- 2 large whole eggs
- ½ cup cooked quinoa

Directions

1. Place a large, deep skillet over medium-high heat and add in the olive oil. Once oil heats, add in the garlic and red pepper flakes and cook for 30 seconds. Add in the kale, season with salt and pepper and cook for about 2 minutes or until it starts to wilt, but not fully. Then, add in the zucchini

noodles and cook for 1 minute and then add in the broth and let cook another 2-3 minutes or until zucchini noodles are cooked to your preference. Stir in the parmesan cheese, remove from heat and then divide into bowls. Top each bowl with quinoa.

2. Meanwhile, add a medium skillet over medium-high heat and coat with cooking spray. Crack in the two eggs and let cook until egg whites set.

3. When eggs and zucchini noodles are done, divide the noodle mixture into two bowls, top with ¼ cup each of quinoa and top each with a fried egg. Garnish with extra parmesan cheese (optional.)

Parsnip Noodles with Leftover Christmas Ham and Butternut Squash-Sage Sauce

Prep Time: *15 minutes* | **Cook Time:** *40minutes* | **Total Time:** *55 minutes* | **Servings:** *3*

Ingredients
- 1/2 tablespoon olive oil
- 6 sage leaves
- 1.5 cups cubed butternut squash
- 1 large shallot, minced
- 2 garlic cloves, pressed
- pinch of red pepper flakes (less than ¼ teaspoon)
- freshly ground sea salt and pepper, to taste
- 2 cups chicken broth
- 3 large parsnips (or 4-5 small ones)
- 3/4 cup cubed leftover Christmas ham (or cubed pancetta)

Directions
1. Heat the oil in a large pot over medium heat. Once the oil heats, add the sage and cook until crispy. Set the sage aside on a paper-towel lined plate.
2. Immediately add in the butternut squash, shallots, garlic and red pepper flakes to the pot and season with salt and pepper. Cook for 5-7 minutes or until onion is translucent. Pour in the broth and raise the heat to bring the mixture to a boil. Once boiling, reduce the heat to a simmer and cook until the squash is softened, 15-20 minutes.
3. While the squash cooks, peel and spiralize the parsnips. Set aside.

4. Once the squash mixture is softened and easily pierced with a fork, transfer to a high-speed blender. Wipe down the pot and set aside. Blend the squash mixture until smooth, about 1 minute. Taste and season with salt and pepper to your preference. If the mixture is too thick, add in vegetable broth.

5. If not using leftover Christmas ham: Set the pot down over medium heat and once heated, add in the ham or pancetta and cook for 5 minutes or until cooked through and starting to brown on edges. Then, add in the parsnip noodles, cover and toss to cook for 5 more minutes or until al dente. Then, add in the squash sauce and toss altogether to warm sauce. Crumble the sage on top and serve immediately.

6. If using leftover Christmas ham: Set the pot down over medium heat and once heated, add in the ham, squash sauce and parsnip noodles, toss and cook for 5-7 minutes or until noodles al dente. Crumble the fried sage on top and serve immediately.

Parsnip Noodles with Ramps, Baby Kale and Ham

Prep Time: 10 minutes | *Cook Time:* 15 minutes | *Total Time:* 25 minutes | *Servings:* 1

Ingredients

- 1 bunch ramps (about 6-8 stalks)
- 1 tbsp olive oil
- 1/3 cup diced ham
- 1 pinch red pepper flakes
- 1/2 cup baby kale
- 1 large parsnip, peeled, Blade C
- salt and pepper, to taste
- 2 tsp grated parmesan cheese

Directions

1. Take your ramps and slice off the reddish stems and leaves. Chop off the root ends, leaving the white parts of the stem and white bulbs. Peel off the outer layer of skin and then roughly chop them, in about 1/2 inch pieces.

2. Place a large skillet over medium heat and add in the olive oil. Once oil heats, add in the ramps and ham. Cook for 2-3 minutes or until ramps begin to soften. Add in the kale, red pepper flakes, parsnip noodles and

season with salt and pepper. Toss to combine and cover, letting cook 4-7 minutes or until parsnip noodles wilt and cook through.

3. When done, pour into a bowl and top with cheese.

Parsnip Spaghetti All'Amatriciana

Prep time: 20 mins | *Cook time:* 60 mins | *Total time:* 1 hour 20 mins | *Serves:* 4

Ingredients

- ½ tablespoon extra virgin olive oil
- 4oz guanciale cut into ¼" strips or pancetta
- 1 onion, diced
- ½ teaspoon red pepper flakes
- 1 (28-ounce) can Tuttorosso diced tomatoes, pureed with juices
- salt, to taste
- 4 parsnips (at least 1.5" in diameter)
- finely grated Pecorino Romano cheese

Directions

1. Place a large pot over medium heat and add in the olive oil. Add in the guanciale (or pancetta) and cook until brown and crispy, about 5-7 minutes. Reserve 1 tablespoon of the meat – set aside in a small bowl.
2. Add in the onions and red pepper flakes and cook for 3-5 minutes or until onions are translucent. Add in the tomatoes and raise the heat to medium-high and bring to a boil. Season with salt, reduce to a simmer at low heat and let cook for 30 minutes.
3. Meanwhile, peel and spiralize the parsnips, using Blade C. After the sauce has cooked for 30 minutes, add in the parsnip noodles, toss to combine thoroughly and let cook for 10 minutes or until parsnips are al dente.
4. Divide the pasta mixture into bowls and garnish with cheese and the reserved meat.

Pasta Arrabbiata with Carrot Noodles

Prep time: 10 mins | *Cook time:* 30 mins | *Total time:* 40 mins | *Serves:* 6

Ingredients

- ¼ cup extra virgin olive oil
- 5 garlic cloves, minced
- 1 (28 ounce) can Tuttorosso® Diced Tomatoes in rich tomato juice
- 1 (28 ounce) can Tuttorosso® Tomato Puree with basil
- 2 teaspoons crushed red pepper
- ½ teaspoon dried oregano
- Salt and black pepper to taste
- 3-4 large carrots, peeled, spiralized using Blade C, noodles trimmed
- ½ cup grated Parmesan cheese
- ¼ cup fresh basil leaves, thinly sliced

Directions

1. Heat oil in large saucepan over medium heat. Add garlic and cook about 3 minutes or until garlic is lightly browned, being careful not to burn. Add in diced tomatoes and tomato puree, bring to a boil.
2. Reduce heat to low, stir in red pepper, oregano, salt and black pepper. Cook uncovered for about 20 minutes, stirring occasionally.
3. Bring a large saucepan filled halfway with water to a boil. Once boiling, add in the carrot noodles and cook for 2-3 minutes or until noodles are al dente. Drain into a colander and set aside.
4. Once sauce is done cooking, remove from heat, fold in the cheese and basil and toss well to combine. Add in the carrot noodles, toss and transfer to a large pasta serving bowl.

Pecorino Butternut Squash Noodles & Cauliflower Steak with Olive, Caper & Chickpea Sauce

Prep Time: *20 minutes* | **Cook Time:** *15 minutes* | **Total Time:** *35 minutes* | **Servings:** *4*

Ingredients

- 1 large cauliflower head, stems removed and cauliflower cut into 1" slices (should make 4 slices)
- olive oil, to drizzle
- salt and pepper, to taste

- 1 tsp garlic powder
- 1 butternut squash, peeled, Blade C
- 1/2 cup freshly grated Pecorino Romano cheese
- 2 tbsp olive oil
- 2 garlic cloves, minced
- 3 shallots, minced
- 3 tbsp capers
- 1/2 cup chopped olives
- 1 cup chickpeas

Directions

1. Preheat the oven to 400 degrees. On a baking tray, place down the cauliflower slices and drizzle lightly with olive oil. Massage the olive oil into the cauliflower "steaks" and then season with salt, pepper and garlic powder. Roast in the oven for 15 minutes, flipping halfway through.
2. Five minutes into roasting the cauliflower, place your butternut squash noodles on a baking tray, drizzle lightly with olive oil and season with salt and pepper. Roast in the oven for 5-7 minutes. When done, remove and toss with the cheese.
3. After you place in the butternut squash noodles, place a large skillet over medium-low heat and add in the olive oil. Then, add in the garlic and cook for 30 seconds. Then, add in the shallots and cook for another 30 seconds. Then, add in the capers, olives, chickpeas and cook for about 3 minutes. When done, toss in the parsley and stir to combine.
4. Plate the butternut squash noodles, top with cauliflower steak and then pour over the olive, caper & chickpea sauce. Enjoy!

Pesto Caprese Zucchini Noodle Salad

Prep time: 25 mins | Total time: 25 mins | Serves: 2

Ingredients

For the pesto:

- 2 teaspoons pine nuts
- 1 packed cup of basil
- 1.5 tablespoons extra virgin olive oil
- 1 small garlic clove
- salt and pepper, to taste

- For the zucchini noodles:
- 1 medium zucchini, Blade D, noodles trimmed

For the caprese:

- 2 half-thick slices of tomato
- 2 quarter-inch thick slice of mozzarella cheese (2oz each)
- 2 teaspoons extra virgin olive oil, to drizzle
- salt and pepper, to taste
- 1 pinch red pepper flakes
- 2 basil leaves, sliced thinly

Directions

1. Place all of the ingredients for the pesto into a food processor and pulse until creamy. Taste and adjust, if necessary.
2. In a large mixing bowl, add in the zucchini noodles and pour in the pesto. Toss together until fully combined.
3. Plate the zucchini noodles into two dishes and top each with a tomato slice. Top the tomato with a slice of mozzarella and drizzle with olive oil (about 1 teaspoon) and season with salt and pepper. Garnish with red pepper flakes and basil.

Pesto Zoodles

"Transform zucchini into long strands that resemble noodles, also known as zoodles. Mix pesto and garbanzo beans into the zoodles for a satisfying, grain-free meal!"

Servings: 2 | Prep: 10 m | Cook: 10 m | Ready In: 20 m

Ingredients

- 1 tablespoon olive oil
- 4 small zucchini, cut into noodle-shape strands
- 1/2 cup drained and rinsed canned garbanzo beans (chickpeas)
- 3 tablespoons pesto, or to taste salt and ground black pepper to taste
- 2 tablespoons shredded white Cheddar cheese, or to taste

Directions

1. Heat olive oil in a skillet over medium heat; cook and stir zucchini until tender and liquid has evaporated, 5 to 10 minutes.
2. Stir garbanzo beans and pesto into zucchini; lower heat to medium-low. Cook and stir until garbanzo beans are warm and zucchini is evenly coated, about 5 minutes; season with salt and pepper.
3. Transfer zucchini mixture to serving bowls and top with white Cheddar cheese.

Nutritional Information

- Calories:319 kcal 6%
- Fat: 21.3 g 33%
- Carbs: 23.1g 7%
- Protein: 12.1 g 24%
- Cholesterol: 16 mg 5%
- Sodium: 511 mg 20%

Pesto Zucchini Noodles with Asparagus and Shrimp

Prep Time: *15 minutes* | **Cook Time:** *10 minutes* | **Total Time:** *25 minutes* | **Servings:** *1*

Ingredients

For the pesto

- 2 packed cups of fresh basil leaves
- salt and pepper
- 1/2 cup of olive oil
- 1/3 cup pine nuts (or a large handful)
- 2 large cloves of garlic, minced

For the rest

- garlic powder
- olive oil cooking spray
- salt and pepper
- 8-10 medium sized shrimp
- 2 medium zucchinis, spiralized
- 6 stalks of asparagus, chopped into thirds

Directions

1. Put all of the ingredients for the pesto into the food processor and blend. Taste with your finger and add anymore of one ingredient to make to your taste (ie if it's too salty, add in more basil/pine nuts/olive oil). Set aside.
2. Place a medium sized saucepan on medium-high heat and spray with olive oil cooking spray. Season with salt and pepper. Once heated, add in the asparagus, spray with olive oil cooking spray and season with garlic powder, salt and pepper. Stir frequently until easily pierced with a fork.
3. While asparagus is cooking, fill a large saucepan full of salted water. Once boiled, add in the zucchini pasta. Cook for about 3-4 minutes or until (test it!) the zucchini is softened a bit. Pour out into a coriander, lay out on paper towels and pat dry.
4. Place a medium sized saucepan over medium-high heat and spray with olive oil cooking spray. Season with garlic powder, salt and pepper. Place in the shrimp, spray with cooking spray and season tops with garlic powder, salt and pepper. Let cook for 1-2 minutes and then flip over and cook another 2 minutes or until completely opaque.
5. Add the zucchini pasta to a large bowl and add in the pesto, asparagus and shrimp and mix thoroughly to combine. I like to take a scissor and cut the long noodles in half so that they are easier to cute and share.
6. Divide onto two plates and enjoy!

Pesto Zucchini Noodles with Asparagus

Prep time: 10 mins | Cook time: 7 mins | Total time: 17 mins | Serves: 2

Ingredients

For the pasta:

*   1 teaspoon extra virgin olive oil
*   4 thick asparagus spears, ends trimmed, sliced on an angle
*   salt and pepper, to taste
*   2 medium zucchinis, Blade D, noodles trimmed
*   ¼ cup jarred vegan pesto or homemade (see below)
*   For the pesto:
*   3 cup basil leaves, packed
*   1.5 talespoons pine nuts
*   3-4 tablespoons extra virgin olive oil
*   salt and pepper

- 1 large clove of garlic, minced

Directions

1. If making homemade pesto, place all of the ingredients for the pesto into a food processor and pulse until creamy. Taste and adjust, if necessary. Set aside.
2. Heat the oil in a medium skillet over medium-high heat. Once oil is shimmering, add in the asparagus and season generously with salt and pepper. Cook for 5-7 minutes or until asparagus is bright green, fork tender, and is browned.
3. Meanwhile, spiralize the zucchinis and place in a large mixing bowl. Pour over the pesto and toss well. Set aside.
4. When asparagus is done, toss it in the bowl with the pesto zucchini noodles and toss well to combine.
5. Divide the pasta into bowls and serve.

Picadillo with Spiralized Green Bell Peppers

Prep time: *20 mins* | **Cook time:** *20 mins* | **Total time:** *40 mins* | **Serves:** *3*

Ingredients

- 1 tablespoon extra virgin olive oil
- 2 green bell peppers, Blade A
- ¾ pound ground beef, lean
- ½ cup chopped white onions
- 2 cloves of garlic, minced
- ½ cup canned tomato sauce
- ¼ teaspoon ground cinnamon
- ½ teaspoon ground cumin
- ½ teaspoon dried oregano
- salt and pepper, to taste
- 3 tablespoons golden raisins
- ¼ cup quartered pitted green olives

Directions

1. Place a large skillet over medium-high heat and add in the olive oil. Once heated, add the bell peppers and season with salt and pepper. Cook for 5 minutes or until al dente (cook longer if you want them softer.)
2. Remove the peppers from the skillet with tongs and transfer to a bowl and set aside.
3. Immediately place in the onions and garlic to the skillet and cook for 5 minutes or until onions soften.
4. Add in the ground beef and cook for 10 minutes or until it browns, crumbling the meat with a wooden spoon.
5. Add in the tomato sauce, cinnamon, cumin, and oregano, season with salt and pepper and stir to combine. Lower the heat, cover and let the mixture simmer for about 5 minutes.
6. Uncover the pan and fold in the raisins and olives, cover and cook for another 5 minutes.
7. Divide the bell pepper noodles into bowls and top with picadillo.

Pomegranate-Maple-Cider Carrot & Cucumber Noodles with Chili Beef and Blue Cheese

Prep Time: *15 minutes* | **Cook Time:** *5 minutes* | **Total Time:** *20 minutes* | **Servings:** *1*

Ingredients

For the pomegranate-maple-cider vinaigrette (makes about 1 cup):

- 3 tbsp fresh pomegranate seeds from 1 pomegranate*
- 1/4 cup apple cider vinegar
- 2.5 tbsp maple syrup
- 3 tsp dijon mustard
- 1/3 cup olive oil
- salt and pepper to taste

For the rest:

- 1/2 cup packed cucumber noodles (Blade C)
- 1/2 cup carrot noodles (peeled, Blade C)
- 2 oz sirloin steak, cut into two strips (or other preferred beef cut)
- 1 tsp chile powder
- salt and pepper, to taste
- 1/2 tbsp olive oil

- 3 tbsp crumbled blue cheese

Directions

1. Prepare your vinaigrette. Add all of the ingredients into a dressing shaker and shake or whisk in a bowl. Taste and add additional ingredients, as preferred. Set aside.
2. Place the carrot noodles in a mixing bowl and drizzle 1 tbsp of the vinaigrette. Toss to combine and set aside.
3. Take your piece of beef and season it with salt, pepper and the chili powder on both sides.
4. Place a medium skillet over medium heat and add in the olive oil. Add in the beef and sear on one side for 1-2 minutes. Flip over and cook until you've reached your preferred "doneness." Take off the heat and set aside.
5. Place your cucumber noodles into the mixing bowl with the carrot noodles, add in the pomegranates and toss to combine.
6. Plate the noodle mixture into a bowl or plate and top with steak, blue cheese and drizzle with 1 more tbsp of the vinaigrette. Enjoy!

Pork Chops with Cherry-Tarragon Sauce and Butternut Squash Fettucine

Prep Time: *15 minutes* |**Cook Time:** *20 minutes* | **Total Time:** *35 minutes* | **Servings:** *2*

Ingredients

For the pork chops and noodles:

- 1 small butternut squash, peeled, Blade B, noodles trimmed
- olive oil cooking spray
- 2 (1" thick) pork loin chops
- salt and pepper, to taste
- 1 teaspoon ground coriander
- 1 teaspoon ground mustard
- 2 teaspoons extra virgin olive oil

For the cherry sauce:

- 1 teaspoon extra virgin olive oil
- 1 cup fresh Bing cherries, pitted and halved

- 1 tablespoon fresh tarragon, roughly chopped
- 2 cloves garlic, minced
- ½ cup red wine
- ¼ cup chicken broth
- salt and pepper, to taste

Directions

1. Heat oven to 400 degrees. Line a baking sheet with parchment paper and lay out the butternut squash noodles. Spray the noodles with cooking spray and set aside.
2. Rinse the pork chops and pat the dry with paper towels. Season generously with salt and pepper and then place the coriander and mustard in a bowl and mix until evenly combined. Rub the spice mixture all over the pork chops, on both sides. Set aside.
3. Olace a medium skillet over medium heat and add in the olive oil. Once oil heats, add in the cherries, tarragon, and garlic. Cook, stirring frequently, for 1 minute and then stir in the wine and broth. Simmer, uncovered, for 10-15 minutes or until the sauce is reduced and thicker. Season to taste with salt and pepper.
4. While sauce is cooking, place a large oven-safe skillet over medium-heat and add in the olive oil. Once oil heats, add in the pork chops and cook for about 4 minutes (about 2 minutes per side) or until bottoms are golden brown.
5. Transfer the pan to the oven, along with the butternut squash noodles and bake until the chops are golden brown, about 7-10 minutes. If using a thermometer, temperature should register at 145 F in the thickest part of each chop. The butternut squash noodles should bake for 8-10 minutes.
6. Divide the butternut squash noodles into plates, top with pork chop, and top with cherry-tarragon sauce.

Pumpkin-Sage Alfredo Carrot Pasta with Crispy Pancetta

Prep time: 20 mins | *Cook time:* 20 mins | *Total time:* 40 mins | *Serves:* 4

Ingredients

- 3-4 large carrots, peeled, Blade D, noodles trimmed
- 4oz pancetta, diced
- 2 sage leaves
- 1 tablespoon minced shallots

- 2 small garlic cloves, minced
- 1 pinch red pepper flakes
- 1 15oz can pumpkin puree
- salt and pepper, to taste
- 1 15oz can full-fat coconut milk, refrigerated overnight
- ½ teaspoon ground nutmeg
- 1 tablespoon chopped parsley, to garnish

Directions

1. Bring a medium pot of lightly salted water to a boil. Once boiling, add in the carrot noodles and let cook 2-3 minutes or until al dente. Drain noodles into a colander and set aside.
2. Place a large skillet over medium heat and add in the ham. Let cook for 5-7 minutes or until ham is cooked and starts to turn crispy. Remove with a slotted spoon and set aside.
3. Immediately place in the sage, shallots, garlic and red pepper flakes and stir frequently, careful not to burn the garlic. If needed, let the skillet cool first. Cook for 30 seconds or until fragrant and then add in the pumpkin and season with salt and pepper. Let cook for 2-3 minutes or until warmed through and then add in the coconut cream from the coconut milk can (the solids only off the top) and nutmeg. Stir to combine and cook for 5 minutes more to absorb the flavors.
4. Divide the carrot pasta into bowls and top with pumpkin sauce and ham. Garnish with parsley.

Quinoa Sweet Potato Noodle Bolognese with Toasted Crushed Almonds

Prep Time: 10 minutes | Cook Time: 25 minutes | Total Time: 35 minutes | Servings: 2

Ingredients

- 3 tbsp dry quinoa
- 1/4 cup + 3 tbsp water
- salt, to taste
- 1 tbsp olive oil
- 2 tsp minced garlic
- 1/4 tsp red pepper flakes
- 1/4 cup chopped celery
- 1/4 cup peeled and chopped carrot

- handful of almonds (less than 1/4 cup)
- 1/4 cup diced red onion
- (1) 14-oz can of diced tomatoes
- 1 tsp oregano flakes
- pepper, to taste
- 1.5 large sweet potato, peeled, Blade C
- olive oil cooking spray
- 1 tsp garlic powder

Directions

1. Place a small saucepan over high heat with the quinoa and water. Add a pinch of salt and bring to a boil and then lower heat and simmer until all water evaporates and quinoa is fluffy. Set aside in a bowl once done.
2. As the quinoa is cooking, place your carrot and celery in a food processor and pulse until no large chunks remain. Set aside.
3. Clean out the food processor and add in the almonds. Crush until chunky. Place a small skillet over medium heat and add in the crushed almonds. Cook for about 3 minutes or until almonds become fragrant. Set aside.
4. Place a large saucepan over medium heat. Add in the olive oil and once it heats up, add in the garlic and cook for 1 minute. Add in the red pepper flakes, cook for 30 seconds, and then add in the celery-carrot mixture and red onions. Cook for about 3-4 minutes or until vegetables soften.
5. Add the diced tomatoes, season with oregano and salt and pepper. Crush tomatoes using the back of a fork or potato masher. Cook for about 10-15 minutes or until sauce is mostly reduced. You want the sauce to be thick but still be juicy.
6. As the sauce is cooking, add the sweet potato noodles to a large skillet over medium heat. Lightly spray the noodles with cooking spray and season with salt, pepper and garlic powder. Toss frequently until noodles have wilted and softened, about 5-10 minutes.
7. Once the sauce is done, add in the cooked quinoa and stir to combine. Add in the cooked sweet potato noodles and toss to combine.
8. Plate the noodles into the bowls and top each with even amounts of toasted crushed almonds. Enjoy!

Roasted Asparagus & Mushroom Butternut Squash Noodles with a Poached Egg

Prep Time: 20 minutes | **Cook Time:** 25 minutes | **Total Time:** 45 minutes | **Servings:** 1

Ingredients

- 4 stalks of asparagus
- 1/2 cup sliced mushrooms (I used white button)
- olive oil cooking spray
- salt and pepper, to taste
- 1 tsp garlic powder
- 3" section of butternut squash, peeled, Blade C
- olive oil, to drizzle
- 1 large egg (or two)

Directions

1. Preheat the oven to 375 degrees.
2. Prepare your asparagus. Snap off one half-inch off the ends and then cut into three sections.
3. Coat a baking tray with cooking spray and place in the asparagus and mushrooms.
4. Let vegetables roast for 20 minutes, flipping halfway through.
5. Place the butternut squash noodles on another baking tray and drizzle olive oil. Mix to combine thoroughly and season with salt and pepper. 5 minutes before the other vegetables are done, add in these noodles. Cook for 5-7 minutes or until softened to your preference.
6. After you put the noodles in the oven, add a medium-sized saucepan filled 1/3 the way with water. Heat until bubbles form on the bottom, almost at boiling level.
7. Lower the heat to a simmer, crack an egg into a small dish, and pour very carefully and slowly into the water.
8. Let cook for about 3-4 minutes. Pull the egg out with a slotted spoon and poke it. If it is jiggly yet firm, it's done. If it's hard to the touch, it's overdone. If it's too delicate, cook for another 30 seconds.
9. Place the spoon on a folded paper towel to drain, while you finish preparing the pasta.
10. Place your butternut squash noodles in a bowl with the roasted vegetables. Top with the drained poached egg. Enjoy!

Roasted Beet Noodles with Pesto and Baby Kale

Prep Time: 10 minutes | Cook Time: 15 minutes | Total Time: 25 minutes | Servings: 3

Ingredients

- 2 medium beets, peeled, Blade C, noodles trimmed
- olive oil cooking spray
- 2 cups baby kale
- For the pesto:
- 3 cup basil leaves, packed
- ¼ cup of pinenuts
- ¼ cup of olive oil
- ½ tsp grinded sea salt
- ¼ tsp grinded pepper
- 1 large clove of garlic, minced

Directions

- Set the oven to 425 degrees. On a baking sheet, spread out the beet noodles and coat with cooking spray and season with salt and pepper. Bake for 5-10 minutes or until beets are cooked to al dente or your preference in doneness.
- While the noodles cook, combine all of the ingredients for the pesto into a food processor and pulse until creamy. Taste and adjust, if needed.
- Once beets are cooked, toss with pesto and the kale. Serve.
- If using hard taco shells: Using pasta tongs, fill the taco shells with zucchini spaghetti mixture and top with olives, a dollop of avocado and a pinch of lettuce.
- If not using hard taco shells: Fill a bowl up with shredded lettuce and top with zucchini noodles (using pasta tongs to let excess moisture drip off), then top with olives and a dollop of avocado. Repeat 3 more times to make 3 taco bowls.
- *Check the ingredients on the taco shells – they should contain nothing more than water, corn (or masa) flour and/or oil.

Roasted Butternut Squash Noodles & Quinoa with Spiced Pumpkin Seeds, Dried Cranberries and Goat Cheese

Prep Time: 15 minutes | **Cook Time:** 20 minutes | **Total Time:** 35 minutes | **Servings:** 1

Ingredients

- 3" piece of butternut squash, peeled, Blade C
- 2 tbsp dried cranberries
- 1 tbsp raw hulled pumpkin seeds
- 1 tbsp chili powder
- 1 tbsp cooked red quinoa
- 1 tbsp cumin
- salt and pepper
- 1 tbsp olive oil
- 2 tbsp crumbled goat cheese
- olive oil cooking spray

Directions

1. Preheat the oven to 375 degrees.
2. Cook the quinoa according to package instructions. Set aside when done.
3. While the quinoa is cooking, coat a baking tray with cooking spray and spread out the pumpkin seeds. Coat the pumpkin seeds with cooking spray and season generously with salt. Then, evenly dust the seeds with the cumin and chili powder.
4. Bake the pumpkin seeds for 5 minutes in the oven. When done, set aside.
5. Change the heat on the oven to 400 degrees.
6. Add the butternut squash noodles onto a baking tray coating with cooking spray. Drizzle half of the olive oil onto the noodles and toss to combine. Season with salt and pepper and bake for 5-7 minutes or until noodles have softened to your preference.
7. Place the noodles in a bowl and toss with cranberries, spiced pumpkin seeds, quinoa, and the rest of the olive oil.
8. Plate onto a bowl and top with goat cheese. Enjoy!

Roasted Butternut Squash Sweet Potato Noodles with Bacon, Crushed Pecans and Spinach

Prep Time: 10 minutes | Cook Time: 45 minutes | Total Time: 55 minutes | Servings: 2

Ingredients

- 2 sweet potatoes, peeled, Blade C
- 1 tbsp olive oil
- 1 tsp garlic powder
- salt and pepper, to taste
- 2 cups cubed skinless butternut squash
- 1 cup packed spinach
- 1/4 cup crushed pecans
- 4 strips of bacon
- olive oil for drizzling
- 1/2 tsp ground cinnamon
- 3/4 cup vegetable broth, low-sodium
- 1/2 cup light unsweetened almond milk

Directions

1. Preheat the oven to 405 degrees. Once preheated, add the cubed butternut squash into a baking tray and drizzle with olive oil. Season with salt and pepper. Dust lightly and evenly with the cinnamon. Mix together to combine and roast for 35 minutes.
2. While the butternut squash is roasting, put a large skillet over medium heat. Add in the tbsp of olive oil and the sweet potato noodles. Season with garlic powder. Cook for about 6-8 minutes or until sweet potato noodles cook through and are soft. Set aside.
3. Place a large skillet over medium heat and add in the bacon strips. Cook the bacon until crispy and set aside on a paper-towel-lined plate.
4. Once the squash is done roasting, add the cubes directly into a food processor. Add in the almond milk and half of the vegetable broth. Pulse until creamy.
5. Place a large skillet over medium heat and add in the squash puree and the rest of the vegetable broth. Cook until the broth reduces and the puree is creamier. Add water or more vegetable broth, if not creamy.
6. Once the sauce is done, add in the spinach and sweet potato noodles and mix to combine thoroughly. Let cook until spinach wilts.
7. Plate the sauced noodles into a bowl and crumble in the bacon. Top with crushed pecans and enjoy!

Roasted Garlic Scape and Tomato Chayote Noodles with Crab

Prep Time: 7 minutes | *Cook Time:* 35 minutes | *Total Time:* 42 minutes | *Servings:* 3

Ingredients

- 15 ounces of tomatoes, cut into 1/2-inch thick slices
- 1.5 tablespoons extra virgin olive oil
- salt and pepper, to taste
- 1/4 teaspoon dried thyme
- 1/4 teaspoon dried oregano
- 4.5 ounces (one large bunch) garlic scapes, diced
- 3 chayotes (about 10.5 ounces each)
- 1 tablespoon lemon juice
- 1 cup jumbo lump crab meat
- 2 teaspoons freshly chopped parsley, to garnish

Directions

1. Preheat the oven to 350 degrees. On one baking tray, place in the tomato slices. Drizzle with 1 tablespoon of the olive oil and season generously with salt and pepper. Sprinkle over the thyme and oregano and set aside.
2. On another baking tray, place in your garlic scapes. Toss with the rest of the olive oil and season with salt and pepper.
3. Bake both the garlic scapes and tomatoes for 25 minutes.
4. As the garlic scapes and tomatoes are baking, spiralize your chayote, using Blade C. Set aside.
5. When the tomatoes and garlic scapes are done, place into a food processor with the lemon juice and pulse until made into a sauce, with the garlic scapes pureed. Taste and adjust with more salt, if needed.
6. Place a large pot over medium heat and pour in the tomato-scape sauce. Let the sauce start to bubble and then add in the chayote noodles and crab meat. Toss to combine and cook, tossing frequently, for 3-4 minutes or until chayote noodles are al dente.
7. Divide into bowls and top with fresh parsley

Roasted Orange & Beet Noodle Pasta with Honey Walnuts & Crispy Baked Kale

Prep Time: 10 minutes | **Cook Time**: 25 minutes | **Total Time**: 35 minutes | **Servings**: 1

Ingredients

For the vinaigrette:

- juice from 1/4 of a large lemon
- one crank of the salt grinder
- two cranks of a pepper grinder
- 1 tbsp olive oil
- 1 tsp red wine vinegar
- 1.5 tbsp orange juice
- 1/2 tsp country dijon mustard

For the rest:

- olive oil cooking spray
- 1 large orange, peeled and sliced into fourths or eighths
- 1 cup of roughly chopped kale leaves (stems removed)
- olive oil, to drizzle
- 1 large beet, peeled, Blade C
- a handful of walnuts
- raw honey, to drizzle

Directions

1. Preheat the oven to 375 degrees. In a baking tray lightly coated with cooking spray, place in the orange slices on one side and the kale on the other. Lightly coat the kale with the cooking spray and season with pepper. Set the timer for 20 minutes. After 10-12 minutes, remove the kale from the baking tray and set aside. Place the baking tray with the oranges back into the oven.
2. In another baking tray, place the beet noodles and drizzle lightly with olive oil. Season with salt and pepper and roast in the oven for 10-15 minutes.
3. While the oranges and beets are roasting, assemble your vinaigrette. Place all ingredients into a bowl and whisk together. Place in the refrigerator.
4. 5 minutes before the oranges are done, place the walnuts on the side of the baking tray that used to hold the kale. Drizzle lightly with honey and toss carefully with tongs. Let roast for the remaining 5 minutes and take out with the oranges.
5. When the beet noodles are done (should be done with the oranges or have another 5 minutes left), place them in a bowl and top with the orange slices, walnuts and kale. Drizzle the vinaigrette over. Enjoy!

Roasted Pork Chops with Pistachio-Parsley Pesto Zucchini Pasta

Ingredients

For the pesto:

- 1/4 cup + 2 tbsp olive oil
- 1/2 cup roasted and salted pistachios (deshelled)
- 1 cup packed fresh parsley leaves
- 1/4 cup grated pecorino romano
- 1 garlic clove, minced
- pepper, to taste

For the rest:

- 2 tbsp olive oil
- 3 boneless pork chops
- salt and pepper, to season
- garlic powder, to taste
- 3 medium zucchinis, Blade A

Directions

1. Preheat the oven to 400 degrees.
2. Season both sides of the pork chops with salt and pepper and a pinch of garlic powder. In batches or using two skillets, sear the pork chops. To do so, place about 1/2 tbsp in the skillet per pork chop and let cook, without moving, for 3 minutes and then flip over and let cook another 3 minutes.
3. Once the pork chops are done searing, place them directly into the oven (still in the skillet). Cook for about 8 minutes or until pork chops register at 140/145 degrees (using a thermometer).
4. While the pork chops are cooking, prepare your pesto. First, place your pistachios into a food processor and pulse until finely ground. Then, add in the rest of the ingredients and pulse until creamy.
5. In a bowl, place in your zucchini noodles and top with your pesto. Toss to combine. Once noodles are coated with pesto, divide them into three plates and top each with a finished pork chop. Enjoy!

Roasted Red Pepper Butternut Squash Pasta with Chicken

Prep Time: 10 minutes | **Cook Time**: 40 minutes | **Total Time**: 50 minutes | **Servings**: 2-3

Ingredients

- 2 whole red bell peppers
- 1 large butternut squash, peeled, Blade C

- olive oil, to drizzle
- salt and pepper, to taste
- 1/2 tsp garlic powder
- 1 tbsp olive oil
- 2 garlic cloves, minced
- 1/4 tsp red pepper flakes
- 3/4 cup diced white onion
- 1/3 cup chicken broth, low-sodium
- 1 cup chopped cooked chicken
- 1 tbsp freshly chopped parsley

Directions

1. Preheat the oven to 400 degrees. Cut the bottom and tops off the bell peppers, remove the seeds inside and place on a baking tray lightly coated with cooking spray. Place the peppers insides up. Roast for 25 minutes.
2. While the peppers are roasting, place your butternut squash noodles on a baking tray. Drizzle the noodles lightly with olive oil and season with salt, pepper and garlic powder. When the peppers are done roasting, place the noodles into the oven and roast for 10 minutes. When done, remove from heat and place into bowls.
3. When the peppers are done roasting, place them into a food processor and pulse until no major chunks are left. Then, place a large skillet over medium heat and add in the olive oil. Then, add in the garlic, red pepper flakes and onions. Let cook for about 3 minutes and then add in the pureed red peppers. Stir to combine and then add in the chicken broth and chicken. Cook for another 2 minutes to heat up the chicken.
4. Pour the red pepper sauce and chicken mixture over the bowls of butternut squash noodles. Top each with freshly chopped parsley, to garnish.

Romesco Garlic Shrimp with Zucchini Noodles

Prep time: 45 mins | *Cook time:* 15 mins | *Total time:* 1 hour | *Serves:* 4

Ingredients

For the pasta:

- 4-6 medium zucchini , Blade C, noodles trimmed
- 2 tablespoons extra virgin olive oil

- ¼ onion, finely chopped
- 2 cloves garlic, minced
- 1 pound large shrimp, peeled and deveined
- salt and pepper, to taste
- 2 teaspoons chopped fresh parsley leaves

For the romesco sauce:

- 2 tablespoons extra virgin olive oil
- ½ cup almonds, chopped
- 1 small onion, diced
- 3 cloves garlic, minced
- 1 teaspoon chili powder
- 1 teaspoon paprika
- 2 tomatoes, seeded and chopped
- 2 tablespoons extra-virgin olive oil
- 1½ teaspoons red wine vinegar
- 1 teaspoon salt
- ½ teaspoon black pepper

Directions

1. MELT the olive oil for the romesco sauce in a large skillet over medium-high heat. When the fat is hot, add the almonds and toast for 3 minutes, stirring often. Add the onion and cook, stirring, for 2 minutes. Add the garlic and cook until aromatic, about 1 minute. Add the chili powder and paprika and cook until the flavors open up, about 30 seconds. Finally, add the tomatoes, mix into the ingredients, and cook, stirring to bring up the tasty bits from the bottom of the pan, until the tomatoes are warmed through, about 2 minutes. Transfer the sauce mixture to a food processor. Add the rest of the ingredients and blend on low speed until the sauce is smooth, then set aside.

2. MELT the olive oil in a large skillet over medium heat, swirling to coat the bottom of the pan. When the oil is hot, add the onion and cook, stirring, until translucent, about 2 minutes. Stir in the garlic and cook until aromatic, about 1 minute. Add the shrimp, toss to coat with the onion and garlic, and cook stirring, for 2 minutes. Add ¼ cup water to the skillet and cover with a lid. Cook until the shrimp form the shape of a "C," 4 to 6 minutes. Transfer to a serving bowl (draining any remaining water), and season with the salt and pepper.

3. AFTER you add the water and cover the shrimp, place a large skillet over medium-high heat. Once heated, add in the zucchini noodles and toss for about 5 minutes or until softened or cooked to your preference. Divide into plates. Top with romesco sauce.

4. SPRINKLE the shrimp with the parsley, toss, and spoon over the dressed zucchini noodles and serve.

Sausage and Peppers with Zucchini Noodles

Prep time: 15 mins | Cook time: 30 mins | Total time: 45 mins | Serves: 4-6

Ingredients

- 5 tablespoons extra-virgin olive oil
- 2 sweet fennel Italian sausage links
- 2 spicy Italian sausage links
- 2 medium yellow onions, peeled, spiralized with blade a, noodles trimmed
- 1 red bell pepper, spiralized with blade a, noodles trimmed
- 1 orange bell pepper, spiralized with blade a, noodles trimmed
- 1½ tablespoons tomato paste
- ¼ teaspoon red pepper flakes
- 4 garlic cloves, minced
- ½ teaspoon dried oregano
- 1 cup low-sodium chicken broth
- Salt and pepper
- 2 tablespoons finely chopped fresh curly parsley
- 2 medium zucchini, spiralized with blade d, noodles trimmed

Directions

1. Heat 2 tablespoons of the olive oil in a large skillet with a lid over medium-high heat. When the oil is shimmering, add the sausages and cover the pan. Cook for about 7 minutes or until just browned on the bottom. Uncover and cook for 5 minutes more, turning, until browned on the outside but not yet cooked through. Using tongs, transfer the sausage to a cutting board and slice into 1-inch pieces. Set aside.
2. Immediately add the remaining 3 tablespoons olive oil, the onion noodles, and the bell pepper noodles to the same skillet. Cook for about 5 minutes or until the vegetables soften. Add the tomato paste, and stir to cook the vegetables. Add the red pepper flakes and garlic and cook for 30 seconds or until fragrant. Return the sausage to the pan and add the oregano and broth. Season with salt and black pepper. Cover the skillet and simmer until the sausage is cooked through, about 10 minutes. Uncover and simmer until the sauce has reduced by a quarter, about 5 minutes more. Stir in the parsley.

3. Transfer to a large serving platter or bowl and add the zucchini noodles. Toss thoroughly until the noodles begin to wilt and are fully incorporated. Serve immediately.
4. Note: If you're serving this dish in the summer, try fresh basil instead of parsley to garnish

Sauteed Green Chard and Tomatoes Zucchini Pasta with Grilled Salmon

Prep Time: 5 minutes | Cook Time: 10 minutes | Servings: 1

Ingredients

- 1.5 zucchinis, Blade A
- half of 1 salmon filet (skinned removed), cut into 2 inch chunks
- 1 tbsp olive oil
- 1 pinch of red pepper flakes
- salt and pepper, to taste
- 5 cherry tomatoes, halved
- 1 garlic clove
- 4 leaves of green chard
- 1/4 cup of vegetable broth, low-sodium
- olive oil cooking spray

Directions

1. Prepare the chard. Cut out the white stem of each leaf and cut into 3 inch pieces. Place aside.
2. Heat up the grill (I used a George Forman grill). Spray both sides with olive oil cooking spray. Once heated, place the chunks of salmon down and season with salt and pepper. Cook until finished (if on George Forman, about 5 minutes) and set aside.
3. While your salmon is cooking, place a small saucepan over medium heat and spray with cooking spray. Place in the tomatoes sliced-side down and cook for about 3-4 minutes, flipping over once. When done, set aside.
4. Place a large skillet over medium heat and add in the olive oil. Once oil heats, add in the garlic, cook for 1 minute and then add in the red pepper flakes and green chard. Cook the chard for about 1 minute and then add in zucchini pasta and vegetable broth. Cook for about 2-3 minutes, stirring frequently until chard wilts and zucchini pasta softens and heats through.
5. Place the pasta and chard in a bowl and top with tomatoes and salmon.

Shaved Asparagus and Sausage Sweet Potato Noodle Pasta

*Prep Time: 15 minutes | **Cook Time**: 15 minutes | **Total Time**: 30 minutes | **Servings**:*
2

Ingredients

- 1.5-2 tablespoons of olive oil
- 2 sweet Italian sausage links, decased, crumbled
- 1 large (350g+) sweet potato, peeled, Blade C
- salt and pepper, to taste
- 1 large garlic clove, minced
- 1/4 tsp red pepper flakes
- 1/2 cup low-sodium beef broth
- 2 tbsp freshly chopped parsley
- 6 asparagus stalks
- optional: grated parmigiano reggiano cheese, to garnish

Directions

1. Place a large skillet over medium heat and add in the olive oil. Then, add in the sausage. Cook the sausage until browned, 5-7 minutes. Continue to crumble the sausage as it cooks. While the sausage is cooking, snap the bottoms off the asparagus and then shave with a vegetable peeler, starting from the bottom of the asparagus tips all the way down to the end of the stalk. When done shaving, chop off the tips and set aside. Set aside all shavings and tips.
2. When the sausage is done, add in the sweet potato noodles, garlic, red pepper flakes and season with salt and pepper. Toss to combine and then add in the broth and parsley. Let cook, stirring occasionally, for 6-8 minutes or until sweet potato noodles are cooked through and soften. After 5 minutes into the noodles cooking, add in the shaved asparagus and asparagus tips. Toss to combine and let the noodles finish cooking.
3. When pasta is done, plate into bowls and garnish with optional grated cheese. Enjoy!

Short Rib Ragu with Sweet Potato Noodles

*Prep time: 15 mins | **Cook time:** 3 hours 15 mins | **Total time:** 3 hours 30 mins | Serves: 6*

Ingredients

- 2.5 pounds bone-in beef short ribs
- 2 tablespoons extra virgin olive oil
- 1 medium yellow onion, diced
- 2 carrots, peeled and diced
- 2 garlic cloves, minced
- 1 tablespoon tomato paste
- ½ teaspoon salt
- pepper
- ½ teaspoon dried rosemary
- 1 teaspoon dried thyme
- ½ teaspoon dried oregano
- 2 bay leaves
- ½ cup dry red wine
- 28oz can diced tomatoes, no salt added
- 4 cups beef broth, low sodium + more as needed
- 3 sweet potatoes
- freshly chopped parsley, for garnish
- grated parmesan cheese, to garnish (optional)

Directions

1. Prepare the meat by trimming the short ribs of any excess fat and then patting dry with paper towels.
2. In a large Dutch over medium-high heat, heat the olive oil. Add the short ribs to the pot and brown on all sides, 10-15 minutes. When browned, transfer the beef and any pan juices to a large platter or pan.
3. Add the onion, carrot, and garlic. Cook until the vegetables are softened, about 10 minutes. Add the tomato paste and stir to coat the vegetables well. Add the short ribs back in and season with salt and season with pepper then add parsley, rosemary, thyme, oregano, bay leaves, wine, diced tomatoes and broth or enough to just cover the meat. Stir the liquid and then cover the pot partially with a lid, reduce the heat to low and let cook for 1.5 hours, uncover, and then cook another 1.5 hours, with the lid off, until fall-off-the-bone tender.
4. Once the short ribs are done cooking, transfer the meat to a cutting board. Using two forks, shred the meat into bite-size pieces. Return the meat to the pot, discarding the bones. Turn the heat down to the lowest setting, cover and keep warm while you cook the sweet potato noodles.

5. Peel and spiralize the sweet potatoes with Blade C. Heat the oil in a large skillet over medium heat. Once oil is shimmering, add the sweet potato noodles, season with salt and pepper, and cook for 7-10 minutes or until cooked through and just al dente.

6. Divide the sweet potato noodles into plates. Uncover the pot with the short rib sauce and using a large spoon, skim the fat off the surface, if necessary. Taste and adjust with more salt and pepper, if needed.

7. Spoon the sauce over the plates of sweet potato noodles and garnish with parsley. Top with cheese, if desired.

Nutrition Information

- Serving size: 6
- Calories: 420
- Fat: 29g
- Saturated fat: 9g
- Trans fat: 0g
- Carbohydrates: 32g
- Sugar: 12g
- Sodium: 1237mg
- Fiber: 6g
- Protein: 17g
- Cholesterol: 47mg

Shrimp Florentine with Zoodles

"Quick, easy and healthy shrimp dinner made with zoodles instead of pasta."

Servings: *4* | **Prep:** *10 m* | **Cook:** *15 m* | **Ready In:** *25 m*

Ingredients

- 1 tablespoon butter
- 1 tablespoon extra-virgin olive oil
- 2 zucchini, cut into noodle-shape strands
- 1/2 large yellow onion, minced
- 1 tablespoon chopped garlic
- 1/2 teaspoon kosher salt
- 2 tablespoons butter
- 1 pound large shrimp, peeled and deveined
- 1 teaspoon minced garlic
- 1 (6 ounce) bag baby spinach

- 1 tablespoon fresh lemon juice
- 1 teaspoon red pepper flakes
- 1/2 teaspoon kosher salt
- 1/2 teaspoon freshly ground black pepper

Directions

1. Heat 1 tablespoon butter and olive oil together in a large skillet over medium heat; cook and stir zucchini noodles (zoodles), onion, chopped garlic, and 1/2 teaspoon salt until zoodles are tender and onion is translucent, about 5 minutes. Transfer zoodle mixture to a bowl.
2. Heat 2 tablespoons butter in the same skillet; cook and stir shrimp and minced garlic until shrimp are just pink, 3 to 4 minutes. Add spinach, lemon juice, red pepper flakes, 1/2 teaspoon salt, and pepper; cook and stir until spinach begins to wilt, 3 to 4 minutes. Add zoodle mixture; cook and stir until heated through, 2 to 3 minutes.

Nutritional Information

- Calories:229 kcal 11%
- Fat: 13.4 g 21%
- Carbs: 7.1g 2%
- Protein: 21 g 42%
- Cholesterol: 195 mg 65%
- Sodium: 781 mg 31%

Shrimp Scampi Zucchini

"A healthy flair to a traditional scampi using 'zoodles.'"

Servings: 4 | **Prep:** 10 m | **Cook:** 20 m | **Ready In:** 30 m

Ingredients

- 3/4 cup butter, divided olive oil
- 1/4 cup diced onion
- 2 tablespoons crushed garlic
- 2 pounds uncooked medium shrimp, peeled and deveined
- 2 cups white wine
- 1 (15 ounce) can diced tomatoes

- 3 tablespoons seafood seasoning (such as Old Bay®)
- 1/2 lemon, juiced
- 4 zucchini, cut into spirals using a spiral slicer salt and ground black pepper to taste
- 1/4 cup grated Parmesan cheese

Directions

1. Melt 1/4 cup butter with olive oil in a large pot over medium-high heat. Saute onion and garlic in hot butter mixture until softened, about 5 minutes.
2. Stir shrimp, wine, diced tomatoes, and seafood seasoning with the onion mixture; cook until shrimp turns pink, about 5 minutes.
3. Stir 1/2 cup butter and lemon juice with the shrimp mixture; cook until the butter melts completely, 1 to 2 minutes. Season the mixture with salt and pepper. Add the zucchini and cook until tender, about 5 minutes more. Top with Parmesan cheese.

Nutritional Information

- Calories:696 kcal 35%
- Fat: 41.8 g 64%
- Carbs: 14.7g 5%
- Protein: 42.5 g 85%
- Cholesterol: 442 mg 147%
- Sodium: 2169 mg 87%

Shrimp Zucchini Pasta Puttanesca

Prep Time: 20 minutes | **Cook Time:** 25 minutes | **Total Time**: 45 minutes | **Servings**: 2

Ingredients

- 1 tablespoon extra virgin olive oil
- 1 large garlic clove, minced
- 3 anchovy filets
- 1/4 teaspoon red pepper flakes
- 1 14.5oz can, whole tomatoes
- 1.5 tablespoons capers

- 3 tablespoons halved kalamata (or green) olives
- 1/2 teaspoon dried oregano
- 1.5 tablespoons freshly chopped parsley + more to garnish
- salt and pepper, to taste
- 2 medium zucchinis, Blade C, noodles trimmed
- 10-12 medium shrimp, deveined, shells removed

Directions

1. Place a large saucepan over medium-low heat and add in the olive oil. Once the oil heats, add in the garlic, red pepper flakes and anchovy filets. Cook for 1 minute, allowing the anchovies to mainly dissolve, and then add in the tomatoes, crushing with your hands as you add them into the saucepan. Make sure to pour all of the juices from the can into the saucepan.
2. Stir the tomatoes and add in the capers, olives, parsley, oregano and season with salt and pepper. Add in the shrimp, cover and cook about 5 minutes or until shrimp are cooked through. Uncover, remove the shrimp with a slotted spoon or pasta tongs and set aside on a plate.
3. Let the mixture reduce fully, about 10 minutes. Once reduced, add in the shrimp and zucchini noodles and cook for 3 minutes, tossing frequently, or until zucchini cooks to al dente.
4. Portion the pasta into bowls and garnish each with additional parsley. Enjoy!

Shrimp, Bacon and Okra 'Creole-Cajun' Zucchini Pasta

Prep Time: 10 minutes | **Cook Time:** 25 minutes | **Total Time:** 35 minutes | **Servings:** 2

Ingredients

- 2 large zucchinis, Blade C
- 1 large tomato, diced
- 3/4 cup chopped red onion
- olive oil, for dabbling
- 1 tsp chili powder
- cooking spray
- 5 pieces of okra, sliced in 1/4 inch pieces
- 8 shrimp
- 4-5 bacon slices

- 3 tsp cajun seasoning
- 1/2 tsp smoked paprika
- 1/4 tsp red pepper flakes (or less, if you don't like spice)
- salt and pepper, to taste
- 1 large garlic clove, minced

Directions

1. Preheat the oven to 400 degrees.
2. Place the ear of corn in a baking tray. Lightly coat with olive oil and season with the chili powder and salt and pepper. Roast for 15 minutes and then set aside.
3. Place the diced tomatoes in a baking tray coated with cooking spray. Season the tomatoes with salt and pepper and roast for 10 minutes, alongside the corn. When done, set aside.
4. While the tomatoes and corn are roasting, place the bacon in a skillet (or skillets) and cook until your crispy preference, about 3 minutes per side.
5. Once the bacon is done, transfer (using tongs or a slotted spoon) to a plate topped with a paper towel.
6. In the same skillet with the bacon fat juices, add in the garlic and cook for 1 minute. Then, add in the red pepper flakes, cook for 30 seconds and then add in the onions and okra.
7. Cook the vegetables for about 3-4 minutes or until okra is softened.
8. Add in the tomatoes, cajun seasoning, smoked paprika and season generously with salt and pepper. Cook for about 2-3 minutes and then add in the shrimp.
9. Cook until the shrimps are just about cooked and then add in the zucchini noodles. Cook the noodles, stirring frequently, for 2-3 minutes.
10. While the noodles are cooking, break up the bacon into pieces. Once the noodles are done, add in the bacon pieces.
11. Plate the pasta into bowls and top with corn by shaving off the kernels with a knife. Enjoy!

Shrimp, Chorizo and Corn Saffron Zucchini Pasta

Prep Time: 3 minutes | Cook Time: 8 minutes | Total Time: 11 minutes | Servings: 2

Ingredients

- 3 zucchinis, peeled, Blade C
- 1 large clove garlic, minced

- 1 chorizo sausage, sliced into 1/2 inch pieces
- 1 pinch crushed red pepper flakes
- salt and pepper, to taste
- 6 shrimp, peeled and deveined
- 1/3 cup vegetable broth
- 4 saffron threads (or a small pinch)
- 1 tbsp chopped parsley to garnish
- 1 tsp chili powder
- 1 ear of corn

Directions

1. Place the corn in a medium saucepan, cover with water and boil. Let boil for about 2 minutes or until the corn is easily pierced with a fork. When done, pour into a colander and then scrape off the kernels with a knife over a bowl. In this bowl, place in the chili powder. Mix to combine and set aside.
2. Place a large skillet over medium heat. Once the pan heats, add in the chorizo slices. Let cook for about 2 minutes.
3. Flip over and add in the garlic and sautee for another minute, stirring frequently, careful not to burn the garlic.
4. Add the shrimp to the pan (season first with salt and pepper). Cook for 1 minute and cook on the other side for another minute.
5. Add in the vegetable broth, saffron, seasoned corn and zucchini pasta. Stir to combine and cook for about 3 minutes or until zucchini softens and heats through.
6. Plate onto dishes and top with parsley!

Sicilian Style Zucchini Spaghetti

Prep time: 15 mins | *Cook time:* 15 mins | *Total time:* 30 mins | *Serves:* 2

Ingredients

- ½ head cauliflower, cored and broken into small florets
- 3 tablespoons extra virgin olive oil
- 1 anchovy fillet, mashed to a paste
- salt and pepper, to taste
- 2 tablespoons golden raisins
- 2 tablespoons pine nuts, toasted
- 1 garlic clove, minced

- 1 pinch red pepper flakes
- 2 medium zucchinis, peeled, Blade D, noodles trimmed
- 3 tablespoons grated parmigiano-reggiano cheese
- 2 tablespoons freshly chopped parsley
- ¼ lemon, juiced + its zest

For the breadcrumbs:

- ¼ cup almond meal
- ¼ teaspoon dried oregano flakes
- ¼ teaspoon dried basil flakes
- ¼ teaspoon dried parsley flakes
- ¼ teaspoon garlic powder
- salt and pepper, to taste
- 2 teaspoons water

Directions

1. Place the cauliflower, 2 tablespoons of the olive oil, and anchovy fillet in a large skillet over medium heat. Cook until the anchovy fillets begin to sizzle; add ¼ cup of water and season with salt.
2. Bring to a simmer, cover, and cook until the cauliflower is just tender, about 5 minutes. Uncover, and cook until the water has evaporated and the cauliflower is golden brown, 5 to 7 minutes. Stir in the raisins and pine nuts, and cook until just heated through. Transfer the mixture to a large mixing bowl and place the skillet back on the stovetop, heat off.
3. While the cauliflower cooks, place the almond meal and seasonings into a small bowl and mix together. Then, add in the water and mix until dough-like. Place a medium skillet over medium-high heat and once heated, crumble in the almond meal dough. Cook until breadcrumb-like and toasted. Set the bread crumbs aside in a small bowl.
4. Turn the heat on underneath the skillet used to cook the cauliflower and add in the remaining olive oil (1 tablespoon.) Once oil heats, add in the garlic and red pepper flakes. Let cook for 30 seconds and then add in the zucchini noodles, tossing occasionally and cook for 3 minutes or until al dente/cooked to your preference. Then, add the noodles to the large mixing bowl with the cauliflower. Stir in the parmesan cheese, parsley, and lemon juice/zest.
5. Sprinkle with almond breadcrumbs and serve immediately.

Sofrito Zucchini Pasta with Beans and Lightly Fried Plantains

Prep Time: 20 minutes | **Cook Time:** 25 minutes | **Total Time:** 45 minutes | **Servings:**

1

Ingredients

- 1 green plantain
- 2 half-tablespoons of olive oil
- salt and pepper
- 2 tsp minced garlic
- 1/4 cup chopped yellow onion
- 3 tbsp chopped red bell pepper
- 3 tbsp chopped green bell pepper
- 2 round red tomatoes, chopped (or 1/2 a 14-oz can of diced tomatoes)
- 1 tsp smoked paprika
- 3 tbsp chopped manzanillo olives or green olives
- 1 heaping tbsp chopped cilantro
- 1.5 medium zucchinis, Blade C
- 1/3 cup pink beans or beans of choice

Directions

1. Chop the ends off your plantain. Slice the skin lengthwise and peel the skin off the plantain. Slice the plantain lengthwise and chop it in four quarters. Set aside.
2. Place a large skillet over medium heat and add in the half tablespoon of olive oil.
3. Once the oil heats, add in the plantain pieces and season with salt and pepper.
4. Let cook for 2 minutes and then flip over, cooking for about another 2 minutes or until plantains are browned on both sides. Set aside on a paper-towel lined plate.
5. Place a large skillet over medium-low heat and add in the other half tablespoon of olive oil.
6. Once the oil heats, add in the garlic, cook for 30 seconds and then add in the chopped onion and chopped peppers. Cook for 2 minutes or until the vegetables soften.
7. Add in the tomatoes, smoked paprika and stir. Cook until the sauce reduces, about 10 minutes. Once the sauce is almost done reducing, add in the cilantro and olives and stir to combine.
8. Add in the zucchini noodles, beans and cook for about 2 minutes or until zucchini softens, tossing frequently.
9. Place the noodles in a bowl and topped with plantains.

Spaghetti alla Puttanesca, Inspired by Jim Carrey

Prep Time: *2 minutes* | **Cook Time:** *15 minutes* | **Total Time:** *17 minutes* | **Servings:**
2

Ingredients

- 1 zucchini, Blade C
- 1 tbsp olive oil
- 1 clove of garlic
- 1 tbsp capers
- salt and pepper, to taste
- 2-3 tbsp chopped parsley
- 1 tsp crushed red pepper
- 1-2 anchovy filets
- 1 (14oz) can of whole peeled tomatoes
- 1/4 cup sliced Kalamata olives*

Directions

1. Place a large skillet over medium heat and add in olive oil. Once oil is heated, add in garlic and anchovy filet(s). Cook until anchovies mainly dissolve into oil.
2. Over the skillet, crush the whole tomatoes with your hands. Pour in about half of the sauce from the can. Use a wooden spoon to further "crush" the tomatoes. Add in about 1 tsp of the oil from the anchovy tin and the rest of the ingredients (parsley, capers, olives and salt and pepper). Simmer for about 10-15 minutes or until liquid from the sauce is evaporated.
3. Once the sauce is evaporated, add in the zucchini noodles and cook for about 2-3 minutes or until zucchini begins to soften. Enjoy!

Spicy Garlic Lump Crab Butternut Squash Pasta with Feta & Parsley

Prep Time: *15 minutes* | **Cook Time:** *10 minutes* | **Total Time:** *25 minutes* | **Servings:**
2

Ingredients

- olive oil, to drizzle
- 1 butternut squash, peeled, Blade C
- salt and pepper, to taste
- 1/4 cup olive oil
- 1 garlic clove, minced
- 1/4 tsp red pepper flakes
- 3/4 cup lump crab meat
- 1/4 cup crumbled feta
- 1 tbsp freshly chopped parsley

Directions

1. Preheat the oven to 400 degrees.
2. In a baking tray, spread out the butternut squash noodles. Drizzle lightly with olive oil and season with salt and pepper.
3. Once the oven preheats, add in the butternut squash noodles. Cook for 7-10 minutes or until softened.
4. Next, in a large skillet, add in the olive oil. Once the oil heats, add in the garlic and cook for 30 seconds. Then, add in the red pepper flakes and crab meat.
5. Cook, stirring frequently, for about 3 minutes or until the crab meat is heated.
6. Place the butternut squash noodles in a bowl and pour in crab meat mixture.
7. Top with parsley and feta. Enjoy!

Spicy Green Harissa Chicken and Golden Beet Noodles

Prep Time: 15 minutes | **Cook Time**: 15 minutes | **Total Time**: 30 minutes | **Servings**: 2

Ingredients

- 1 boneless skinless chicken breast, cubed
- 3 tablespoons Mina Harissa Spicy Green Pepper Sauce
- 1 large garlic clove, minced
- 1 large shallot, peeled, minced
- 1/4 cup chicken broth

- 2 large golden beets with green tops attached, peeled, Blade C, noodles trimmed and 2 cups of chopped greens reserved
- salt and pepper, to taste
- 2 teaspoons minced parsley to garnish

Directions

1. Place the chicken in a bowl with the harissa sauce. Set aside.
2. Place a large skillet over medium heat and add in the olive oil. Once the oil heats, add in the garlic and shallots. Let cook for 30 seconds or until garlic is fragrant. Then, add in the chicken with sauce and the chicken broth. Let cook for about 3 minutes or until the sauce thickens.
3. Add in the beets, beet greens and season generously with salt and pepper. Toss to combine and cover, letting cook for about 5 minutes, or until beet noodles are al dente. Uncover to toss occasionally.
4. Once done, plate into bowls and top with parsley.

Spicy Moroccan Chickpeas with Beet Noodles

Prep Time: 15 minutes | Cook Time: 25 minutes | Total Time: 40 minutes | Servings: 4

Ingredients

- 3-4 large beets, peeled, Blade C, noodles trimmed
- 2 tablespoons extra virgin olive oil
- 2 teaspoons minced garlic
- ½ red onion, finely chopped
- 7 dried apricots, small cubed
- 1 teaspoon garam masala
- 1 teaspoon cumin
- salt and pepper, to taste
- ¼ teaspoon crushed red pepper
- 1 tablespoon lemon juice
- 1 14oz can chickpeas, rinsed, drained, patted dry
- 1 14oz diced tomatoes, no salt added
- 1 tablespoon chopped fresh mint

Directions

1. Preheat the oven to 400 degrees.
2. Lay out the beet noodles evenly in a baking tray and drizzle with 1 tablespoon of the olive oil. Season with salt and pepper and bake for 10-15 minutes or until wilted.
3. Heat a large skillet over medium-high heat. Add in the rest of the olive oil and once it heats, add in garlic. Cook the garlic for 30 seconds or until fragrant.
4. Add the onions, lemon juice, apricots, garam masala, red pepper flakes and season with salt and pepper. Cook for 5 minutes or until onion begins to slightly brown.
5. Add in the chickpeas and tomatoes and bring to a boil. Reduce the heat and simmer for 5-7 minutes, stirring occasionally, to reduce.
6. Once reduced, stir in the mint.
7. Divide the beet noodles onto 4 plates and top each with hearty scoops of the chickpea mixture.

Spicy Parmesan-Garlic Zucchini Pasta with Sausage and Kalettes

Prep time: 20 mins | *Cook time:* 15 mins | *Total time:* 35 mins | *Serves:* 2

Ingredients

- 2 spicy Italian sausage links, decased and sliced into ½" thick chunks
- 2 garlic cloves, minced
- ⅓ cup diced sweet onion (or red onion)
- ¼ teaspoon red pepper flakes (or less/omit if you don't like spicy)
- 1 tablespoon extra virgin olive oil
- 2.5 cups halved kalettes
- 2 medium zucchinis, Blade C
- ⅓ cup grated parmesan cheese + more for garnish (if desired)

Directions

1. Heat a large skillet over medium-high heat. Add in the sausage, cooking for 10-12 minutes or until it browns and cooks completely. Remove the sausage with a slotted spoon and set aside on a plate.
2. Immediately add in the garlic, onions, red pepper flakes, olive oil and kalettes. Let cook for 2-3 minutes or until kalettes begin to cook. Then, add in the zucchini pasta and toss for 2-3 more minutes or until noodles are al dente.

3. Add in the parmesan cheese and sausage and toss until combined and cheese is melted.
4. Divide into bowls and serve, garnished with additional parmesan, if desired.

Spicy Sausage and Basil Potato and Zucchini Pasta

Prep time: 15 mins | *Cook time:* 20 mins | *Total time:* 35 mins | *Serves:* 3

Ingredients

- 1.5 tablespoons extra virgin olive oil
- 1 medium Yukon gold potato, peeled, Blade D, noodles trimmed
- Salt and pepper, to taste
- ¼ teaspoon garlic powder
- 2 link spicy sausages, caseings removed and cut into ½ inch chunks
- 1.5 cups seeded and chopped tomato
- 1 large zucchini, Blade D, noodles trimmed
- ⅓ cup chopped basil + more for garnish
- 1 large garlic clove, finely minced
- ¼ teaspoon red pepper flakes
- 3 tablespoons grated parmesan cheese

Directions

1. Place a large skillet over medium-high heat and add in 1 tablespoon of the olive oil. Once oil heats, add in the potato noodles and season with salt, pepper and garlic powder. Cook for 7 minutes or until potatoes are cooked to al dente. Transfer the potatoes to a plate and immediately add in the sausage. Cook the sausage for 7-10 minutes or until sausage is cooked through and browned. Add in tomatoes, season with salt and pepper and cook for another minute. Transfer the tomato and sausage mixture to the plate with the potato noodles.
2. Immediately add the zucchini noodles, basil, garlic, red pepper flakes and remaining olive oil and cook for 2-3 minutes or until zucchini softens. When cooked, add in the potato noodles, sausage and tomatoes and toss for 1 minute.
3. Remove from heat and toss thoroughly to combine. Plate the pasta onto dishes and serve garnished with any leftover chopped basil and the cheese.

Spinach Zucchini Noodle Lasagna

Prep Time: 15 minutes | **Cook Time:** 1 hour | **Servings:** 6

Ingredients

- 1 tbsp olive oil
- 2 garlic cloves, minced
- ¼ tsp red pepper flakes
- ¾ cup diced red onion
- 2 (14oz) canned diced tomatoes, no salt added
- 1 tsp dried oregano flakes
- 8 basil leaves, chopped
- salt and pepper, to taste
- 3-4 cups of spinach
- 3 medium zucchinis, Blade A
- 1 large egg, beaten
- 1/3 cup grated parmesan cheese (grated not shredded!)
- 1.5 cups ricotta cheese
- 1 cup shredded mozzarella cheese

Directions

1. Preheat the oven to 400 degrees.
2. In a large skillet over medium heat, place in the olive oil. Then, add in the garlic and red pepper flakes. Let garlic cook for 30 seconds and then add in the red onions. Let onions cook for 2 minutes and then add in the canned tomatoes, oregano, basil and season with salt and pepper. Stir to combine and then let cook, stirring occasionally, until the sauce is fully reduced, about 15 minutes. The sauce should have no excess liquid, almost to the point where it sticks to the bottom of the pan. This is important to avoid a watery lasagna at the end.
3. While the sauce reduces, place a large skillet over medium heat and add in the spinach. Cook until completely wilted and set aside in a plate. Then, cook the zucchini noodles for 2 minutes, tossing frequently. Place the cooked noodles in a colander and pat dry to remove as much moisture as possible. Set aside once done.
4. While the sauce is still cooking, add the ricotta, parmesan and egg to a bowl. Whisk together and set aside.
5. Once the sauce is done, gather all of your prepared ingredients. Take out a casserole dish (I use 4.2 quart) and add a layer of the tomato sauce to the

bottom. Then, add a layer of zucchini noodles. Then, add a layer of the ricotta mixture. Then, add in a layer of

6. tomato sauce. Then, add in a layer of spinach, using all of the spinach. Then, add a layer of the ricotta mixture. Then, add in a layer of zucchini noodles. Then, add in the last of the tomato sauce, in a layer. Then, top with all of the mozzarella cheese.

7. Cover the casserole dish with tinfoil and bake in the oven for 40 minutes. After 40 minutes, take the dish out of the oven, remove the tinfoil top and let rest for 5-10 minutes. After resting, carefully and slowly pour out as much excess liquid as possible. Then, carefully cut the lasagna into 6 equal portions. Remove these portions and plate immediately or save in individual containers in the refrigerator (or freezer). This is very important to avoid excess moisture. Enjoy immediately!

Spinach, Mushroom and Turkey Bacon Pasta (Zucchini Pasta)

Prep Time: 13 minutes | Cook Time: 13 minutes | Servings: 1

Ingredients

- 2 zucchinis, Blade A
- 4 pieces of turkey bacon
- 4 cups of spinach leaves
- 1 cup of sliced baby portabello mushrooms
- 1 tbsp olive oil
- 1/2 cup chicken broth
- salt and pepper, to taste
- 1 shallot, minced
- 1 large clove of garlic, minced
- olive oil cooking spray
- grated Parmesan cheese, for garnish

Directions

1. Place a large skillet over medium heat and coat with cooking spray. Once heated, add in strips of bacon. You may have to do this in batches if your bacon doesn't fit. Let cook on each side for about 3 minutes or until bacon is cooked, but not leathery. Set aside.

2. Add olive oil to the same skillet and then garlic. Cook for 30 seconds and then add in the shallots. Cook shallots for 1 minute and then add in the

mushrooms. Cook the mushrooms, stirring frequently, for about 2 minutes and then add in 1/4 cup of the chicken broth.
3. Cook mushrooms for another minute and then add in the zucchini pasta, spinach and remaining chicken broth. Toss to combine thoroughly and season with salt and pepper. Cook for about 2 minutes or until spinach is completely wilted and zucchini pasta has softened. Add in turkey bacon and cook for about 30 seconds to warm.
4. Divide onto plates and enjoy, garnished with a little Parmesan cheese!

Spiralized Butternut Squash with Curried Lentils and Pumpkin Seeds

Prep time: 20 mins | *Cook time:* 30 mins | *Total time:* 50 mins | *Serves:* 3

Ingredients

- 1 medium-large butternut squash, peeled, Blade C, noodles trimmed
- ½ cup dry green lentils, rinsed
- 1 tablespoon pumpkin seeds
- 1 tablespoon extra virgin olive oil
- ¼ cup diced onion
- 1 garlic clove, minced
- ½ teaspoon minced ginger
- 1 small teaspoon red curry paste
- 8oz tomato sauce
- ½ teaspoon garam masala
- ½ teaspoon curry powder
- 1 pinch turmeric
- 1 pinch cayenne pepper

Directions

1. Preheat the oven to 400 degrees. Line a baking sheet with parchment paper. Lay out the butternut squash noodles on the sheet and set aside.
2. Place the lentils in a medium pot and add in 1.5 cups of water. Bring to a boil and once boiling, reduce to a simmer and let cook for 15 minutes or until lentils are cooked but not mushy, adding water as needed to keep the lentils moist.
3. While lentils cook, place a small skillet over medium-high heat and once heated, add in the pumpkin seeds. Let seeds cook until golden brown and toasted. Set aside in a small bowl.

4. When lentils are just about done, transfer the butternut squash noodles to the oven and bake for 15 minutes or until cooked to your preference.
5. Meanwhile, place a large skillet over medium heat with the oil and once oil heats, add in the onion, garlic and ginger and let cook until translucent, about 3 minutes. Add in the curry paste and swirl until onions are covered in the paste. Add the tomato sauce, garam masala, curry powder, turmeric, cayenne, and stir until combined. Add in the lentils and let cook for 5 more minutes to strengthen the flavors.
6. Remove the butternut squash noodles from the oven, divide into bowls and divide the lentil mixture over the bowls and garnish with pumpkin seeds.

Spiralized Carrot Spaghetti with Shrimp and Shaved Asparagus

Prep time: 15 mins | Cook time: 10 mins | Total time: 25 mins | Serves: 2

Ingredients

- 1 large carrot (or 2 medium), peeled, Blade D, noodles trimmed
- 1.25 cups Victoria Organic Toasted Garlic pasta sauce
- 8 asparagus spears, shaved, tips reserved
- 8 ounces shrimp, peeled and deveined
- salt and pepper

Directions

1. Bring a medium pot filled halfway with water to a boil. Once boiling, add in the carrot noodles and cook for 2-3 minutes or until al dente or cooked to your preference. Drain into a colander and set aside.
2. Meanwhile, place a medium skillet over medium heat and add in the tomato sauce. Season the shrimp with salt and pepper and set aside. Stir the asparagus tips into the sauce and bring to a simmer and then add in the shrimp, cover, and let cook until shrimp turn C-shaped and opaque, about 2-3 minutes per side. Add the asparagus shavings, carrot noodles and toss just to coat the carrots and asparagus shavings in the sauce, about 1 minute.
3. Divide the pasta into bowls and serve, garnishing with extra pepper.

Spiralized Kohlrabi with Vegan Alfredo and Cajun Shrimp

*Prep time: 20 mins | **Cook time:** 10 mins | **Total time:** 30 mins | **Serves**: 3*

Ingredients

For the sauce:

- ½ cup raw cashews, soaked for at least 2 hours and then drained
- ½ teaspoon garlic powder
- 1 tablespoon nutritional yeast
- 1 teaspoon lemon juice
- ¼ cup vegetable broth + 2 tablespoons + more for thinning if needed
- salt and pepper, to taste
- For the pasta:
- 2 large kohlrabi, peeled, Blade C, noodles trimmed
- salt and pepper
- ½ pound shrimp, cleaned, deveined, deshelled
- 1 tablespoon extra virgin olive oil
- 2 teaspoons Cajun seasoning (or mix together ½ teaspoon garlic powder, ½ teaspoon paprika, ¼ teaspoon onion powder, ¼ teaspoon cayenne pepper, ½ teaspoon dried oregano)
- chopped parsley, to garnish

Directions

1. Make the sauce: add all the ingredients for the sauce into a blender and blend until creamy. Pour into a small saucepan and place over medium-high heat, bringing to a simmer. Once simmering, reduce heat to low and keep warm.
2. Heat the oil in a large skillet over medium-high heat. Once oil is shimmering, add the kohlrabi noodles, season with salt and pepper, and cook until al dente, about 5 minutes.
3. While kohlrabi cooks, add the shrimp to a medium mixing bowl along with the olive oil, Cajun seasoning, salt and pepper. Toss to combine. Set aside.
4. Once kohlrabi is done cooking, transfer with tongs to a medium mixing bowl, tent with foil to keep warm, and place the skillet back over medium-high heat. Add the seasoned shrimp and cook about 2 minutes per side or until c-shaped and opaque.
5. Meanwhile, pour the heated sauce over the bowl of kohlrabi noodles and toss well to combine. Divide onto two plates and top each plate with the cooked shrimp. Garnish with parsley and serve immediately.

Spiralized Parsnip Noodles with Roasted Butternut Squash, Kale and Feta

Prep time: 15 mins | Cook time: 40 mins | Total time: 55 mins | Serves: 2

Ingredients

- 1 cup cubed butternut squash
- 1 tablespoon + 2 teaspoons of extra virgin olive oil, divided
- salt and pepper, to taste
- ½ teaspoon paprika
- 2 parsnips, peeled, Blade D, noodles trimmed
- 2 cups chopped kale
- 1 garlic clove, sliced thinly
- ¼ cup crumbled feta
- ½ teaspoon red pepper flakes, to garnish

Directions

1. Preheat the oven to 400 degrees, line a baking sheet with parchment paper and lay out the butternut squash. Drizzle with 2 teaspoons of the oil and season with salt, pepper and paprika. Toss to combine and once oven is preheated, roast for 30-35 minutes or until fork tender.
2. Ten minutes before the squash is done, place a large skillet over medium-high heat and add in the rest of the olive oil. Add in the parsnip noodles and let cook for 5-7 minutes or until cooked through. Transfer the parsnip noodles to a plate and add in the kale and garlic. Let cook until wilted, about 5 minutes and then add back in the parsnip noodles. Toss to combine and then divide onto two plates and top with butternut squash, feta and the red pepper flakes.

Spiralized Parsnips with Pesto, Roasted Red peppers and Chickpeas

Prep time: 15 mins | Cook time: 15 mins | Total time: 30 mins | Serves: 4

Ingredients

For the pasta:

- 4 parsnips, peeled, Blade D, noodles trimmed
- salt and pepper, to taste
- 1 cup jarred roasted red peppers, drained and sliced into ¼" thick slivers and then halved
- 1 cup chickpeas, rinsed and drained
- For the pesto:
- 3 cup basil leaves, packed
- 2 tablespoons pine nuts
- ¼ cup extra virgin olive oil
- salt and pepper
- 1 large clove of garlic, chopped

Directions

1. Place a large skillet over medium-high heat and once it heats, add in the parsnip noodles and season with salt and pepper. Toss and then cover, letting cook for 5-7 minutes or until parsnip noodles are cooked through. Uncover, stir in the red peppers and chickpeas and let cook another 2 minutes or until heated through.
2. Meanwhile, place all of the ingredients for the pesto into a food processor and pulse until creamy. Taste and adjust to your preferences, if necessary.
3. Transfer the mixture to a large bowl and add in the pesto. Toss to combine thoroughly and divide onto two plates.

Spiralized Potato Noodle Cups with Meatballs and Tomato Sauce

Prep time: 15 mins | Cook time: 30 mins | Total time: 45 mins | Serves: 6

Ingredients

- 1 tablespoon extra virgin olive oil
- 2 large russet potatoes, peeled, Blade D, noodles trimmed
- salt and pepper, to taste
- ½ teaspoon garlic powder
- 2 large eggs, beaten
- ¾ cup jarred tomato sauce (I used Victoria Fine Foods Tomato Herb sauce)
- 6 pre-cooked meatballs, defrosted (homemade or otherwise)

Directions

1. Preheat the oven to 425 degrees. Grease a large muffin tin with cooking spray.
2. Heat oil in a large skillet over medium-high heat. Once oil is shimmering, add in the potato noodles. Season with salt, pepper and garlic powder and toss. Let cook for 7-10 minutes or until cooked through and lightly browned. Transfer to a medium mixing bowl. Let cool for 2 minutes.
3. Add in the eggs to the bowl and toss thoroughly to combine. Pack the potato noodles into the muffin holes, trying your best to create a cavity in the center. Bake in the oven for 15 minutes or until potato mixture has set.
4. While potato cups bake, pour the tomato sauce into a small skillet and bring to a strong simmer. Add in the meatballs and let heat while potato cups cook.
5. When potato cups are done, remove and align on a platter.
6. If serving immediately, place one meatball on top of each potato cup and top with extra sauce, if desired.
7. If not serving immediately, transfer the cooked meatballs to a serving bowl along with pasta tongs. Let guests make their own meatball cups and serve themselves!

Spiralized Red Bell Peppers with Sundried Tomato Cream Sauce and Andouille Sausage

Prep time: *20 mins* | **Cook time:** *25 mins* | **Total time:** *45 mins* | **Serves:** *4*

Ingredients

- 2 andouille sausage links, sliced into ¼" rounds
- 1 teaspoon olive oil
- 2 garlic cloves, minced
- 2 teaspoons minced shallots
- ½ cup chopped and drained oil-packed sun-dried tomatoes
- ½ cup coconut cream (solids) from can of full-fat coconut milk*
- ¼ teaspoon red pepper flakes
- ¼ teaspoon dried basil
- ¼ teaspoon dried oregano
- salt and pepper, to taste
- ½ cup vegetable (or chicken) broth, low sodium
- 4 red bell peppers, Blade A
- 2 tablespoons freshly chopped parsley

- *Scoop out ½ cup of the solids off a 15oz can of full-fat coconut milk. Reserve the rest for future use.

Directions

1. Place a large skillet over medium heat and once heated, add in the sausage. Cook the sausage until browned and cooked, about 7 minutes. Transfer the sausage to a plate and immediately add in the oil, garlic and shallots and cook for 1 minute or until fragrant. Then, add in the tomatoes, coconut cream, red pepper flakes and season with basil, oregano and salt and pepper. Bring to a boil and then reduce to a simmer for 2 minutes. Transfer to a high speed blender or food processor with the broth and pulse until creamy. Set aside.
2. Add the red bell peppers noodles into the skillet and cook for 5-7 minutes or until cooked to your consistency preference.
3. Once bell peppers are cooked, pour in the sauce and sausage to heat up, stirring for about a minute.
4. Divide the pasta into plates and garnish with parsley.

Spiralized Rutabaga Pasta and Salmon with Spicy Marinara

Prep time: 15 mins | Cook time: 15 mins | Total time: 30 mins | Serves: 2

Ingredients

- 1 medium rutabaga, peeled, Blade C, noodles trimmed
- 2 teaspoons extra virgin olive oil
- 1.25 cups jarred marinara sauce (Victoria Fine Foods Premium Marinara)
- ¼ teaspoon red pepper flakes or more
- 1 4oz salmon filet, skinless
- salt and pepper

Directions

1. Preheat the oven to 425 degrees F. Spread out the rutabaga noodles on a non-stick baking sheet and drizzle with the olive oil and season with salt, pepper and garlic powder. Toss together to combine thoroughly and roast the rutabaga for 12-15 minutes or until cooked through, but still al dente.
2. Heat the marinara sauce and red pepper flakes in a medium skillet over medium-high heat. Season the salmon with salt and pepper. Bring the

sauce to a solid simmer and then add in salmon, spooning some of the marinara sauce on top. Cover and cook, uncovering to break up the salmon with a spatula as it cooks, about 10-15 minutes.

3. Once rutabaga and salmon are done, divide the rutabaga into bowls and top with salmon sauce. Garnish with extra red pepper flakes if you really love spice!

Spiralized Sweet Potato Pizza Bake with Turkey Bacon

Prep time: 15 mins | Cook time: 35 mins | Total time: 50 mins | Serves: 4

Ingredients

For the sweet potatoes:

- 1 tablespoon extra virgin olive oil
- 2 medium sweet potatoes, peeled, Blade C
- salt and pepper, to taste
- 1 teaspoon garlic powder
- For the casserole:
- 1.5 cups marinara sauce (I like Rao's)
- ½ teaspoon dried oregano
- 1.25 cups shredded mozzarella cheese
- 12 turkey pepperoni slices
- 2 tablespoons chopped basil, to garnish
- 1 tablespoon grated parmesan cheese, to garnish

Directions

1. Preheat the oven to 425 degrees and grease a 10" cast-iron skillet or square casserole dish.
2. Place a large skillet over medium-high heat and add in the olive oil. Once oil heats, add in the sweet potato noodles and season with salt, pepper and garlic powder. Let cook for about 5 minutes or until noodles begin to soften.
3. Transfer the cooked noodles to the casserole dish and pour over the tomato sauce. Sprinkle the dried oregano over the tomato sauce evenly and then layer over with the mozzarella cheese. Place the pepperoni slices on top in rows.
4. Bake in the oven for 20-25 minutes or until cheese melts through and is slightly golden brown.

5. Remove from the oven, garnish with basil and parmesan cheese.

Spiralized Turnip Mushroom and Tomato Risotto

Prep time: 20 mins | *Cook time:* 20 mins | *Total time:* 40 mins | *Serves:* 4

Ingredients

- 1 tablespoon extra virgin olive oil
- 1 medium white onion, diced
- 2 garlic cloves, minced
- ¼ teaspoon red pepper flakes
- 3 large turnips, peeled and spiralized using Blade C
- 16 ounces baby portobello mushrooms, sliced
- 1 teaspoon dried oregano
- Salt and black pepper to taste
- 1 (28 ounce) can Tuttorosso® Crushed Tomatoes with basil
- ¼ cup Parmesan cheese
- ¼ cup Pecorino Romano cheese
- 1 tablespoon finely chopped flat-leaf parsley, to garnish

Directions

1. Place the turnip noodles into a food processor and pulse until rice-like.
2. Place a large pot over medium heat and add in the olive oil. Once oil heats, add in the onion, mushrooms, garlic and red pepper flakes and cook for 5 minutes or until onions turn translucent and mushrooms begin to wilt.
3. Add in the turnip rice and season with oregano, salt and pepper. Stir to combine and add in the tomatoes.
4. Cook, uncovered, for 10 minutes, stirring frequently, or until turnip rice softens and cooks to your preference. Once cooked, fold in the cheese and stir until fully combined.
5. Transfer to a serving dish, garnish with parsley and serve immediately.

Spiralized Vegetarian Bibimbap with Quinoa

Prep time: 20 mins | *Cook time:* 25 mins | *Total time:* 45 mins | *Serves:* 2

Ingredients

- ⅓ cup dry quinoa
- 1 cup water
- 3 teaspoons sesame oil
- ½ large carrot, peeled, Blade D, noodles trimmed
- salt, to taste
- 1 cup bean sprouts
- 1.5 cups Asian mushrooms (or mushrooms of choice)
- 2 cups spinach
- 1 teaspoon minced garlic
- 1 large zucchini, Blade D, noodles trimmed
- 2 whole eggs
- sriracha, to garnish

Directions

1. Place the quinoa and water in a small saucepan, cover and bring to a boil. Once boiling, reduce to a simmer and let cook for 10-15 minutes or until quinoa is fluffy. When done, fluff up with a fork and transfer to a bowl.
2. While quinoa is cooking, get a large tray or plate ready for assembling the bibimbap and set aside next to the stovetop. Or, just have a few plates ready to hold the various vegetables.
3. Place a large skillet over medium heat and add in 1 teaspoon of sesame oil. Add the carrots and season with salt. Cook for 2 minutes or until softened. Transfer to the tray/plate and set aside.
4. Add the bean sprouts to the skillet, season with salt and cook for 2 minutes or until softened. Transfer to the tray/plate and set aside.
5. Add in another teaspoon of sesame oil and add in the mushrooms and season with salt. Cook for 3-5 minutes or until mushrooms wilt. Transfer to the tray/plate and set aside.
6. Add in the last teaspoon of sesame oil and then add in the spinach, garlic and cook for 3 minutes or until wilted. Transfer to the tray/plate and set aside.
7. Add the zucchini noodles. Cook for 3-5 minutes or until cooked to your preference. Transfer to the tray/plate and set aside.
8. Now, it's time to assemble! Portion out of all the veggies and quinoa into two separate bowls. Traditionally, it is served in a circular manner (like the picture.) Once all the vegetables are portioned into bowls, cook the eggs.
9. Heat the same large skillet over medium-high heat and crack in two eggs. Let cook for 3-5 minutes or until egg whites are set.
10. Top each bowl with the fried egg. Drizzle with sriracha and serve.

Spooky Sweet Potato "Worms" with Oozing Beef "Eyeballs"

*Prep Time: 20 minutes | **Cook Time:** 25 minutes | **Total Time:** 45 minutes | **Servings:** 3*

Ingredients

For the meatballs:

- ½ pound 90% lean ground beef
- 1 tablespoon freshly minced parsley
- 1/2 teaspoon dried oregano flakes
- 1.5 tablespoons grated parmesan cheese
- salt and pepper, to taste
- 1 garlic clove, finely minced

For the eyeballs:

- 3 small mozzarella pearls, sliced in half (about ½ inch in diameter)
- 3 jumbo pitted black olives, sliced width-wise into two hollow circles
- For the pasta and sauce:
- 1 tablespoon extra virgin olive oil
- 2 garlic cloves, minced
- ¼ teaspoon red pepper flakes
- ½ cup diced red onion
- 1 15oz cans crushed tomatoes
- 2 teaspoons tomato paste
- salt and pepper, to taste
- 1 teaspoon dried oregano flakes
- ½ teaspoon dried basil flakes
- 1 large sweet potato, peeled, Blade C, noodles trimmed

Directions

1. Preheat the oven to 375 degrees. Line a baking tray with parchment paper.
2. Place all of your ingredients for the meatballs into a bowl and mix together. Using your hands, mold into slightly larger than golfball sized meatballs, about 6. Arrange on the baking tray. In each meatball, press your fingertip into the center to create a cavity for the "eyeball." Set aside.
3. In a large saucepan over medium heat, add in the olive oil. Once the oil heats, add in the garlic. Let garlic cook for 30 seconds and add in the red pepper flakes and onions. Let cook for 2 minutes or until onions begin to

soften. Add in the tomatoes, tomato paste and season with salt, pepper, basil and oregano.

4. Stir to combine the seasonings, lower heat to a simmer and cook for about 2 minutes to allow flavors to develop. Reserve 3 teaspoons of the sauce in a bowl and then turn off the heat on the stovetop, but leave the skillet there.

5. Place a half-teaspoon of the reserved sauce into the eyeball cavities of the meatballs. Top with a mozzarella piece and top with an olive slice. Cook for 18-20 minutes or until meatballs are cooked through and eyeball cheese is oozing.

6. Five minutes into cooking the meatballs, turn the heat back to a low simmer and then add in the sweet potato noodles, toss and cook for 10 minutes or until sweet potato noodles are cooked through.

7. Divide the noodles onto plates and top with 2 meatballs.

Spring Prosciutto Parsnip Pasta with Snap Peas

Prep time: 15 mins | Cook time: 15 mins | Total time: 30 mins | Serves: 2

Ingredients

- ½ tablespoon extra virgin olive oil
- 1 garlic clove, minced
- 1 pinch red pepper flakes
- ½ cup chicken broth, low sodium
- 3oz sugar snap peas, sliced in half
- 2 large parsnips, peeled, Blade C/D, noodles trimmed
- salt and pepper, to taste
- 4 pieces of prosciutto, thinly sliced
- 2 tablespoons freshly grated parmigiano reggiano cheese (or parmesan)
- parsley to garnish

Directions

1. Place a large skillet over medium heat and add in the oil. Once oil heats, add in the garlic and red pepper flakes. Let cook for 30 seconds or until fragrant and then add in the chicken broth. Let broth come to a boil and then add in the snap peas and cook for 5 minutes or until liquid evaporates by ½.

2. Then, remove the snap peas and add in the parsnip noodles, season with salt and pepper and toss thoroughly. Cover and let cook for 5 minutes or until parsnip noodles are al dente. Uncover, add back in the snap peas, add

in the prosciutto and sprinkle with cheese and toss thoroughly to combine or until cheese is melted.

3. Divide into bowls and garnish with parsley.

Spring Zucchini Pasta with Peas, Leeks & Watercress

Prep Time: 10 minutes | *Cook Time:* 10 minutes | *Total Time:* 20 minutes | *Servings:* 1

Ingredients

- 1/2 tbsp of olive oil
- 1 clove of garlic, minced
- 1 small pinch of red pepper flakes
- 1/4 cup diced white onion
- 1 leek stalk, green tops removed and white bottoms sliced thinly (about 1/3-1/2 cup)
- salt and pepper, to taste
- 1.5 zucchinis, Blade C
- 1/2 cup packed watercress
- 2 tbsp cooked green peas
- 1/2 whole lemon
- 1 tsp grated parmesan cheese, to garnish

Directions

1. Place a large skillet over medium heat and add in the olive oil. Then, add in the garlic and red pepper flakes. Let cook for 30 seconds and then add in the white onion and leeks. Season with salt and pepper and cook for about 3 minutes or until leeks start to brown.
2. Then, add in the zucchini noodles and watercress. Toss frequently for about 3 minutes or until zucchini noodles have softened and warmed. When done, add in the peas and squeeze lemon over the skillet. Toss the pasta once more to combine and then plate into a bowl. Top with parmesan cheese and enjoy!

Squash Blossom and Kohlrabi Pasta with Grilled Steak

Prep Time: 15 minutes | *Cook Time:* 15 minutes | *Total Time:* 30 minutes | *Servings:*
2

Ingredients

- 12 squash blossoms
- 1/2 pound of thin steak (hanger, skirt)
- 2 tablespoons extra virgin olive oil
- salt and pepper, to taste
- half a white onion, thinly sliced
- 1 large garlic clove, minced
- 2 medium kohlrabis, peeled, Blade C
- ½ pint cherry tomatoes
- 2 tablespoons grated parmigiano reggiano cheese

Directions

1. Slice the bottoms of the squash blossoms and let the bud fall out. Discard the buds and bottoms and then set the squash blossoms aside.
2. Brush steak with 1 tablespoon of the olive oil and season very generously with pepper and some salt.
3. Place a grill pan or skillet over medium-high heat and coat with cooking spray. Once heated, add in the steak and cook 3 minutes on each side and then set aside.
4. Place a large skillet over medium heat and add in the other tablespoon of olive oil. Once the oil heats, add in the onions, red pepper flakes and garlic and cook for 2-3 minutes or until onions begin to soften. Then, add in the kohlrabi noodles, squash blossoms, tomatoes and season with salt and pepper. Toss the noodles and then cover, letting cook for 5-7 minutes, shaking the pan with the lid on, or until tomatoes burst.
5. Uncover the skillet. Using a fork, crush about half of the tomatoes. Sprinkle in the parmigiano reggiano and toss to combine all of the flavors, letting the cheese melt into the noodles.

Sundried Tomato Pesto Zucchini Noodle Mason Jars

Prep time: 30 mins | *Total time:* 30 mins | *Serves:* 2

Ingredients

For the salad:

- 1 large zucchini, Blade C, noodles trimmed
- ¼ cup pitted and halved kalamata olives
- 2 packed cups baby spinach
- ¾ cup canned chickpeas (drained and rinsed)
- ¼ cup crumbled feta cheese
- ¼ small red onion, sliced thinly
- 1 cup canned artichoke hearts, drained and quartered

For the pesto:

- ½ cup sundried tomatoes
- 1 tablespoon pine nuts
- ¼ cup extra virgin olive oil
- salt and pepper, to taste (about 5 cranks of a salt grinder)
- 1 teaspoon red wine vinegar

Directions

1. Place all of the ingredients for the pesto into a food processor and pulse until creamy. Taste and adjust to your preference. If it's not creamy enough, you can add some water or more oil.
2. If eating same-day: Toss the zucchini noodles in a medium mixing bowl with the pesto. Top, in this order, with artichoke hearts, red onion, chickpeas, olives, feta cheese and finally the spinach. Refrigerate for later use. To serve, pour into a bowl and toss together.
3. If letting sit overnight or more than 24 hours: in the bottom of the mason jar, add in the pesto. Top, in this order, with: artichoke hearts, red onion, chickpeas, spinach, olives, feta cheese and finally, the zucchini noodles. Refrigerate for future use. To serve, pour into a bowl and toss together.

Sweet Potato Mac and Cheese

Prep Time: 10 minutes | Cook Time: 10 minutes | Total Time: 20 minutes | Servings: 3

Ingredients

- 1 large (350g+) sweet potato, peeled, Blade B

- 2 tbsp vegan butter
- 1 tbsp coconut flour
- 1/3 cup plain almond milk
- 1/2 cup grated sharp cheddar cheese
- 1/4 cup grated parmesan cheese

Directions

1. Take your spiralized sweet potato noodles and cut with a scissor, if they are not in half-moon shape. Set aside.
2. In a large skillet, coat with cooking spray and add in the sweet potato noodles. Cook, tossing frequently, until cooked, for 5-7 minutes. When done, set aside.
3. In a large saucepan, add in the vegan butter and let melt. Once melted, add in the coconut flour and whisk together until flour absorbs butter and becomes thick. Then, add in the almond milk and whisk together constantly until mixture thickens.
4. Once the mixture thickens, add in the sweet potato noodles and stir to combine. Once combined, add in the cheese and stir again to combine. If it is too thick, add in more almond milk. Once the cheeses have melted into the noodles and consistency is to your preference, divide into bowls and enjoy!

Sweet Potato Noodle Carbonara

Prep Time: *15 minutes* | ***Cook Time:*** *10 minutes* | ***Total Time:*** *25 minutes* | ***Servings:*** *4*

Ingredients

- cooking spray
- 2 large (325g+) sweet potatoes, peeled, Blade C
- 2 tbsp olive oil
- 2 tsp minced garlic
- 1/4 tsp red pepper flakes
- 1/2 cup diced red onion
- 1 cup cubed pancetta
- For the sauce:
- 2 eggs
- 1/2 cup grated parmesan cheese
- salt and pepper, to taste

Directions

1. Place a large skillet over medium heat and coat with cooking spray. Add in your sweet potato noodles and cook for about 5-7 minutes, tossing frequently, or until noodles are cooked to your preference.
2. In a separate skillet (while you cook the sweet potato noodles), add another large skillet over medium heat and add in the olive oil. Once the oil heats, add in the garlic and red pepper flakes. Cook the garlic for 30 seconds and then add in the onion. Cook the onion for 2-3 minutes or until it begins to soften and then add in the pancetta cubes. Cook, stirring often, until cooked through, about 5 minutes.
3. While the pancetta and noodles are cooking, combine the eggs and parmesan cheese in a bowl and whisk together until not very clumpy. Season with the salt and pepper and set aside.
4. Once the noodles are done, add to the skillet with the pancetta, toss to combine and then turn off the heat.
5. Slowly, pour in the sauce, stirring constantly, over the noodles. It's important to do this slowly and stir constantly so that the eggs cook while they heat up in the noodles. Use as much sauce as you want until the pasta has enough sauce for your preference.
6. Serve into bowls and enjoy!

Sweet Potato Noodles with Brussels Sprouts and Lentil Ragu

*Prep time: 15 mins | **Cook time:** 25 mins | **Total time:** 40 mins | **Serves:** 4*

Ingredients

- ½ cup dry brown lentils
- 1 bay leaf
- 1.5 cups water
- 3 medium sweet potatoes, peeled, Blade D, noodles trimmed
- 2 tablespoons extra virgin olive oil
- ¼ teaspoon garlic powder
- salt and pepper
- 1 small red onion, peeled and diced
- 2 garlic cloves, minced
- 2 celery stalks, diced
- 2 small carrots, diced
- 2.5 cups shredded brussels sprouts

- 1.5 cups Victoria Fine Foods Organic Marinara sauce (or similar jarred sauce)
- chopped parsley to garnish
- grated parmesan cheese, if desired (to garnish)

Directions

1. Place the lentils, bay leaf, and water in a small saucepan over high heat and bring to a boil. Once boiling, reduce heat to low, cover and let simmer for 15 minutes or until lentils are cooked through, adding more water as needed.
2. Meanwhile, cook the sweet potato noodles. Heat half of the olive oil in a large skillet over medium-high heat. Once oil is shimmering, add the sweet potato noodles and season with garlic powder, salt, and pepper. Cook, tossing occasionally, until cooked through and al dente, about 7 minutes. When done, transfer noodles to a plate and tent with foil to keep warm.
3. Place the skillet back over medium-high heat and add the remaining olive oil. Once oil is shimmering, add the onions, garlic, celery, and carrots and cook for 5 minutes until vegetables soften. Add the brussels sprouts and cook until browned, about 5 minutes. Add the lentils and tomato sauce and let cook for 5 more minutes, letting flavors mend together.
4. Divide the sweet potato noodles into bowls and top with equal amounts of the ragu. Garnish with parsley and cheese (if desired.)

Sweet Potato Noodles with Chicken and Tomato Basil Sauce

Prep time: 5 mins | Cook time: 20 mins | Total time: 25 mins | Serves: 2

Ingredients

- 2 tablespoons extra virgin olive oil
- ½ pound boneless chicken breasts
- salt and pepper, to taste
- ¼ teaspoon oregano
- ¼ teaspoon garlic powder
- 1 large sweet potato
- 1 cup Rao's tomato basil sauce (or favorite tomato sauce brand)
- 1 tablespoon chopped curly parsley, to garnish
- optional: grated parmesan cheese, to garnish

Directions

1. Place a large skillet over medium-high heat and add in 1 tablespoon of the olive oil. While oil heats, season the chicken with salt, pepper, oregano and garlic powder. Once oil heats, add in the chicken. Cover and cook for 10 minutes or until chicken is cooked through and no longer pink on the inside.
2. While chicken cooks, peel and then spiralize the sweet potato with Blade D on the Inspiralizer. Set aside.
3. Set the chicken aside on a plate and cover to keep warm. Then, carefully wipe down the skillet and add in the other tablespoon of olive oil. Then, add in the sweet potato noodles, season with salt and pepper and cook, tossing frequently, until al dente, about 7 minutes.
4. While sweet potato noodles cook, place a small pot on medium heat and heat up the tomato basil sauce. Let simmer while sweet potato noodles finish cooking.
5. When sweet potato noodles are done, divide onto two plates. Top the noodles with tomato basil sauce and then chicken. Garnish with parsley and optional parmesan cheese.

Sweet Potato Noodles with Garlic Kale and Pork Chops

Prep time: 10 mins | Cook time: 20 mins | Total time: 30 mins | Serves: 2

Ingredients

- For the pork chops:
- 2 boneless pork chops, 3oz each
- salt and pepper
- 3 teaspoons extra-virgin olive oil
- For the sweet potatoes and kale:
- 1 medium sweet potato, peeled, Blade D, noodles trimmed
- 1 tablespoon + 2 teaspoons extra virgin olive oil
- 3-4 cups chopped kale
- 2 garlic cloves, thinly sliced
- salt and pepper, to taste

Directions

1. Preheat the oven to 400°F.
2. Rub each pork chop with 1 teaspoon of the olive oil, then season with salt and pepper. Set the chops aside.

3. Set a large oven-safe skillet over medium-high heat and add in the last teaspoon of olive oil. Add the pork chops to the skillet for about 3-4 minutes per side until golden brown.

4. Transfer the pork chops to the oven and roast until cooked through, about 7-9 minutes (if using a thermometer, the pork chops should register at 140 degrees in the thickest part.) Transfer the cooked pork chops to a plate and pour any pan juices into a small bowl and reserve. Let the pork chop stand for least 5 minutes, undisturbed.

5. Once you transfer the pork chops into the oven, also place a large skillet over medium-high heat. Add in 1 tablespoon of olive oil and then add in the sweet potato noodles and season with salt and pepper. Let cook for 7 minutes or until cooked to your preference and then divide into two plates and immediately add in the rest of the olive oil and kale into the skillet. Cook the kale for 1 minute and then add in the garlic. Cook the kale and garlic for 3-5 more minutes or until kale is wilted and cooked. Divide the kale into the plates with the sweet potato noodles.

6. Top each plate with a pork chop and drizzle over the sweet potatoes and kale with the reserved pan juices. Serve immediately.

Sweet Potato Pasta with Chicken Sausage and Corn

*Prep time: 10 mins | **Cook time:** 20 mins | **Total time:** 30 mins | **Serves:** 2*

Ingredients

- 1 tablespoon extra virgin olive oil
- 1-2 chicken sausage links, sliced into about ½" thick rounds
- kernels from 1 ear of corn
- ¼ teaspoon red pepper flakes
- 1 medium sweet potato, peeled, Blade D, noodles trimmed
- salt and pepper
- ¼ teaspoon garlic powder

Directions

1. Heat the oil in a large skillet over medium-high heat. Once oil is shimmering, add the chicken sausage, corn and red pepper flakes. Cook for about 8 minutes or until browned and cooked through. If using pre-cooked sausage, cook for about 3-5 minutes or until golden brown on both sides. Using a slotted spoon or tongs, transfer the chicken sausage and corn to a plate and immediately add in the sweet potato noodles. Season with salt,

pepper, and garlic powder and cook the noodles for 7 minutes or until cooked through and al dente.

2. Add in the chicken sausage and corn back into the skillet (along with any pan juices) and toss together with the sweet potato noodles.

3. Divide into bowls and serve immediately.mediately.

Thick Bacon, Kale and Goat Cheese Butternut Squash "Fettucine"

Prep Time: 15 minutes | Cook Time: 15 minutes | Total Time: 30 minutes | Servings: 2

Ingredients

- 1 small butternut squash, peeled, Blade B, noodles trimmed
- ½ tablespoon extra virgin olive oil
- pepper, to taste
- 3 slices thick-cut bacon, cubed
- 2 cups finely chopped curly kale
- salt, to taste
- 1 large garlic clove, sliced thinly
- ¼ cup crumbled goat cheese

Directions

1. Preheat the oven to 400 degrees. Line a baking sheet with parchment paper and lay out the squash noodles. Drizzle with the olive oil, season with pepper and roast for 8-10 minutes or until al dente.

2. Place a large skillet over medium heat and once heated, add in bacon. Let bacon cook until crispy about 5-7 minutes per side. Once cooked, transfer to a plate with slotted spoon and leave a little more than half of the bacon grease in the pan. Immediately add in the garlic and kale and season with salt and pepper. Cook, tossing occasionally, for 5 minutes or until wilted and cooked.

3. Divide butternut squash noodles into bowls and top with equal amounts of kale, bacon and goat cheese.

Tomato Basil Zucchini Pasta with Goat Cheese and Asparagus

Prep time: 20 mins | Cook time: 35 mins | Total time: 55 mins | Serves: 2

Ingredients

- 1 tablespoon extra virgin olive oil
- 1 large clove of garlic, minced
- ⅓ cup diced red onions
- 1 14oz can diced tomatoes with juices
- salt and pepper, to taste
- 5 large asparagus spears
- 2 medium zucchinis
- 1 tablespoon chopped basil + more to garnish
- 2oz goat cheese
- red pepper flakes, to garnish

Directions

1. Place a large skillet over medium heat and add in the olive oil. Once oil heats, add in the garlic and onions and cook for 2-3 minutes or until onions start to soften and become translucent.
2. Add in the tomatoes and season with salt and pepper. Bring to a boil and then reduce heat and simmer for 20-25 minutes.
3. While sauce cooks, spiralize the zucchinis and shave the asparagus by peeling it into strips with a vegetable peeler. Keep the asparagus tips for future use and toss the remaining asparagus stalks. You can also include the asparagus tips, if you'd like, but I didn't.
4. Once sauce is done, place another large skillet over medium-high heat and once heated, add in the zucchini noodles and asparagus. Let cook for 2-3 minutes or until al dente.
5. While zucchini cooks, add in the basil to the tomato sauce and stir for 1 minute. Then, remove from heat and stir in the goat cheese.
6. When noodles are done, add to the pan with the sauce and toss to combine (alternately, you can combine both in a large mixing bowl and toss that way, if you don't have a wide enough skillet to accommodate the noodles.)
7. Divide the pasta mixture into bowls, top with remaining goat cheese and garnish with extra basil and red pepper flakes.

Tomato Zucchini Spaghetti with Shrimp, Kale and Feta

Prep Time: 5 minutes | Cook Time: 15 minutes | Total Time: 20 minutes | Servings: 1

Ingredients

- 1.5 zucchinis, Blade C
- 3/4 of a 14oz can of diced tomatoes
- 1 tbsp olive oil
- salt and pepper
- 1 medium clove of garlic, minced
- 1 tbsp dried oregano flakes
- 1-2 tsps garlic powder
- 1/2 of a medium onion, chopped
- 1 tsp red pepper flakes
- 4-5 medium sized shrimp, deveined and deshelled
- 1.5 cups chopped kale
- 1/4 cup of feta or less to top (optional)

Directions

1. Place a large skillet over medium heat and pour in olive oil. Season with salt and pepper. Once oil heats, add in garlic. Cook for 1 minute and then add in the red pepper flakes. Cook for 30 seconds and then add in the tomatoes, oregano and season with more salt and pepper. I like my tomatoes crushed, so I took a potato smasher and smashed the tomato chunks - you can do this with a fork!
2. Let the mixture cook for about 10-15 minutes or longer, until the sauce reduces and most of the juices are gone. Then, add in the kale and zucchini pasta and cook until the kale is wilted and the zucchini softens. When you add in the kale and zucchini, put a medium skillet over medium heat and spray with cooking spray. Once skillet heats, add in shrimp and season with garlic powder, salt and pepper. Cook for 1-2 minutes and then flip on the other side for another 1-2 minutes or until shrimp is cooked through and opaque.
3. Pour the pasta mixture into your dish, and top with the shrimp and feta.

Tomatokeftedes (Tomato Balls) with Tzatziki Zucchini Pasta

Prep Time: 17 minutes | Cook Time: 25 minutes | Total Time: 42 minutes

Ingredients

For the tzatziki sauce

- 1/2 of a cucumber

- 1/3 cup 0% plain Greek Yogurt (I used Chobani)
- 1 garlic clove, very minced
- 1/2 tbsp olive oil
- 1/2 tbsp red wine vinegar
- 1/2 tbsp fresh dill, chopped
- 1 tsp lemon juice
- a few (3-4) cranks of a sea salt grinder
- a couple cranks (2-3) of the peppercorn grinder, to taste
- For the tomato balls and pasta
- 1 large zucchini, peeled, Blade C
- 1 cup baby vine tomatoes, chopped
- 3-4 tbsp spring onion, chopped
- 1 tbsp warm water
- 1 tbsp mint, chopped
- 1 pinch of oregano
- 1/4 cup of whole wheat flour
- 1/4 cup of Pecorino Romano cheese (recipe calls for kefalotyri, but normal grocery stores don't carry it so this will do)
- salt and pepper, to taste

Directions

1. Preheat the oven to 405 degrees.
2. Take the cucumber and peel it. With a teaspoon, scrape out the seeds in the inside of the cucumber and discard.
3. Time to prepare the tzatziki sauce. Loosely chop the cucumber and put it into a food processor. Pulse until big chunks are gone. If you don't have a food processor, finely chop the cucumber. When done, place into a bowl with the rest of the ingredients for the sauce (Greek yogurt, garlic, olive oil, red wine vinegar, dill, lemon juice, salt, pepper). Place in the refrigerator.
4. Next, prepare the tomato ball mixture. In a large bowl, place in all of the ingredients and mix together with hands until the mixture is thick and sticky enough to create about 2 large tomato balls. If needed, add more flour and water. Form the tomato balls with your hands.
5. Spray a baking sheet with cooking spray and place on the tomato balls. Bake in the oven for 10 minutes, flip over and bake for another 10-15 minutes or until tomato balls are browned on the outside and don't easily fall apart with poked with a fork. When done, take out of the oven and set aside.
6. Pour the tzatziki sauce over the zucchini pasta and mix thoroughly to combine. Place in a bowl. Top with tomato balls and enjoy!

Tuna Pasta with Olives and Arugula

*Serving size: 1 | **Time to prepare**: 2 minutes | **Time to cook**: 3 minutes*

Ingredients

- 1 can of solid white albacore tuna
- 1 can of halved black olives
- 1 can of Rao's tomato basil sauce (or your favorite)
- 1 container or bag of baby arugula
- 1 large zucchini

Directions

1. Place a large skillet over medium-high heat.
2. Measure 3/4 cup tomato sauce and pour into skillet.
3. Open can of tuna and pour out liquid.
4. Pour drained tuna into skillet and stir to break up and combine.
5. Prepare your zucchini and then spiralize it, Blade C.
6. Add zucchini noodles to the skillet and mix thoroughly to combine.
7. Open can of black olives.
8. Take a handful of olives (or desired amount) and put into the skillet. Mix to combine.
9. Let zucchini cook, stirring frequently to combine and make sure sauce covers all noodles.
10. Once done, pour into a pasta bowl, top with a handful of arugula and enjoy!

Turnip Noodles with Roasted Butternut Squash, Toasted Pine Nuts and Goat Cheese

*Prep Time: 15 minutes | **Cook Time**: 25 minutes | **Total Time**: 40 minutes | **Servings**: 2*

Ingredients

- 1.5 cups cubed butternut squash
- 1.5 tablespoons extra virgin olive oil

- salt and pepper, to taste
- 2 tablespoons raw pine nuts
- 1 large garlic clove, minced
- pinch of red pepper flakes
- 2 medium turnips, peeled, Blade C, noodles trimmed
- 1/3 cup crumbled goat cheese

Directions

1. Preheat the oven to 425 degrees. Place the butternut squash on a parchment paper lined baking tray, drizzle with ½ tablespoon of the olive oil and toss together. Season with salt and pepper and roast for 20 minutes or until easily pierced with a fork.
2. While butternut squash is roasting, place a small skillet over medium-high heat and add in the pine nuts. Let cook for 3-5 minutes, tossing the pan occasionally to avoid burning the nuts. Once golden brown, transfer to a small bowl or plate and set aside.
3. Place a large skillet over medium heat and add in the rest of the olive oil. Once oil heats, add in the garlic, red pepper flakes and cook for 30 seconds or until fragrant. Then, add in the turnip noodles, cover and cook for 5-7 minutes, uncovering to toss the noodles occasionally, until turnip noodles are al dente.
4. Once turnip noodles are cooked, remove from heat, add in the butternut squash and goat cheese and toss until goat cheese softens and melts into the noodles.
5. Portion the noodles into two bowls and top with toasted pine nuts.

Tuscan Kale and Sausage Ragu with Butternut Squash Fettuccine

Prep time: 20 mins | *Cook time:* 60 mins | *Total time:* 1 hour 20 mins | *Serves:* 4

Ingredients

- .75 pound spicy Italian sausage, decased and crumbled
- 1 small sweet onion, diced
- 2 garlic cloves, minced
- ¼ teaspoon red pepper flakes
- 1 (28 ounce) cans Tuttorosso Peeled Plum Tomatoes – No Salt Added
- 1.5 tablespoons tomato paste
- ¼ cup red wine (or beef broth)
- 1 teaspoon dried basil

- 1 teaspoon dried oregano
- 1 bay leaf
- salt and pepper, to taste
- 4 cups chopped Tuscan kale
- 1 cup canned white beans, drained and rinsed
- 2 medium butternut squash
- olive oil, to drizzle
- fresh basil, to garnish
- parmesan cheese, to garnish

Directions

1. Preheat the oven to 400 degrees.
2. Place a large pot over medium heat and add in the sausage. Crumble the sausage further with a wooden spoon and cook until browned, about 10 minutes. Then, add in the onions, garlic and red pepper flakes and let cook for 2-3 minutes or until onions turn translucent.
3. Using your hands, crush the tomatoes over the pot. Using a wooden spoon, further crush the tomatoes so that no large chunks remain. Then, add in the tomato paste, wine (or broth), basil, oregano, bay leaf and season with salt and pepper. Raise the heat to medium-high and bring to a boil and then reduce heat to medium-low to a simmer. Cook for 30-35 minutes or until reduced by half and then stir in the kale and beans. Cook for another 5 minutes or until kale wilts and sauce is thick like a ragu.
4. Peel and spiralize the butternut squash, using Blade B. Line a baking sheet with parchment paper and lay out the butternut squash noodles.
5. Drizzle with olive oil and massage it into the squash with your hands.
6. Once you add the kale to the ragu, season with salt and pepper and roast for 8-10 minutes or until cooked to al dente.
7. Divide the butternut squash noodles into bowls and top with the ragu, making sure to discard the bay leaf. Garnish with basil and Parmesan cheese.

Vegan Buffalo Cauliflower with Sweet Potato Noodles

Prep Time: *20 minutes* | **Cook Time:** *30 minutes* | **Total Time:** *50 minutes* | **Servings:** *4*

Ingredients

- 1 medium head of cauliflower, chopped into florets (about 8 cups)

- salt and pepper, to taste
- olive oil cooking spray
- 3 tablespoons coconut oil
- ¼ cup raw cashews, soaked in water for at least 2 hours
- vegetable broth, if needed
- 2 large sweet potatoes, peeled, Blade B, noodles trimmed
- 1 tablespoon chopped parsley, to garnish
- For the buffalo pasta sauce:
- 3-4 tablespoons hot sauce (I use Tessemae's)
- 1 teaspoon garlic powder
- 1 teaspoon paprika
- 1 tablespoon freshly squeezed lemon juice
- 1 tablespoon apple cider vinegar
- salt, to taste

Directions

1. Preheat the oven to 400 degrees. Arrange the cauliflower on a baking sheet, season with salt, pepper and coat lightly with cooking spray. Roast for 20-25 minutes or until beginning to brown.
2. On another baking sheet, lay out the sweet potatoes and coat lightly with cooking spray and season with salt and pepper. Roast for 17-20 minutes or until cooked through, but still al dente (taste test.)
3. While the cauliflower and sweet potato roasts, puree the cashews in a high-speed blender or food processor until creamy. Set aside.
4. In a medium pot over medium heat, melt the coconut oil. Add the coconut oil to the cashew cream along with the other ingredients for the buffalo sauce and puree again until creamy. If needed, add in vegetable broth until reached a sauce-like consistency (not runny, but not too thick.) Cover and set aside, to keep warm.
5. In a large mixing bowl, toss together the cauliflower florets with half of the buffalo sauce mixture, keeping the remaining sauce in the pot. Spread the cauliflower back out on the baking sheet and cook for 5 more minutes or until sauce begins to bubble.
6. Plate the sweet potato noodles and top with cauliflower florets. Stir the buffalo sauce and then drizzle over plates. Serve immediately, garnished with parsley.

Vegan Butternut Squash Noodles and Toasted Almonds with Pumpkin-Sage Sauce

Prep Time: 20 minutes | Cook Time: 15 minutes | Total Time: 35 minutes | Servings:

4

Ingredients

For the pasta:

- 1 large butternut squash, peeled, Blade C*
- 1 tablespoon extra virgin olive oil
- ¼ cup slivered or sliced almonds
- For the sauce:
- ½ tablespoon extra virgin olive oil
- 6 fresh sage leaves
- 1 large garlic clove, minced
- ¼ teaspoon red pepper flakes
- 1 large shallot, minced
- 1 tablespoon tomato paste
- 1 15oz can pumpkin puree
- ½ cup unsweetened almond milk or vegetable broth (if nut allergy)
- optional: 2 teaspoons nutritional yeast flakes**
- salt and pepper, to taste

Directions

1. Preheat the oven to 400 degrees. Line a baking sheet with parchment paper. Lay out the butternut squash noodles, drizzle with the olive oil and season with salt and pepper. Bake for 8-10 minutes, tossing halfway through, or until butternut squash is no longer crunchy and is al dente (check after 8 minutes to make sure you don't overcook- ovens are finicky!)
2. While the butternut squash is cooking, prepare the pumpkin sage sauce. Place a large pot over medium heat and once heated, add in the olive oil. Once oil is shimmering, add in the sage and fry until crispy (about 3 minutes) and then remove with a slotted spoon and set aside on a paper towel lined plate. Add in the garlic, red pepper flakes, shallots and cook for 1-2 minutes or until shallots are translucent. Add the tomato paste and pumpkin and stir to combine thoroughly. Then, add in the milk, season with salt and pepper and stir until sauce thins out and absorbs the milk. Then, add in the nutritional yeast flakes, if wanted. Raise heat to high and bring to a boil. Lower to a simmer, crumble in the sage, stir and let flavors develop, while the butternut squash finishes cooking.
3. While sauce is simmering, place a small skillet over medium-high heat and add in the slivered almonds. Toast for 3-5 minutes or until lightly browned

on all sides and fragrant. Be careful not to burn. When done, transfer to a small plate and set aside.

4. When the butternut squash is finished, portion into bowls and pour over pumpkin sauce. Top each bowl with a tablespoon of the toasted almonds. Alternately, toss the pasta in a large mixing bowl with the almonds and sauce to combine and then portion out to serve.

Vegan Creamy Ginger-Coconut Kale Zucchini Spaghetti

Prep Time: 15 minutes | *Cook Time*: 15 minutes | *Total Time*: 30 minutes | *Servings*: 6

Ingredients

- 1/2 tablespoon extra virgin olive oil
- 3 garlic cloves, minced
- 2 1/2 tablespoons fresh ginger, peeled and minced
- 1 15 ounce can lite coconut milk
- 2 teaspoons lemon juice
- red pepper flakes, to taste
- kosher salt and freshly ground pepper, to taste
- 3 cups chopped kale
- 1/4 cup packed fresh basil
- ¼ cup raw cashews
- 6 medium zucchinis, Blade C, noodles trimmed
- 3/4 cup defrosted green peas

Directions

1. In a large pot over medium heat, add in the olive oil. Once heated, add the garlic and ginger and cook for 1-2 minutes or until fragrant.
2. Add in the coconut milk, lemon juice, red pepper flakes and season with salt and pepper. Stir to combine and then add in the kale. Cover and cook until the greens have wilted, about 5 minutes.
3. Transfer the kale mixture to a high-speed blender and add in the basil and cashews. Blend until smooth and creamy and set aside.
4. Wipe down the pot and place back over medium heat. Add in the zucchini noodles and peas and toss for 3-4 minutes or until cooked to al dente or your preference. Once cooked, divide into bowls and top with green sauce. Serve immediately.

Vegan Kale and Rutabaga Lasagna

Prep time: 15 mins | *Cook time:* 50 mins | *Total time:* 1 hour 5 mins | *Serves:* 6

Ingredients

- 1 large rutabaga or 2 small rutabagas, peeled
- 3.5 cups tomato basil sauce
- ½ tablespoon extra virgin olive oil
- 8 cups chopped kale
- 3 cloves of garlic, minced
- ¼ teaspoon red pepper flakes
- 1 large shallot, minced
- salt and pepper, to taste
- For the cashew cheese:
- 1.5 cups cashews, soaked in water for at least 2 hours (preferably overnight) and drained
- 2 tablespoons nutritional yeast
- ½ teaspoon dried oregano
- ½ teaspoon dried basil
- ½ teaspoon dried parsley
- ½ teaspoon garlic powder
- 3 tablespoons freshly squeezed lemon juice
- salt and pepper, to taste
- ½ cup vegetable broth

Directions

1. Preheat the oven to 425 degrees.
2. Slice halfway through the rutabaga, just to the center (careful not to go further.) Spiralize the rutabaga, using Blade A.
3. Place a medium pot over medium-high heat, add in the tomato sauce and bring to a simmer. Once simmering, lower heat to low to keep warm on the stovetop.
4. Place all of the ingredients for the cheese into a high-speed blender or food processor and process until creamy. Taste and adjust with more salt, if needed. Set aside.
5. Place a large skillet over medium heat and add in the olive oil. Once oil is shimmering, add in the kale, garlic, red pepper flakes, shallots and season

with salt and pepper. Cook the mixture for 2-3 minutes or until kale is wilted.

6. Gather all of your prepared ingredients to build the lasagna. Take out a casserole dish (I use 4.2 quart) and add about ½ cup of the tomato sauce on the bottom. Then, add a layer of the rutabaga on top. Then, add a layer of the cheese mixture. Then, add in a layer of the kale mixture. Top with tomato basil sauce and spread it around with the back of a spatula or otherwise. Top with a layer of rutabaga. Then, add the cashew cheese. Then, add a layer of kale mixture. Then, add in a layer of the tomato basil sauce. Top with a layer of the rutabaga and then, top with the remaining tomato sauce.

7. Cover the casserole dish and bake in the oven for 40-45 minutes. After 40 minutes, poke the top layer and if you can easily pierce through the rutabaga, it's done. If you can't, bake another 5 minutes.

8. Once the lasagna is done, carefully cut into 4 very large pieces or 6 medium pieces.

Vegan Taco Bolognese Zucchini Spaghetti

Prep time: *30 mins* | **Cook time:** *15 mins* | **Total time:** *45 mins* | **Serves:** *4*

Ingredients

For the pasta:

- 1 ear of corn, shucked
- 1 tablespoon extra virgin olive oil
- ½ cup diced white or red onion
- 1 teaspoon diced jalapeno
- 1 large garlic clove, minced
- salt and pepper, to taste
- 1.5 tablespoons tomato paste
- 1 14.5oz can peeled whole tomatoes, drained
- 3 large zucchinis (or 4 medium), Blade D, noodles trimmed
- ½ cup halved medium black olives
- 1 avocado, insides sliced
- 2 tablespoons chopped cilantro
- 1 lime quartered, to serve

For the taco "meat":

- 1 cup walnuts

- ½ teaspoon chile powder
- ½ teaspoon ground cumin
- ¼ teaspoon smoked paprika
- 1 pinch of cayenne pepper
- salt and pepper, to taste

Directions

1. Place the corn in a medium pot, cover with water and a pinch of salt and bring to a boil. Once boiling, cook for another 1-2 minutes or until fork-tender. Drain into a colander, shave the kernels off the cob with a knife and set aside.
2. Place the walnuts into a food processor along with all of the spices, season with salt and pepper and pulse until chunky-ground. Set aside.
3. Heat the olive oil in a large skillet over medium heat. Once heated, add in the onion and jalapeno and cook until onions begin to soften, about 2 minutes. Then, add in the garlic, season with salt and pepper and cook for 30 seconds. Then, add in the tomato paste and stir to combine for about 1 minute. Then, add in the taco meat and crush the tomatoes by hand (from the canned tomatoes) and stir to combine and cook for 2 minutes or until heated through. Fold in the corn and let cook for 30 seconds to heat.
4. Remove half of the taco meat and add in half of the zucchini noodles and cook for 3-5 minutes or until zucchini noodles cook to al dente or to your preference. Transfer to a bowl and set aside. Add back in the rest of the taco meat and the rest of the zucchini noodles and cook again for 3-5 minutes or until cooked to your preference.
5. Divide all of the the zucchini pasta into four bowls, garnish with olives, avocado and cilantro and serve with lime wedges.

Vegetarian Bell Pepper Fiesta Skillet

Prep time: 25 mins | *Cook time:* 15 mins | *Total time:* 40 mins | *Serves:* 3

Ingredients

For the skillet:

- 1 large ear of corn, shucked
- pinch of salt
- 1 tablespoon extra virgin olive oil
- 1 small yellow onion, sliced

- 2 large bell peppers, stem removed, Blade A (I used yellow and red)
- 2 roma tomatoes, seeded and chopped
- 2 garlic cloves, minced
- 1 15oz can black beans, drained and rinsed and patted dry
- 1 tablespoon chopped cilantro
- ½ cup Mexican blend cheese
- 1 avocado, peeled, pitted and sliced thinly

For the fajita seasoning:

- ¼ teaspoon cayenne pepper
- 1 teaspoon chili powder
- ¼ teaspoon garlic powder
- ½ teaspoon paprika
- ½ teaspoon smoked paprika
- ½ teaspoon onion powder
- ¼ teaspoon cumin
- ¼ teaspoon salt
- ¼ teaspoon oregano

Directions

1. Preheat the oven to 450 degrees.
2. Place the corn halves into a medium pot and cover with water and a pinch of salt. Bring to a boil and let cook for 2-3 minutes or until corn is cooked through (easily pierced with a fork.) Drain into a colander and set aside to cool.
3. Once water boils, place a medium cast-iron skillet (or regular skillet will do) over medium heat and add in the olive oil. Once oil heats, add in the onions and bell peppers and cook for 5 minutes or until peppers and onions begin to soften. Then, add in the tomatoes, garlic, black beans and 1 tablespoon of the fajita seasoning. Toss and let cook for 2-3 minutes and then add in the cilantro and corn, shaving the corn off the cob into the skillet with a knife.
4. Remove the skillet from the heat and sprinkle over with cheese. Place in the oven for 5 minutes or until cheese melts.
5. Serve immediately, garnished with avocado slices.

Vegetarian Zucchini Spaghetti Tacos

Prep Time: 15 minutes | Cook Time: 15 minutes | Total Time: 30 minutes | Servings: 6 hard taco shells

Ingredients

- 1 ear of corn
- ½ cup canned tomato sauce
- 1 avocado, peeled and cored
- 1 tablespoon finely minced cilantro
- salt and pepper, to taste
- 2 medium zucchinis, Blade C, noodles trimmed
- ½ cup black beans
- 1 cup shredded lettuce (romaine or spinach works best)
- Optional, if not using hard taco shells: 3 cups of shredded lettuce
- 6 yellow or blue corn taco shells*

For the taco seasoning:

- 1/2 tablespoon chili powder
- 1/8 teaspoon garlic powder
- 1/8 teaspoon onion powder
- 1/8 teaspoon dried oregano
- 1/4 teaspoon smoked paprika
- 1 teaspoon ground cumin
- 1/4 teaspoon ground coriander
- salt and pepper, to taste

Directions

1. Place the corn in a medium saucepan and cover with water. Bring to a boil and once boiling, let cook for 2 minutes or until corn is easily pierced with a fork. Once done, drain into a colander and shave off corn with a knife. Set shaved kernels aside.
2. While the water is heating up, combine all of the taco seasoning spices together and whisk until thoroughly combined. Set aside.
3. Once the corn is done, heat a large skillet over medium heat. Once the skillet heats, add in the tomato sauce and pour in taco seasoning mix. Stir to combine and lower the heat, simmering for 5 minutes for the flavors to develop.
4. While tomato sauce is simmering, smash the avocado in a bowl, add in the cilantro and season with salt and pepper. Stir to combine and set aside.
5. Add in the zucchini noodles, corn and beans and cook for 2-3 minutes or until noodles are cooked through.
6. If using hard taco shells: Using pasta tongs, fill the taco shells with zucchini spaghetti mixture and top with olives, a dollop of avocado and a pinch of lettuce.

7. If not using hard taco shells: Fill a bowl up with shredded lettuce and top with zucchini noodles (using pasta tongs to let excess moisture drip off), then top with olives and a dollop of avocado. Repeat 3 more times to make 3 taco bowls.
8. *Check the ingredients on the taco shells – they should contain nothing more than water, corn (or masa) flour and/or oil.

Winter Kale, Sausage and Butternut Squash Lasagna

Prep Time: 20 minutes | **Cook Time**: 60 minutes | **Total Time:** 1 hour 20 minutes | **Servings:** 6

Ingredients

- 1 medium butternut squash
- 1/2 tablespoon extra virgin olive oil
- 6 fresh sage leaves
- 4 sausage links, decased
- 5 cups chopped kale
- 3 cloves of garlic, minced
- ¼ teaspoon red pepper flakes
- 1 large shallot, minced
- salt and pepper, to taste
- 1.5 cups ricotta cheese
- 1/3 cup grated parmesan cheese (grated not shredded!)
- 1 large egg, beaten
- 1 cup shredded gruyere cheese

Directions

1. Preheat the oven to 425 degrees.
2. Cut the bulbous bottom off the butternut squash (the seeded part.) Slice the top off to ensure that it's perfectly flat. Peel the butternut squash entirely. If the butternut squash is longer than 6 inches, slice it into two manageable pieces. Slice halfway through the butternut squash, just to the center (careful not to go further.) Spiralize the squash, using Blade A.
3. Place a large skillet over medium heat and add in the olive oil. Once oil heats, add in the sage leaves and cook until crispy, careful not to burn. Transfer the sage leaves to a small paper towel lined plate and set aside.
4. Immediately crumble in the sausage to the skillet and cook until browned, 5-7 minutes. Then, add in the kale, garlic, red pepper flakes, shallots and

season with salt and pepper. Cook the mixture for 2-3 minutes or until kale is wilted.

5. While the sausage is cooking, add the ricotta, parmesan and egg to a bowl. Whisk together and set aside.

6. Once the sausage is done, gather all of your prepared ingredients. Take out a casserole dish (I use 4.2 quart) and add a layer of the butternut squash to the bottom. Then, add a layer of the kale and sausage mixture. Then, add in a layer of ricotta mixture. Top with a layer of butternut squash. Then, add a layer of the kale and sausage mixture. Then, add in a layer of ricotta mixture. Top with a layer of the butternut squash and then, top with all of the gruyere cheese.

7. Cover the casserole dish with tinfoil and bake in the oven for 40-45 minutes. After 40 minutes, poke the top layer and if you can easily pierce through the butternut squash, it's done. If you can't, bake another 5 minutes.

8. After the 40 minutes of baking, take the dish out of the oven, remove the tinfoil top and immediately sprinkle with sage topping. Then, let rest for 5 minutes. After resting, carefully cut the lasagna into 6 equal portions.

Yellow Squash with Ricotta Salata and Grilled Tomatoes

Prep Time: *30 minutes* | **Cook Time:** *10 minutes* | **Total Time:** *40 minutes* | **Servings:** *2*

Ingredients

- 2 bamboo skewers
- 1 dozen cherry tomatoes
- 2 tablespoons extra virgin olive oil
- 1 tablespoon balsamic vinegar
- salt and pepper, to taste
- 2 garlic cloves, finely minced
- 1 large garlic clove, minced
- 1 pinch red pepper flakes
- 2 yellow squashes, julienned or spiralized (Blade C)
- 1.5 tablespoons chopped basil
- 1 oz shaved ricotta salata

Directions

1. Soak 2 bamboo skewers in water for 30 minutes (if using a grill.)

2. While skewers are soaking, place the tomatoes in a bowl with 1 tablespoon of the olive oil, balsamic and garlic and season with salt and pepper. Let marinade for 10 minutes.
3. While tomatoes are marinating, spiralize or julienne your squashes. Set aside.
4. Once skewers are finished soaking (if applicable), place 6 marinated tomatoes on each skewer.
5. If using a grill:
6. Heat up a grill to medium/high heat. Grill tomatoes for 3-4 minutes or until they are cooked. Set aside on a plate, covered with tinfoil.
7. If using a grill pan or skillet:
8. Place a large grill pan or skillet over medium heat. Once the pan is heated, add on the skewers. Cook for 2 minutes, flip over and cook another 2-3 minutes or until tomatoes are cooked. Set aside on a plate, covered with tinfoil.
9. Once the tomatoes are cooked, place a large skillet over medium heat and add in the other tablespoon of olive oil. Once the oil heats, add in the garlic, red pepper flakes and cook for 30 seconds or until fragrant. Add in the squash noodles and basil and toss for 2-3 minutes or until al dente.
10. Divide the squash noodles into two bowls and top each with a tomato skewer and the ricotta salata. Top with freshly cracked pepper.

Zoodles ala Carbonara

"A twist on the traditional carbonara using zucchini squash noodles and omitting the cream for a gluten-free, low-carb, high-protein dish."

Servings: 2 | Prep: 15 m | Cook: 5 m | Ready In: 20 m

Ingredients

- 2 eggs 1 egg yolk
- 2/3 cup shredded Pecorino cheese, or to taste
- 2 tablespoons olive oil
- 2 ounces cubed pancetta, or to taste
- 1 extra large zucchini, cut into noodle-shape strands
- 2 tablespoons grated Parmigiano-Reggiano cheese
- 2 teaspoons ground black pepper

Directions

1. Whisk eggs and egg yolk together in a bowl. Add Pecorino cheese and mix well.
2. Heat olive oil in a large wok or skillet over medium heat; cook and stir pancetta until cooked through but not crispy, 2 to 3 minutes. Add the zucchini noodles (zoodles); cook and stir until zoodles are warmed but not soft and pancetta is slightly crispy, 3 to 5 minutes. Remove wok from heat.
3. Pour egg mixture over zoodles and stir until evenly coated. Top zoodles with Parmigiano-Reggiano cheese and black pepper.

Nutritional Information

- Calories:414 kcal 21%
- Fat: 30.5 g 47%
- Carbs: 13.8g 4%
- Protein: 22.5 g 45%
- Cholesterol: 316 mg 105%
- Sodium: 634 mg 25%

Zucchini Noodle Alfredo

"A great alternative to pasta. Top with grilled chicken for a well-rounded meal."

Servings: 4 | **Prep:** 10 m | **Cook:** 15 m | **Ready In:** 25 m

Ingredients

- 1/4 cup pine nuts, or to taste (optional)
- 4 zucchini, sliced
- 2 tablespoons extra-virgin olive oil
- 1 (8 ounce) package sliced fresh mushrooms
- 1 cup chopped asparagus
- 2 ounces prosciutto, chopped
- 1 cup Alfredo sauce, or as desired
- 1/2 cup frozen peas, thawed
- 1/2 cup cherry tomatoes, halved
- 1 pinch white pepper
- 1 pinch nutmeg
- 1 tablespoon chopped fresh basil, or to taste

Directions

1. Heat a skillet over medium heat; cook and stir pine nuts until fragrant and toasted, about 5 minutes.
2. Slice zucchini into noodle-shaped strands using a spiralizing device.
3. Heat olive oil in a skillet over medium heat; cook and stir mushrooms, asparagus, and prosciutto until vegetables are tender and prosciutto is slightly crisp, 6 to 8 minutes.
4. Stir Alfredo sauce, peas, and zucchini into vegetable-prosciutto mixture; toss gently and simmer over low heat until sauce is heated through, 2 to 3 minutes. Mix tomatoes into zucchini mixture and remove skillet from heat.
5. Ladle zucchini mixture into bowls and season with white pepper and nutmeg. Sprinkle basil and pine nuts over each.

Nutritional Information

- Calories:400 kcal 20%
- Fat: 34.2 g 53%
- Carbs: 15.1g 5%
- Protein: 12.9 g 26%
- Cholesterol: 37 mg 12%
- Sodium: 913 mg 37%

Zucchini Noodle and Arugula Salad with Bacon, Corn and Ricotta

Prep time: *15 mins* | **Cook time:** *15 mins* | **Total time:** *30 mins* | **Serves:** *2*

Ingredients

- 1 ear of corn
- 4 strips of bacon
- 2 medium zucchinis, Blade D, noodles trimmed
- ¼ teaspoon red pepper flakes
- ½ teaspoon garlic powder
- 1 tablespoon freshly squeezed lemon juice + ¼ teaspoon zest
- ¼ cup ricotta cheese
- 1 cup arugula
- pepper, to taste

Directions

1. Place the corn in a medium pot, cover with water and a pinch of salt and bring to a boil. Once boiling, cook another 2 minutes or until easily pierced with a fork. Drain into a colander and set aside.
2. While the corn is cooking, set a large skillet over medium-high heat and once heated, add in the bacon. Cook for 5-7 minutes or until crispy and then transfer to a paper towel lined plate.
3. Pour out half of the bacon grease and immediately add in the zucchini noodles. Season with red pepper flakes, garlic powder, lemon, zest and cook for 3 minutes or until cooked to your preference.
4. Shave the corn into the skillet with the zucchini noodles. Toss to combine and then divide into bowls. Top with equal amounts of ricotta, seasoned with fresh cracked pepper, arugula and bacon and serve.

Zucchini Noodles and Shrimp with Spicy Vodka Sauce

Prep time: 15 mins | **Cook time:** 25 mins | **Total time:** 40 mins | **Serves:** 4

Ingredients

- 2 tablespoons extra virgin olive oil
- 1 pound shrimp, peeled, deveined
- salt and pepper, to taste
- 1 medium onion, diced
- 2 garlic cloves, minced
- 1 teaspoon red pepper flakes (or less if you don't like it too spicy)
- 1 (14.5 ounce) can crushed or diced tomatoes
- ¼ cup vodka (I used Stolichnaya)
- ¼ teaspoon dried oregano
- ¼ cup coconut cream from a can of lite coconut milk
- 4 medium zucchinis, Blade C, noodles trimmed
- 3 tablespoons chopped fresh basil leaves

Directions

1. Heat the olive oil in a large skillet over medium-high heat. Once oil is shimmering, add in the shrimp, season with salt and pepper and cook for 1-2 minutes per side or until C-shaped and opaque. Transfer the shrimp to a large plate with a slotted spoon or tongs and cover with foil or something to keep warm.

2. Immediately add in the onions, garlic and red pepper flakes to the skillet used to cook the shrimp and cook for 3-5 minutes or until onions soften. Add in the tomatoes, vodka, and oregano. Bring to a boil and then lower to medium-low and simmer until the sauce thickens, about 10 minutes. Stir in the coconut milk and let cook for 3 more minutes to thicken a bit.

3. Meanwhile, place another large skillet over medium-high heat and once heated, add in the zucchini noodles. Cook the noodles, tossing frequently, until al dente, 3-5 minutes. Drain into a colander and then divide into four plates and set aside.

4. Once sauce is done, add back in the shrimp and toss to coat. Stir in the basil, season with more salt if needed, and portion out over the bowls of zucchini noodles. Garnish with extra red pepper flakes.

Zucchini Noodles and Summer Vegetables with Sweet Pepper Chicken Sausage

"Fresh from the farmer's market! A light and flavorful blend of farm-fresh summer vegetables and sweet pepper chicken sausage."

Servings: 4 | **Prep:** 15 m | **Cook:** 12 m | **Ready In:** 27 m

Ingredients

- 2 zucchini, cut into noodle-shape strands
- 2 tablespoons extra-virgin olive oil, divided
- 1/2 cup chopped green bell pepper
- 1/3 cup chopped white onion
- 1 tablespoon seasoned salt (such as Spike® seasoning)
- 1 pinch sea salt and freshly ground black pepper to taste
- 2 sweet pepper chicken sausages, sliced
- 1 cup lightly torn fresh spinach
- 2 tablespoons chopped fresh basil 1 teaspoon garlic paste
- 1 large tomato, diced
- 1/4 cup shredded Parmesan cheese

Directions

1. Bring a pot of lightly salted water to a boil. Cook zucchini noodles (zoodles) in the boiling water until tender yet firm to the bite, about 3 minutes; drain.

2. Heat 1 tablespoon olive oil in a skillet over medium heat; cook and stir green bell pepper, onion, seasoned salt, and sea salt for 3 minutes. Add chicken sausage and cook until sausage is lightly browned, 4 to 5 minutes. Add spinach, basil, garlic paste, and seasoned salt to taste; cook until spinach is wilted, 2 to 3 minutes.
3. Place zoodles on a serving plate and toss with remaining 1 tablespoon olive oil and sea salt. Add sausage mixture and tomatoes and top with Parmesan cheese; season with salt and pepper.

Nutritional Information

- Calories:208 kcal 10%
- Fat: 13.6 g 21%
- Carbs: 9.2g 3%
- Protein: 11.7 g 23%
- Cholesterol: 40 mg 13%
- Sodium: 1407 mg 56%

Zucchini Noodles Pad Thai

"A healthier adaptation of a Pad Thai recipe. Serve with extra lime wedges."

Servings: 4| Prep: 45 m | Cook: 12 m | Ready In: 57 m

Ingredients

- 3 large zucchini
- 1/4 cup chicken stock
- 2 1/2 tablespoons tamarind paste
- 2 tablespoons low-sodium soy sauce
- 2 tablespoons oyster sauce
- 1 1/2 tablespoons Asian chile pepper sauce
- 1 tablespoon Worcestershire sauce
- 1 tablespoon fresh lime juice
- 1 tablespoon white sugar
- 2 tablespoons sesame oil
- 1 tablespoon chopped garlic
- 12 ounces skinless, boneless chicken breasts, cut into 1-inch cubes
- 8 ounces peeled and deveined shrimp
- 2 eggs, beaten
- 2 tablespoons water, or as needed (optional)

- 3 cups bean sprouts, divided 6 green onions, chopped into 1-inch pieces
- 2 tablespoons chopped unsalted dry-roasted peanuts
- 1/4 cup chopped fresh basil

Directions

1. Make zucchini noodles using a spiralizer.
2. Whisk chicken stock, tamarind paste, soy sauce, oyster sauce, chile pepper sauce, Worcestershire sauce, lime juice, and sugar together in a small bowl to make a smooth sauce.
3. Heat sesame oil in a wok or large skillet over high heat. Add garlic and stir until fragrant, about 10 seconds. Add chicken and shrimp; cook and stir until chicken is no longer pink in the center and the juices run clear, 5 to 7 minutes.
4. Push chicken and shrimp to the sides of the wok to make a space in the center. Pour eggs and scramble until firm, 2 to 3 minutes. Add zucchini noodles and sauce; cook and stir, adding water if needed, about 3 minutes. Add 2 cups bean sprouts and green onions; cook and stir until combined, 1 to 2 minutes.
5. Remove wok from heat and sprinkle peanuts over noodles. Serve garnished with remaining 1 cup bean sprouts and fresh basil.

Nutritional Information

- Calories:370 kcal 19%
- Fat: 14.5 g 22%
- Carbs: 28.1g 9%
- Protein: 35.6 g 71%
- Cholesterol: 222 mg 74%
- Sodium: 671 mg 27%

Zucchini Noodles with Chicken, Feta and Spinach

Prep Time: 5 minutes | **Cook Time:** 10 minutes | **Total Time:** 15 minutes | **Servings:** 1

Ingredients

- 2-3 chicken breast tenderloins (strips), cut into chunks
- salt and pepper, to taste

- pinch of red pepper flakes
- 1/2 tsp garlic powder
- juice of half a lemon
- 1 packed cup of spinach
- 1 large zucchini, Blade C
- 5 small cubes of feta cheese (less than 1/4 cup)

Directions

1. Place a large skillet over medium heat. Coat with cooking spray and add in your chicken. Season with salt and pepper and let cook for about 3 minutes and then flip over, cooking another 3-5 minutes or until the chicken is cooked through. Then, add in the lemon juice, spinach, zucchini and garlic powder. Let cook, tossing frequently, until spinach is wilted and zucchini noodles soften, about 3 minutes.
2. When done, use pasta tongs to transfer to a bowl. Season with pepper, top with feta and enjoy!

Zucchini Noodles with Creamy Avocado Lime Cilantro Dressing, Corn and Tomatoes

Prep time: 15 mins | Cook time: 5 mins | Total time: 20 mins | Serves: 2

Ingredients

For the sauce:

- 1 lime, juiced
- 1 ripe avocado, peeled and pitted
- 2 tablespoons chopped cilantro
- 1 teaspoon minced jalapeno
- 1 small clove of garlic, minced
- water to thin, if needed
- salt and pepper
- For the rest:
- 2 teaspoons olive oil
- 1 medium ear of corn, kernels shaved off
- ½ teaspoon chili powder
- salt and pepper, to taste
- 2 medium zucchinis, Blade D, noodles trimmed

- 1 cup halved cherry tomatoes

Directions

1. Heat the oil in a medium skillet over medium-high heat. Once oil is shimmering, add the corn and season with salt, pepper, and chili powder. Cook for 5 minutes or until corn is cooked through and fork tender. Set aside when done.
2. Place all of the ingredients for the sauce into a food processor and pulse until creamy. Taste and adjust, if needed.
3. Place your zucchini noodles into a bowl, pour over the creamy sauce and mix to combine thoroughly.
4. Divide the dressed noodles into two to three plates and top with corn and tomatoes.

Zucchini Noodles with Fire Roasted Tomato and Crunchy Almond Pesto

Prep Time: 15 minutes | Cook Time: 10 minutes | Total Time: 25 minutes | Servings:
4

Ingredients

For the pasta:

- 4 medium zucchinis, peeled, Blade C
- For the pesto sauce:
- 1/4 cup slivered almonds
- 1/4 cup extra-virgin olive oil
- 14 ounce can diced fire-roasted tomatoes, drained
- 1/2 cup fresh basil leaves
- 3 teaspoons red wine vinegar
- ¼ cup freshly grated Parmesan cheese
- salt, to taste
- 1 small pinch crushed red pepper flakes

Directions

1. Place a large skillet over medium-high heat and once heated, add in the almonds, stirring frequently, until golden and fragrant, 3-5 minutes. Allow them to cool slightly.

2. Transfer the almonds to a food processor and process until ground into chunks. Set aside in a small bowl and then, in the same food processor, add in the olive oil, tomatoes, basil, vinegar, cheese, salt and crushed red pepper. Pulse until creamy, add in the almonds and then pulse lightly until combined.
3. If you'd like to have this raw: just serve zucchini noodles, topped with pesto sauce!
4. If you'd like to have this cooked: place a medium pot over medium-high heat and add in the pesto. Cook the pesto, stirring occasionally, until heated through, about 3-5 minutes.
5. While pesto heats, place a large non-stick skillet over medium-high heat. Once heated, coat with cooking spray and add the zucchini noodles. Toss until al dente, 2-3 minutes, or until cooked to your preference.
6. Serve the zucchini noodles topped with the pesto sauce.

Zucchini Pasta alla "Skinny Jeans" Vodka with Grilled Chicken

Prep Time: 5 minutes | Cook Time: 20 minutes | Total Time: 25 minutes | Servings: 2

Ingredients

- 1.5 zucchinis, Blade A
- 1.5 garlic cloves, minced
- salt and pepper
- olive oil
- 14oz can of diced tomatoes
- 1/2 medium red onion, chopped
- 1 tbsp red pepper flakes
- 1-2 boneless chicken breasts, grilled
- 1/4 cup of vodka (I used Tito's)
- 3 tbsp 2% Greek yogurt (I used Fage brand)
- 1/3 cup Parmesan cheese and more for topping*
- 1/3 cup chopped Italian flat leaf parsley
- 2 tsp dried oregano flakes

Directions

1. Place a large skillet over medium heat and add in two glugs of olive oil, seasoned with salt and pepper. Once oil heats, add in garlic and cook for 1 minute. Then, add in red pepper flakes and red onion. Cook by stirring

frequently until onions are translucent and softened. Add in Earth Balance butter and stir to melt.

2. Crush your can of diced tomatoes by placing them in a food processor and pulsing a few times until crushed. Add to the skillet and season with salt, pepper and the oregano flakes. Stir to combine, remove from heat and then add in vodka. Simmer for about 10 minutes or until the liquid is almost all absorbed.
3. Add in Greek yogurt, Parmesan cheese and stir to combine and cook for 1 minute. The sauce should turn a more pinkish color.
4. Add the zucchini pasta to the sauce, stir to combine and then add in the chicken, continuing to stir to combine. Let cook for about 1-2 minutes or until zucchini pasta starts to absorb sauce and softens. Stir in a few pinches of chopped parsley.
5. Plate onto two dishes and top with Parmesan cheese (optional) and more chopped parsley!

Zucchini Pasta Alla Norma

Prep time: 25 mins | Cook time: 20 mins | Total time: 45 mins | Serves: 2

Ingredients

- 3 tablespoons extra virgin olive oil
- 2 cups diced eggplant
- salt and pepper, to taste
- 1 tablespoon chopped garlic
- ¼ teaspoon red pepper flakes
- 1 14.5 oz can diced tomatoes
- 1 teaspoon dried oregano flakes
- 2 tablespoons pine nuts
- 2 medium zucchinis, Blade D, noodles trimmed
- 1 tablespoon chopped fresh parsley

Directions

1. Place a large skillet over medium heat and add in the olive oil. Once oil heats, add in the eggplant and season with salt and pepper. Cook until eggplant is browned and soft. When done, transfer to a plate (do not line with paper towels.)
2. In the same skillet, add in garlic and red pepper flakes and let cook for 30 seconds or until fragrant. Then, add in the tomatoes and then season with

oregano, salt and pepper. Lower heat to a simmer and let cook for 10 minutes. Right when the sauce is done, fold in the eggplant.

3. Meanwhile, place a small skillet over medium-high heat. Once the skillet heats, add in the pine nuts and let cook for 3 minutes or until golden brown, shaking the pan to ensure the nuts don't burn. When done, set aside.

4. Five minutes into cooking the sauce, add another large skillet over medium-high heat and coat with cooking spray. Once the pan is heated, add in the zucchini noodles and let cook, tossing occasionally, for 3-5 minutes or until cooked to your preference.

5. Plate the noodles into bowls and top with equal amounts of sauce. Garnish with parsley and pine nuts

Zucchini Pasta Made for Men

Prep Time: *10 minutes* | **Cook Time:** *25 minutes* |**Total Time**: *35 minutes* | **Servings:** *1*

Ingredients

For the pasta:

- 1 zucchini, Blade C
- 3/4 cup marinara sauce OR 1 cup of my tomato basil sauce (below)
- 1 egg, beaten
- 1 piece of whole wheat bread
- 1/4 tsp oregano flakes
- 1/4 tsp garlic powder
- salt and pepper, to taste
- 1 chicken breast
- 1 long ball of mozzarella cheese
- cooking spray
- 3 tbsp grated Parmesan cheese

For the tomato basil sauce (makes 1 cup)

- 1/3 cup of chopped onions
- 1 (14oz) can of diced tomatoes, no salt added
- 1 pinch of red pepper flakes
- 2 tsp oregano flakes
- salt and pepper to taste
- 1 tbsp olive oil

- 1 clove of garlic, minced
- 1/3 cup loosely packed basil

Directions

1. Preheat the oven to 405 degrees.
2. Place your piece of bread into a food processor and pulse into breadcrumbs. Pour into a bowl and season with the oregano, garlic powder and then salt and pepper to taste. Take out a baking dish or tray and pour the breadcrumbs onto the tray. Add in Parmesan cheese and mix thoroughly to combine. Set aside.
3. Start your sauce. Place a large skillet over medium heat and pour in olive oil. Once oil heats, add in garlic. Cook for 30 seconds and then add in red pepper flakes. Cook for 10 seconds and then add in onions. Cook, stirring frequently, for about 2 minutes or until onions begin to soften and are translucent. Add in diced tomatoes, oregano and season with salt and pepper. Crush tomatoes with a potato crusher, stir and lower heat. Simmer for 15 minutes.
4. Coat a baking dish with cooking spray. Dredge your chicken in the beaten egg then dip in the breadcrumb-Parmesan mixture. Dip on both sides and pat breadcrumbs into any crevices on the chicken breast. Place on the baking tray and put into the oven for 17-20 minutes, depending on how thick the chicken breast (thicker = longer).
5. Continue to simmer the tomato sauce until all the juice is absorbed, adding in the basil at the end. Once done, reserve half of the sauce and keep the rest in the skillet, but turn off the heat.
6. After the chicken is done, take out, pour on the half cup of tomato basil sauce, top with mozzarella slice and place back in the oven for 5 minutes or until the cheese melts and starts to lightly brown on top.
7. While the chicken is cooking for the last 5 minutes, turn the skillet back on, throw in the zucchini spaghetti, and toss to combine, cooking for 3 minutes or until zucchini softens and sauce is heated. Place the zucchini pasta down on a plate and set aside.
8. Top the pasta with the chicken parmesan and enjoy.

Zucchini Pasta Primavera

Prep Time: 15 minutes | *Cook Time:* 20 minutes | *Total Time:* 35 minutes | *Servings:*
3

Ingredients

- 1.5 cup broccoli florets
- 1 tablespoon extra virgin olive oil
- 3 teaspoons minced garlic
- ¼ teaspoon red pepper flakes (or just a pinch)
- 1 cup cherry tomatoes, halved
- ½ small red onion, peeled, thinly sliced
- 1/2 cup defrosted green peas
- 1 bell pepper, seeds and top removed, thinly sliced
- salt and pepper, to taste
- 2 tablespoons freshly chopped parsley
- 2 medium zucchinis, Blade C
- 2 medium carrots, peeled and then shaved with a vegetable peeler
- 2 tablespoons lemon juice
- 1/2 cup grated parmesan cheese + more to garnish

Directions

1. Bring a medium pot filled halfway with lightly salted water to a boil. Once boiling, add in the broccoli and cook for 2 minutes or until tender but still crunchy. Drain into a colander, pat dry and set aside.
2. Place a large skillet over medium heat and add in the olive oil. Once the oil heats, add in the garlic, red pepper flakes and onions. Cook the onions for 2-3 minutes or until translucent. Then, add in the tomatoes, green peas and bell pepper and season with salt and pepper. Cook for about 3 minutes or until the bell pepper softens.
3. Add in the zucchini noodles, carrot shavings, lemon juice and parsley and toss for 2-3 minutes or until the zucchini noodles are al dente.
4. Add in the broccoli and parmesan cheese and toss completely to spread the cheese.
5. Plate into bowls and top with additional parmesan cheese, to garnish.

Zucchini Pasta Tower with Lentils, Escarole and a Fried Egg

Prep Time: 5 minutes | Cook Time: 40 minutes | Total Time: 45 minutes | Servings: 2

Ingredients

- 1.5 large zucchinis, Blade C

- 2 eggs
- olive oil, salt and pepper
- 1/3 - 1/2 cup of Parmesan Reggiano, grated (optional)
- 2 tsp red pepper flakes
- 1/2 cup lentils, cooked
- 8-10 leaves of escarole
- 2 garlic cloves, minced
- 3/4 cup vegetable broth

Directions

1. Cook your lentils according to package directions. Typically, cooking lentils takes about 30 minutes, so take this into consideration when timing this meal. Set aside when done.
2. Rinse off your escarole. Once rinsed, tear off the leaves you're using (about 8-10 - they wilt just like spinach!) Chop off the hard white parts on the bottom. Once done, set aside.
3. Once the lentils are finished and set aside, place a large skillet over medium heat and place in 2-3 glugs of olive oil and season with salt and pepper. Once oil heats, add in garlic and cook for 1 minute, stirring frequently so that the garlic doesn't have a chance to brown. Add in the red pepper flakes, stir for 30 seconds, and then add in your escarole. Cook for about 1 minute and once it begins to wilt, add in zucchini pasta and vegetable broth.
4. Cook for about 2-3 minutes or until zucchini begins to soften. While cooking, place a medium skillet on medium-low heat and add in a (small) glug of olive oil. Crack two eggs into the pan and make sure they are on separate sides of the skillet. Season with salt and pepper, cover, and cook for about 2-3 minutes or until just about "eggs over medium."
5. While eggs are cooking, pour your finished cooked zucchini pasta into a bowl and mix in Parmesan Reggiano cheese.*
6. Then, divide onto two plates evenly and top with 1/4 cup each of lentils and of course.... a fried egg! Enjoy your pasta tower....

Zucchini Pasta with Roasted Red Pepper Sauce and Chicken

"Zucchini subs in for traditional pasta in this great veggie-rich dish.

Servings: 2| **Prep:** 1 h | **Cook:** 30 m | **Ready In:** 1 h 30 m

Ingredients

- 6 roma tomatoes
- 3 red bell peppers, chopped
- 1 large sweet onion, halved
- 3 tablespoons extra-virgin olive oil
- 4 cloves garlic
- 1 (28 ounce) can crushed tomatoes
- 1 cup tightly packed fresh basil leaves, chopped
- salt and ground black pepper to taste
- 2 yellow summer squash, cut into spirals using a spiral slicer
- 2 zucchini, cut into spirals using a spiral slicer
- 2 cooked chicken breast halves, cubed
- 1 tablespoon grated Parmesan cheese, or to taste

Directions

1. Preheat grill for medium heat and lightly oil the grate.
2. Grill tomatoes, bell peppers, and onion halves on the preheated grill until well charred, about 15 minutes. When peppers are cool enough to handle, split with a knife and remove seeds.
3. Heat olive oil in a large skillet; cook and stir garlic until fragrant, about 1 minute. Stir canned crushed tomatoes, basil, grilled tomatoes, bell peppers, and onion into skillet; bring to a boil, reduce heat, and simmer until vegetables are tender, about 10 minutes. Puree vegetable mixture with a stick blender; season with salt and pepper and keep at a simmer.
4. Bring a large pot of water to a boil; drop in summer squash and zucchini spirals and cook until tender, about 3 minutes. Drain water from pot; lay spirals on paper towels to drain completely.
5. Place squash spirals on individual plates; top with a portion of cooked chicken, a generous amount of red pepper sauce, and Parmesan cheese.

Nutritional Information

- Calories:352 kcal 18%
- Fat: 16 g 25%
- Carbs: 33.4g 11%
- Protein: 23.3 g 47%
- Cholesterol: 42 mg 14%
- Sodium: 369 mg 15%

Zucchini Spaghetti alla Marinara

"This is a great gluten-free, grain-free, and uncooked recipe. Add cheese of your choice, if desired."

Servings: *4* | **Prep:** *15 m* | **Ready In:** *27 m*

Ingredients

Marinara Sauce:

- 2 ripe tomatoes, chopped
- 1/2 (8 ounce) can tomato paste
- 1/2 cup water, or as needed
- 2 tablespoons simple syrup
- 2 tablespoons chopped garlic
- 2 tablespoons balsamic vinegar
- 1 tablespoon olive oil
- 1 teaspoon sea salt
- Spaghetti: 4 zucchini, peeled and spiralized

Directions

1. Blend tomatoes, tomato paste, water, simple syrup, garlic, balsamic vinegar, olive oil, and sea salt together in a high-speed blender until smooth. Add more water if sauce is too thick.
2. Place spiralized zucchini in a bowl; add sauce and toss to coat.

Nutritional Information

- Calories:125 kcal 6%
- Fat: 4 g 6%
- Carbs: 21.6g 7%
- Protein: 4.4 g 9%
- Cholesterol: 0 mg 0%
- Sodium: 690 mg 28%

Zucchini Spaghetti and Quinoa Crusted Chicken Parmesan Meatballs

Prep Time: 15 minutes | *Cook Time:* 1 hour | *Total Time:* 1 hour, 15 minutes |
Servings: 4

Ingredients

- 2/3 cup cooked quinoa
- 1/4 cup dijon mustard
- olive oil cooking spray
- 1 tablespoon extra virgin olive oil
- 1 large garlic clove, minced
- 1 pinch of red pepper flakes
- 2 teaspoons of dried oregano flakes
- 2 14.5oz cans of crushed tomatoes
- 1 tablespoon tomato paste
- salt and pepper, to taste
- ¼ cup shredded mozzarella cheese
- 3 medium zucchinis, Blade C, noodles trimmed

For the meatballs:

- 1 pound ground chicken
- 4 tablespoons finely minced parsley + more to garnish
- 2 tablespoons grated parmesan cheese + more to garnish
- salt and pepper, to taste
- 1 teaspoon garlic powder
- 1 tablespoon dried oregano flakes
- 1 tablespoon dried basil flakes
- 1/2 cup finely chopped white onion

Directions

1. Preheat the oven to 300 degrees. Spread the cooked quinoa out on a parchment lined baking sheet. Bake the quinoa for 25-30 minutes. Let cool and then transfer to a mixing bowl, breaking up any clumps. Afterwards, immediately, set the oven to 425 degrees.
2. While the quinoa is baking, place all of the ingredients for the meatballs together in a mixing bowl and mix until combined. Form 10-12 golf sized meatballs from the mixture and set aside on a plate.
3. Once the quinoa is done cooking, lightly coat the meatballs with the mustard and then dip the meatballs in the quinoa, coating well on all sides. Place the prepped meatballs back on a baking tray with a new sheet of parchment paper.
4. Spritz the meatballs with cooking spray and bake until cooked through, 15-20 minutes.

5. While the meatballs are baking, place a large skillet over medium heat and add in the olive oil. Once the oil heats, add in the garlic and red pepper flakes and cook for 30 seconds or until fragrant. Then, add in the crushed tomatoes, tomato paste, oregano and season with salt and pepper. Cook for 10-15 minutes or until sauce fully reduces. Once done, set aside.

6. Once the meatballs are done (around same time as sauce) set aside and immediately set the oven to a high broil. Place about a teaspoon of the sauce on top of each meatball. Then, sprinkle the tops of the meatballs with the mozzarella cheese (the sauce should help the mozzarella keep in place) and place back into the oven. Cook for 1 minute or just until the cheese melts.

7. Plate the zucchini noodles into bowls and top with equal amounts of sauce and top finally with meatballs (3 meatballs per plate). Garnish with additional parmesan cheese and parsley.

Zucchini Spaghetti and Sriracha Fried Eggs

Prep Time: 5 minutes | *Cook Time:* 7 minutes | *Total Time:* 13 minutes | *Servings:* 1

Ingredients

- 1 large zucchini, Blade C
- 1 tbsp olive oil
- salt and pepper, to taste
- sriracha, to drizzle
- 2 pinches of red pepper flakes (or one, if you don't like spicy!)
- 2 tsp grated Parmesan cheese & more to garnish
- 2 eggs
- 1-2 tsp garlic powder
- 1/2 piece of whole wheat bread
- olive oil cooking spray

Directions

1. Place bread in food processor and pulse into breadcrumbs. Set aside.
2. Place a small skillet on medium-high heat and place in half of the tbsp of olive oil. Once heated, add in the breadcrumbs and cook, stirring frequently for about 2-3 minutes or until crumbs are "toasted." Set aside.
3. Put a large skillet on medium heat and coat with cooking spray. Add in the zucchini pasta and season generously with salt and pepper. Toss to combine and then add in red pepper flakes and garlic powder. Cook for

about 2-3 minutes or until zucchini softens. Place onto a plate, sprinkle with the Parmesan cheese and set aside.

4. While the zucchini spaghetti is cooking, place a medium skillet over medium heat and add in the other half tbsp of olive oil. Once heated, crack the eggs into the skillet, trying to keep them separate. They will flow into one another, so when they begin to set, divide with your spatula. Let cook for about 2-3 minutes or until eggs are fried but yolks are still runny (the whites should be fully set).

5. Place the fried eggs on top of the zucchini spaghetti and garnish with the Parmesan cheese and top with breadcrumbs.

Zucchini Spaghetti with Gluten-Free Vegetarian Meatballs

Prep time: 20 mins | Cook time: 1 hour 10 mins | Total time: 1 hour 30 mins | Serves: 4

Ingredients

For the meatballs:

- 1 cup lentils
- 1 tablespoon extra virgin olive oil + more to drizzle (about ½ tablespoon)
- ½ red onion, chopped
- 1 carrot, chopped
- 1 celery stalk, chopped
- 1 garlic clove, minced
- ½ teaspoon dried thyme
- salt and pepper, to taste
- 1 pinch red pepper flakes
- 1.5 tablespoons tomato paste
- 4 ounces button mushrooms, sliced
- 1 egg + 1 egg white
- ¼ cup grated Parmesan cheese + more to garnish
- ¼ cup chopped fresh parsley
- 2 tablespoons finely chopped walnuts

For the breadcrumbs (makes about ¼ cup):

- 4 tablespoons almond flour
- 2 tablespoon water
- For the pasta:
- 4 medium zucchinis

- 1.5 cups favorite canned tomato sauce (I love Rao's Tomato Basil sauce)

Directions

1. Combine the lentils and 4 cups of water in a medium stockpot and bring to a boil over high heat. Reduce the heat to low and simmer until the lentils are soft but not falling apart, about 20 minutes. Drain the lentils and allow to cool.
2. Meanwhile, add the olive oil to a large skillet and cook the onions, carrots, celery, garlic, thyme and season with salt and pepper over medium-high heat, stirring frequently, for about 7 minutes, until the vegetables are tender and just beginning to brown. Add the tomato paste and continue to cook, stirring constantly, for 3 minutes. Add the mushrooms and cook, stirring frequently, for 15 more minutes, or until all the liquid is absorbed. Transfer the mixture to a large bowl and allow to cool to room temperature. When cool, add the lentils to the vegetable mixture.
3. In a small mixing bowl, add in the almond flour and water and massage with hands until dough-like. Place a medium skillet over medium-high heat and once heated, add in the dough, crumbling into pieces with your fingers. Break the dough up with a wooden spoon or spatula and let toast until breadcrumb-like, yielding about ¼ cup. Set aside.
4. Add the eggs, Parmesan, prepared breadcrumbs, parsley and walnuts to the cooled vegetables and lentils and mix by hand until thoroughly incorporated. Place in the refrigerator for 25 minutes. Preheat the oven to 400 degrees.
5. Drizzle the olive oil into a baking dish and use your hand to evenly coat the entire surface. Set aside.
6. Roll the mixture into round golf ball-size meatballs (about 1½ inches), making sure to pack the vegetable mixture firmly. Place the balls in the prepared baking dish, in rows.
7. Roast the meatballs for 30 minutes, or until the meatballs are firm and cooked through. Allow the meatballs to cool for 5 minutes in the baking dish before serving.
8. Meanwhile, spiralize the zucchinis with Blade D and trim the noodles. Set aside.
9. Ten minutes before the meatballs are done roasting, place a large skillet over medium heat and once heated, add in half of the zucchini noodles. Cook for 3 minutes or until cooked to your preferences. Set aside in a large mixing bowl and then cook the remaining zucchini noodles.
10. Meanwhile, place a medium pot over medium-high heat and add in the tomato sauce. Cook to heat up, about 5 minutes. Place at a simmer until ready to use.
11. Once zucchini noodles, sauce and meatballs are cooked, prepare your bowls. Divide the zucchini into four bowls, top with equal amounts of sauce and then top with 3 meatballs each. Top with parmesan cheese.

Zucchini Spaghetti With Parsley, Tuna and Lemon

Prep time: 10 mins | *Cook time:* 10 mins | *Total time:* 20 mins | *Serves:* 2

Ingredients

- 2 tablespoons extra virgin olive oil
- 1 garlic clove, minced
- 1 pinch red pepper flakes
- 2 medium zucchinis, Blade D, noodles trimmed
- 2 tablespoons freshly chopped parsley
- ½ lemon juiced + zest
- 3 oz canned tuna in water
- ¼ cup pitted and halved kalamata (or other) olives

Directions

1. Heat the olive oil in a large skillet over medium heat. Once heated, add in the garlic, red pepper flakes and let cook until fragrant, about 30 seconds. Add in the zucchini noodles and cook for 3-5 minutes or until al dente/cooked to your preference.
2. Once cooked, stir in the parsley, lemon juice/zest, tuna and olives. Toss to combine and heat up the tuna.
3. Serve.

Zucchini Spaghetti, Crispy Prosciutto and Roasted Cauliflower with Lemon-Parmesan Sauce

Prep Time: 5 minutes | *Cook Time:* 25 minutes | *Total Time:* 30 minutes | *Servings:* 2-3

Ingredients

- 2 cups cauliflower florets
- 1 tablespoon extra virgin olive oil
- 1/4 teaspoon garlic powder

- salt and pepper, to taste
- 2 garlic cloves
- 1 large shallot
- olive oil cooking spray
- 4 pieces of prosciutto
- 1 tablespoon extra virgin olive oil
- 1 pinch red pepper flakes
- 2 medium zucchinis
- 1 tablespoon minced parsley, to garnish

For the lemon dressing:

- 1/4 teaspoon lemon zest
- 1.5 teaspoons lemon juice
- 1/4 cup plain non-fat Greek yogurt
- 1.5 tablespoons grated Parmesan cheese
- salt and pepper, to taste

Directions

1. Preheat the oven to 450 degrees. Line a baking tray with parchment paper and set aside.
2. Toss the cauliflower in a medium bowl with the olive oil, garlic powder and season with salt and pepper. Lay the cauliflower out on the prepared baking tray and roast for 20 minutes or until easily pierced with a fork and lightly browned.
3. While the cauliflower is roasting, combine all of the ingredients for the lemon dressing and set aside. Mince the garlic and shallot and set aside. Spiralize the zucchini, using Blade C and trim the noodles.
4. Place a large skillet over medium heat and coat with cooking spray. Lay in the prosciutto slices and cook for 3-5 minutes or until crispy. Transfer to a paper towel lined plate and set aside.
5. Allow the skillet to cool down for at least 2 minutes and then place the skillet back over medium heat and add in the olive oil. Once oil heats, add in the garlic, shallots and red pepper flakes. Cook for 30 seconds or until fragrant and then add in the zucchini noodles.
6. Cook, tossing frequently, for 3-5 minutes or until zucchini noodles are al dente. Add in the cauliflower and crumble the prosciutto over the skillet, with your fingers. Give a toss and then remove from heat and stir in the Greek yogurt mixture. Toss to combine thoroughly and divide into bowls. Sprinkle with parsley, to garnish.

Zucchini Spaghetti

"Fooled my husband into eating his vegetables. When fully cooked, the texture is like an al dente pasta. You can turn this vegetarian by omitting the ground beef."

***Servings**: 3 | **Prep**: 10 m | **Cook**: 20 m | **Ready In**: 30 m*

Ingredients

- 1 pound ground beef
- 1 teaspoon ground black pepper
- 1 (15 ounce) can tomato sauce
- 1 (14.5 ounce) can whole peeled tomatoes
- 1 tablespoon salt, or more to taste
- 1 teaspoon dried basil
- 1/2 teaspoon dried oregano
- 1/2 teaspoon garlic powder
- 1/2 teaspoon onion powder
- 1/4 teaspoon ground thyme
- 1/4 teaspoon red pepper flakes
- 1 (6 ounce) can tomato paste
- 3 zucchini, cut into long strands

Directions

1. Heat a large skillet over medium-high heat. Cook and stir beef and black pepper in the hot skillet until browned and crumbly, 5 to 7 minutes; drain and discard grease.
2. Mix tomato sauce, tomatoes, salt, basil, oregano, garlic powder, onion powder, thyme, and red pepper flakes into ground beef; cook and stir until sauce is warmed through, about 2 minutes. Stir tomato paste into sauce.
3. Mix zucchini "noodles" into sauce, pressing down to fully submerge them; simmer over medium-low heat until zucchini is tender, about 10 minutes.

Nutritional Information

- Calories:449 kcal 22%
- Fat: 24.6 g 38%
- Carbs: 29.4g 9%
- Protein: 32.1 g 64%
- Cholesterol: 93 mg 31%

- Sodium: 3801 mg 152%

Chapter 9: Soup

***

BBQ Pork Turnip Noodle "Ramen" for Two

***Prep Time:** 2 hours | **Cook Time:** 30 minutes | **Total Time:** 2 hours 30 minutes | Servings: 2*

Ingredients

For the pork:

- 1 large garlic clove, minced
- 1/2 inch fresh ginger
- 1 scallion, diced
- ½ pound pork tenderloin (ask butcher)
- 2 tablespoons low-sodium soy sauce
- 1.5 tablespoons dry sherry
- 1/4 teaspoon Chinese Five-Spice
- 1/2 tablespoon honey

For the ramen:

- 3 scallions, diced + 1 scallion diced for garnish
- 1 inch piece of ginger, peeled and minced
- 2 garlic cloves, halved
- ½ tablespoon extra virgin olive oil
- 4 cups chicken stock
- 1 large egg
- 1.5 tablespoons low-sodium soy sauce
- 1.5 oz champignon mushrooms
- 2-2.5oz snap peas
- 1 large turnip or 2 medium turnips, Blade C, noodles trimmed
- 1 medium carrot, peeled, Blade C, noodles trimmed
- cilantro leaves, to garnish

Instructions

1. In a Ziploc bag or shallow dish, mix the garlic, ginger, green onions, soy sauce, sherry, Chinese Five-Spice, ½ tablespoon of the honey, and pork. Seal the bag or cover the pan and marinate, refrigerated for at least 2 hours. Shake the bag to mix up the marinade occasionally.
2. Preheat the oven to 450 degrees. Place a cast iron skillet (or oven-safe skillet) into the oven as you set it to preheat to heat for about 15 minutes.

Once heated, remove with oven mitts and add in the pork, place back in the oven and let cook for 10 minutes. Remove from the oven, baste with any pan juices and then let cook for another 10-15 minutes. The pork is done when the internal temperature is 140-145 degrees. Remove from the oven, tent with foil and let rest for a least 10 minutes before you slice it thinly.

3. While pork roasts, hard boil the eggs: in a small pot, add in the eggs and cover with about ½-1" of water and bring to a boil. Once boiling, cover and let cook for 12 minutes. Run under cold water gently and then once ready to handle, peel eggs and halve.

4. While pork roasts and eggs boil, place a large pot over medium-high heat and add in olive oil. Once heated, add in the scallions, ginger and garlic and cook for 1 minute or until fragrant. Then, pour in the chicken stock, cover and bring to the boil, then simmer, covered for about 10 minutes. Then, add in the soy sauce and mushrooms, letting cook for 1-2 minutes. Then, add the snap peas and turnip noodles and cook for 2-3 more minutes or until noodles are cooked to al dente or your preference.

5. Using pasta tongs, carefully transfer the noodles to two serving bowls and ladle over with the broth mixture. Top with the sliced barbecue pork and half an egg each. Garnish with carrot noodles and then cilantro, if desired.

Butternut Squash Noodle Soup with Turkey

"Using spiralized butternut squash as an alternative to pasta, this soup is loaded with fall flavors and gets its smoky spiciness from ground chipotle. The ideal soup to warm you up on cold winter days. Perfect for using up leftover turkey."

*Servings: 8 | **Prep:** 20 m | **Cook:** 28 m | **Ready In:** 48 m*

Ingredients

- 6 cups low-sodium chicken broth
- 3 ribs celery, chopped
- 1/2 white onion, chopped
- 1 teaspoon chopped garlic
- 3/4 teaspoon Mexican oregano
- 1/4 teaspoon ground chipotle chile pepper, or to taste
- 3/4 butternut squash, peeled and cut into noodle shapes
- 2 cups diced cooked turkey
- 1 teaspoon chopped fresh cilantro, or more to taste

Directions

1. Combine chicken broth, celery, onion, garlic, Mexican oregano, and ground chipotle in a large pot; bring to a boil. Cover and reduce heat; simmer until vegetables are softened, about 20 minutes.
2. Stir butternut squash and turkey into the broth mixture; simmer until turkey is heated through, 3 to 5 minutes. Garnish with cilantro.

Nutritional Information

- Calories:125 kcal 6%
- Fat: 2.2 g 3%
- Carbs: 13.4g 4%
- Protein: 13.9 g 28%
- Cholesterol: 30 mg 10%
- Sodium: 132 mg 5%

Chicken Zoodle Soup

"With the winter months approaching fast my niece and I co-conspired to come up with this warm and comforting soup using 'zoodles' that's easy on the waistline."

Servings: *6 |* **Prep:** *20 m |* **Cook:** *25 m |* **Ready In**: *45 m*

Ingredients

- 2 tablespoons olive oil
- 1 cup diced onions
- 1 cup diced celery
- 3 cloves garlic, minced
- 5 (14.5 ounce) cans low-sodium chicken broth
- 1 cup sliced carrots
- 3/4 pound cooked chicken breast, cut into bite sized pieces
- 1/2 teaspoon dried basil
- 1/2 teaspoon dried oregano
- 1 pinch dried thyme (optional) salt and ground black pepper to taste
- 3 zucchini squash, cut into 'noodles' using a spiral slicer or vegetable peele

Directions

1. Heat olive oil in a large pot over medium-high heat. Saute onion, celery, and garlic in hot oil until just tender, about 5 minutes.
2. Pour chicken broth into the pot; add carrots, chicken, basil, oregano, thyme, salt, and pepper. Bring the broth to a boil, reduce heat to medium-low, and simmer mixture until the vegetables are tender, about 20 minutes.
3. Divide zucchini 'noodles' between six soup bowls; ladle broth mixture over the 'noodles.'

Nutritional Information

- Calories:208 kcal 10%
- Fat: 9.5 g 15%
- Carbs: 8.9g 3%
- Protein: 21.6 g 43%
- Cholesterol: 48 mg 16%
- Sodium: 257 mg 10%

Creamy Roasted Tomato Basil Zucchini Noodle Soup with Kale Chips

Prep Time: *7 minutes* | **Cook Time:** *25 minutes* | **Total Time:** *32 minutes* | **Servings:** *2*

Ingredients

For the kale chips:

- olive oil, for drizzling
- 1/8 tsp of garlic powder
- sea salt grinder
- 3-4 pieces of kale
- For the soup:
- 1 zucchini, Blade A
- 1 tbsp olive oil + more olive oil for drizzling
- pepper grinder, to taste
- 1/4 tsp red pepper flakes (or more, if you like spice)
- 2 garlic cloves, minced
- 6 tsp finely chopped basil
- 1/2 cup chopped red onions

- 10 campari tomatoes
- 1 cup vegetable broth, low-sodium
- 2 tbsp 0% non-fat plain Greek Yogurt (Chobani, preferably)
- 2 slices of crusty whole grain bread, optional (for dipping)

Instructions

1. Preheat the oven to 375 degrees.
2. Slice your tomatoes in half and lay, cut sides up, on a baking tray. Drizzle with olive oil and season with salt and pepper. Roast for 20 minutes.
3. After 10 minutes of roasting the tomatoes, prepare your kale chips. Coat a baking tray with cooking spray and lay down your pieces of kale (make sure they are completely dry!)
4. Drizzle the kale lightly with olive oil and massage oil into kale leaves, with your hands.
5. Season the kale very lightly with salt and garlic powder. Use about 1-2 cranks of the sea salt grinder.
6. Place the kale into the oven for 5-7 minutes, monitoring after 4 minutes to make sure they don't burn. When ready, take out and set aside.
7. Five minutes before the tomatoes are done roasting, place a large saucepan over medium-low heat and add in the olive oil. Once oil heats, add in the garlic and red pepper flakes and cook for 1 minute.
8. Add in the onions and cook for about 1-2 minutes or until they soften. When done, pour into a food processor, along with the tomatoes (with any juices from the baking tray).
9. Pour the puree back into the large saucepan, over medium heat, and add in the vegetable broth and chopped basil. Bring soup to a boil and then let simmer for 10 minutes.
10. Add in the zucchini noodles and cook for 2 minutes.
11. Once noodles are done, stir in the Greek Yogurt and simmer for another 1 minute to let it heat in.
12. Pour the soup into bowls, top with kale chips, and serve with warmed bread (optional).

Easy Clear Onion Soup with Carrot Noodles

*Prep time: 15 mins | **Cook time:** 15 mins | **Total time:** 30 mins | **Serves:** 4*

Ingredients

- 1 large white onion, diced

- 2 teaspoons extra virgin olive oil
- salt, to taste
- 2 celery stalks, diced
- 2 garlic cloves, minced
- 6 cups water
- ¼ teaspoon ground white pepper
- 8oz button mushrooms, thinly sliced
- 1 large carrot, peeled, Blade D, noodles trimmed
- 3 scallions, diced
- salt and pepper, to taste

Instructions

1. Place a large skillet over medium heat and add in the oil. Once oil heats, add in the onions and cook for 5-7 minutes or until onions soften.
2. Add in the celery, garlic, water, pepper and bring to a boil. Once boiling, reduce heat and let simmer for 1 minute. Then, strain the vegetables from the broth and add in the mushrooms and carrot noodles.
3. Bring the heat up to a rapid simmer and let cook for 2-3 more minutes or until carrot noodles are cooked to your preference. Stir in the scallions and let simmer for 1 more minute and then divide into bowls and serve.

Garlic Ginger Zucchini Noodle Bowl with Salmon and Bok Choy

Prep Time: 3 minutes | *Cook Time:* 25 minutes | *Total Time:* 28 minutes | *Servings:* 1

Ingredients

- 1.5 zucchinis, peeled, Blade C
- 2 oz salmon, skinless
- pepper to taste
- 1/2 tbsp canola oil
- 4 stalks bok choy
- 1 small clove of garlic, minced
- 1 tsp ginger, minced
- 1 tbsp soy sauce
- 2 tsp sesame oil
- 1 cup, vegetable broth
- 1/4 cup chopped scallions

Instructions

1. Cook your salmon anyway you prefer – grill it, sautee it, poach it, steam it, bake it. While cooking, follow the remaining steps.
2. Put a large skillet on medium-high heat and add in a the canola oil.
3. Once oil is heated, add in garlic. Cook for 30 seconds and then add in minced ginger. Stir for 1 minute.
4. Cut the white stems off the bok choy, cut into 4 inch pieces and add it to the skillet, season with salt and pepper and stir around so that bok choy is coated in mixture. Stir for about 2 minutes or until bok choy begins to wilt.
5. Add in sesame oil, vegetable broth and soy sauce and stir for 1 minute.
6. Add in zucchini noodles, season with salt and pepper, and let cook uncovered for about 3-5 minutes or until liquid boils for 1 minute and zucchini noodles soften and are cooked. Right before the noodles are done, mix in the scallions.
7. Pour the noodle mixture into a large bowl and sprinkle with half of the green onions. Mix to combine.
8. Pour noodle mixture into a bowl, top with piece of salmon and garnish with remaining green onions.

Ginger Seared Salmon in Miso Broth with Jalapeno-Scallion Relish and Zucchini Noodles

Prep Time: 15 minutes | **Cook Time:** 15 minutes | **Total Time:** 30 minutes | **Servings:** 2

Ingredients

For the salmon:

- 1 tablespoon extra virgin olive oil
- 1 teaspoon crushed ginger
- 2 3oz pieces of salmon, skinless
- For the soup:
- 1-1.5 cups water
- 1-1.5 cups low sodium vegetable broth
- 1 tablespoon miso paste
- 1 teaspoon soy sauce
- 1 medium/large zucchinis, Blade C, noodles trimmed

For the relish:

- 1 tablespoon finely minced jalapeno (seeds removed)
- 3 tablespoons diced scallions
- 1 tablespoon lime juice

Instructions

1. Place the jalapeno, scallions and lime juice in a bowl and set aside in the refrigerator.
2. Season both sides of the salmon pieces with salt and pepper. Place a large skillet over medium-high heat and add in the olive oil. Once oil heats, add in the crushed ginger, stir and add in the salmon. Cook for 3 minutes, flip over, and cook another 5 minutes or until salmon flakes easily with a fork.
3. While the salmon is cooking, place a medium saucepan over high heat, add in the vegetable stock and water, and bring to a boil. Once the soup is boiling, ladle out about 1/3 cup of the soup into a bowl. In that bowl, add the miso paste and whisk until it dissolves. Pour this miso broth back into the saucepan and lower the heat to a high simmer. Add the soy sauce, zucchini noodles and pepper to the soup. Let cook for 2-3 minutes or until zucchini noodles soften to al dente or your preference.
4. Ladle the soup into two bowls, add the seared salmon and top with jalapeno-green onion relish.

Hearty & Healthy Beef Stew with Zucchini Noodles

Prep Time: *15 minutes* | **Cook Time:** *1 hour, 25 minutes* | **Total Time:** *1 hour, 40 minutes* | **Servings:** *3-4*

Ingredients

- 1 lb beef stew chunks
- 1/2 red onion, diced
- 1/4 tsp red pepper flakes
- 2 garlic cloves, minced
- 3 celery stalks, diced
- 3 carrots, peeled and diced
- 3 tbsp worcestershire sauce
- 1 tsp thyme
- 1/2 tsp cayenne pepper
- salt and pepper, to taste

- 1 (14oz) can of diced tomatoes
- 4 cups low-sodium beef broth
- 1-2 bay leaves
- 4 large zucchinis, Blade A
- freshly chopped parsley, to garnish

Instructions

1. Place a large saucepan over medium heat and add in the olive oil. Add in the beef chunks and cook until browned. Remove from the saucepan and set aside in a bowl.
2. In the juices left in the pan from the beef, add in the garlic and cook for 30 seconds. Then, add in the red onions and red pepper flakes. Cook for 1 minute and then add in the celery and carrots. Cook for 2 minutes to let the vegetables sweat and then add back in the beef chunks. Add the worcestershire sauce, thyme, and cayenne pepper and stir to combine. Then, season with salt and pepper and add in the beef broth and diced tomatoes. Place the bay leaves on top and cover to bring to a boil.
3. Once brought to a boil, lower to a simmer and cook for 40 minutes, covered. Then, remove the cover and let simmer uncovered for 35 more minutes or until the stew thickens.
4. Divide the zucchini noodles into bowls and top evenly with spoonfuls of the stew. Let the stew cook a couple minutes over the zucchini noodles and enjoy, garnished with a bit of fresh parsley!

Italian Wedding Soup with Zucchini Noodles

Prep time: 20 mins | Cook time: 25 mins | Total time: 45 mins | Serves: 6

Ingredients

For the meatballs:

- 1 pound lean ground turkey
- 1 teaspoon garlic powder
- ½ teaspoon dried basil
- ¼ teaspoon dried oregano
- 1 tablespoon freshly chopped parsley
- salt and pepper, to taste
- For the soup:
- 7 cups low-sodium chicken broth

- 1 large garlic clove, minced
- 2 medium zucchinis
- 1 egg
- salt and pepper, to taste
- 1 tablespoon freshly grated Parmesan cheese
- 1 tablespoon Pecorino Romano cheese
- ¼ teaspoon red pepper flakes
- 2 tablespoons chopped parsley

Instructions

1. Make the meatballs: combine all of the meatball ingredients into a large mixing bowl and stir together. Then, shape the meat mixture into 1-inch-diameter meatballs, about 16. Place on a baking sheet and set aside.
2. Start the soup: Bring the broth and garlic to a boil in a large pot or deep pan. Add the meatballs, lower the heat and simmer until cooked through, about 7-10 minutes.
3. While the meatballs are cooking, slice your zucchinis lengthwise halfway and then spiralize them, using Blade D.
4. Once the meatballs are about done, add in the zucchini noodles and let cook 2-3 minutes or until al dente. Then, whisk the eggs and cheese in a medium bowl to blend and season with salt and pepper. Stir the soup in a circular motion. Gradually drizzle the egg mixture into the moving broth, stirring gently with a fork to form thin stands of egg, about 1 minute. Season the soup to taste with salt and pepper.
5. Ladle the soup into bowls and serve. Finish soup with red pepper flakes and parsley.

Jalapeno-Lime Chicken, Bean & Avocado Zucchini Noodle Soup

Prep Time: 15 minutes | **Cook Time:** 30 minutes | **Total Time:** 45 minutes | **Servings:** 2

Ingredients

- 1 chicken breast
- olive oil to drizzle
- salt and pepper, to taste
- 1 tsp cumin
- 1 tsp chili powder
- 1 tsp paprika

- 1 tbsp olive oil
- 2 tsp minced garlic
- 1/3 cup diced red onion
- 1/2 pepper, seeds removed, diced
- 2 tsp freshly squeeze lime juice
- 14oz can diced tomatoes
- 1/2 cup black beans
- 3 cups chicken broth, low-sodium
- 1 tsp Mediterranean oregano (or regular oregano will work)
- 1 tbsp chopped cilantro
- 1 avocado, insides cubed
- 2 medium zucchinis, Blade C

Instructions

1. Preheat the oven to 350 degrees.
2. Place the chicken breast on a baking tray lightly coated with cooking spray. Drizzle lightly with olive oil and massage into skin. Season lightly with salt and pepper on both sides.
3. In a small bowl, mix together the cumin, chili powder and paprika. Dust both sides of the chicken with about half of the mixture. Save remaining spices and set aside.
4. Bake the chicken for 20-25 minutes, turning once. Since we'll be shredding the chicken later, test after 20 minutes to see if the chicken is cooked through. If not, cook another 2-5 minutes. Once done, set aside to cool.
5. While the chicken is cooking, heat the olive oil in a large saucepan/pot. Once the oil heats, add in the garlic and cook for 1 minute. Add in the onion and cook until the onions begin to soften, about 2 minutes.
6. Add in the jalapeno pepper and lime juice and cook for about 1 minute. Add in the tomatoes, remaining spice mixture, black beans and cook for about 2 minutes.
7. Add in the chicken broth, oregano and cover. Bring the soup to a boil and then reduce the heat to a simmer and cook for about 10-15 minutes, stirring occasionally. Half way through, add in the cilantro.
8. While the soup is simmering, take your cooked chicken and shred it with your hands and a fork.
9. When soup is done simmering, add in the shredded chicken, zucchini noodles and avocado and stir for about 2 minutes to let the avocado and zucchini soften.
10. Pour the soup into two bowls, add salt and pepper to taste and top with tortilla strips. Enjoy!

Kao Soi Gai with Zucchini Noodles

Prep time: 20 mins | *Cook time:* 30 mins | *Total time:* 50 mins | *Serves:* 4

Ingredients

For the paste:

- 5 dried red Thai chillis
- 4 garlic cloves, peeled
- 2 small shallots, peeled
- skin from ½ Kaffir lime (or regular lime)
- 3" piece of ginger, peeled and sliced
- 1.5" piece of turmeric, sliced
- 1 lemongrass stalk, tough end trimmed off and then sliced
- 1 teaspoon shrimp paste (or 1 tablespoon fish sauce)
- 1 teaspoon mild curry powder

For the curry:

- 4 pieces bone-in chicken drumsticks + 2 bone-in thighs
- (1.5) 13.5 oz cans lite coconut milk, can shaken first
- 4 cups chicken broth
- 1 tablespoon fish sauce
- 3 medium zucchinis, Blade C, noodles trimmed
- 1 large handful cilantro, lightly chopped
- ¾ cup diced scallions, green parts only
- 1 lime quartered, to garnish
- crispy noodles, optional to garnish (I omitted)

Directions

1. Soak the chilis in water for 5 minutes.
2. First, prepare the paste. There are a few ways to do this. The authentic way is with a mortar and pestle, so if you have one: smash together the lemongrass, turmeric and lime skin until they're broken down. Add the chilis (after they've been soaked) and ginger and mash until all combined. Add the garlic, shallot, and yellow curry powder and keep mashing. Finally, add the shrimp paste (or fish sauce) and mix together so there are no chunks and it's all one paste.
3. If you don't have a mortar and pestle, to make the paste: mash all of the ingredients except for the shrimp paste (or fish sauce, if that's what you're using) on a cutting board using anything you have that's heavy (meat

tenderizer works). Add this to a food processor and pulse until combined and paste-like. Remove, transfer to a bowl and stir in the fish sauce and stir well until paste-like, smashing again if needed.

4. After the paste is made, prepare the curry. Add a large pot over medium-high heat and once the pot is hot, add the coconut milk and the prepared paste. Stir to melt the paste into the coconut milk. Add the chicken, chicken broth, fish sauce, and stir the liquid. Cook the chicken until well-cooked, about 15 minutes. Remove the chicken and slice through the thickest piece to make sure it's no longer pink on the inside. If it's still pink, cook for another 5 minutes. If it's ready, add the zucchini noodles to the pot and meanwhile, shred the chicken off of the chicken thighs and some of the drumsticks (try to leave the drumsticks mostly intact.) Add the pulled meat and drumsticks back into the pan and let everything cook for 3-5 minutes or until zucchini noodles are wilted.

5. Using tongs, divide the drumsticks into four bowls and then divide the curry and noodles on top. Top with the cilantro, scallions, and if desired, the crunchy noodles.

Lentil Soup with Spiralized Turnips

Prep time: 20 mins | Cook time: 35 mins | Total time: 55 mins | Serves: 6

Ingredients

- 2 tablespoons extra virgin olive oil
- 1 medium yellow onion, diced
- 2 celery ribs, diced
- 2 carrots, peeled and diced
- salt and pepper, to taste
- 3 garlic cloves, minced
- ½ teaspoon dried basil
- 1 teaspoon dried thyme
- ½ teaspoon dried oregano
- 1 28-ounce can of diced tomatoes
- 1 cup lentils (any color but red), rinsed
- 6 cups vegetable broth
- 2 bay leaves
- ¼ - ½ teaspoon red pepper flakes (depends on how spicy you like it!)
- 2 small turnips
- 2 teaspoons freshly squeezed lemon juice

Instructions

1. Heat the oil in a large pot over medium heat.
2. Once the oil is shimmering, add the onion, celery, carrot, season with salt and pepper, and cook, stirring often, until the onion has softened, 3-5 minutes. Add the garlic, basil, thyme and oregano. Cook until fragrant while stirring constantly, about 30 seconds. Add the tomatoes and stir thoroughly to combine.
3. Add the lentils, broth, and bay leaves. Season with red pepper flakes, salt and pepper. Raise the heat to high and bring the mixture to a boil, then cover the pot partially and reduce heat to medium-low and let simmer for 20 minutes or until lentils are almost tender.
4. While the soup cooks, peel and spiralize the turnip using Blade C and trim the noodles. Set the noodles aside. After 20 minutes, remove the bay leaves, add in the turnip noodles, stir to combine and let cook for 5-7 minutes more or until lentils are fully tender and turnip noodles soften.
5. Stir in the lemon juice and serve.

Minestrone Zucchini Noodle Soup with Parmesan-Rosemary Quinn Popcorn

Prep Time: *20 minutes* | **Cook Time:** *25 minutes* | **Total Time:** *45 minutes* | **Servings:** *2*

Ingredients

- 2 tbsp olive oil
- 1 garlic clove, minced
- 1 small pinch of red pepper flakes
- 1/2 cup diced carrots
- 1/2 cup diced red onion
- 1/2 cup diced celery
- 1 (14oz) can diced tomatoes
- salt and pepper, to taste
- 1/4 tsp dried oregano
- 1/2 tsp chopped fresh rosemary
- 4 sprigs of fresh thyme
- 1/4 tsp dried basil
- 3 cups vegetable broth, low-sodium
- 1 large zucchini, Blade C
- 1/2 cup red kidney beans
- 1/2 cup cannellini beans

- 1/4 cup popped Parmesan-Rosemary Quinn Popcorn

Instructions

1. Place a large saucepan over medium heat and add in the olive oil. Once the oil heats, add in the garlic and red pepper flakes. Cook for 30 seconds and then add in the onion, carrots, and celery.
2. Cook the veggies for about 5 minutes or until they begin to soften.
3. Add in the diced tomatoes, crush lightly with the back of a fork, and season with salt, pepper, oregano, rosemary, thyme and basil. Stir to combine and add in the vegetable broth.
4. Bring the soup to a boil and then lower to simmer. Cover the saucepan and cook for 15 minutes.
5. Uncover the saucepan and add in the beans and zucchini noodles. Cook for about 3 minutes or until zucchini noodles soften.
6. Spoon into bowls, top with popcorn and enjoy!

Pesto and Chicken Sausage Soup with Zucchini Noodles

Prep time: 20 mins | Cook time: 15 mins | Total time: 35 mins | Serves: 4

Ingredients

For the soup:

- 1 tablespoon extra virgin olive oil
- 4 chicken sausage links, decased
- ¼ teaspoon red pepper flakes
- 2 cloves of garlic, minced
- ½ red onion, diced
- 2 celery stalks, diced
- salt and pepper, to taste
- 6 cups chicken broth, low sodium
- 2 medium zucchinis, Blade D, noodles trimmed

For the pesto:

- 1 tablespoon pine nuts
- 2 packed cups of basil
- 2 tablespoons parmesan cheese
- 1 tablespoon extra virgin olive oil

- 1 large garlic clove, chopped
- salt and pepper, to taste

Instructions

1. Place a large soup pot over medium-high heat and add in the olive oil. Once oil heats, add in the chicken sausage, crumble with a wooden spoon and cook for 5 minutes or until the sausage starts to brown on the edges. Add in the red pepper flakes, garlic, onions and celery, season with salt and pepper and let cook until onions are translucent, about 3 minutes.
2. Add in the broth and bring to a boil. Once boiling, let cook for 5 minutes and then add in the zucchini noodles and cook for another 5 minutes or until cooked to your preference.
3. Meanwhile, add all of the ingredients for the pesto into a food processor and pulse for 30 seconds. The pesto shouldn't be like a normal pesto, it should be thicker and not as creamy.
4. When soup is done cooking, add in the pesto and stir to combine. Serve immediately.

Ribbolita with Spiralized Carrots

Prep time: 15 mins | Cook time: 45 mins | Total time: 1 hour | Serves: 4

Ingredients

- 1 tablespoon extra-virgin olive oil
- 1 small yellow onion, chopped
- 1.5 stalks celery, chopped
- 2 garlic cloves, minced
- 1 (15-ounce) can crushed tomatoes
- 4 cups low-sodium vegetable broth (use chicken if not vegan)
- 1 bay leaf
- 2 fresh sage leaves
- 2 sprigs fresh thyme leaves
- ¼ teaspoon freshly ground black pepper
- 1 15-ounce can cannellini beans, rinsed and drained
- 3 cups chopped kale leaves (curly, lacinato, or Tuscan)
- salt
- 4 slices day-old crusty whole grain bread, roughly torn into 1-inch pieces (4 ounces total, about 2 cups)
- 1 large carrot, peeled, Blade D, noodles trimmed

- If not vegan: ¼ cup grated Parmesan cheese

Directions

1. In a large pot, heat the oil over medium heat. Add the onions, and celery, and stir to coat the vegetables in the oil. Cook, stirring occasionally, until the vegetables are beginning to soften, 5-7 minutes. Add the garlic and cook, stirring constantly, until fragrant, about 30 seconds. Add the tomatoes, broth, bay leaf, sage, thyme, and black pepper, increase the heat to medium-high, and bring to a simmer. Add the beans and kale, season with salt, cover the pot, reduce the heat to low, and simmer for 25 minutes. Uncover, stir in the carrot noodles and bread, and simmer for 5 more minutes.
2. Ladle the soup into bowls and serve. If not vegan, Andie's original recipe calls for a garnish of parmesan cheese (see ingredients.)

Salmon Red Coconut Curry with Turnip Noodles

Prep time: *25 mins* | **Cook time:** *15 mins* | **Total time:** *40 mins* | **Serves:** *4*

Ingredients

- 1 tablespoon coconut oil or extra virgin olive oil
- 2 garlic cloves, minced
- 2 teaspoons minced ginger
- 3 scallions, diced (white and green parts divided)
- 2-3 teaspoons Thai red curry paste
- 1 13.5-ounce canned coconut milk
- 1.25 cup vegetable broth
- 2 medium turnips, Blade D, noodles trimmed
- 5 oz green beans
- 6oz skinless salmon, cut into chunks
- handful of thai basil leaves or cilantro

Instructions

1. Heat the oil in a large pot over medium-high heat, and once oil heats, add the garlic, ginger, and white part of the scallions. Cook for 30 seconds or until fragrant and then add in the curry paste (be careful – the paste will fry, which is good, but can get on your clothes.)

2. Scoop the thickened coconut solids out of the top of the can of coconut milk, leaving the watery milk below. Add these solids to the skillet, stir to combine and let cook for 1 minute.
3. Add the rest of the coconut milk, vegetable broth, stir and bring to a boil. Once boiling, add in the turnip noodles, green beans and salmon chunks. Reduce heat to a low simmer and cover and let cook for 5 minutes, uncover and test to see if the salmon is done – if it flakes easily, it's done. If not, let it cook another 5 minutes.
4. Portion into bowls and garnish with green scallions, cilantro or thai basil and serve.

Sesame-Ginger Daikon Noodle Soup with Bok Choy, Snow Peas and Shiitake Mushrooms

Prep Time: 15 minutes | *Cook Time:* 20 minutes | *Total Time:* 35 minutes | *Servings:* 3

Ingredients

- 3 eggs
- 2 bunches of baby bok choy
- 1 medium daikon radish
- 1 tablespoon sesame oil
- 2 teaspoons peeled and minced ginger
- 1/3 cup diced scallions
- 3.5oz container shiitake mushrooms, stems removed and tops sliced into ¼" slivers
- 3.75 oz snow peas
- salt and pepper, to taste
- 4 cups of low-sodium chicken broth
- 1 tablespoon low-sodium soy sauce
- 1 tablespoon mirin
- 1 tablespoon lime juice
- ¼ cup cilantro leaves

Instructions

1. Place three eggs in a medium saucepan and cover with water and a pinch of salt. Bring to a roaring boil and then turn off the heat and let sit for 12-

14 minutes. Rinse the eggs under cold water until they are easily handled. Peel and slice in half. Set aside.

2. While the eggs are cooking, peel and spiralize the daikon radish, using Blade C and set aside. Chop the ends off the baby bok choy and cut the remainder into 1" pieces. Set aside.

3. After the eggs are cooked, pour the oil in a large skillet over medium heat and let melt. Once melted, add in the ginger, half of the scallions and cook for 30 seconds or until fragrant. Add in the bok choy, mushrooms and snow peas, season with salt and pepper and cook for 2-3 minutes or until mushrooms sweat. Stir and then add in the chicken broth, raise heat to high and bring to a boil. Once boiling, add in the daikon noodles, soy sauce, mirin, lime juice, lower to medium heat and let cook for 2 minutes or until daikon softens to al dente.

4. Stir in the cilantro and portion into soup bowls. Top each bowl with a sliced boiled egg and the rest of the scallions.

Spicy Asian Chicken Turnip Noodle Soup

Prep Time: *5 minutes* | **Cook Time:** *1 hour* | **Total Time:** *1 hour 5 minutes* | **Servings:**
3

Ingredients

- 1 12 -ounce chicken breast (with bones), skin discarded
- 6 cups low-sodium chicken broth
- 2 cups of water
- 1 red bell pepper
- 5 scallions
- 2 teaspoons red curry paste
- 2 large turnips
- ¼ cup cilantro leaves
- 1 lime, cut into wedges for serving

Instructions

1. Place a medium saucepan over medium heat and bring the chicken, broth and two cups of water to a simmer.

2. Lower the heat to low, cover and simmer until the chicken is cooked through, about 30 minutes. Remove the chicken and let cool.

3. While the chicken is cooking, deseed and then thinly slice the red bell pepper and slice the scallions on an angle. Then, peel the turnips, spiralize them using Blade C and trim them for ease of serving. Set all aside.
4. Then, shred the chicken and set aside, returning only the bones back into the simmering broth and raise the heat to bring to a boil. Then, let cook uncovered and reduce down by about one-third, about 10-15 minutes.
5. Once reduced, strain the broth by scooping out the bones with a slotted spoon. Whisk the curry paste into the broth and return to a simmer over medium-high heat. Add the turnip noodles and bell pepper and cook until the noodles are just tender, about 3 minutes. Then, stir in the shredded chicken and scallions.
6. Ladle the soup into bowls and top with cilantro leaves. Serve with the lime wedges.

Spicy Ginger Pork Soup with Flat Zucchini Noodles

Prep time: *20 mins* | **Cook time:** *20 mins* | **Total time:** *40 mins* | **Serves:** *4*

Ingredients

- 1.5 tablespoons sesame oil
- ¾ pound ground pork (lean)
- 1 garlic clove, minced
- 3 teaspoons minced ginger
- 4-5 large scallion stalks, diced, whites and green parts separated
- ½ teaspoon red pepper flakes
- salt, to taste
- 1.5 oz enoki mushrooms (or other type of mushroom)
- 4 cups low-sodium chicken broth
- 4 cups chopped bok choy
- 1.5 tablespoon low-sodium soy sauce
- 1 teaspoon fish sauce (Bob's)
- 2 medium zucchinis, Blade A, noodles trimmed
- 1 ear of corn

Instructions

1. Place a medium pot over medium-high heat and add in the sesame oil. Once oil heats, add in the pork, breaking it up in the pan. Once broken, add in the garlic, ginger, the whites of the scallions and red pepper flakes. Season with salt and cook until browned. When the pork is just about

browned. Add in the chicken broth, bok choy, soy sauce, fish sauce and bring to a boil. Then, add in the zucchini noodles and mushrooms and let cook for 3-5 minutes or until the noodles are cooked to your preference.

2. Meanwhile, place the corn in a small pot and cover with water and a pinch of salt. Bring to a boil. Once boiling, cook until fork-tender, about 2-3 minutes. Drain into a colander and shave the kernels off with a knife and set aside.

3. Divide soup into four bowls and top with corn and remaining scallions.

Spicy Ginger Scallion & Egg Drop Zucchini Noodle Bowl

Prep Time: *10 minutes* | **Cook Time:** *15 minutes* | **Total Time:** *25 minutes* | **Servings:** *1*

Ingredients

- 1/2 large zucchini, Blade C
- 3/4 tbsp extra virgin olive oil
- 1 tbsp minced ginger
- 3 tbsp dried seaweed
- 1/2 cup chopped scallions
- 1/4 tsp red pepper flakes
- 2 tsp sherry vinegar
- 1 tbsp low-sodium soy sauce
- 2 cups vegetable broth
- 1/2 cup water
- 1 large egg, beaten
- pepper to taste (from a peppercorn grinder)

Instructions

1. Place a large saucepan over medium heat and add in the oil. Once oil heats, add in the ginger and cook for about 1 minute.
2. Add in the red pepper flakes, sherry vinegar, soy sauce, vegetable broth and water. Bring to a boil.
3. Once broth boils, add in the seaweed. Then, slowly add in the egg while stirring the broth.
4. Add in the zucchini noodles, scallions, season with pepper, and cook noodles for about 2 minutes.
5. Plate into a bowl and enjoy!

Spicy Sausage and Kale Soup with Carrot Noodles

Prep time: *10 mins* | **Cook time:** *25 mins* | **Total time:** *35 mins* | **Serves:** *4*

Ingredients

- .75 pound sweet Italian sausage, decased
- 2 garlic cloves, minced
- ½ cup diced onions
- salt and pepper, to taste
- 4 cups curly kale, chopped
- 6 cups chicken broth, low sodium
- 1 teaspoon dried oregano
- 1 large carrot or 2 medium carrots, peeled, Blade D, noodles trimmed
- ¼ cup shredded parmesan cheese (optional)
- 1 teaspoon red pepper flakes

Instructions

1. Place a large saucepot over medium-high heat and once the pan heats, add in the sausage, crumbling with a wooden spoon. Cook for about 10-15 minutes or until browned on all sides. Add in the garlic and onions, season with salt and pepper and let cook for 3 minutes or until onions begin to soften. Add in the kale and cook for 1 minute to combine the flavors. Add in the chicken broth and oregano and raise heat to high and bring to a boil. Once boiling, add in the carrot noodles and stir to combine. Reduce heat to low and let cook for 5 minutes or until carrot noodles are cooked through.
2. When done, divide into bowls and garnish with parmesan cheese and red pepper flakes.

Spiralized Daikon Ramen with Portobello Mushrooms and Soft Boiled Egg

Prep time: *10 mins* | **Cook time:** *20 mins* | **Total time:** *30 mins* | **Serves:** *2*

Ingredients

- 1 egg
- 2 teaspoons sesame oil
- 2 scallions, diced, white and green parts separated
- 1 inch piece of ginger, peeled and minced
- ½ yellow onion, thinly sliced
- 1 garlic clove, minced
- 4 cups vegetable broth
- 2 tablespoons low-sodium soy sauce
- 1 large portobello mushroom caps, ribs scooped out, sliced into ½" thick strips
- 1 medium daikon radish, Blade C, noodles trimmed
- 3 cups chopped curly kale
- sesame seeds, to garnish
- hot sauce, to garnish

Directions

1. Place the egg in a small saucepot and cover with water. Cover the pot, place over high heat and bring to a boil. Once boiling, remove from heat and let sit (still covered) for 7 minutes. Then, rinse with cold water until able to be handled and peel. Slice in half.
2. Meanwhile, place a large skillet over medium-high heat and add in the oil. Once oil is shimmering, add the white scallions, ginger, onion and garlic to the skillet and cook for 5 minutes or until onions soften. Then, pour in the stock and soy sauce, cover and bring to the boil. Add the mushrooms, lower to a simmer and let cook for 5 minutes or until mushrooms are softened. Then, add the daikon noodles and kale and let cook for 5-7 more minutes or until noodles are softened and kale wilts.
3. Divide the soup into two bowls. Garnish with green scallions, sesame seeds and hot sauce. Top with half of the egg per bowl.

Spiralized Vegan Ramen Soup with Zucchini Noodles

Prep time: 15 mins | Cook time: 30 mins | Total time: 45 mins | Serves: 2

Ingredients

- 2 teaspoons sesame oil
- ½ tablespoon white or yellow miso paste

- 7oz baby bok choy, ends trimmed and leaves separated
- 2 scallions, diced, white and green parts separated
- 1 inch piece of ginger, peeled and minced
- ½ yellow onion, cut into ½" slices
- 1 garlic clove, minced
- 4 cups vegetable stock
- 2 tablespoons low-sodium soy sauce
- 3.5 oz shiitake mushrooms, halved
- 1 large zucchini or 2 small zucchini, Blade D, noodles trimmed
- hot sauce, to garnish (optional)
- ¼ teaspoon black sesame seeds + ¼ teaspoon white sesame seeds, mixed together

Instructions

1. Place a large skillet over medium-high heat and add in half of the oil. While oil heats, rub the bok choy with the miso paste using your fingers to cover completely. Once heated, add in the bok choy and cook 3 minutes per side or until charred. Remove the bok choy and set aside and then immediately add in the rest of sesame oil, white scallions, ginger, onion and garlic to the skillet and cook for 5 minutes or until onions soften. Then, pour in the stock and soy sauce, cover and bring to the boil. Then, add in the mushrooms, lower to a simmer and let cook for 5 minutes or until mushrooms soften. Then, add the zucchini noodles and cook for 2-3 more minutes or until noodles are cooked to al dente or your preference.
2. Using pasta tongs, carefully transfer the noodles to two serving bowls and top with the bok choy. Then, ladle over with the broth mixture. Garnish with green scallions, sesame seeds and hot sauce, optional and serve immediately

The Best Chicken Zucchini Noodle Soup, Ever!

Prep Time: 15 minutes | Cook Time: 45 minutes | Total Time: 1 hour | Servings: 4 very hearty bowls

Ingredients

- ½ heaping cup diced red onion
- 2 celery ribs, diced
- 1 large carrot, diced
- 2 garlic cloves, minced

- 1 small pinch of red pepper flakes
- 3 teaspoons fresh thyme (or 1 teaspoon dried thyme)
- 3 teaspoons fresh oregano (or 1 teaspoon dried oregano)
- 4 chicken thighs, bone-in, about 1.75 pounds
- 2 bay leaves
- 6 cups chicken broth, low-sodium
- 2 cups water
- 3 medium zucchinis

Instructions

1. Place a large soup pot over medium heat and add in the onions, celery, carrots, garlic and red pepper flakes. Cook for 3-5 minutes or until vegetables "sweat" and onions are translucent. Add in the thyme and oregano and cook for another 1 minute, stirring frequently.
2. Place in the chicken thighs and bay leaf and pour in the chicken broth, water and cover and let come to a boil. Once boiling, lower to a steady simmer and cook for 30 minutes. After 30 minutes, remove the chicken and peel off the skin and discard. Then, shred the chicken off the bone and set aside, with any juices. Place the bones back into the soup pot and simmer for 10 more minutes, uncovered.
3. While the bones simmer, slice the zucchinis halfway lengthwise. Then, spiralize them, using Blade C. Set aside.
4. Remove the bones and bay leaves and discard. Add the reserved shredded chicken back to the pot along with the zucchini noodles. Cook for 5 minutes or until zucchini is al dente or cooked to your preference. Serve warm.

Tom Saab Goong with Spiralized Zucchini (Spicy Clear Soup with Shrimp)

*Prep time: 15 mins | **Cook time**: 10 mins | **Total time**: 25 mins | **Serves**: 1*

Ingredients

- 1.5 cups water
- 1 small piece of galangal (if you can't find, sub in ginger)
- 1 lemongrass stalk, tough end trimmed off and other end smashed
- 3-4 Kaffir lime leaves, ripped (if you can't find, omit – there's unfortunately no good substitute)

- 1 grilled shallot, sliced thinly (if you can't grill the shallot, just heat it up in a pan or the oven until charred)
- ½ small zucchini, Blade D, noodles trimmed
- 4 medium shrimp, peeled and deveined
- ¼ teaspoon chili powder
- ¼ teaspoon salt
- 1 tablespoon fish sauce
- 2 small Thai red chilis, sliced into ¼" thick rounds (or thinner for more spice)
- 2-3 leaves Thai parsley (if you can't find this, sub in cilantro or flat-leaf parsley)
- ¼ - ½ lime, juiced

Directions

1. Place a medium pot over medium-high heat and add the water. Once water starts to simmer, add in the galangal, lemongrass, Kaffir lime leaves and shallot. Bring the soup to a boil.
2. Once soup is boiling, add the zucchini noodles, shrimp, chili powder, salt, fish sauce, and mix together. Let shrimp cook for 3 minutes or until opaque and c-shaped. Then, add in the chilis and parsley. Stir well and add the lime juice. Remove the galangal and lemongrass before eating. Serve hot.

Tortilla Soup With Jicama Noodles

Prep time: *20 mins* | **Cook time:** *20 mins* | **Total time:** *40 mins* | **Serves:** *4-6*

Ingredients

- 1 tablespoon extra virgin olive oil
- 1 small white or yellow onion, diced
- 1 large garlic clove, minced
- 1 large jalapeno, seeded and finely diced
- 6 cups low-sodium vegetable broth (or chicken broth, if not vegan)
- 1 (14.5-ounce) can fire roasted diced tomatoes
- 1 (14.5-ounce) can black beans, rinsed and drained
- 1 teaspoon ground chili powder
- 1 teaspoon oregano flakes
- ½ teaspoon ground cumin
- ¼ teaspoon smoked paprika
- 1 avocado, pitted, sliced

- 2 small limes, juiced
- 1 cup roughly chopped fresh cilantro leaves
- 1 medium jicama, Blade C
- salt and pepper, to taste

Instructions

1. In a large saucepan heat the olive oil. Add the onions and cook for 2 minutes. Once the onions have softened add the garlic and jalapenos and cook for another minute.
2. Pour the chicken broth, tomatoes and beans into the pot and bring to a boil. Once at a boil lower heat to simmer and add avocado, lime juice, and fresh cilantro to the pot, letting cook for 2-3 more minutes to let the flavors deepend. Season with pepper and salt.
3. Ladle soup into bowls and top each with about ½ cup of jicama noodles.

Vegan Curry with Spiralized Potatoes

Prep time: 20 mins | *Cook time:* 25 mins | *Total time:* 45 mins | *Serves:* 4

Ingredients

- 1 tablespoon coconut oil
- 2 teaspoons peeled and minced ginger
- ½ white onion, diced
- 2 garlic cloves, minced
- 2 carrots, peeled and diced
- 2.5 cups broccoli florets
- 1 tablespoon curry powder
- ¼ teaspoon ground cumin
- ¼ - ½ teaspoon red pepper flakes
- 1 14.5 oz can lite coconut milk
- 1 14.5oz can diced tomatoes, drained
- 1.5 cups vegetable broth
- salt and pepper, to taste
- 1 medium red potato
- ¼ cup cilantro leaves, optional to garnish

Instructions

1. Place a medium saucepot over medium-high heat and add the oil. Once oil is shimmering, add the ginger, onion and carrot and let cook for 3 minutes or until onions begin to soften. Add in the garlic and cook for 30 seconds or until fragrant.
2. Add in the broccoli, curry powder, cumin, and red pepper flakes and stir constantly until the vegetables are coated with the spices.
3. Add the coconut milk, tomatoes, vegetable broth, and season with salt and pepper. Increase the heat to high and bring the mixture to a boil. Once boiling, reduce the heat to medium-low and let simmer for 5 minutes to begin to soften the vegetables.
4. While curry cooks, peel and spiralize the potatoes with Blade D. Trim the noodles with kitchen shears and place in a bowl of cold water and set aside until ready to use, if necessary.
5. After cooking the curry for 5 minutes, drain the potato noodles (if you submerged them in water) and add them into the curry. Stir to combine and let simmer for 7 minutes or until potato noodles are cooked through and al dente.
6. Fold in the cilantro, if using, and then ladle the curry into bowls.

Vegetarian Lemongrass Green Coconut Curry Soup with Zucchini Noodles

Prep Time: 15 minutes | Cook Time: 20 minutes | Total Time: 35 minutes | Servings: 2

Ingredients

- 1 tablespoon extra virgin olive oil (or virgin coconut oil)
- 1 lemongrass stalk, diced
- 1 garlic clove, minced
- ½ teaspoon minced ginger
- 1 pinch red pepper flakes
- 1 tablespoon Thai green curry paste
- 2 cups vegetable broth
- 1/2 cup water
- 1.5oz mushrooms of choice (a large handful)
- 2oz snow peas
- 2oz baby bok choy, chopped in 3" pieces
- 1/3 cup diced scallions
- ½ cup small-cubed tofu

- 1 tablespoon freshly squeezed lime juice
- 1 large zucchini or 2 medium zucchinis, Blade C
- salt and pepper, to taste

Instructions

1. Heat oil in a medium saucepan over medium heat. Add in the lemongrass, garlic, ginger, red pepper flakes and green curry paste. Cook until fragrant, about 2 minutes.
2. Add the broth and water and bring to a boil. Once boiling, add in the mushrooms, snow peas, bok choy, scallions, tofu, lime juice and zucchini noodles.
3. Let cook for 3-4 minutes or until vegetables are tender. Once tender, add in the cilantro, season generously with salt and pepper and stir to combine and serve into bowls.

Vegetarian Sweet Potato Rice & Bean Chili

Prep Time: *15 minutes* | **Cook Time:** *40 minutes* | **Total Time:** *55 minutes* | **Servings:** *4-6*

Ingredients

- 1 large sweet potato (340g+), peeled, Blade C
- 2 large garlic cloves, minced
- 3/4 cup diced red onion
- 2 tbsp olive oil
- 1 cup diced celery
- 1 cup diced carrots
- 1 cup diced red bell pepper (or green)
- 1 tsp cumin
- 1 tsp oregano flakes
- 1/2 tsp chili powder
- salt and pepper, to taste
- 2 cups low-sodium vegetable broth
- 2 cups water
- 2 (14oz) cans of diced tomatoes
- 1 (14oz) can of white beans (cannellini)
- 1 (14oz) can of red kidney beans
- 2 tbsp freshly chopped parsley

- 4-5 avocados, insides cubed

Instructions

1. Place your spiralized sweet potato noodles into a food processor and pulse until made into rice-like bits. Set aside.
2. Place a large saucepan over medium heat and add in the olive oil. Once oil heats, add in the garlic and let cook for 30 seconds. Then, add in the onions and cook for about 2 minutes or until translucent.
3. Next, add in the carrots, celery, peppers, and season with cumin, chili powder, salt, pepper and oregano. Stir to combine and let cook for 5 minutes, stirring frequently.
4. Then, pour in the vegetable broth, water, tomatoes and beans. Cover, raise heat and bring to a boil. Once boiling, uncover, reduce to a simmer, stir in the fresh parsley and let cook for 20 minutes, uncovered.
5. After 20 minutes, add in the sweet potato rice, stir to combine and let cook, uncovered for 10 minutes.
6. Once done, ladle into bowls and enjoy garnished with a few avocado chunks (about 1/2 avocado per bowl).

Watermelon Gazpacho with Beet Noodles

Prep Time: 30 minutes | Servings: 4

Ingredients

- 4 cups finely diced seedless watermelon
- 1/2 medium seedless cucumber, finely diced
- 1 large tomato, pureed
- 2 tablespoons minced red onion
- 1/4 cup chopped fresh basil, dill, or mint
- 1/4 cup chopped parsley
- 1 tablespoon red-wine vinegar
- 1 tablespoon sherry vinegar
- 2 tablespoons lime juice
- 1 tablespoon extra-virgin olive oil
- salt and pepper, to taste
- ½ jalapeno, diced
- 2 medium beets, peeled, Blade C

Instructions

1. Mix all but 1 cup of the watermelon and the cucumber, jalapeno, basil (or dill), parsley, lime juice, tomato, onion, vinegars, oil and salt and pepper in a large bowl.
2. Puree the mixture in a blender or food processor until to your desired consistency (I like a thicker gazpacho).
3. Refrigerate* and serve chilled. When serving, top with a quarter cup of watermelon and a handful of beet noodles.
4. You can serve immediately, but soup tastes best extra chilled.

Winter Kale Vegetable Stew with Rutabaga Noodles

Prep Time: 25 minutes | **Cook Time**: 40 minutes | **Total Time:** 1 hour 5 minutes | *Servings: 5*

Ingredients

- 1 large rutabaga, peeled, Blade C, noodles trimmed
- 3 cups roughly chopped Tuscan kale
- 1 tablespoon extra virgin olive oil
- ½ cup diced sweet Vidalia onion
- 3 garlic cloves, minced
- ½ teaspoon red pepper flakes
- 1 cup carrot, diced
- 1 cup celery, diced
- 1 15oz can diced tomatoes
- 2 cups low sodium vegetable broth
- 1 15oz can cannellini beans, drained, rinsed
- 1 teaspoon thyme flakes
- 1 teaspoon oregano flakes
- 1 bay leaf
- salt and pepper, to taste
- ¼ cup red wine

Instructions

1. Preheat the oven to 425 degrees. Line a baking tray with parchment paper and add in the rutabaga noodles. Spray with cooking spray and season with salt and pepper. Set aside.

2. Place a large pot over medium heat, coat with cooking spray and add in the kale. Tossing frequently, cook until wilted, about 5 minutes. Set aside on a plate and place pot immediately back over medium heat.
3. Add the olive oil to the pot. Once oil heats, add in the onions, garlic, red pepper flakes, carrots and celery. Cook for 5-7 minutes or until vegetables soften, stirring frequently. If the vegetables stick to the bottom, add a few drops of water.
4. Add in the tomatoes, vegetable broth, cannellini beans, thyme, oregano, bay leaf, red wine, cooked kale, season with salt and pepper and stir. Cover, bring to a boil and then reduce heat to low and let simmer, uncovered for 20-30 minutes or until vegetables are tender and stew thickens, stirring occasionally.
5. Once the stew is simmering, place the rutabaga noodles into the oven for 15-20 minutes or until cooked to al dente. When done, portion into bowls and set aside.
6. Once stew is cooked, remove the bay leaf and spoon portions over the cooked rutabaga noodles. Garnish with parmesan cheese, if preferred.

Conclusion

Thank you again for downloading this book!

I hope you enjoyed reading about my book!

Finally, if you enjoyed this book, please take the time to share your thoughts and post a review on Amazon. It'd be greatly appreciated!

Write me an honest review about the book – I truly value your opinion and thoughts and I will incorporate them into my next book, which is already underway.

Leave your review of my book here:

https://www.amazon.com/dp/B01N9BK07R

Thank you!

If you have any questions, feel free to contact at *contact@smallpassion.com*

An Awesome Free Gift for

You

Download Gift

http://www.smallpassion.com/awesome-gift

I want to say "**Thank You**" for buying my book so I've put together a few, awesome free gift for you **Tips and Techniques for Cooking like a Chef & Delicious Desserts!**

This gift is the perfect add-on this book and I know you'll love it.

So click the link to go grab it.

Read more my book here:

http://www.amazon.com/author/anniekate

http://www.smallpassion.com/my-cookbooks

Annie Kate

Founder of www.SmallPassion.com

* * *

Made in the USA
Las Vegas, NV
05 July 2022

51133622R00275